The Faerie Queene as
Children's Literature

THE LATCH KEY

The Faerie Queene as Children's Literature

Victorian and Edwardian Retellings in Words and Pictures

VELMA BOURGEOIS RICHMOND

McFarland & Company, Inc., Publishers
Jefferson, North Carolina

ALSO BY VELMA BOURGEOIS RICHMOND
AND BY MCFARLAND

*Chivalric Stories as Children's Literature:
Edwardian Retellings in Words and Pictures* (2014)

*Shakespeare as Children's Literature:
Edwardian Retellings in Words and Pictures* (2008)

*Chaucer as Children's Literature: Retellings from
the Victorian and Edwardian Eras* (2004)

Frontispiece: An idealized family read from *The Latch Key* (1921), volume six of Olive Beaupré Miller's *My Book House*, an American home library that featured literature. The questing knight marks enthusiasm for chivalric romances like Spenser's *The Faerie Queene*, while Dryden's statement epitomized the importance of good children's literature in the formation of character and success.

LIBRARY OF CONGRESS CATALOGUING DATA ARE AVAILABLE

Names: Richmond, Velma Bourgeois, author.
Title: The Faerie Queene as children's literature : Victorian and Edwardian retellings in words and pictures / Velma Bourgeois Richmond.
Description: Jefferson, North Carolina : McFarland & Company, Inc., Publishers, 2016. | Includes bibliographical references and index.
Identifiers: LCCN 2016023718 | ISBN 9781476666174 (softcover : acid free paper) ∞
Subjects: LCSH: Spenser, Edmund, 1552?-1599. Faerie Queene. | Spenser, Edmund, 1552?-1599—Adaptations—History and criticism. | Children's literature, English—History and criticism. | Spenser, Edmund, 1552?-1599—Appreciation—English-speaking countries. | Children—Books and reading—English-speaking countries—History—19th century. | Children—Books and reading—English-speaking countries—History—20th century.
Classification: LCC PR2358 .R52 2016 | DDC 821/.3—dc23
LC record available at https://lccn.loc.gov/2016023718

BRITISH LIBRARY CATALOGUING DATA ARE AVAILABLE

ISBN (print) 978-1-4766-6617-4
ISBN (ebook) 978-1-4766-2587-4

© 2016 Velma Bourgeois Richmond. All rights reserved

No part of this book may be reproduced or transmitted in any form or by any means, electronic or mechanical, including photocopying or recording, or by any information storage and retrieval system, without permission in writing from the publisher.

Front cover: Britomart, a warrior knight who pursues adventures and is also a woman in love, wears exquisite armor when she rescues lovely Amoret, bound captive by magician Busirane. His Oriental costume marks him as other, as does his position outside the frame. Art Nouveau details characterized Frank C. Papé's beautiful illustrations for Emily Underdown's *The Gateway to Spenser* (1911).

Printed in the United States of America

*McFarland & Company, Inc., Publishers
Box 611, Jefferson, North Carolina 28640
www.mcfarlandpub.com*

For Fr. Michael Sweeney, O.P.
Founder of College of Fellows
Dominican School of Philosophy and Theology
Berkeley, California

Table of Contents

Preface   1

1. Contexts and Criticism   5
2. Victorian Beginnings   25
3. Edwardian Extravagance   57
4. American Difference   140
5. Schoolbooks   181
6. Literary Histories   224

Epilogue   250
Chapter Notes   255
Bibliography   264
Index   267

Preface

Among many ways to discover the complexity of literary and cultural history, the studying of adult works and how they were retold for children provides richer understanding of both the original and adapted texts. The classic objectives to teach and to delight become clearer because those who wrote for children were especially concerned with moral purpose (patriotic, social, and religious) and engaging storytelling. In their number, variety, and excellence, books of canonical literature retold in the late Victorian and Edwardian eras are an unsurpassed treasure of words and pictures. Moreover, this canon embraced popular literature, chapbooks and ballads, as well as recognized masterpieces. Indeed the romance, a genre designation that is fluid over the centuries, was favored as well as major authors. My first books about traditional literature retold for children considered the most important English authors, *Chaucer as Children's Literature: Retellings from the Victorian and Edwardian Eras* (2004) and *Shakespeare as Children's Literature: Retellings in Words and Pictures* (2008). *Chivalric Stories as Children's Literature: Edwardian Retellings in Words and Pictures* (2014), much wider in scope, was devoted to medieval stories (romances, ballads, epics, and legends) that defined ideals of Christendom throughout Europe. The present study continues that literary history with Edmund Spenser's *The Faerie Queene*, the early modern Protestant romance / epic that refashioned medieval romance and marked its end.

The medieval romance has been the subject of much of my research, especially its chivalric ideals, commitment to service at the heart of Christianity, and belief in an eternity after life in this world.[1] My study of the reception of the most popular romance *Guy of Warwick*, adapted in a variety of literary forms, showed how this hagiographical romance underwent changes across centuries. The greatest diversity came with early modern writers who wanted to maintain the medieval Catholic romance yet render it appropriately current by introducing changed attitudes and beliefs of Renaissance and Reformation.[2] Recent histories of Tudor England have revised long held beliefs in a dominant Protestantism that replaced an effete and corrupt Catholicism.[3] A corollary has been many lively arguments, both scholarly and popular, about Shakespeare and religion, an obvious issue in an age of intense religious controversy and nationalism when allegiances were often veiled. In *Shakespeare, Catholicism, and Romance* (2000) I argued for a "Catholic habit of mind."[4] Spenser's Protestantism was overt.

The Faerie Queene (1589 and 1596) has a canonical place in English literature as the great sixteenth-century romance / epic informed by Protestant allegory. Edmund Spenser, who wrote for a court audience, ranks below only Chaucer, Shakespeare, and Milton in the hierarchy of authors. Thus *The Faerie Queene* was frequently retold for late Victorian and Edwardian children. England's Saint George as the Red Cross Knight was exalted, but as a Protestant icon not a Catholic saint.

A study of Spenser's early modern romance serves several purposes. Selection of narrative episodes, treatment of characters, and purposeful comments expressed adult response to *The Faerie Queene* and assumptions about what will appeal to and inform children, as well as encourage further reading of the original text when they are adults. This is true of all retold literature for children but especially significant for a canonical work. Those who retold *The Faerie Queene* did not simply affirm these expectations. Introductory and pedagogical material offered an apology for the length and complexity of Spenser. Indeed affinity was established with adults who, it was acknowledged, seldom read the whole. Because Spenser's work was informed by aggressive Protestant religious beliefs it provides a case study for how entertainment and didacticism were balanced for children. His multiple levels of allegory—moral, religious, social, and political—are demanding even for adults. This literary technique involves a statement of meaning through abstraction, characters that personify qualities that children do not always readily understand. Yet Spenser retold could not avoid allegory completely; adaptation varied from quick reference and immediate ignoring to elaborate exposition.

Chapter 1, "Contexts and Criticism," offers ways to understand the adult world in which Spenser lived and wrote. There are three sections: "Protestant and Catholic Imagining of Romance," "Humanist and Protestant Objection," and "Children's Enthusiasm." Particular attention is paid to statements of the influence of childhood reading and listings of romances read. This serves as background to subsequent chapters that discuss in detail books that retold *The Faerie Queene* for children in words and pictures.

Chapter 2, "Victorian Beginnings," first considers the poem as a Protestant statement and its relation to medieval romances, followed by analysis of representative adaptations for adults: *Spenser Redivivus* (1687), John Upton's commentary for his two volume edition (1758), and J. E. Rabbeth's *The Story of the Faerie Queene* (1889). Brief reference is made to Victorian paintings inspired by Spenser's work. A second section examines books: *Knights and Enchanters: Three Tales from The Faerie Queene* (1873), M. H. Towry's *Spenser for Children* (1878/1885), Sophie H. Maclehose's *Tales from Spenser* (1890/1905), and R. A. Y.'s *The Story of the Red Cross Knight* (1891).

Chapter 3, "Edwardian Extravagance," discusses the extraordinary number and rich quality of children's books of *The Faerie Queene* published in the fifteen years before World War I. They range from Books for the Bairns, paper pamphlets that sold for a penny, to expensive reward / prize books with color illustrations. Authors were women (Mary Macleod, Jeanie Lang, and Emily Underdown) and men (A. J. Church and Lawrence H. Dawson) devoted to making literature accessible to children. Collections of stories by Andrew Lang, Dorothy M. Belgrave and Hilda Hart, Christine Chaundler, and H. A. Guerber also gave *The Faerie Queene* a place. Pictures were as important as words, whether reproduced paintings by G. F. Watts, John Gilbert, Briton Rivière or illustrations by A. G. Walker, Gertrude Demain Hammond, T. H. Robinson, Frank C. Papé, Brinsley Le Fanu, and H. J. Ford.

While American literature was treated as part of English literature, national responses diverged. Chapter 4, "American Difference," shows that *The Faerie Queene* was less favored in the United States than in Britain: only three books—one was a reprint of an English version—as compared with thirteen English, and three collections compared with five. Home libraries, much relied upon at the start of the twentieth century, somewhat balanced the difference. In contrast to Spenser's *The Faerie Queene* that sought favor at court, John Bunyan's Protestant allegory *The Pilgrim's Progress* (1678), written in colloquial language and with simplicity, was intended for ordinary people and easily read by children; it suited American Puritans. Pedagogical studies and advice from librarians clarify American attitudes.

Chapter 5, "Schoolbooks," considers how they introduced and promoted *The Faerie Queene* as a canonical work, part of national inheritance in Britain and the Empire. Series, Romance Readers and Graded Schoolbooks presented prose stories, with occasional verse quotations, and engaging pictures. Readers that selected and modernized Spenser's verse were available for older children. Thomas Nelson and Edward Arnold, principal publishers of schoolbooks, offered different contexts and several ways to study Spenser.

Chapter 6, "Literary Histories," examines how children learned more about Spenser and *The Faerie Queene* in a tradition of English and American literature. Many alternatives provided historical context and biography, but usually told a story and evaluated the relation between story and allegory. Again there were national differences in emphasis and enthusiasm. Children's Spenser facilitated and encouraged reading of *The Faerie Queene*. The Epilogue shows how this continues, whether in a picture book, prose retellings, or modernized text.

Many have influenced my studies of children's literature. My Edwardian parents and teachers instilled what J. B. Priestly identified as the optimism of those who survived the Great War, "almost tiny but very compact and somehow indestructible. It encourages us to engage in all manner of doubtful ventures."[5] Waldo F. McNeir's graduate seminar fully introduced Spenser, and Don Cameron Allen and Helen Gardner enriched my understanding. Honors students at Holy Names braved a seminar in *The Faerie Queene*. The British Library, the National Library of Scotland, the Huntington Library, and Doe Library, University of California, Berkeley, have always been hospitable. Antiquarian booksellers—many online—made it possible for me to acquire most of the books here discussed. As always, I am most grateful for my husband's support.

1

Contexts and Criticism

Medieval chivalric romances reached a vastly expanded audience with the invention of printing and ever increasing literacy and availability of texts. Along with religious titles William Caxton (1415/24?-1491), England's first printer, favored many romances and books of chivalry, thus continuing the combination of religion and romance marked by medieval manuscript collections like the Auchinleck (National Library of Scotland Adv MS 19.2.1), compiled in a London bookshop in the 1330s, and the Thornton (Lincoln Cathedral MS 91), collected by Robert Thornton in Yorkshire in the fifteenth century. Caxton's successors Wynkyn de Worde (d.1534) and Richard Pynson (d.1530) sustained interest in romances developed in somewhat modernized retellings. Later printers produced simplified versions as chapbooks. Since romances were an essential part of the Catholic ethos and work of publishers, a Protestant poet needed to deploy their medieval chivalry for early modern Protestant readers. With *The Faerie Queene* (1589 and 1596), Edmund Spenser (1552-1599) by epitomizing Protestant advocacy and English nationalism secured his place in the traditional canon of English literature albeit below Chaucer, Shakespeare, and Milton. Later Italian romancers Ariosto and Tasso were influences; however, Spenser relied heavily on English medieval romances—Arthur and St. George but also *Bevis of Hamtoun* and *Guy of Warwick*. Moreover, allegory that defined religion and nation made *The Faerie Queene* an obvious choice for late Victorian and Edwardian children, who sustained enthusiasm for the old romances long after adults had forsaken them. However, the poem's size, allegorical complexity, elaborate verse, and deliberate use of archaic language—difficult even for many adults—required major adjustments to become an accessible prose story for children.

Spenser, who positioned himself as continuing the poetic tradition of Geoffrey Chaucer, also allied *The Faerie Queene* to medieval narratives and their popular adaptation through ballads and chapbooks for an increasingly large literate readership.[1] His most celebrated hero was the Red Cross Knight / St. George, patron saint of England. Chivalry was not from the distant past.[2] It survived in Renaissance displays like the meeting of Henry VIII and Francis I at the Field of the Cloth of Gold in 1520, Elizabeth I's pageantry, eulogies of Sir Philip Sidney, especially his generosity as he died in 1586, and of Sir Walter Raleigh, who courteously placed his rich cloak on a puddle so that Queen Elizabeth would not soil her shoes. These sixteenth-century knights became paragons of chivalry in many children's history books. As a canonical text *The Faerie Queene* flourished in an array of late Victorian and Edwardian elegant books, often illustrated by major artists and given as Rewards / Prizes, and in schoolbooks. Its combination of chivalric adventure—worthy knights defeating evil knights and dreadful monsters—with religious and moral allegory as well as patriotism provided both instruction and pleasure in large measures.

Edmund Spenser's elegant Elizabethan portrait introduced a sensitive poet in Clara L. Thomson's *Tales from The Faerie Queene* (1902), an early reader prepared for use in school, but attractively printed with illustrations by Helen Stratton. Like many others, Thomson told Spenser's first two books, stories of the Red Cross Knight and of Sir Guyon.

Protestant and Catholic Imagining of Romance

Scholarly interest in the place of religion in early modern England has burgeoned during recent decades with recovery of much historical record and revised understanding and attitudes about Catholicism in sixteenth-century England.[3] Thus the happy triumph of Protestantism over a decadent and evil Roman Catholic Church has been challenged and simple anti-Catholicism eschewed to recognize an era in England when religious beliefs and practices were not only difficult and dangerous but also complex and problematical. Moreover, a case has been made for the role of Catholics in shaping national identity.[4] The question "Was Shakespeare a Catholic?" has engaged scholars and spawned public and academic interest. The significance of Shakespeare's romances, especially the late plays, has been crucial in these discussions.[5] A few similar studies of the relation between religion and early modern romance evaluate how Protestant and Catholic loyalties and affinities influenced later development that combined sacred and secular and presented the marvelous, the supernatural that was readily believed. Spenser has long been hailed as the dominant Protestant advocate who transformed "romance" through allegory and contributed *The Faerie Queene*, a great "epic," to the canon of English literature.[6] Nevertheless, extensive adherence to the Catholic ethos coexisted, and some early modern romances preserved qualities of older romances, subtly and through equivocation—to cite contemporary Jesuit practice. Recent studies have explored their religious ambiguity.

Donna B. Hamilton's *Anthony Munday and the Catholics, 1560–1633* (2005), which eloquently argued how this prolific author moved circumspectly between Protestant and Catholic adherents, provided a case study for understanding complexity of religious allegiances faced by writers in sixteenth-century England.[7] Munday (c.1560–1633) has been largely recognized for work in the theatre and controversial pamphlets, including ones about the Jesuit Edmund Campion and *The English Romayne lfye* (1582). However, he was also an indefatigable translator of Spanish romances.[8]

Tiffany Jo Werth's *The Fabulous Dark Cloister: Romance in England after the Reformation* (2011) established ways to understand changes in the writing and reception of chivalric romance—"such a confusing, vexed, elusive, and often critically slighted genre"—and to identify its developments as "a perfect register of the hybridity that spans Catholicism and Protestantism."[9] Principal texts were Spenser's *The Faerie Queene*, Sidney's *Arcadia*, Shakespeare's *Pericles*, and Lady Mary Worth's *Urania*. Werth's argument focused on "a particular moment in England, in the late sixteenth and early seventeenth centuries, when authors strove to reformulate romance" (161). Her "Coda: Exceptional Romance" claimed these romances significant as "evidence of cultural change," yet recognized elements they sought to reform "remained by and large the most compelling strand of stories. The texts I have studied represent the exception to the ongoing legacy of romance rather than the rule. Their reformations were bafflingly piecemeal and strangely abortive" (161). Nevertheless, criticism typically defined Spenser as the Protestant / Puritan author along with Milton and Bunyan in the seventeenth century.

Analogous criticism stressed *The Faerie Queene* was greatly influenced by Italian Renaissance continuations, especially Ariosto's *Orlando Furioso*

(1516, rev. 1521 & 1532). Yet Spenser's indebtedness to medieval romance has long been recognized. Thomas Wharton (1728–17970), poet laureate and literary historian who wrote both *Observations on the Faerie Queene* (1754) and *The History of English Poetry* (1774–1781), identified *Bevis of Hampton* as the basis for St. George / Red Cross Knight's slaying of the dragon. Only more recently has Spenser's deep indebtedness to medieval English romances been explored. In *The Faerie Queene and Middle English Romance: The Matter of Just Memory* (2000) Andrew King identified an early religious tradition that prefigured Protestantism and an historical sense that furthered English nationalism because of a providential history adapted by Spenser to advocate an English Church as distinct from Rome. King found this quality in narratives preserved in the Auchinleck Manuscript, most notably *Guy of Warwick* and *Sir Bevis of Hampton* but also *King Horn, Horn Childe, Havelok, Of Arthour and of Merlin, Richard Coeur de Lion*.[10] Moreover, the "Books of *The Faerie Queene*—relatively separate narrative units … recall the sequences of individual, juxtaposed romances, separated usually by spacing and titles in manuscript-anthologies such as Auchinleck and the Lincoln Thornton MS" (38). Detailed analyses argued "Spenser's insightful perception that the native romances offer specific narrative patterns which are uncannily appropriate for a dramatization of both the Calvinist paradigm of salvation and the Protestant historical interpretation of the English Reformation" (129). Bevis's achievement foreshadowed Protestant St. George; "Holiness was not a new achievement for the Reformed English nation, but the correct remembering of something much older and derived from God rather than human invention" (145). *Guy of Warwick*, another slayer of dragons and giants, was a similarly essential inspiration, especially for Sir Guyon in Book II, albeit Spenser's hero differed significantly from the hagiographical champion.

Adapting native romances to Protestant theology was demanding:

> The heroic exploits which are an expected feature of the romance mode would seem more adaptable to the representation of Catholic spirituality, where the good works of the individual can be efficacious or co-operative with God's grace in reducing purgatory and eventually attaining salvation. It is difficult to imagine a romance where the hero is powerless [126–127].

Citing "Calvinist emphasis on God's grace as the sole agent of salvation, with the implied notion that humans can do nothing to alter the determination of their salvation or damnation, decreed by God before time," King quoted Book I. x.1 of *The Faerie Queene* (127). There were, of course, differences in theological discourse—Erasmus and Hooker as compared with Calvin and Cranmer.[11] Nevertheless, Spenser's firm statement of predestination ("If any strength we haue, it is to ill, / But all the good is Gods, both power and eke will") exemplified the major influence of Calvinist theology and corollary challenges to reconcile Catholic medieval romances. Spenser's "refusal to settle for phantastic, propagandistic solutions" in Book I that clearly extended the providential narrative beyond this world (the medieval ethos) contrasted with Books II and V: "Memory of the historical experience of a large, complex nation, or really nations, produces a complicated and erratic session of events with no obviously discernible providential structure" (212). Early modern chivalric romances faced a current history that was a far cry from an ethos of the temporal and eternal that informed medieval romances.[12] Yet there lingered a Catholic "habit of mind"—Hilaire Belloc's phrase.

Helen Cooper's *The English Romance in Time* (2004), a study of motifs through centuries, documents how a range of medieval romances, the most sophisticated secular fiction, was readily available and widely read by Spenser's generation. For a poet there was an intensity of response, awareness of a traditional literary and religious foundation and concurrent desire to transform that Catholic ethos into a Protestant one. Some changes were straightforward. St. George had been England's patron saint for centuries, the champion against dragon evil and inspirer on the battlefield—albeit other nations also claimed him. Concurrent with Spenser was Richard Johnson's prose romance *The Seven Champions of Christendom* (1596/7, with parts added 1608 and 1610), in which St. George surpassed six European counterparts; all fought Saracens, a common enemy.[13] Moreover, Johnson's St. George was born in Coventry, and his eldest son was Guy of Warwick.[14] Guy renounced the world, but Sir Guyon, his namesake in Book II, was Temperance, accompanied by a palmer (Reason). Gloriana, the Virgin Queen of England on this earth replaced Roman Catholic Blessed Virgin Mary in Heaven, and referenced Catholic honoring of virgin martyrs. Cooper centered a case for adapted fairy lore on Scotland's Thomas of Erceldoune as political prophecy. Perhaps her most significant argument concentrated on Britomart, woman warrior and questing lover, to express Spenser's advocacy of a religious theology of God-given sexuality, a Neo-platonic understanding that wise earthly love and beauty can move the soul to God. This was subtler and more sophisticated than fighting monsters and enemy knights—and less obvious material for children. However, a woman knight had feminist appeal. Britomart's quest, because it proceeds through several books with many characters and episodes, required more adjustment than those of the Red Cross Knight or Sir Guyon, but her adventures still became favorites for children.

Among four main romances discussed by Werth only *The Faerie Queene* flourished as children's literature. Book I's St. George / Red Cross Knight was the archetypal hero familiar to children; Sir Guyon and Britomart were next:

Holiness, Temperance, and Chastity were virtues significantly redefined by Protestantism. Other knights and diffuse narrative of later books were less amenable to adaptation. Seeing how *The Faerie Queene* was adjusted as children's literature enhances understanding of early modern chivalric romance.

Humanist and Protestant Objection

Early modern pedagogical expectations and practices differed markedly from late Victorian and Edwardian enthusiasm for chivalric stories.[15] Humanist antipathy to medieval romances was intense. Erasmus (1466–1536) objected to *fablae stultae et aniles*, stories of Lancelot and Arthur, because they distracted students from classical history and poetry. Juan Luis Vives (1493–1540) included a dimension of gender to his rejection of romances with *De Institutione feminae christianae* (1523), dedicated to Queen Catherine of Aragon. Vives, having been invited to England by Henry VIII (to whom he dedicated his commentary on Augustine's *City of God*) was tutor to Princess Mary Tudor. To Vives's list of forbidden romances translator Richard Hyrde (d. 1523) added popular English examples: Parthonope, Generydes, Ipomedon, Lybaeus Desconis, Arthur, Guy, and Bevis. Thomas Paynell's translation from "De Disciplina Feminae" in Vives's *De Officio Mariti* (1546), observed: "These books do hurte both man and woman, for they make them wylie & Craftye, they kindle and styr up covetousness, inflame anger, & all beastly and filthy desire."[16] Vives, who was born and educated in Valencia, moved to the Netherlands where he was a friend of Erasmus, and subsequently to England where he frequented the household of Thomas More. His objection to Henry VIII's divorce led to a loss of favor; Vives died in Bruges.

While Protestantism induced intense religious and moral objections to chivalric romances, this judgment predated the early modern period. John Wycliffe (c.1320–1384), a pre-Reformation reformer of the Catholic Church and translator of the Bible into English, deemed courtly romances and epic songs "lascivious" stories of the temporal world and thus condemned them.[17] Memorable early modern expressions were those of Roger Ascham (1515–1568), Princess Elizabeth's tutor in Latin and Greek. In *Toxophilus* (1545) he wrote:

> In our fathers tyme nothing was red, but books of fayned chivalrie, wherein a man by redinge should be led to none other ends, but only manslaughter and baudrye. Yf any man suppose they were good enough to passe the tyme with al, he is decyved. For surelye vayne woordes doo worke no small thinge in vayne, ignoraunt, and younge mindes, specially yf they be given any thynge thereunto of theyre owne nature. These bokes (as I have heard say) were

made the moste parte in Abbayes and Monasteries, a very lickely and fit fruite of suche an ydle and blynde kinde of lyvying.[18]

The reference to "younge myndes" was a significant expression of Ascham's commitment to pedagogy. His revised denunciation in *The Scholemaster* (1570) added more specific anti-Catholic judgment:

> In our forefathers tyme, whan Papistrie, as a standing poole, couuered and ouerflowed all England, fewe bookes were read in our tong, sauying certaine bookes Cheualrie, as they sayd, for pastime and pleasure, which, as some say, were made in Monasteries, by idle Monkes or wanton Chanons: as one for example, *Morte Arthure*: the whose pleasure of which booke standeth in two speciall poyntes, in open manslaughter, and bold bawdrye[19]:

This expressed greater awareness of national identity—English works and Malory—as well as Protestant zeal.

Similar was the view of Edward Dering (c.1540–1576), a Puritanical preacher whose *A Bryfe and Necessary Catechisme or Instruction, Verie Needefull to Bee Knowne of All Householders* (1572) began with regret and distress about current taste for books "full of synne and abominations" that continued the "wickedness" of forefathers who "had their spiritual enchantments, in which they were bewitched, Bevis of Hampton, Guy of Warwicke, Arthur of the round table, Huon of Burdeaux, Oliver of the Castle, the foure sonnes of Amond, and a great many other such childish follye."[20] Dering, who longed for imitators of the Ephesians inspired by St. Paul, wanted such books burned. He also associated romance with childishness—augury of the audience that sustained chivalric stories.

Thomas Nashe (1567–c.1601) in *The Anatomie of Absurdity* (1589) both railed against "the fantastical dreames of those exiled Abbie-lubbers" that told of heroes like Arthur, Tristram, Huon, and the four sons of Aymon and scoffed at absurd rimes in metrical romances like Bevis. Ronald Crane neatly pointed the conflict between medieval romances and sixteen-century classicism and rationalism: "Their remoteness from reality, their improbability, their extravagant idealism were bound to offend tastes formed on the literature of antiquity."[21]

Nevertheless, even opponents of romance recognized its qualities for instruction. Written in 1583, Sir Philip Sidney's *An Apology for Poetry* (1595) acknowledged efficacy in some circumstances:

> I dare undertake, Orlando Furioso, or honest King Arthur, will never displease a soldier [151]. ...
>
> Chaucer, undoubtedly, did excellently in his Troilus and Cressida, of whom, truly, I know not whether to marvel more, that he in that misty time could see so clearly, or that we in this clear age walk so stumblingly after him. Yet had he great wants, fit to be forgiven in so reverent antiquity [154]. ...
>
> Truly, I have known men that even with reading *Amadis de Gaule* (which God knoweth

wanteth much of a perfect poesy) have found their hearts moved to the exercise of courtesy, liberality, and especially courage [144].[22]

Spenser chose King Arthur as his central hero. Moreover, Sidney cited Chaucer's great romance, albeit with surprise and grudging admiration for such achievement by a medieval Catholic poet. In short, Spenser's task was to transform Catholic romance into Protestant, what could be identified as "moral romance" or "poetical ethics." The circumstance was analogous to the change from mystery and cycle plays of Corpus Christi to morality plays that taught through allegory instead of stories from Scripture and saints' lives.[23]

Records from the seventeenth century that describe childhood reading and continuing enthusiasm for the old favorite medieval romances explain why they appealed. In 1614 Sir Robert Ashley (1565–1641) left a remarkable account of the place of romance amidst the classical education of an Elizabethan youth. He described how he denied work, sleep, and play to read chivalric stories:

> I remember how when I was a boy and my masters kept me hard at work, if by chance some book fell into my hands that contained some fabulous and useless fictions such as were told about Bevis of Hamtoun or Guy of Warwick, or the history of Valentine and Orson, or the life of Arthur of Britain and his knights of the Round Table, or portents and monsters of a kind that never existed, or else indeed were useless and vain things surpassing all belief added in by monks with nothing better to do (made up in an earlier age to entrap the ignorant common man and ensnare him with pleasures).[24]

Ashley, who continued his education at Oxford and law at the Middle Temple, served as a Member of Parliament, learned several continental languages, and bequeathed a substantial library to the Middle Temple. Reading medieval romances did not forestall his career—however much they were "fabulous and useless fictions."

That Ashley was but one of many delighted—distracted—by romances explained the intensity of *An Easy and Compendious Introduction for Reading All Sorts of Histories* (1648) by Mathias Prideaux (c.1625–1646?), son of the Bishop of Worcester, who edited and published it with a dedication to Sir Thomas and Lady Katherine Reynell, "FOR THE USE of their Towardly young Sonnes." Prideaux, who served as a Royalist captain and was killed during the Civil War, attacked "Romance's, or the Bastard sort of Histories … not for any great uses … but for manifold abuses." First was "In wasting pretious time which might be better imployed," followed by "stuffing the Fancy and Memory with ridiculous Chimerah's, and wandering Imaginations," and "transporting and deluding the affections, with languishing Love, impossible attempts and victories, stupendous inchantments, wherewith the weake Reader is often so taken."[25]

Prideaux, who identified seven types of "Such Brats of Invention, and Spawne of Idle houres," made lists with the range of popular chivalric stories. Two types were: "Rude, those may be reckoned, which neither favour of Ingenuity, Language, or Invention, ... and Endlesse...." Another was pointedly germane:

> To the Tattle of depraved Romances belong such Peeces as we have of King Arthur, and his Knights of the Round Table, Guy of Warwick, Bevis of Southampton, to which may be added Father Turpins, Rolando or Orlando, Sir William Wallis and the like, Who though they were truly Famous in their times, and deserved an Homer or Virgill to set them forth, yet falling into the hands of Illiterall, and sordid Monkes, their Stories are so depraved, that the Persons are made ridiculous.

Blurring genres, Prideaux followed Rude, Endless, and Depraved with

> superstitious Romances, of whose impudency, and doltish forgery, their own men complaine, yet Dominus opus habet. Popery must have such props to uphold its policy, and hoodwinke the vulgar, and therefore the like Wares are at this day set forth to sale ... where the stuffe is the same, though the dresse be neater, the cuts more artificiall, and a new glosse set upon it.

Offending hagiographers ranged from Jacobus de Voraigne (c.1230-c.1298) and John Capgrave (1393–1464) to Jesuit Pedro De Ribadineira (1527–1611) and "our Miracle-mongers in English." Edwardians recognized romances as a fluid genre.[26] Affinities between knights of romance and saints of legends were particularly strong.

Set against his catalogues of stories of medieval knights and saints was Prideaux's catalogue of early modern romances:

> The wandring Knights, Spencers Fairy Queene, Sir Philip Sydnies Arcadia, with other pieces of the like straine may passe with singular Commendations for morall Romances, being nothing else but Poeticall Ethicks, that with apt contrivance, and winning Language, informe Morality. ... Informes us better for our compleat behavior.

Citing classical precedents—Heliodorus, Statius, Homer, and "exquisite Athenian Philosophers"—Prideaux reiterated humanist advocacy of classical superiority. Moreover, as Catholic texts were earlier denigrated, so Protestant early modern romances were lauded. A sixth type, "Romances that point at Policy" included Thomas More's *Utopia*, *Reynard the Fox*, and "diverse passages in Chaucer." Finally, "The vanity of the foure first kinds is wittily scourged by" the seventh type, "Satyricall Romances of Don Quichot, ... and the like."

Prideaux's concluding paragraph summarized his judgment and wishes for reform:

> 1. The Ruder, Endlesse, Depraved, and Superstitious were utterly abolished, or restrained at least from Youth of both kinds, for preventing of Fantasticall impressions. 2. That the

multiplying of new Follies ... as pernicious as the former, were strictly forbidden, and 3. That the Morall, Politicall, and Satyricall, might be permitted only to those that can read them with judgement, and make use of them with discretion.

An Essay and Compendious Introduction for Reading All Sorts of Histories was a remarkable survey; it identified chivalric romances, medieval and early modern, while recording intense objections to their widespread influence, especially potential harm to young readers. Prideaux added religious concern to humanist anxieties. As Dale B. J. Randall and Jackson C. Boswell documented in their magisterial *Cervantes in Seventeenth-Century England: The Tapestry Turned* (2009), alliance between Catholicism and romance, with Don Quixote as an apex, was frequently argued—with corollary condemnation.[27]

While many linked medieval and some later romances, *The Faerie Queene* was seldom in such lists. A few examples suggest variety of responses. Robert Burton (1577–1640), an erudite physician, was moderate and kindly rather than polemical in *The Anatomy of Melancholy* (1621). He simply warned that too great indulgence in reading could exacerbate depression:

> such Inamoratoes as read nothing but play-bookes, Idle Poems, Jests, *Amadis de Gaul*, the *Knight of the Sun*, the seven Champians, *Palmerin de Oliva*, *Huon of Burdeaux*, &c Such many times prove in the ende as mad as *Don Quixot*. Study is only prescribed to those that are otherwise idle, troubled in mind and carried headlong with vaine thoughts and Imaginations to distract their cognitations.[28]

John Taylor (1578–1652), a boatman on the Thames called himself "The Water Poet"; in *The Great O Toole* (1622) he mocked "Arthurus Severus O'Toole," a soldier who fought for Elizabeth in Ireland. Taylor's knowledge of popular romance heroes was impressive; he named several from France, England (Sir Bevis was one), Scotland, and Spain; however, "amongst the Grecians" was a vague classical reference.[29]

A somewhat later sophisticated and sympathetic response to chivalric romances was in Peter Heylyn's *Cosmographie in Four Bookes* (1652). Heylyn (1599–1662), a poet, historian, and leading churchman, wrote this expansion of *Microcosmus* (1621) during the turmoil of the Civil War. After the Restoration he served at Westminster Abbey, where he is buried near the stall he occupied—a situation envisioned in a dream of Charles I. As part of his survey of geography, Heylyn considered "Unknown Parts of the World": "THE LANDS OF CHIVALRIE are such *Islands*, *Provinces*, and *Kingdoms* in the Books of *Errantry*, which have no being in any *known* part of the World and therefore must be sought in this." He concluded with a positive judgment of romances as children's literature:

> And yet I cannot but confess (for I have been a great student in these Books of *Chivalrie*) that they may be of very good use to children or young boys in their *Adolescency*. For besides

that they divert the minde from worse cogitations, they perfect him that takes pleasure in them in the way of *reading*, beget in him a habit of *speaking*, and *animate* him many times to such high conceptions as really may make him fit for great undertakings.³⁰

Like Sir Robert Ashley, Heylyn—also Oxford educated—recognized pedagogical advantages in reading romances, their significance in forming moral character. Absence of *The Faerie Queene* suggests its Puritan character meant it was perhaps already viewed as *sui generis*.

Religious differences occasioned Anglican and Puritan conflict as well as Protestant and Catholic confrontation. An anonymous tract *Bartholomew Faire* (1641) recorded actions of a "precise puritan" who ventured to London and startled bystanders. Feeling "just anger and holy indignation" when he discovers images of Christ, Apostles, Saints, and Mary in Christ Church Cloisters (Aldergate), he "most furiously makes an assault, and battery upon the poore innocent pictures" until shopkeepers turn him over to a Constable who places him in the stocks. In September 1641 Parliament ordered all pictures of Jesus, God, and Mary removed.³¹ Fifty years after Spenser's vigorous verbal attacks in *The Faerie Queene* corollary physical action continued. Curiously ambivalent were William London's remarks in *A Catalogue of the Most Vendible Books in England* (1657), "which lists an estimated 4,500 titles," including romances acknowledged as good for sales but unacceptable. However, "I do indeed take less paines to promote their study though I hinder not their sale.... They are the least usefull of any." London's cited authority was Montaigne, who averred as a youth he never read Romances.³² Reference to romances sold by London, were often in Anglo Catholic attacks.

The Anglo-Catholic Bishop of Durham John Cosin (1595–1672) introduced an extraordinary view of attitudes toward romances in *A Scholastical History of the Canon of the Holy Scripture* (1657). Responding amidst a plea for tolerance Peter Talbot (1618/20–1680), Roman Catholic Archbishop of Dublin in *A Treatise of Religion and Government with Reflexions upon the Cause and Cure of Englands Late Distempers and Present Dangers* (1670), pointed out his misrepresentation of St. Augustine's view that "the most profane books, and Romances, *Esop's Fables*, and Don *Quixote*, may be received by the Church for holy Scripture, as well as *Machabees*."³³ Reformation vilification of Roman Catholic affinity to romances became even stronger after mid-century.

Attacks linking romances and Catholicism were far reaching. John Dryden (1631–1700), Poet Laureate, became a Roman Catholic in 1685 and defended this faith in *The Hind and the Panther* (1687). This provoked Thomas Brown in *The Late Convert Exposed; or, The Reasons of Mr. Bays's Changing His Religion Considered in a Dialogue. Part the Second* (1690) to attack Dryden's presentation of his new faith as a milk-white female deer. Using a name given Dryden in a lampoon, Brown asserted Roman Catholic intolerance and linked romances with persecutions and a pagan god:

> Certainly, Mr. *Bays*, you were not well awake when you made Good Nature and Clemency one of the distinguishing characters of your Catholic *Hind*. Why surely you think, we never traveled farther in history than the *Seven Champions*, and *Don Quixot*, or never heard of the *Albigenes*, the *Vaudois* ... thousands of which were sacrificed to the *Roman Moloc*, and whose Posterity are duly every year delivered into the Devils hands, by your Pious Pastor.[34]

A corollary anxiety about Catholic influence through children's literature was occasioned by Sir Roger L'Estrange's *The Fables of Aesop and the Eminent Mythologists: with Morals and Reflections* (1692)—and his visible and diverse political experiences. L'Estrange (1616–1704), whose complicated career included a death sentence, time in prison, and exile, was an active pamphleteer, Licenser of the Press as a Royalist after the Restoration, and Member of Parliament. His most extensive translations of stories were presented as a way to use an impressionable quality of young minds—John Locke's view of the child mind as a white paper—to teach moral duties. Reverend Samuel Croxall (1688/9–1752) prefaced his own translation of Greek and Latin fables with a fierce attack on L'Estrange, "a tool and hireling of the popish faction":

> What sort of children therefore are the *Blank Paper*, upon which such Morality as this ought to be written? Not the children of *Britain*, I hope; for they were born with free Blood in their Veins, and suck in Liberty with their very Milk.... Let the Children of *Italy, France, Spain*, and the rest of the Popish countries furnish him with Blank Paper for Principles, of which free-born *Britons* are not capable.[35]

Here religious difference again informed nationalism. Because *The Faerie Queene* brilliantly infused chivalric stories of English knights with Protestant advocacy, the poem allowed its readers to delight in adventures of chivalric combats and destroying monsters, as had readers of Catholic romances of the Middle Ages.

Children's Enthusiasm

Belief in the strong link between reading and religion continued to instigate "appropriate" texts, of which *The Pilgrim's Progress* by John Bunyan (1628–1688) was the most popular success, rivaling the Bible. While *The Faerie Queene* was left to sophisticated and academic readers, *The Pilgrim's Progress*, inspired by Bunyan's youthful enthusiasm for chapbook romances, especially *Bevis of Hampton*, became the preferred Protestant text, read by children as well as adults, widely disseminated by the Religious Tract Society.

Elizabeth Godfrey (pseudo. Jessie Bedford) in *English Children in the Olden Time* (1907) vividly described early appeal:

> It was no wonder that in such a dreary waste the children seized on *The Pilgrim's Progress* with avidity. It presented, it is true, the same narrow and distorted view of the religious life; but the children did not trouble about the divinity; it was a story, and a story was what they wanted, and its vivid descriptions, its quaint personifications of qualities after the manner of the old Mysteries and Moralities, above all, the series of exciting adventures and hair-breadth escapes which befell Christian on his journey, were just what appealed to the imagination of children, and when embellished with wood-cuts, however rude, it was a delight indeed; and the crowning delight was that it was permitted on Sundays, that day, to them, of weary gloom.[36]

This was a period where Catechisms and books like *Token for Children*—urging conversion since original sin damned all—by James Janeway (?1636-1674) prevailed. Not surprisingly, as literary histories reiterate, children claimed three immortal works, *The Pilgrim's Progress*, *Gulliver's Travels*, and *Robinson Crusoe*, as their own. Juliet Dusinberre's *Alice to the Lighthouse: Children's Books and Radical Experiments in Art* (1987) analyzed a late nineteenth-century shift to irreverence. According to "an inquiry into the popularity of children's books," made by the *Pall Mall Gazette* in 1898, Lewis Carroll's *Alice in Wonderland* (1865) and *Through the Looking Glass and What Alice Found There* (1871) had replaced *The Pilgrim's Progress* as most frequently quoted, second only to Shakespeare.[37]

Although Spenser's masterwork retold for children might have counterbalanced enthusiasm for chapbook versions of medieval Catholic romances and Spanish favorites, it was not until Victorian and Edwardian development of children's literature that *The Faerie Queene* was widely adapted for them. Yet these efforts have been little recognized. F. J. Harvey Darton's seminal *Children's Books in England: Five Centuries of Social Life* (1932) cites *The Faerie Queene* only in connection with Oberon's genealogy.[38] In contrast, he declared: "Bunyan, in respect of children's books, as in adult literature, is alone. It would be impertinent here to discuss *The Pilgrim's Progress*, or even *The Holy War*, which I confess to reading rapturously—as an adventure story—when I was a boy" (63). Humphrey Carpenter and Mari Prichard in their magisterial *The Oxford Companion to Children's Literature* (1984) refer to *The Faerie Queene* in a single paragraph and cite only two examples, Mary Macleod and A. J. Church.[39] There is no reference to *The Faerie Queene* or Spenser in *A Critical History of Children's Literature* (1953), edited by Cornelia Meigs in the United States. However, Bunyan's work was discussed at length and its role among Puritans in the United States recognized: "*Pilgrim's Progress* was for a weary time the only work of imagination available to conscientious small readers."[40]

Sir Bevis of Southampton, with its exciting adventures in the Orient, dragon slaying, giant killing, and romantic love, was one of the most popular medieval romances. Scholars early identified it as one inspiration for *The Faerie Queene*, and children eagerly read the story retold in chapbooks. An especially well illustrated version was in *The Home Treasury of Old Story Books* (1859), above, a collection that combined those chosen by "Felix Summerly" (Sir Henry Cole) and "Ambrose Merton" (William J. Thoms), both distinguished public servants in England who were influential in establishing children's literature that was not primarily didactic.

There was, of course, a concurrent tradition of chapbooks, simplified versions of romances that children read avidly in the seventeenth and eighteenth centuries. They were among the first books offered as children's literature by Victorians, most notably by "Felix Summerly" [Sir Henry Cole

(1808–1882)] in *The Home Treasury* (1843) that "purposed to cultivate the Affections, Fancy, Imagination, and Taste of Children." Cole was a distinguished civil servant—Public Records Office, work for the Great Exhibition of 1851, and first director of the South Kensington [Victoria and Albert] Museum. His efforts explicitly countered those of "Peter Parley" [Samuel Goodrich (1793–1860], American promulgator of instructive literature for children who was widely imitated in England. In 1846 the Home Treasury series added Charles Cole's *Tales from the Faerie Queene*.[41] Henry Cole's successor was "Ambrose Merton" [William J. Thoms (1803–1885)], an antiquary especially interested in myth and folklore (he coined the term). Thoms, Deputy Librarian to the House of Lords, founded *Notes and Queries* in 1849 and served as editor. Although he also edited early modern texts in *Early Prose Romances* (1827–1828), with an enlarged second edition in 1858, Thoms did not make *Tales from the Faerie Queene* one of twelve items in *The Home Treasury of Old Story Books* (1859), which combined Felix Summerly's Fairy Tales from "The Home Treasury" with Merton's "Old Story Books of England" and five ballads.[42] This delightful volume had fifty engravings by Dalziel and reached a broader audience than the original books printed by Joseph Cundall, exquisite items that resembled medieval manuscripts.

Chapbook versions of medieval romances were separate from canonical Spenser. *Tales from the Faerie Queene* was also not chosen for later collections. In *Nursery Stories and Pictures for the Young* (1878) Ward, Lock reprinted *Guy, Earl of Warwick* and *Sir Bevis, of Southampton*, as well as *Tom Hickathrift, the Conqueror* and *Patient Grisssel*. My copy was a prize given to a seven-year-old at Boys' National School Wrexham: "Presented for success in the Government Examination, October 20, 1887." Children's books typically combined chapbook romances with fairytales. Included in forty *Merry Tales for Little Folk* (c.1855), edited by Madame de Chatelain, were *Sir Guy of Warwick, Tom Hickathrift the Conqueror, Bold Robin Hood, Tom Thumb, Jack the Giant Killer*, and *Jack and the Beanstalk*—all traditional tales of old England. In the United States, *Bo-Peep Story Books* (c.1860), a small book, printed only these six favorites.[43] Those who retold *The Faerie Queene* could depend upon children's knowledge and delight in the chapbook romances that Spenser read. Some chapbook versions of medieval romances, popular for centuries, were reprinted as schoolbooks in the twentieth century.[44]

Robert Laneham's letter of 1575 named items in the library of Captain Cox, a mason of Coventry, often cited for evidence of early modern readership.[45] The list included seventeen romances such as *Arthur, Four Sons of Aymon*, and *Bevis of Hampton*—but not *Guy of Warwick*, an obvious item for local patriotism; this suggests Laneham's list was probably not complete.

Several recorded influence. Francis Kirkman (1632–c.1680), who probably wrote *The Wits or Sport upon Sport* (1662) with its famous frontispiece of theatre and characters, left an account of schoolboys' reading that parallels Ashley's early in the century. Kirkman was a publisher, bookseller, bibliographer, author and translator. *The Unlucky Citizen* (1673), allegedly autobiographical, presented a London merchant's son:

> Once I happened upon a Six Pence, and having lately read that famous book of the *Fryar and the Boy*, and being hugely pleased with that, as also the excellent History of the *Seven wise Masters of Rome*, and having heard great commendation of *Fortunatus*, I laid out all my money for that, and thought I had a great bargain ... now having read this book and being desirous of reading more of that nature; one of my School-fellows lent me *Doctor Faustus*, which also pleased me, especially when he traveled in the Air, saw all the World, and did what he listed. ... The next Book I met with was *Fryar Bacon*, whose pleasant Stories much delighted me: But when I came to Knight Errantry, and reading *Montelion Knight of the Oracle*, and *Ornatus* and *Artesia*, and the famous *Parisimus*; I was contented beyond measure, and (believing all I read to be true) wished myself Squire to one of these Knights: I proceeded on to *Palmerin of England*, and *Amadis of Gaul*; and borrowing one Book of one person, when I read it myself, I lent it to another, who lent me one of their Books: and thus robbing Peter to pay Paul, borrowing and lending from one to another, I in time had read most of these Histories. All the days I had from School, as Thursdays in the afternoon, and Saturdays, I spent in reading these Books; so that I being wholly affected to them, and reading how that *Amadis* and other Knights not knowing their Parents, did in time prove to be Sons of Kings and great Personages; I had such a fond and idle Opinion, that I might prove to be some great Person, or at leastwise be Squire to some Knight.[46]

While the excitement of magic and science were cited, knights and chivalry were cherished for deeds still deemed in the realm of possibility—and speculation about uncertainty of parentage, traditional romance theme of the fair unknown. Two points are significant. Kirkman recorded that many schoolboys shared enthusiasm for chapbooks and devised patterns of trading copies.[47] Second, many titles were Spanish rather than English-French romances, a shift in taste. Peninsula romances influenced works like Sidney's *Arcadia*, written in the 1570s and subsequently revised to be more like *Amadis*. Kirkman introduced his translation of the second part of Jerónimo Fernández's *The Honour of Chivalry; or, The Famous and Delectable History of Don Bellianis of Greece* (1664) with "Epistle" addressed "To the Courteous and Discourteous Reader." Set against his fascination with knight-errantry that might lead to its being "censured" as "wild and extravagant" was a claim that he wrote his translation "in a few days; for in the invention and writing I spent not a full week" and an expectation that readers "will find somewhat of a recreation." Kirkman then advanced his defense:

> Many people love Romances, but some are grown so squeamish, that there must be nothing of improbability, neither Giant nor Enchantment, because there is none in our age. To whom I answer, That this History is not of people of our time, but many ages past, and we know

that sacred Writ mentions both and Poetry allows of them.... This is no translation but fancy: we have many pleasant and ingenious Romances in the English tongue, but we are obliged to other nations for their invention of them: very few have been written originally in English, and only Sir *Philip Sidneys Arcadia* hath had the success to be not onely approved of in our own language, but rendered into French and other languages.[48]

Publishers early recognized change and continuity in fashion. *Cupids Sport and Pastimes* (1684), a chapbook in Samuel Pepys's collection of *Penny Merriments*, began with a rationale: "The Histories of Guy and Bevis are grown very old, therefore new conceits may be more pleasing."[49] Pepys (1653–1703), a successful naval administrator and Member of Parliament, has a secure place in literary study because of his "unique" confessional diary (1660–1669). However, he is also crucial to the study of popular literature because of his extraordinary collections of ballads and chapbooks, mostly from the 1680s, now at Magdalen College, Cambridge. *Penny Merriments* has 115 titles, more than 3,000 pages, including old "histories" of Friar Bacon, Guy of Warwick, Robin Hood, Dick Whittington, and Tom Hickathrift. Other titles were early modern: Johnson's *Tom Thumb* and *Life & Death of the Famous Champion of England, St. George, Famous History of Don Quixote de la Mancha*.

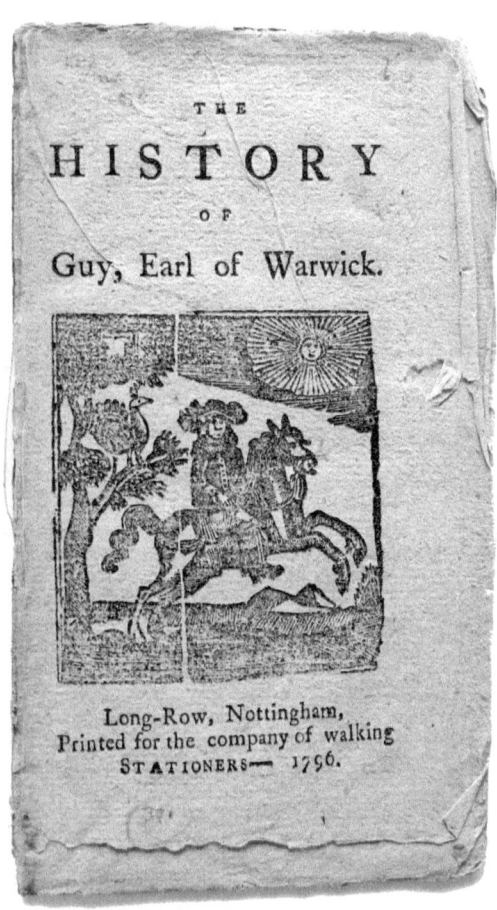

Among medieval romances none enjoyed wider reception or more varied adaptations than *Guy of Warwick*, a significant influence on Spenser's early modern romance / epic. *The History of Guy, Earl of Warwick* (1796) was one of many chapbooks that retold medieval romances for the newly literate and children, as well as sophisticated collectors like Samuel Pepys. Eighteenth-century clothes for a medieval champion showed publisher's expediency in use of woodcuts at hand, as did distribution by itinerant sellers.

Richard Steele, writing as Isaac Bickerstaff in *The Tatler* #95, for Thursday, November 17, 1709, specified titles read by his eight-year-old godson, who having rejected *Aesop's Fables* as not true, had

> very much turned his Studies for about a Twelvemonth past, into the Lives and Adventures of Don *Bellianis of Greece, Guy of Warwick*, the *Seven Champions*, and other Historians of that Age. ... He would tell you the Mismanagements of *John Hickathrift*, find Fault with the passionate Temper in *Bevis* of *Southampton*, and loved St. *George* for being Champion of England; and by this Means had his Thoughts insensibly moulded into the notions of Discretion, Virtue, and Honour.[50]

His was a case that romances not only delighted but also fostered moral character. That he "loved St. *George* for being a Champion of England" marked national commitment; however, this chapbook St. George was from Richard Johnson's *The Seven Champions of Christendom*, not the Red Cross Knight of Spenser's *The Faerie Queene*.

This was still the case at mid century. In *Tristram Shandy* (1759–1767) Laurence Sterne (1713–1768) recorded the place of chapbooks of chivalric heroes in the creation of Uncle Toby's character and career. "My Uncle Toby's Apologetical Oration" declared:

> If, when I was a school-boy, I could not hear a drum beat, but my heart beat with it—was it my Fault?—Did I plant the propensity?—Did I sound the alarm within, or Nature?
>
> When Guy, Earl of Warwick, and Parismus and Parismenus, and Valentine and Orson, and the Seven Champions of England, were handed around the school,—were they not all purchased with my own pocket-money? [Book VI, Chapter 32].[51]

Only after this inspiration does he refer to responses to the story of Greeks and Trojans. That schoolboys shared such books, "purchased with my own pocket money," marked the same enthusiasm expressed by Ashley in the sixteenth century and Kirkman in the seventeenth.

Such childhood reading did not fade; with Romanticism came efforts to revive and develop chivalric romances. William Godwin (1756–1836)—husband of Mary Wollstonecraft (1759–1797), author of *A Vindication of the Rights of Women* (1792), and father of Mary Wollstonecraft Godwin (1797–1851), who married Percy Bysshe Shelley (1792–1822) and wrote *Frankenstein* (1818)—is regarded as a political philosopher but was also a publisher who favored imaginative literature for children. He printed a collection of Benjamin Tabart's *Popular Fairy Tales* (1818), edited by the second Mrs. Godwin, and Lamb's *Tales from Shakespeare* (1807). Godwin's letter to William Cole in 1802 united fairy tale and romance; he advised Charles Perrault and *The Seven Champions of Christendom*.[52] A letter from Samuel Taylor Coleridge (1772–1834) to Thomas Poole raised the question and positively answered: "Should children be permitted to read Romances & Relations of Giants & Magicians & Genii?—I know all that has been said against it; but I have formed my faith in the affirmative."[53] Class and education did not limit the benefits of such reading.

Thomas Holcroft (1745–1809), a peddler's son who worked as a stable boy and a teacher, became a writer of plays and novels and the friend of leading Romantic authors. In a remarkable tribute to childhood reading he reported inspiration derived from chapbooks in *Memoirs of the Late Thomas Holcroft* (1816), completed by William Hazlitt. A gift of *Parismus and Parismenes* and *The Seven Champions of Christendom*, two battered chapbooks, fired his imagination and were "an inestimable treasure," remembered as well as "my catechism, or the daily prayers I repeated kneeling before my father."[54] As in medieval manuscripts and early printed books romances and religion were juxtaposed.

In the nineteenth century books vastly increased in number, not least because of cheap printing costs.[55] In 1830 James Bowd, a seven-year-old farm laborer's son, was suffering from scarlet fever and swellings when a doctor gave him a "new Halfpenny or Penney Book as a distraction from the application of leeches." Thus a chapbook *Bluebeard* became his introduction to imaginative literature.[56] Similarly transformative was an example at the end of the century. Because of a small library purchased by his mother John Eldred, a stonemason's son who grew up in a London tenement, began an experience of literature that he expanded with purchases in second-hand bookshops in Charing Cross Road. Eldred's record of items showed his precise memory and initial breadth of interest: "I open each of the newly-purchased volumes with a thrill, handle it gently and reverently. I remember all the titles—a mixed assortment"[57]: He named older classic works, current fiction, travel books, and books encouraging moral improvement—*Pilgrim's Progress* was first named. The only romance was *Don Quixote*.

With the waning of enthusiasm for John Bunyan's *The Pilgrim's Progress* the moment was right for late Victorians and Edwardians to retell an early modern romance that drew on medieval tradition, while advocating Protestant values and patriotism. Moreover, *The Faerie Queene* was a sophisticated literary masterpiece, placed by its author in the tradition from Chaucer, praised and imitated by poets, and respected by sophisticated readers. It was, of course, also a challenge to adapt.

Over centuries simplification of *The Faerie Queene* has been constant; Spenser's sheer complexity and struggle to redefine medieval romance, signed by his archaic language, almost immediately created a need for adult adaptations. Major adjustments of a literary work express admiration for the original but also apprehension about its currency and accessibility. One early attempt was *Spencer Redivivus: containing the first book of the Fairy Queen:*

his essential design preserv'd, but his obsolete language and manner of verse totally laid aside. Deliver'd in heroic numbers. By a person of quality, published by T. Chapman in London in 1687. While the "person of quality" may have hoped to "revive" the entire epic and simply began with Book I, it is also probable that he / she was only interested in the most famous portion, with its explicit affirmation of Protestantism and nationalism and the legend of St. George. Heroic couplets replaced Spenserian stanzas and contributed clarity and classical elegance to suit current aesthetics.

Much of the prefatory material was a discussion of style. Rewriting was justified as advocacy of current aesthetics but also needed intelligibility. The opening paragraph described reception of *The Faerie Queene* in 1686. "There are few of our Nation that have heard of the Name of Spencer, but have granted him the repute of a famous Poet." Although esteem marked the poet's place in English literary canon, how Spenser's reputation was secured left much to be desired; it came

> from an implicite or receiv'd Concession, [rather than] than a knowing Discernment paid to the Value of this Author: Whose Design, in his Books of the *Fairy Queen*, howsoever admirable, is so far from being familiarly perceptible in the Language he deliver'd it in, that his style seems no less unintelligible at this Day, than the obsoletest of our English or Saxon Dialect [A3].

Having noted Spenser's imitation of Chaucer, the reviver concluded, "peruse him here ... in more fashionable *English* and Verse. And I hope without Diminution to his Fame in any regard" (A7v). In short, he / she valued the substance of *The Faerie Queene* but deemed the accidents of Spenser's style unlikely to be understood or admired.

In 1758 John Upton (1707–1760), an accomplished classical and literary scholar and a Church of England clergyman, edited *The Faerie Queene* in two volumes with glossary and notes. This work affirmed Spenser's style and explained its complexity. Upton's critical observations were printed in J. E. Rabbeth's *The Story of Spenser's Faerie Queene*, a monumental prose version (1889) for adults, concurrent with Victorian children's versions.

2

Victorian Beginnings

Extravagance often characterized late Victorian and Edwardian England, not least books that fostered national tradition. Editions of Spenser's *The Faerie Queene*, both the original poem sumptuously illustrated and unadorned prose translation, encouraged encounters with this early modern romance / epic, Most dazzling were six volumes issued by G. Allen from 1894–1897, edited by T(homas) J(ames) Wise (1859–1937) and illustrated by Walter Crane (1845–1915). Crane, renowned for his role in the Arts and Crafts Movement and pictures of fairytales, provided illustration, ornamentation, and decorative design. One thousand copies were on handmade paper and twenty-five on Japanese vellum, one of which is in the British Library. In 2011 the Folio Society printed a facsimile, one thousand copies in three volumes. Carol Belanger Grafton selected and arranged Crane's work—352 illustrations and ornaments, in a Dover facsimile (1999).[1]

The Allen edition combined work by a noted bibliophile and a skilled artist. While Wise subsequently became notorious as a thief and forger, Crane's reputation steadily increased, not simply for his artistic work but for a role in establishing the Socialist League with William Morris and fostering decorative arts in Britain. Crane served as Master of the Art-Workers Guild, twice President of the Arts and Crafts Exhibition Society, and in 1898 Principal of the Royal College of Art.

Of the Decorative Illustration of Books Old and New (1896) originated in three lectures Crane gave to the Society of Arts in 1889. The expanded book surveyed the artist's role in writing manuscripts, early printed books through the sixteenth century, "modern illustration" that began with William Blake (1757–1827), and Victorians who developed the art, particularly William Morris (1834–1896), now identified as the Soul of Arts and Crafts.[2] Edward Burne-Jones was a major influence. Without Morris's Kelmscott Press books like Crane's *The Faerie Queene* would have been less likely. It was his exemplar in "Of General Principles in Designing Book Ornaments and Illustrations: Considerations of Arrangement, Spacing, and Treatment." Included were three full pages from *The Faerie Queene* to show harmony of type and illustration: a heading (218), a partial page illustration (219), and a full page with border and subsidiary figures (220). Crane explained his method: "the full-page designs are all treated as panels of figure design, or pictures and are enclosed in fanciful borders. In which subsidiary incidents of characters of the poem are introduced or suggested, somewhat on the plan of medieval tapestries" (222). An immediately recognizable style expressed "my own feeling—and designing must always finally be a question of individual feeling" (217). Crane's density of work and pictorial storytelling would fascinate children. Though some subjects—many nudes—were risqué, Belphoebe in a diaphanous short hunting dress might have met their gaze as well as Timias's (27); many female figures were modestly draped in Burne-Jones's style.

For *The Faerie Queene* Crane made 88 full-page woodcut illustrations, 132 head and tailpieces, and many capitals, displaying his imaginative response to Spenser's vast company of characters, creatures, and episodes. Inevitably much was conventional; however, introduction of characters in borders of full pages increased visual interest and added comment. The border for a splendidly mounted and armed Red Cross Knight with Una had lilies in upper corners, but a hideous hag (Errour) at lower right, and an ambiguous hermit (Hypocrisie) on the left side (2). In the House of Pride two black attendants fan enthroned Lucifera with peacock feathers; a dragon serpent is coiled at her feet (7). In the border the Seven Deadly Sins ride their allegorically significant mounts. Fascination with the Orient, especially Egypt, informed "Isis Church" where Britomart, in armor but with helmet off, sits pensively (103). Since Spenser's Christian knights often battle pagans, Crane contrasted armor (8, 95,105). Red Cross Knight slays the dragon (18), but is also betrothed to Una in a scene reminiscent of medieval manuscripts (20). Imaginatively different monsters, giants, mermaids, nymph, sea god, wild man, and satyrs vie with fighting knights and lovely ladies. Smaller decorations were ships, castles, heraldry, and people. Intellectually inspiring was Prince Arthur reading the chronicle of Britain's Kings and rolls of Elfin Emperours (40).

Purchasers were probably more attracted to Crane's illustrations than to Spenser's original text. Certainly modern reprints and citations attest this. Less admired has been a rival edition, three volumes with vellum binding, published by J. M. Dent (1896–1897) and a companion to Dent's *Le Morte D'Arthur* (1893–1894) illustrated by Aubrey Beardsley (1872–1898). Wood engraved illustrations by Louis Fairfax-Muckley (1862–1926), whose Art Nouveau style was also influenced by Edward Burne-Jones, lacked the appeal of Crane's decoration and storytelling.

Over centuries simplification of *The Faerie Queene* has been constant; Spenser's density and struggle to redefine romance to advocate Protestant religion and political circumstances, created a need for adaptation antecedent to tales and stories retold for children. The intention of J. E. Rabbeth's *The Story of Spenser's Faerie Queene* (1889) was to increase accessibility of a poem where deliberately archaic vocabulary, complex allegory, and vast numbers of characters and episodes are daunting. Many revered Spenser's poetic skill, but others found it a hindrance. The title page of Rabbeth's tome of 491 pages identified his work as "edited."³ Contents gave titles with allegorical meanings; for example, "Book I.—Containing the Legend of the Redcross Knight, or of Holiness." In addition Chapters were listed with summary contents, not unlike Spenser's introductory verses for cantos. Rabbeth's dedication marked a labor of love: "This Version of a Great Poem which Presents a Picture of Human Life, under the Similitude of Knightly Heroism, Devoted to the Pursuit of a High Ideal of Duty." A preface cited Dr. Church, Dean of St. Paul's, whose highest praise was for "the music and melody" of Spenser's verse, its "wonderful, almost unfailing sweetness of numbers." Then Rabbeth asked, "What is it that gives the 'Faerie Queene' its hold on those who appreciate the richness and music of the English language, and who in temper and moral standard are quick to respond to English manliness and tenderness?" Style was essential but so were "the quaint stateliness of Spenser's imaginary world and its representatives" and "the intrinsic nobleness of his general aim" (ix). Rabbeth modestly but firmly justified his version by defining his audience:

> whilst those who require no aid to understand and appreciate Spenser will, very probably, regard this experiment with disfavour, it is hoped that the far larger number who for one reason or another are unwilling or unable to read the "Faerie Queene" will not consider the attempt to make them acquainted with its story ill conceived, however, they may regard the manner of its execution ... the charm and grace of his style, would have no power at all to please any longer than the sound of it lingered in the ear, except that the ideas to which he gave expression were, as Dr. Church says, real and beautiful, and his aim noble and pure [x].

Granting delight and instruction, Rabbeth affirmed the latter; after each book were John Upton's evaluations from his two volumes edition (1758). Annotations made more than a century earlier, marked continuity. Typical of Upton's thought-provoking comments was one that suggested resemblance to a tragedy, admired varied and masterly characterizations and scenes, and found moral achievement in Book I:

> Should we presume to lift up the mysterious veil, wrought with such subtle art and ornament as sometimes to seem utterly to hide, sometimes lying so transparent as to be seen through; should we take off, I say, this fabulous covering, under it we might discover a most useful moral—the beauty of truth, the foulness of error, sly hypocrisy, the pride and cruelty of

false religion, holiness completed in virtues, and the church, if not in its triumphant, and triumphing state. ... And always we must look for more than meets the eye or ear; the words carrying one meaning with them, and the secret sense another matter [73].

If adults' access was demanding, retelling for children was more challenging. Nevertheless, children's Spenser increased recognition. A recent generic article referred adult readers to a children's version—Mary Macleod's *Stories from the Faerie Queene* (1897), which comes "to the rescue" and should be read before attempting Spenser's "intricate and allegorical plot."[4]

Because Victorians admired historical painting, especially scenes from great literature, there were splendid resources. Visual interpretation of *The Faerie Queene* was well established. Eighteenth-century master George Stubbs (1724–1806) painted Isabella Saltonstall in gleaming white as Una; the lion and donkey displayed his skill with animals (1782). American John Singleton Copley (1783–1815), famous for his portraits, painted *The Red Cross Knight* (1793). Henry Fuseli (1741–1825) imagined *Prince Arthur and the Faerie Queene* (c.1788) in characteristically Gothic style. *Britomart Redeems Faire Amoret* (1833), a painting by William Etty (1787–1849) was provocative in juxtaposing a female nude and a knight in armor. John Gilbert (1817–1897), prolific illustrator of Shakespeare and historical battle scenes, created pictures of *The Faerie Queene* later used in children's schoolbooks.

Subjects in the public competition for frescoes to decorate the new Palace of Westminster (Houses of Parliament), rebuilt after the fire of 1834, were English literature, Arthur, and British history. Eight wall paintings in the Poet's Hall (Upper Waiting Hall) indicate mid-nineteenth century interest and canonical status. Illustrated works were by Chaucer, Spenser, Shakespeare, Milton, Dryden, Byron, and Scott. G. F. Watts's contribution was *St. George Overcoming the Dragon* (1853). Later Watts also painted *The Red Cross Knight and Una* (1869) and *Britomart and Her Nurse* (1878). Edward Burne-Jones made drawings for *The Masque of Cupid* seen by Britomart but not a finished work. Alternatively Burne-Jones, famously devoted to King Arthur, and Dante Gabriel Rossetti depicted *St. George with Sabra* from Richard Johnson's *The Seven Champions of Christendom*. Pre-Raphaelite influence was strong. Some chose less obvious characters and more adult subjects. John Dixon Batten (1860–1932), who illustrated fairy tales and myths, painted *The Garden of Adonis—Amoretta and Time* (1887) early in his career. *Acrasia* (c.1888) by John Melhuish Strudwick (1841–1937) imagined the tempting Bower of Bliss. Interested over many years, Briton Rivière (1840–1920) followed *Una and the Lion* (1880) with *St. George and the Dragon* (1908). Phoebe Ann Traquair (1852–1936), who was Irish but worked in Edinburgh, is regarded as the first major professional woman artist in Scotland. A leader of the Arts and Crafts Movement, she worked in different media from murals to embroidery and manuscript illumination. Spenser was her subject in *St. George Slaying the Dragon* (1904), *St. George Riding with Una* (1907), and *St. George in Armour Being Kissed by Una* (1914).

Books of children's stories from Spenser sometimes drew upon this visual tradition with reproductions of great paintings instead of newly commissioned illustrations. Interlace of literature and art in schoolbooks became increasingly strong, while schoolbooks of literature and history were often coordinated. Because there were major differences in audience, publishing values, and prices, books of Edwardian extravance and schoolbooks are discussed in later chapters. As with Chaucer and Shakespeare, although reward / prize books and schoolbooks were different, major authors of English literature were given to children of dissimilar social classes and ages.

The presence or absence of allegory suggests how adaptors treated issues of religion in *The Faerie Queene*. Often difficulty was avoided; allegorical meanings were either not given, or simply stated, while adventures thrilled young readers. Since children do not like uncertainty, adherence to Spenser's facing of theological and political issues was avoided. Simplified prose narratives abound in familiar and engaging elements: knights and ladies, fairies, dwarfs, dragons, monsters, witches—all rich subjects for illustrators. While names were often retained, a theme of good versus evil did not require Spenser's complex allegory. Moreover, Arthur and St. George were well known. Talus, Spenser's original creation, was an Iron Man, an amusing anticipation of the Tin Man in *The Wonderful Wizard of Oz* (1900), a new fantasy created by L. Frank Baum (1856–1919) since traditional fairy tales had only 'historical' interest; Baum Americanized their European motifs.

Not surprisingly Book I was most favored for children; it combined patriotic myth with youthful recovery of identity and promised happy ending. Book II offered similar appeal, while Britomart's story (in several books) celebrated women. Although the Red Cross Knight, Sir Guyon, and Britomart are strenuously challenged, their stories are more straightforward and reassuring than those in later books. Volumes were usually sequential, some with six tales to encompass Spenser's original cantos, but always modified, and typically suitable for older children. Four writers made quite different judgments about what to select and emphasize. *Knights and Enchanters: Three Tales from Spenser* (1873) presented Red Cross Knight, Sir Guyon, and Britomart as exemplars of Holiness, Temperance, and Purity. M. H. Towry's *Spenser for Children* (1878), elegantly printed and illustrated, was valued as a prize for many years; my copy (1885) was awarded in 1907. Sophia H. Maclehose's *Tales from Spenser: Chosen from The Faerie Queene* (1890), which had many Edwardian editions, were simple stories; she made no claims for allegory or completeness. R. A. Y.'s *The Story of the Red Cross Knight* (1891), cast as a storytelling experience by a worthy aunt to several children, both recounted the story and offered moral / religious explanations.

Knights and Enchanters: Three Tales from The Faerie Queen *(1873)*

Knights and Enchanters: Three Tales from The Faerie Queen (1873) by the author of "Old Friends from Fairyland" was dedicated to "dear nephews" who requested its publication. "May their love of deeds knightly and noble commend to them the Christian virtues Holiness, Temperance, and Purity, from which they spring."[5] This plain book (4¼ × 6¾ inches), gold title and black floral frame on a brown cloth cover and gold design on the spine, had small print, no pictures or explanatory notes. Occasional quoted verses in modern spelling varied simple prose; chapter divisions focused events, free of Spenserian elaboration and complications.

A rationale for actions explained the book's title. The old hermit, Archimago, a wicked magician in disguise,

> hated the champions of the Fairy Queen because they were the sworn foes of all evil enchantments and magicians, and if possible, he hated the Princess Una still more, for the fame of her truth and goodness had reached his ears, and such virtues were as hateful to him as light is to those venomous reptiles which can only live in darkness [14].

Red Cross Knight failed to perceive because "he was honest and true-hearted himself, and suspected no deceit in others, and how could he dream that this fair-seeming lady was in truth a powerful and wicked witch?" (22). Naiveté has dire consequences.

"Fair Una and Her Knight" began with a paean of chivalry in a world of romance:

> Long, long ago, in the days when King Arthur and his brave knights of the Round Table set before the eyes of all men an example of the highest and noblest chivalry, all who sought the honour of knighthood, vowed to protect the weak and to fight to the death against all kinds of wrong and oppression. ... men.... Giants, Fairies and Enchanters.... Many were the strange adventures which befell these brave knights, many were the perils they encountered, and fierce and powerful were their enemies [5].

Una praised his defeat of Error: "'Brave knight, ... well worthy art thou of thy golden spurs, and of thy good armour; thou hast won great renown this day and thy first adventure has ended gloriously. May all thine enterprises be as successful'" (11).

Details of armor and court added distinction. At Lucifera's Palace:

> [Red Cross Knight] arrayed himself in his armour, looking carefully as he did so to see that each plate was firm and strong and each rivet in its place. When he came into the large hall where all the company were assembled, he was soon followed by the Saracen, who was clothed in a suit of strong chain mail, curiously wrought. ... The songs of minstrels resounded through the lofty hall, and pages brought goblets of the rich spiced wines of Greece and Arabia to inflame the courage of the two champions, which was indeed needless; and each swore a solemn oath that they would obey the laws of arms in their combat [34].

Comparison with Spenser (I.v.1–4) shows omitted similes and details of chronicles, abbreviated description of the palace, but added information about armor. There was no procession of the Seven Deadly Sins. Red Cross Knight is "full of youthful activity and the true courage of a noble heart fighting for the right" (34), yet sorely wounded before Duessa whisks fallen Sansjoy away in a cloud.

Twelve cantos of verse became eight chapters of prose, alternating between Red Cross Knight and Una, early separated and accompanied by enchanted false knight and lady. Forsaken Una meets a lion, is made captive by Sansloy, is rescued by Satyrs and Fauns, hears a false report of Red Cross's death but acquires a champion in Sir Satyrane, who fells Sansloy. Red Cross, who drinks from a fountain with enchanted water, becomes so drowsy that hideous giant Orgoglio overcomes him. Prince Arthur is needed.

This singular knight had special arms: an ebony spear, glittering armor, jeweled baldrick, ivory sheath for sword with gold hilt, golden helmet with plumes held in place by a golden dragon, an enchanted shield—made by Merlin from "one entire diamond" and impenetrable, "before it all false things faded away, and appeared as they really were" (47–48). Arthur comforts Una, "for the bravest and noblest are ever the most gentle and tenderhearted" and gravely counsels, "'Despair cannot remain where Faith is firm'" (48). He kills Orgoglio by gradual dismemberment (arm, leg, head). Una's gratitude is effusive, "'Oh noble Prince! The flower of chivalry'" (53). They search the castle and find Red Cross much weakened. Arthur counsels not "'to talk of miseries or perils that are past ... but learn wisdom to avoid them in future; ... grieve not over thy past misfortunes'" but proceed practically. Stripped, Duessa is "a hideous misshapen old hag" (56). The knights exchange gifts—a precious balsam to heal wounds and a book "the history of his Lord"—explicit reference to Holiness (57) before Red Cross Knight resumes the main quest.

In Chapter VIII Una joyfully returns to her native land with her champion, who immediately confronts a "dreadful beast" that half flies and half moves on its feet, remarkable because of the

> immense size of his hideous body, which was entirely covered with scales like the strongest coat of mail, so closely did they lie together that no bare place was to be seen which sword

or spear might pierce: and as an eagle ruffles up all her plumage when she sees her prey, so he shook up all his horrid scales with a noise like clashing of armour. His great wings, when he spread them out were like two sails, and his huge tail, which was knotted into a hundred folds, ended in two stings, sharper far than the most deadly dagger—but sharper far even than these, were his fearful claws, nothing could escape if once caught in them. His tremendous jaws were armed with three rows of teeth, and his hollow, flaming eyes were ever glaring round on the look out for his prey. As if rejoicing at the sight of a fresh victim, he reared his haughty head and lifted aloft his speckled breast, shaking his scales as if ready for battle and bidding defiance to every enemy [59–60].

While this simplified Spenser's poetry, similes of eagle and sails still distinguish this "fearful dragon." The fight filled five pages; sustained by "Well of Life" and "Tree of Life" Red Cross slays the dragon on the third day. King and Queen rejoice; by his "noble chivalry" Red Cross has won daughter and kingdom. Having put aside her black mantle for a white robe, Una is "as fair and fresh as a flower in May" (66). Archimago's last deception is quickly exposed. A paragraph noted the marriage and knight's return to the Queen of Fairyland to fight "her enemy, the Paynim King" (68).

In "Sir Guyon and the Palmer" the knight, who accepts a deceitful account of betrayed chivalry, is engaged to fight until he recognizes "a shield which bears the holy sign of the blood-red Cross, that indeed would have been a shame to all my vows of chivalry" (72). Guyon and the palmer meet a dying and despairing lady, wife of Sir Mordant who was enslaved in the Bower of Bliss where enchantress Acrasia's charm killed him. Guyon tries to wash the lady's blood from "a beautiful babe [who] was playing all unconsciously" beside her. He, "one of the chosen knights of the Fairy Queen," is to vanquish Acrasia (79).

The tone changed in Chapter II; "a vain, idle man named Braggadochio, who knew nothing of true honour or chivalry, but was full of foolish vanity and self-conceit" (80), terrifies Trompart into becoming his squire. When the braggart hears a lady huntress' horn, he hides, and then unsuccessfully tries to flatter her.

In Chapters III and IV Sir Guyon mastered Furor and his hagmother: "not blinded by passion, but cool and skilful," he defeats Pyrocles, who "fought like a madman" (91). Sir Guyon chivalrously yields his prisoners to Pyrocles, who injudiciously releases them, only to be attacked by Furor. The palmer argues against such "vain pity" (93) before he and Guyon ride toward the Bower of Bliss. Phedria takes Pyrocles's twin Cymocles into her gondola to another part of Acrasia's kingdom, where a "magic liquid" renders him prisoner. Sir Guyon, courteous but impervious to Phedria's wiles, lands at the island where Cymocles jealously attacks him. Phedria intervenes and ferries Sir Guyon where he wished. As Atin waits on the shore, Pyrocles, burning with inward flames, a wound from Furor, casts himself into "the slimy waves" (99); the squire follows. Fortuitously Archimago arrives and restores Pyrocles's wounds with "mighty spells."

Spenser's lines—"Fair shields, gay steeds, bright armes be my delight; / Those be the riches fit for an advent'rous knight"—introduced Mammon's temptation in Chapter V. Sir Guyon quickly rejects proffers of gold: "'I have vowed to spend my days in knightly deeds, and it ill suits with the spirit of chivalry to care for the hoards of worldly pelf'" (102). Offers of finest armor and a display of treasure hold no attraction, nor does Mammon's beautiful daughter Philotimé. Exhausted and hungry, temperate Guyon even refuses magic food; he is finally free of Mammon.

The palmer finds Sir Guyon lying senseless, but watched by "a youth of more than mortal beauty, whose snow white wings of dazzling purity shewed him to be one of those blessed Spirits sent for a while from their own bright home, on some errand of mercy, to succour those faithful knights who have fallen into sudden and great dangers" (107). In Chapter VI Prince Arthur again must aid a knight of the Fairy Queen. Archimago fears "Prince Arthur, the flower of chivalry, the bravest knight alive" (109), but Pyrocles seizes Guyon's shield and Arthur's sword Mordure. Combat is difficult: Arthur fights on foot with only a spear, and then only a shield, until the palmer gives him Guyon's sword; the twins fall before his "strong arm." As with the Red Cross Knight, Prince Arthur modestly and courteously assures Sir Guyon: "'Dear knight, ... why should good turns be counted between one true knight and another? Are we not all bound by our oaths of chivalry to withstand oppression and wrong? I have done no more than thou would'st have done for me'" (113). Fellowship, divine and human, sustains a knight.

Sir Guyon and the palmer reach the Bower of Bliss after sailing for two perilous days—whirlpool, rocks, floating islands, enticing female, narrow passage, quicksand, sea monsters, enticing mermaids, dangerous landing—with the palmer ever cautioning against intemperate response. So alluring is Acrasia that Guyon glances only once before tossing over her the palmer's magic net. Destruction of her bowers and release of "strange creatures"— men who were tempted and transformed—complete Sir Guyon's vow. Prince Arthur waits on the shore to hear the story of his "strange adventures" (121).

"Britomart and the Enchanted Spear" signaled a maiden knight's prowess: "All my delight on deedes of armes is sett, / To hunt out perilles and adventures hard, / By sea, by land, whereso they may be mett" (122). Chapter I explained how King Ryence's daughter beheld "the figure of a noble knight.... Brave and wise he looked, and tall and strong; his splendid armour was somewhat ancient in fashion and design, and was all inlaid with gold, and on his shield he bore the device of an ermine (the emblem of purity), crowned with gold" (123). Britomart responds with alacrity to her nurse Glaucé's suggestion that a royal maiden may be needed to rescue him. Merlin claimed his magic determined all. Chapter II reiterated Britomart's role as knight:

> "I have from my earliest years been brought up in a warlike land, amidst brave knights, and I have learnt to use shield and spear, and to manage a horse, and the life that most women lead seemest tame and dull to me in comparison, for all my delight is in deeds of arms. I have been told that here in Fairy-land are many famous knights and ladies, and many strange adventures to be found, in which great honour may be won, and for this reason I have come to this country" [128–129].

Only after this declaration does she ask Sir Guyon, unhorsed by her ebony spear, for tidings of the Knight of the Ermine, "'who hath been the cause of great grief to me'" (129)—a delicious ambiguity. After the palmer reassured Guyon he fell because of the princess's enchanted spear, Guyon praises the knight she seeks. At the seashore, Britomart fells Marinel, a sea-nymph's son who challenged and defeated all comers.

Chapters III and IV told of Florimel the Fair's long love of Marinel and his mother's fearing a prophecy and training him to eschew women. News of Marinel's death occasioned Florimel's haste. She seeks a night's rest in a hag / witch's cottage, where the son, idle and slothful, wants her to serve him. Florimel flees to the beach and escapes in a boat; the witch's beast devours her horse before Sir Satyrane rides up and kills it. Assuming Florimel is dead, the witch creates false Florimel for her son. Later Braggadocio takes this lady from the lazy youth, but abandons her when challenged.

In Chapter V Britomart still searches for Sir Artegal but joins Sir Scudamour whom she hears lamenting his wife's abduction by the enchanter Busirane. At Busirane's magnificent castle, with entry through "sulphurous fumes," they see rich furnishings, two doors ("Be bold" and "Be not too bold"), and a strange procession. In two days Britomart observes, rescues Amoret, and forces the enchanter to remove spells that bound her.

In Chapter VI all assemble at Sir Satyrane's tournament to honour his lost Florimel—the prize is her golden girdle. He defeats challengers except the Knight of the Forest, who is then overthrown by the Knight of the Ebony Spear. Neither Britomart nor Sir Artegal knows the other's identity. Awarding the girdle proves erratic. After champions Knight of the Ebony Spear and Knight of the Forest refused false Florimel and rode away, Sir Satyrane lets her decide: she chooses Braggadocio.

Britomart's greatest challenge comes in the forest from Knight of the Forest, whom she defeated, and Sir Scudamour, who believes she stole his lady Amoret. The Knight of the Ebony Spear unseats Sir Scudamour. In a harder fight her helmet is struck open: "instead of a hardy knight, he saw the delicate face of a beautiful maiden whose long golden hair fell over her shoulders in thick curls!" (158). Astonished Knight of the Forest falls on his knees and begs pardon for the outrage of fighting a woman, as does Sir Scudamour. Glaucé quickly convinces the princess knight to declare a truce. When Knight of the Forest removes his helmet Britomart recognizes Sir Artegal and lowers her sword: "joy and timid fear took the place of her proud courage" (159). Her attempts to be stern to conceal her love are futile; Glaucé proposes forgiveness and a penance for Sir Artegal. Britomart, who decrees he return to her father's court and help against his enemies, is delighted that Merlin's commands led to such a happy end.

The conclusion sorted remaining characters. True Florimel, held prisoner in a crystal cave by an old fisherman, laments her fate and lost love Marinel. Overhearing her, he repents his lack of love. His sea-nymph mother intercedes with the Sea King, who orders Florimel released. Marinel holds a tournament to celebrate their wedding and proves his prowess, until he ventures too far. Sir Artegal, who exchanged shields with Braggadocio, rescues him. This precipitates the coward's foolish claim of victory and superiority of his own "snow maiden" (false Florimel). When Sir Artegal exposes the boaster, true Florimel and false Florimel are brought together; the latter disappears, leaving only Florimel's girdle. Sir Guyon temperately restrains Sir Artegal from severely chastising the braggart. A final paragraph cited where each couple goes, only Sir Scudamour and Amoret return to the Fairy Queen.

Knights and Enchanters, planned to appeal to boys, stressed heroic knights—their shining armor, noble character, adventures, perseverance in adversity, and triumphs. Eschewing Spenser's religious and political allegory, it retold stories of the victory of good over evil. An alternative rendering was a more beautiful and complicated book.

M. H. Towry, Spenser for Children *(1878/1885)*

Published two years after Mrs. Haweis's *Chaucer for Children: A Golden Key* (1876), M. H. Towry's *Spenser for Children* (1878) was a similarly handsome large volume: 7½ × 10 inches, 177 pages, with a dark green cloth cover stamped in red and black.[6] At the upper left a lady kneels to pray for a mounted knight who thrusts his lance into a dragon's mouth; two watch from a moated castle's tower. The title page repeated this image with figures identified: Una, Red Cross Knight, Dragon, King of Eden. A decorated capital began each tale, and several small devices added interest. Drawings for Contents—three seated children read a book—and Finis—a child points to a picture in a book set against helmet, lance, sword, and shield—were iconic. Six full-page illustrations by Walter J(enks) Morgan (1847–1924) used subtle colors of chromoxylography, woodblock printing perfected by Edmund Evans. Towry's modest preface characterized his efforts:

> The work of one of our greatest poets has not been approached in an irreverent spirit, nor with any intention of vulgarizing his fictions by relating them in a familiar and mocking manner—a style too often supposed to be the most attractive to the young. Many of the episodes in the poem, though comprising some of the finest descriptive parts, have little or no action, and have, therefore, been necessarily omitted. In Books III. and IV. of the "Faerie Queene" the plot is so entangled that it would be difficult for young readers to follow the threads of the different adventures which are here given separately, but entirely without repetition.
>
> The volume can only give a most imperfect foretaste of the pleasure to be afterwards enjoyed from the original work; and is designed to serve as an incitement to turn to it. Children read on account of the interest of the narrative; beautiful thoughts and artistic excellence of composition are not perceived until a riper age, when the Poems themselves can be enjoyed [v-vi].

Concise guides, blocks within the text, were helpful in the first four tales, but absent from the last two. Even with elaborate similes simplified, and discursiveness and repetition lessened, readers might struggle to persevere. Occasionally lines of poetry added variety.

Spenser completed six books, and Towry wrote six tales; however, Towry chose unusual episodes, sometimes neglected principal knights, and reordered. Thus "the things that befell Arthegall in his adventure shall be told in the history of Talus, or the Iron Man" (116), or "The episode of Prince Arthur and Gerioneo is omitted, as the incidents, a fight with a giant and a monster, are without novelty" (n171). *Spenser for Children* did not stress exemplified virtues. Towry began with language familiar in fairy tales: "In the distant kingdom of Fairyland.... Once upon a time ... (1); There was once a knight ... (81); In ancient times there was a king ... (88); Among many kingdoms of Fairyland, there lay upon the sea-shore..." (117). Titles—several used "history," as did chapbook medieval romances—promised danger and the exotic:

> I. History of the Knight of the Red Cross, containing his Adventures in the Wandering Wood, the House of Pride, and His Encounter with the Dragon of Tartary
>
> II. The Perilous Voyage of Sir Guy in Search of the Bower of Bliss
>
> III. History of Cambel and Triamond; or The Ring of Canacee
>
> IV. History of Britomart; or, the Magic Mirror and the Enchanter Busyrane
>
> V. The Fair Florimell; or, The Sea-King's Palace
>
> VI. Talus; or, The Iron Man [iii].

Towry adhered to Book I's interlacing of episodes, many characters and disguises, and various scary monsters. Morgan's frontispiece "Una and the Red Cross Knight" was a typical chivalric image of knight in armor and modest lady riding in English countryside with daisies and daffodils, a massive limestone castle in the background, and a distant peasant.

Towry turned Spenser's descriptions into simple prose. "Errour, a vile monster"

> ... opened her mouth, and poured out a flood of poison, horrible and black, mixed with frogs and toads without eyes, who crawled away into the weedy grass. The smell of all this sickened and nearly choked the knight, which when the fiend perceived, she opened her maw again, and discharged a flood of small serpents and foul deformed monsters, black as ink, which swarmed and crawled over him. Upon this the knight, half furious, resolved either to win or lose at once; so with a sudden and mighty stroke, he severed her head from her body. The corpse fell back, and poured forth a stream of coal-black blood. The brood of young monsters gathered round it, and, horrible to relate, devoured it so ravenously that they forthwith burst in pieces: thus the knight needed not to slay them also [5].

His "frogs and toads without eyes" is less daunting than "great lumpes of flesh and gobbets raw." Missing was Errour's "vomit full of bookes and papers" (I.i.20), anti–Papal allegory. But "horrible to relate" promised grizzly details, and gore was abundant. Spenser devoted Canto XI to slaying the dragon. Towry took six pages (39–44) and identified the hero "St. George" (41).

Sir Guy (Anglisized name) was hero of Spenser's Book II and Towry's Tale II.[7] Spenser's initial description of his "demure and temperate" countenance (II.i.6) became "grave"; "Well could he tourney and in lists debate" was generalized to "great in deeds of arms." Guy's "perilous voyages" commence after a lady relates how Acrasia, "who dwells on a wandering island, which floateth in a deep and perilous gulf" enchanted her knight (51). An interlude at the castle of Extremes introduced comic antics of Braggadochio and Trompart. Sir Guy defeats opponents but separates from the palmer when he enters the boat of the Maiden of the Idle Lake. Spenser's "'Faire shields, gay steeds, bright arms be my delight; / These be the riches fit for advent'rous knight'" marked rejection of Mammon (62). However, weakened Guy collapses, so that paynim twins Pyrrhochles and Cymochles would rob his corpse.

At the center of the tale was "the bravest knight alive, Prince Arthur, the flower of chivalry, who hath killed a thousand Saracens" (67) and adds two to that number. In Alma's castle Guy and Arthur received hospitality and instruction—"Sir Guy found an ancient register named 'Briton Moniments,' and Prince Athur a book called 'Antiquities of Faerieland'" (71). Outside Arthur fights a "monstrous rabble of misshapen creatures." Their captain Maleger—"his body was made of a thin, airy substance, cold and snakelike to the touch, so that he seemed more like a ghost than a man"—rides a tiger and is renewed when he falls to earth. Arthur throws him in the lake and drowns him (72–74).

A perilous voyage—the Gulf of Greedyness, Rock of Foul Reproach, Wandering Isles, Whirlpool of Decay, death fish, and singing mermaids—inspired "This is the port of rest from troublous toyle" (77). In a boat with wind-filled sail and straining oarsman, the palmer holds the rudder and Guy—who asked the boatman to go slowly—stands to gaze at three adolescent mermaids (two wave and one holds a harp). Once landed Guy and palmer proceed to the Bower of Bliss, where enchantress Acrasia holds young knight Verdant captive. They bind her and free him, then destroy palace and bowers. Finally the palmer restores "the crowd of wild beasts ... lately men who had been decoyed to the bower by the enchantress" (80). Not all are pleased; Grill chooses to be a pig—a warning for greedy children.

Tales I and II filled nearly half the book; Tale III was brief, Cambel's tournament to win his sister Canacee, "the most learned of ladies; she knew every science and every secret work of nature" (81). Priamond, Diamond, Triamond—brothers protected by the Three Fatal Sisters who agreed to passing of life from eldest to youngest—pose a threat. Moreover, their sister Cambina, also child of a fairy, rides into the lists to help wounded Triamond. In Morgan's "A Lady bright and fair, and of angelic race" Canacee and her ladies watch from the lists when Cambina drives her chariot, pulled by two splendid lions, between knights poised to fight with sword and axe.

> In her right hand she carried a rod of peace entwined with two serpents, which were crowned with one olive garland. In her left was a cup, filled with nepenthe to the brim. Nepenthe is a drink which assuages all grief and anguish, and calms all rage, instilling peace and quiet into the heart. Few are allowed by the gods to drink of it, but such as may, find eternal happiness [86].

With a drink from the "wondrous" cup "bitter foes became true friends," Cambina weds Cambel and Canacee marries Triamond; "since their days such lovers have not been found elsewhere" (87).

Britomart's history, Tale IV, paralleled male adventures. They seek fair ladies, and her quest is for a future husband seen in a magic mirror. She and her nurse Glaucé consult Merlin, who identifies Arthegall, prophesies victory over Paynims, marriage and joint reign. Resourceful Glaucé remembers "armour, fretted with gold and rich array, that had belonged to Angela, the Saxon queen"—spoils taken by Britomart's father King Ryence of South Wales (91). Included are a mighty ebony spear—magically endowed to unseat all who ride against it—and a shield. Glaucé dons armor and rides as squire. With Red Cross Knight, met by chance, Britomart defeats six knights. At Castle Joyous, they find its luxury oppressive and seek other adventure.

Cambina's dramatic entry in a chariot drawn by lions interrupted the combat between Cambel and Triamond at the tourney held to decide who will marry fair Canacee. Spenser, who completed Chaucer's unfinished "Squire's Tale" in *The Canterbury Tales*, was acclaimed as his successor. These knights exemplified Friendship in Book IV. In M. H. Towry's *Spenser for Children* (1878/1885) W.J. Morgan combined charming lions with spectacular armor, a lovely lady with a golden serpent-entwined magic wand and cup of Nepenthe—that assuages grief and anguish.

Britomart chases giant Ollyphant away from a young knight and listens to Scudamour's story of his love Amoret, held by Busyrane, an enchanter. They enter his splendid castle, proceed from room to room, and finally rest. At midnight after an iron door opens, they behold "The Masque," a procession of costumed figures, and a magnificent chamber that match the verbal text (96). Having observed carefully, on the second night, "the championess" defeats the enchanter and forces him to lift the spell. Britomart and Amoret ride as knight and lady. Outside another castle Britomart defeats a young knight that demanded Amoret as his lady. Britomart "unlaced her glittering helmet, whereupon her yellow locks fell all around her like a golden veil, and her fair countenance was plainly shown" (101)—a declaration of gender. The young women, showing "frank affection," talk of their loves.

At Satyrane's tournament Britomart overthrows Arthegall, not knowing who he is. When Scudamour and Arthegall meet they join forces against Britomart, now alone because Amoret wandered off in the forest. Fierce fighting between Britomart and The Savage Knight (Arthegall) ensues; even without the magic lance, she fights well with sword and shield until a stroke splits her helmet; the knight "did homage to her as a goddess. But she, sternly standing over him, bade him rise or die, threatening to strike him again" (105). Scudamour and Glaucé secure a truce. When Arthegall lifts his visor, Britomart sees the knight of the magic glass. Although he finds Britomart daunting, "so full of princely gravity and modesty," they are soon betrothed. Inevitably Arthegall must undertake further adventures for three months. Thus Britomart joins Scudamour's search for Amoret, stolen by a wild cannibal. After running away Amoret meets Timias, Arthur's squire, out hunting with the nymph Belphoebe, who fells the monster but rushes away out of jealousy over the squire's attention to Amoret. Timias hastens after her; Æmylia tends wounded Amoret, until Prince Arthur finds them.

Arthur's next feat was to kill a "giant of flaming eyes" that swears by Mahound. Placidas relates how the giant's daughter Pœana loved a captive squire, Amyas, whose escape Placidas managed. They return to the giant's castle with his corpse, Arthur releases prisoners, finds treasure, reforms the doting lady, and convinces Placidas not to scorn her love. Again there are two weddings. Narratives connect when Arthur intervenes in an unfair combat—Britomart and Scudamour against four knights provoked because of her success at the tourney, a repetition of male competition. Arthur leads Scudamour to his love Amoret, while Britomart thinks longingly of Arthegall.

Britomart resolved Florimell and Marinell's story in Tale V. Marinell, son of sea-nymph Cymoënt and a mortal knight Dumarin, challenged any who landed on his shore; his mother feared a prophecy that a virgin will defeat her son. Britomart defies Marinell's challenge and deftly unhorses him with her lance. Nereus, who pities the grieving mother, calms waves; a flotilla of nymphs and monsters recover the wounded knight. Morgan's "Cymoënt and Marinell" is a kind of Pièta in a sea-shell chariot drawn by two dolphins with a boy holding reins; gulls fly above and a nymph swims in azure water (120).

Florimell, who loves Marinell, escapes a pursuing forester and finds shelter at a cottage where a witch and "wicked son, a lazy loon" threaten. Florimell leaves, but "a hideous beast, horrible in aspect, monstrous, misshapen, and with a back speckled with a thousand spots of different colors" pursues her (123). Although she escapes in a small boat, the beast devours her palfrey. Satyrane, who happens along, binds the monster with Florimell's girdle. After it escapes and returns to the cottage, Florimell is presumed dead. To assuage her son's despair the witch creates false Florimell, later stolen by knight Braggadochio and his squire Trompart. Meanwhile, true Florimell is captive in the sea king's palace; Proteus, an aged sire capable of shape changing, woos her in vain.

As in Tale III, resolution came at a great three-days tournament: "all the knights there showed their utmost prowess, which was well seen by their wounds, their shivered spears, their shattered shields, their swords all strewn about, and their steeds running loosely about" (131). Satyrane, who held it for love of Florimell, triumphs until a stranger knight (Arthegall) prevails, only to be bested by another stranger knight (Britomart). At the feast beauty's prize goes to false Florimell. Exposed when the golden belt falls from her, she ties it about her. Many claim this fairest one; she chooses Braggadochio.

During a feast for the wedding of the Thames and Medway, half-fairy / half-man Marinell overhears captive Florimell's love lament. He first pities her and then becomes ill with love. His mother intercedes with Neptune, Proteus releases Florimell, and soon Marinell presides over a tournament to celebrate his wedding. Arthegall, using Braggadochio's shield to conceal his identity, rescues him. Then he has to challenge coward Braggadochio's boastful claims and support Sir Guyon's recovery of his horse. Tale V ended as the braggart was

> driven from the hall, and his beard shaved off, his shield overturned, his arms taken from where they were hung, and dispersed, his sword broken in two. Such was the disgrace of this traitor to true knighthood, and infamous vagabond, who, as he went away, was gibed and jeered at by all the people; and the knights and ladies laughed to think what a glorious show he had made through his knavery [141].

Public humiliation is just reward for betrayers of chivalry, a lesson for young readers.

Tale VI reviewed Arthegall's early history and education in justice from the goddess Astræa, but the titular and practical hero was Talus, "a man made of iron instead of flesh, immovable and resistless. He always carried in his hand an iron flail, with which he threshed out falsehood and unfolded truth" (143). Arthegall's task is to succour Princess Irena from Grantorto, a usurping tyrant, but first he and Iron Man meet a squire bewailing the headless corpse of a lady, killed by a knight who deemed his lady less fair and stole the squire's love. With Talus combat is decisive. Sir Sanglier

> set his spear, and ran at Talus with all his force. It moved him no more than would stones thrown at a rock; but he, leaping forward, gave the knight such a blow that he fell on the ground. Before he could rise, Talus seized him in his iron grip, and he found himself so ill-hurt that he could scarcely walk, so Talus dragged him along, and forced the lady to return also [144].

Solomon-like Arthegall tests knight and squire. Because the squire who loves his lady accepts shame to spare her life, Arthegall metes out justice: Sir Sanglier must bear the head of his lady whom he killed, while the squire secures the living lady.

Arthegall next vanquished a cruel and thieving Saracen whose daughter abetted his crimes through magical arts. This involved falling through a trapdoor in a bridge and swimming: "Arthegall was very skilful in swimming, and could venture in water at any depth, as every knight should be able" (146). Talus, who batters through the castle's door, drags the lady "by her fair locks, without pity. Though Arthegall felt compassion, yet he would not change the course of justice, which Talus always executed" (147–148). Iron Man tosses her into "the slimy river," seizes all "that mucky pelf, and ill-gotten spoil," burns it, and tosses the ashes into the water. At the Castle of the Rich Strand justice was less drastic; Arthegall arbitrated two brothers' dispute over inherited land, a lady, and a treasure chest cast up by the sea.

Iron Man's advantages are realized in a different way when Arthegall meets a band of Amazons poised to torment Sir Turpin, their prisoner: "as he would not attack womankind himself, he sent Talus to them, who with a few strokes of his iron flail soon dispersed them all" (150). Such chivalry does not extend to battle against Radigund, "proud Amazonian queen," who defeats Fairyland's knights, forces them to women's work—"spinning, carding, sewing, washing, and wringing" for the pitiful sustenance of bread and water—and hangs those who resist. Arthegall rescues Turpin from Radigund, whom he stuns but is unable to defeat because her "warlike maidens" separate them. Humiliated and wrathful, Radigund sends Clarinda with a challenge to single combat. Arming is elaborate and fighting intense. Arthegall fells Radigund; however, moved to pity by her beauty, he throws away his sword and forbears striking off her head. The woman is not so chivalrous; recovered from fainting, she rushes at the weaponless knight and forces him to submit. "So he was overcome, yet not by her, but of his own accord; for by throwing away his weapon he wilfully lost all that he had attained" (155). With Turpin hanged and Arthegall Radigund's vassal, Talus leaves.

Talus's report leads Britomart to assume her love untrue, and she rides with Talus as squire to seek revenge—this parallels Radigund's initial motive, rejection by a knight. At the temple of Isis Britomart dreams, and a priest interprets as had Merlin—marriage and joint reign. Two great women warriors who engage, "like a lioness and tigress," shed much blood. Britomart does not hesitate to decapitate the Amazon; yet she orders Talus to stop slaughtering Radigund's followers. Prisoners are released and Arthegall briefly restored to joyful Britomart before resuming his quest.

With Prince Arthur he rescues two damsels from Paynims before Arthur fights the Sultan, who attacks from his chariot. "They flew into combat with equal fierceness, but different motives; for the proud sultan sought only slaughter and vengeance, the prince did battle for honour and right, against lawless power, and trusted more in the truth of his cause than in his strength" (165–166). Discrepancy between chariot and horse made this a remarkable encounter that ends when Arthur uses his shield to spook the chariot's horses that dash about until the Pagan is torn to pieces. Sultaness Adicia, trying to avenge, rushes into the woods where she becomes a tigress. Damsel Samient describes villain Malengine and leads the knights to rescue Queen Mercilla. By subterfuge they gain entry; the "carle" flees, and Arthegall dispatches Talus, who must flail against shape changing, but ultimately kills the snake. Sadly, Morgan provided no picture of Talus.

When Arthegall finally meets the old warrior who came to Fairy Court to request aid to save his lady from tyrant Grantorto, he learns she will be lost in ten days. Further definition of chivalry comes with a reproach to Sir Burbon, who was dubbed by Red Cross but threw away his shield, "the greatest disgrace that can happen to any knight, to lose the badge that displays his deeds." Nevertheless, he assists in an attack against peasants holding Burbon's lady. Arthegall and Talus take a boat to the Savage Isle, where Grantorto gathers an army against them. Once more Talus slays many before Arthegall bids him stop and sends a challenge for single combat. The tyrant's weapon of choice, a fearsome axe, lodges in the shield of Arthegall, who is dragged about. But he drives at Grantorto, who is trying to free his axe, and fells him; sword Chrysaor "lightly reft off his head" (175). Fair Irena receives homage of her people, Talus discovers hidden crimes and punishes justly before knight and squire journey to the Fairy Court. Hags Envy and Detraction defame

Arthegall and set the Blatant Beast against him. Nonetheless, he rides on serenely, receives honor from Queen Gloriana, joins his bride Britomart, and returns to her kingdom to fulfill the prophecies. With this happy ending, *Spenser for Children* stopped. The book was challenging but an attractive prize. My copy of the new edition of 1885 was awarded in 1907 in D Class for History, Geography, and Arithmetic.

Sophia H. Maclehose, Tales from Spenser (1890/1902)

Sophia H. Maclehose's *Tales from Spenser Chosen from The Faerie Queene* (1890/1902) was a quietly elegant book, 4¼ × 6½ inches, 195 pages, with relatively small print. James Maclehose and Sons, publishers to Glasgow University, offered this modest children's book, with cloth spine and hard boards.[8] The cover featured a printed title and unusual illustra-

Sophia H. Maclehose's modest *Tales from Spenser* (1890/1905), written to amuse and delight, also served in schools. Una and her Lion were often featured, a mark of interest in women but also praise of Truth.

tion of "Una and the Lion" in the Art Nouveau style of Glasgow. The only other illustration was on the title page; two similar ladies hold a shield identifying title, author, and publisher. Between them slender tree trunks frame a radiant sun; other trees bear fruit and leaves. The back cover for the fifth edition (1902) quoted laudatory reviews of Maclehose's *The Last Days of the French Monarchy* (1901).

Maclehose's preface declared her modest purpose:

> In writing these Tales from "The Faerie Queene," no attempt has been made to interpret their allegorical or explain their historic bearing. Intended for children, the stories are related simply as stories, and therefore only those episodes in the poem most interesting and most complete in themselves have been chosen. In no case do the Tales pretend to relate the whole that Spenser tells of their heroes and heroines [v].

Like the illustrations, "heroines" intimated attention to women; the running title for the archetypal event was *"Una* and the Dragon" (italics mine). Dedication "To my nephews Hamish and Crawford" tempts one to discover an underlying pedagogical intent.

While her preface did not include tpical Edwardian arguments that early experience of stories from great literature will lead to reading the original when older, Maclehose provided precise notations before each of eleven stories; exact references located events and characters in *The Faerie Queene*:

> "Una and the Lion," Book I, Cantos I, III, VI (1–20)
> "Prince Arthur helps Una to find the Red-cross Knight," Book I, Cantos VIII, X (21–40)
> "How the Red-cross Knight slew the Dragon," Book I, Cantos XI, XII (41–56)
> "Britomart and the Magic Mirror," Book III, Cantos II, III (57–73)
> "Britomart and Amoret," Book III, Cantos XI, XII (74–88)
> "The Story of Marinell and Florimell," Book III, Cantos IV, VII, VIII; Book IV, Canto XII; Book V, Canto III (89–109)
> "Braggadochio," Book II, Canto III; Book III, Canto VIII; Book IV, Canto V; Book V, Canto III (110–129)
> "How Britomart found Artegall," Book IV, Cantos IV, V, VI (130–145)
> "Cambello and Triamond," Book IV, Cantos II, III (146–157)
> "The Story of Timias," Book III, Canto V; Book IV, Cantos VII, VIII; Book VI, Canto V (158–170)
> "Calidore and Pastorella," Book VI, Cantos I, IX, X, XI, XII (171–195)

Numbers in parentheses indicated each story's length, usually about twenty pages.

Tales from Spenser were three in number and included Book I but not Book II. Sir Guyon, subject of strenuous temptation, was merely mentioned: during Arthur's rescue of Florimell from the pursuing forester (95), and at Marinell's tournament to claim his stolen horse; he also demonstrates temperance by calming Artegal's anger against the coward's ravings (127). Britomart and Artegal's adventures combined portions of Books III and IV with a conclusion both wishful and reassuring:

> How Sir Artegal did at last return from his enterprise and marry the Princess Britomart, Spenser does not say, for he did not live to end all the tales he had begun. But we know that they were married and lived happily, for Merlin prophesied this when Britomart and Glaucé went together to his cave [145].

Rapport between author and reader was a reminder of earlier action and a reiteration of the wonder and satisfaction of fairy tale.

Maclehose made separate tales of some of the most exotic briefer episodes. Boys would have enjoyed colorful accounts of three tournaments (119, 130, 150) as well as cumulative anxiety as Britomart puzzled over what she found beyond the fire, watched through nights, and decided when to "Be bold" (78–86) against enchanter Busyran. Timias, Arthur's squire, was likely to create empathy. Youthful frustration led to extreme behavior: Timias breaks his weapons and makes a "foolish vow" to become a hermit. But living "wild"—hair uncut, clothes unwashed, surviving in the woods (albeit barely)—could excite. Nevertheless, Maclehose judged his decision, "wasting his youth in selfish solitude" (165). Even if love sick Timias seemed silly, his longing inspired marvelous sympathy with a turtledove—a female messenger that resolves dissension. Moreover, Timias loves a huntress, Belphoebe; she rides and shoots but is also nurturing, so skilled at salving his wounds as to seem "an angel or a goddess" (162).

Interest in and praise of women centered on Britomart, a knight errant with inherently appealing adventures, plus the fascination of women warriors—Amazons, Brunhilde, Boadicea, Joan of Arc. Glaucé defined prowess when she and Britomart armed themselves:

> "Thou art tall and large of limb, and armour will befit thee well, and practice will soon bring thee the needful skill in handling weapons. ... it ought to inflame thy courage to remember how many women of thy house—a house inferior to none—have done deeds to rival those of the bravest men. Remember bold Bundeca, brave Gwendolin, Martia, and Emmeline; and more than these, let the example of the Saxon Virgin incite thy courage. ...
> Men call her fair Angela, ... for she is as fair as she is courageous in battle: she is more dreaded than all the Saxons by her foes, and so beloved by her people that they call themselves by her name. Therefore, fair child, take her example for thine, and equal her in courage" [70–71].

While love sickness weakened Britomart, her female heritage promised amazing action.

Women's intellect was praised in Canacée, Cambello's sister, who "was very beautiful, and was the most learned lady of her day. She was skilled in the works of nature and in magic arts; she understood the virtues of herbs and the sounds of beasts and birds, and was as good as she was learned" (146). Cambina exemplified women's use of knowledge for good when she drove her chariot into the tournament where Cambello and Triamond were in deadly combat. Although she attempts to stop them with feminine pleading, she does not hesitate to employ her knowledge of magic to achieve harmony:

> with tears [she] prayed to them by all that was dear to them to cease. Her entreaty availing not, she touched them with her wand, whereupon their swords fell from them, and as they stood doubtful whether or not to resume them, she handed them the soothing draught, and they being very thirsty, drank it eagerly.

> Then was a wonder wrought, for the two fierce combatants ceased fighting, and kissed each other, and plighted hands as friends for evermore [156].

Woman's traditional role to mitigate man's physical violence became a transforming magic based on learning. In spite of female displays of haughty indifference to men's wooing, heroines like Britomart and Belphoebe were sympathetic actors, not objects.

Since tales exist within contexts, Maclehose established Spenser's Fairyland in several ways. The opening line was "Once upon a time, while goblins still lingered in the forests of Merry England, a great queen named Gloriana reigned over Fairyland." Acknowledging Shakespeare's *A Midsummer Night's Dream*, she defined personages as "not tiny creatures like Oberon and Titania" (1). "Britomart and the Mirror" began "Once upon a time there lived in Cambria" (57); and "Once upon a time there lived a knight named Cambello, who had a sister called Canacée" again evoked fairy tale (146). Maclehose's last words were: "and we may be very sure that they were, as the old story-books say, 'happy ever after'" (195).

This also culminated her alliance with child readers, established through sharing superior knowledge denied characters in the narrative. When Una met Arthur, she "told the Prince the story you already know" (29); "soon after this the true Florimell was married, as you have already heard, to Marinell" (124); "You may remember that the good Prince Arthur had a squire named Timias" (158). Circumstances were often unexplained, with transitions typical of romance—"now it happened … it chanced … meanwhile … some time after this"—and "met with many adventures" provided needed compression as well as promise.

On only four occasions did Maclehose quote poetry. Modernized lines added emphasis and stressed didactic points, two in Britomart's story. Glaucé anticipates her paean of women's accomplishments and patriotic role when she encourages Britomart to reveal the cause of her melancholy—which Glaucé already discerns as love:

> "But be it worthy of thy race and royal seed,
> Then I avow by this most sacred head
> Of my dear foster-child to ease thy grief
> And win thy will" [61].

Wise Merlin, who already knows of Britomart's love for the knight in the mirror, crisply observes: "'Who help may have elsewhere / In vain seeks wonders out of magic spell'" (66). He speaks cogently about the relation of free will and Providence: "'true is it that naught can shake the heavenly destiny, nevertheless men must make their own endeavour to work it out'" (68).

Knights exercise this obligation, or suffer dire consequences. Brisk judgment of the Red-cross Knight when he abandons Una was a sober warning and urging to duty: "In leaving her he followed a false imagination put into his mind by Archimago, instead of remaining strictly true to the charge given him by Gloriana, Queen of Faeryland, and this one false step led him into much misfortune" (23). Recognition comes only after he has slain the dragon, married Una, and returned to Gloriana's court to complete his service. "After this he was no longer known as the Red-cross Knight, but as St. George, the slayer of the dragon—the great Saint George whom England made her patron saint" (56).

Two explicitly didactic verse passages expressed Spenser's religious sense of providence. Florimell, another maiden whose love is unaware of her, speaks her grief and fearful aloneness after Proteus brought her to his undersea dungeon:

> Heaven, that unto all lends equal ear,
> Is far from hearing of my heavy plight,
> And lowest hell, to which I lie most near,
>   Cares not what evils hap to wretched wight,
>   And greedy seas do in the spoil of life delight [105].

Finally Timias, having escaped three brothers who attacked and seriously wounded him, finds himself

> in a sad plight all alone in the forest, but—
> Providence heavenly passeth living thought,
> And doth for wretched man's relief make way [161].

Although Maclehose eschewed allegory, she could not tell tales from *The Faerie Queene* without some indications. Comments were simple: "Sansloy, who had no compassion in his soul, made no attempt to render him assistance" (14). The giant's demise was thrilling: "Lo! Orgoglio's body shrank away, and nothing was left but an empty dried-up skin—such is the end of pride" (34). Maclehose relied heavily on named creatures, most extensively in Busyrane's castle, where seeking to rescue Amoret, Britomart watches through nights before seeing

> a band of minstrels, followed by a troop of masquers.... Fancy and Desire, dressed in silk and embroidery; Doubt and Danger in more sober garb; Fear, armed from head to foot; Hope, with golden locks and samite robes; Suspicion and Deceit, Grief and Fury, Pleasure and Displeasure—six couples in all. Behind these came a fair lady, led by Cruelty and Despight, who goaded and tormented her as she walked. After these rode the winged god, mounted on a lion, and closely followed by Reproach, Shame, and Repentance, while a confused rabble brought up the rear [81–82].

This was her fullest rendering of Spenser's allegorical scenes. By comparison Book I offered less, lacking details of Error and the Seven Deadly Sins. After

Arthur rescues the Red-cross Knight, Una takes him to "the House of Holiness, in which she knew they would have a kind welcome and good food" (39). Children, usually eager for the latter, could empathize. Lady Charity was named but not her daughters, the knight's recovery merited only two paragraphs; one described how "the knight rejoiced greatly as he heard that he was descended from ancient Saxon kings, and was destined to do great deeds for his native land" (40).

Much of Spenser's appeal for children was variety of monsters. The Red-cross Knight's triumph over the dragon required days of fighting and recovery, Una's anxiety and prayers (42–53), and a typical description of a monstrous creature (42–43). The dragon engendered early fear and thrills, while the Blatant Beast provoked fascination at the end of *Tales from Spenser*. Moreover, this "hideous monster" that attacked Timias and was the object of Sir Calidore's quest was Spenser's creation:

> so terrible ... that even the wicked race from which it sprang dreaded and hated it.
> This monster had iron teeth, and within the iron teeth were a thousand tongues—of dogs, cats, bears, and tigers,—but the greatest number were human tongues, and these uttered cruel scandals, caring not when or where. There were also serpents' tongues, with three-forked stings, which spat out poison and said hateful things of any who interfered with the Beast. Indeed the delight of this horrid creature was to annoy and injure and destroy good men and women. It was the very plague and curse of mankind, whom it bit and wounded and tormented with its venomous teeth and wicked tongues [171–172].

Stopping the Blatant Beast required prolonged struggle—not least because Sir Calidore abandoned his quest to enjoy Pastorella's charms and pastoral life. This failure of duty, prompted by love, was judged lesser than Red-cross Knight's abandoning Una. "Now all this time the Blatant Beast was ranging at will, no one stopping or restraining his course. And Sir Calidore deemed it high time to follow his quest once more, although he must first secure the safety of his love" (189). The effort was great—"With ceaseless pains and toils Sir Calidore resumed his task"—albeit the Blatant Beast's increased "spoil and havoc" made his trail easier to follow (190).

Physical combat between knight and monster proceeded apace with sounds of "the thousand yelling, barking, back-biting tongues" in "its ugly mouth" (191). The Blatant Beast's final effort was not physical: "it began to reveal its deepest, most wicked nature, and used its tongue no longer to spit out blood or venom, but to speak reproaches and to utter wicked lies of Sir Calidore" (193). Although the struggle increases, Sir Calidore muzzles the Blatant Beast, so that lies cease. Since saying mean things and lying are among the first behaviors children are taught to avoid as wrong, they could readily understand. With this last knightly victory, Maclehose left a didactic message they could act upon: "Sir Calidore rid the world during his lifetime of a scandalous pest, although after his days the Beast broke its chain and ranged once more at liberty" (194). While Maclehose made tales from Spenser accessible and entertaining, and introduced ideals children might attain, another had children participate in the storytelling.

R. A. Y., The Story of the Red Cross Knight *(1885/91)*

R. A. Y. employed personal conversation to manage challenges. *The Story of the Red Cross Knight* (1885 /1891) was told in a sequence of Aunt Alice's conversations with nieces Daisy and Ruth and nephews Sydney and George,

Both title page and frontispiece were devoted to Una, riding her modest donkey, accompanied by the Red Cross Knight and her lamb or by the lion that protects. R. A. Y.'s *The Story of the Red Cross Knight* (1891) used a combination of an aunt's engaging storytelling to her nieces and nephews with subtle moral exposition of Spenser's allegory.

the Ingoldsby children.⁹ A Preface stated an intention to bring "in simple language, the old story so beautifully narrated by Spenser. While full of stirring incidents and containing many noble lessons, the 'Fairy Queen' is, perhaps, hardly known as widely as it deserves." R. A. Y. promised pleasure and learning but added "the earnest hope that it may help to inspire some with a love for the true and beautiful, and induce them to search for themselves the works of our great authors" (vii). Introductory Note joined criticism with reference to Raleigh's letter:

> The six books form a descending scale of merit. The first two have the fresh bloom of genius upon them; the third contains some exquisite pictures of womanhood, coloured with the light of poetic fancy; but in the last three the divine fire is seen only in fitful and uncertain flashes. It was not that the poet had written himself out, but he had been tempted to aim at achieving too much. Not content with giving us the most exquisite pictures of chivalrous life that have ever been limned in English words, and at the same time enforcing with some success lessons of true morality and virtue, he attempted to interweave with his bright allegories the history of his own day. Thus Gloriana the Faerie Queene, Belphœbe the huntress, represent Elizabeth; Artegall is Lord Grey; Envy is intended for Mary Stuart.—*From Collier's History of English Literature* [xiii].

This justified telling Book I and limiting allegory. Children's expectations and preferences were established in Chapter I "Listeners and a Story," balanced by a final Chapter IX "What Is the Story?" Seven interim chapters reiterated circumstances for storytelling with a few interlaced comments from aunt and children, but essentially told Spenser's story. Seven drawings added interest and emphasis.

R. A. Y. presented an idyllic picture of Victorian childhood, opening traditionally ("It had been a hot but lovely day in May—one of those days when everything seems happy" 15) and describing play in a glorious natural world, including Daisy's suggestion of its affinity to fairyland and request that aunt tell a fairy story. Differences of age and gender were immediately voiced. "'Oh no!' said Sydney; 'what a girl's taste! Now if you asked for something sensible, like knights fighting, and taking care of ladies, and seeking adventures, it would be something like a tale.'" Ruth likes "*true* stories.... Fairytales are nice, but you don't know that they really happened'" (17). Aunt Alice immediately responds; she can "satisfy you all.... Daisy ... a fairy tale ... and it shall be about knights and ladies, Sydney.—And what is better, Ruth, it has truth hidden in it'" (18). She identified neither author nor title, but recounted the feast of Gloriana, the beautiful Queen of Fairyland, where a lady asks help to free her royal parents of "a huge, terrible dragon." An untried young man who asks for this "errand" succeeds when he puts on the armor the lady brought; he is made a "Knight of the Red Cross." Aunt observed, "'As the knight rode along, you boys would have admired him, for his armour gleamed and flashed in the sunlight;" and described it and the landscape in detail (19-20).

The first pictured encounter was "In the Den of Error" (23). A youthful knight in armor kneels with his sword ready to strike as he holds a writhing serpent at arm's length. In the background Una raises her hands in prayer. Hermit / enchanter Archimago takes them to his dwelling to rest, but arranges for Morpheus to send Red Cross Knight a dream. In it Una chides him for "'sleeping in carelessness'" while she "'cannot sleep ... but waste the night in sorrow.'" This innocuous adjustment meant Archimago must tell Red Cross Knight "the fair Una ... was false and wicked" (27). He rides away and soon meets "a fierce-looking knight.... Sansfoy, or Infidelity" whose lady urges him to fight. When the Christian kills the pagan, the lady flees but turns back and identifies herself as Fidessa with a tale of pagan oppression that leads Red Cross Knight to beome her protector. At this dramatic moment, Aunt asks rhetorically, "'Had the knight so soon forgotten his poor Una? We shall see'" (29).

She asks Sydney how he likes her knight:

> "O Aunt Alice, I think he is a real jolly fellow to beat that old dragon as he did. What did you say its name was?"
> "Error, dear boy,—which can only be vanquished by such arms as this knight used.—George, what do *you* say to my fairy tale?"
> "I like it very much; only I do think it was mean of the knight to leave Una. I wouldn's have done so" [34].

George's immediate response made clear what interests boys. Use of a frame story allowed audience response, not unlike what students might make in class. Since the children want more of the story, Aunt gladly promises, provided they remember "it is not only a fairy story; there are beautiful meanings in it which you can find out if you will'" (34). Teaching began with a reply to Ruth—the most sophisticated child—who asks the meaning of Una's name: "'truth,' because truth is always single and straightforward. ... so beautiful in every one, whether old or young." Aunt, who calls attention to the sunset—"'like a Christian's life, ending in glory and peace,'"—sends the children home with promise of more story on the morrow (35). Chapter I ended with a family scene: telling mother of the day's play and that aunt told them a story, repeating all when Mr. Ingoldsby entered, and going to bed tired but protesting.

"Una in Distress" was "'a chapter for the girls ... but perhaps the boys will like it as well'" (39). Certainly Una's adventures provided excitement: meeting a lion that dotes on her and kills Kirk-Rapine but is slain when protecting her from Sansloy; rescue by satyrs, who serve and learn from her,

Satyrane's arrival and report of Red Cross Knight's death, and information from a pilgrim—"'You may guess this pilgrim was no other than the deceiver Archimago, who led Satyrane to Sansloy, who was resting by the fountain'" (51). Woman's vulnerability was pictured in "The Combat, The Terror" (49). Una, in flowing gown and mantle, flees as Satyrane duels Sansloy. The pilgrim (enchanter "enjoying the contest") was not easily identified. Skillfully managing suspense, Aunt reported Archimago followed Una "to try to work her further woe"—but the story must return to her knight. R. A. Y. ended with gentle teaching when asked who Archimago represents: "'the spirit of evil which is abroad in the world, which men call 'lying,' or 'deceit,' which is always at war with 'truth,' seeking to overcome it'" (51). Explanation of the lion, a response to Ruth, was subtler: "'reason is a very good servant when truth is its mistress, but even reason sometimes fails, ... while truth itself has never been, and never will be, destroyed.'" George declares had he been a knight he would have liked to meet Una and take her to a safe place. Aunt assures him he can *seek* truth and guard her, always confident "'for she *never* deceives *any one.*'" With "eyes kindled" he is resolved.

This served as smooth transition to "The House of Pride," an explicitly didactic section, introduced by a typical chivalric illustration: mounted Red Cross Knight in armor pauses as a lady gestures toward a path leading to a castle with strong walls and turret (55). Inside they meet Lucifera in her great hall, where steward Vanity attends. The center of Chapter III was devoted to Lucifera's coach drawn by six animals, with allegorical names and disturbing descriptions of their excesses (59–61). Sansjoy's arrival means combat with Red Cross Knight that ends when Duessa's mist saves Sansjoy. This circumstance provoked Sydney to ask, "'What had become of Sansjoy?'" and commiserate, "'What a disappointment to the good knight not to be able to find him.'" The storyteller reassured, "'You shall hear'" (64). Told by his page of those condemned to Lucifera's dungeons, Red Cross Knight left but is soon challenged when Duessa encourages him to drink from a fountain. He immediately loses his strength; giant Orgoglio fells him, places him in a dungeon, and woos Duessa for himself. Narrative threads rejoined when Una's dwarf reports her knight's situation, and she sets out to find him. Una meets Arthur, who gently reassures her. Young listeners heard of Arthur's magnificent armor (70–72). Readers could be inspired by "The Goodly Knight's Vow" (75). A thoughtful knight with plate armor, exotic helmet, sword, and shield stands beside seated Una who joins her hands prayerfully. Chapter III stopped at this turning point. Moreover, suspense increased when the children invited their aunt to the family's holiday excursion to Lyndhurt Tower.

Chapter IV "The Picnic" afforded respite from storytelling; on another fine day the children explore nature; combat is between a spider and a fly. With visting Uncle Will they ramble about and cook potatoes, search for Neddy, a temporarily lost donkey that carried their basket. R. A. Y. observed, "Who can forget, who has once known the delights of a country ramble, the utter enjoyment of such a time?" (84).

A few days later Aunt Alice resumed storytelling—after R. A. Y. explained why children were so fond of her—a selfless Christian woman given to charitable works, a friend and wise teacher. Sydney recalls she "'left off just in an interesting part, where that grand, brave knight went up to the giant's castle'" (89); he is keen to know whether Arthur's shield was uncovered. "The Rescue" described a fierce fight in which it was, and the giant's head cut off. Although the old man, Ignorance, is not helpful, Arthur searches the castle. "Found" showed him descending a stair at the foot of which lies weakened Red Cross Knight (95). Delivered to Una, Duessa has her finery removed to reveal "an old and ugly hag" (97). When Una asks the saviour knight his name, Daisy "triumphantly" declares, "'did I not tell you I thought this was King Arthur?'"—and is reminded he is yet Prince Arthur (97). Una calls him "the flower of chivalry" and hears of his dream and quest for the Fairy Queen (98). Aunt's character ended Chapter V:

> the type of true nobility ... represented here, in this splendid magnificence, to give the idea of a perfect man ... gathers all the virtues into himself, and so is used here to portray a higher grace than man has. Just as the Red Cross Knight could not deliver himself, but was rescued by Arthur, so man cannot fight alone, but needs a stronger arm than his to lean upon [99-100].

Daisy understands: "'Magnificence seeks Gloriana; and when a man is perfect, he truly seeks the glory of God'" (100). The children repeat admiration of Una as Truth.

With increasing understanding of allegorical meanings children were ready for lessons in "The House of Holiness." Because Red Cross Knight overestimates his strength when he responds to Sir Terwin's tale of a knight who committed suicide, he seeks Despair. Despair's argument, the strife of life plus personal guilt for abandoning Una, leads Red Cross Knight to seize a dagger. Only Una's intervention saves him; she stops his dagger thrust and takes him to the House of Holiness for help by Dame Cœlia and her daughters Fidelia, Speranza, and Charissa. Knight and lady meet Humility, Zeal, and Reverence who gently lead them to Dame Cœlia, who has Obedience take the knight to his room and sends two doctors (Patience and Repentance) to ease his troubled conscience. Charissa, with whom the learning experience culminates, is pictured with her children and helper Mercy (108). Mercy leads Red Cross Knight to "a holy house of entertainment in which seven good men always waited, spending their lives in doing good to all around" (108). Next Mercy leads him to an old man Contemplation, who takes him to a high hill. In "In View of 'The City of the Great King'" the knight in armor kneels as a monkish figure points to the New Jerusalem (115). He explains the knight must first deliver "'this royal maid from the deadly foe'"; then "'thou shalt be the friend and patron of thy country, and shalt be called 'St. George of Merry England'" (117). The once awkward young man learns his heritage: descended from Saxon kings, stolen by a fairy, found by a ploughman who gave the name "George," and desire for fame that led him to Gloriana. Gradually the knight returned to earth; no comments from Aunt or children broke the moment.

Chapter VII "The Combat" provided thrills. Red Cross Knight bids Una wait on a hill when he faces the dragon:

> And what an enemy! His enormous body was covered with scales so thick and close together that neither spear nor sword could get between them; and they shook and clashed as he moved, like armour. His wings, when they were expanded, were like two immense sails; and the pinions resembled the yard-arms of a ship for size and strength. When he flew, the very clouds were chased away, as if in dread. His huge tail, wound in many folds, was nearly three furlongs in length, and had two stings at the end, fearfully sharp, with which he could inflict grievous wounds. As to his claws, there was little hope of anything that once got within their reach being released, for they were sharper than any stings or steel. His mouth, which was deep and wide, armed with three rows of teeth, sent forth flames and smoke. Then his eyes burned like two fires; while they were set so far in his head that the light from them seemed to cast a shade around [119–120].

"The Combat with the Dragon" visually emphasized the woman (121). In a valley beneath a castle on a hilltop mounted St. George aims his lance at the dragon; both are small figures. In the foreground a large Una watches from a hill. Nevertheless, Sydney and George were probably not disappointed; R. A. Y. followed iconic description with an equally vivid blow-by-blow account of the fight. Anxiety when the knight falls prompts George to interrupt:

> "Oh, was the knight really conquered?" asked George. "I did so hope he would have won this battle that no one else could."
> "Wait a bit and you shall hear" [124].

"The Well of Life" and "The Tree of Life" restore Red Cross Knight, who slays the dragon on the third day. Aunt praises his perseverance and corollary kindness and gentleness. Moreover, she sought direct involvement: "'And, George, he bore your name; I should think you feel honoured.'" The boy, who quickly declares he could not have so persevered, searches for the word for "'those who are bravest and really fight the best are most—'" (127). "'Chivalrous?'" is Aunt's reply. Ruth and Daisy voice admiration and understanding of allegorical meanings; Daisy announces Aunt reminds her of Mercy and begs to learn her secret. The answer is learning to forget oneself and to live giving for others, persevering with confidence. Then Aunt says, "'Now, goodnight, my children, and don't dream of dragons and battles'" (129)—a gentle reminder that allegory may be lost in the excitement of chivalric romance.

Chapter VIII "The Reward of Victory" continued Spenser's report of the people's response, welcome by Una's parents, a banquet when events are recapitulated, Red Cross Knight's betrothal to a now dazzlingly arrayed Una, Archimago's last futile attempt to prevent the marriage of Truth and Holiness, joy, followed by the knight's honoring his vow to serve another six years, and anticipation of a happy reunion. Aunt's final lessons informed Chapter IX "What Is the Story?" When the children ask for meanings, she offers a simple universal answer: Red Cross Knight is "'a picture of the soul ... striving after Holiness which is at last united to Truth? You might call it the Legend of Holiness'" (139). George relates *The Faerie Queene* to Ephesians 6: "'The girdle of truth—breastplate of righteousness—helmet, the hope of salvation—shield of faith—sword of the Spirit, which is the word of God'" (139). A few additional allegorical figures, a sketch of Queen Elizabeth's court, mention of Shakespeare but special attention to Spenser's friends Sir Philip Sidney and Sir Walter Raleigh—historical knights of chivalry—completed a hope the children, when older, will enjoy the poem as much as the story (138). There is always more to learn, "heart-knowledge" and "head-knowledge" ever increasing, "if love to God and man is what we seek most to cultivate" (142).

3

Edwardian Extravagance

Late Victorian and Edwardian extravagance led to a remarkable variety of engaging and imaginative books for children that extended delight and mitigated didactic lessons. In this "Golden Age of Children's Literature" retold major English authors paralleled now revered classics by Beatrix Potter, Kenneth Graham, James Barrie, and E. Nesbit.[1] Many retold *The Faerie Queene*. Mary Macleod's *Stories from the Faerie Queene* (1897) numbered six. Wells Gardner, Darton's small series printed two as *The Red Cross Knight and Sir Guyon* (1908). Macleod's *Stories* became *The Story of the Faerie Queene* (1902), edited by Edward Brooks, discussed in Chapter 4 American Difference. E. Edwardson's *The Courteous Knight and Other Tales* (1899) drew upon Malory and later books of *The Faerie Queene* for "adaptations." Jeanie Lang's *Stories from the Faerie Queen* (1906), Told to the Children Series, published by T. C. and E. C. Jack, reordered and selected to suit younger children, while Lawrence H. Dawson's *Stories from the Faerie Queene Retold from Spenser* (1909), Harrap's Told through the Ages Series suited older. A. J. Church's *The Faery Queen and Her Knights* (1910) extended his retold classical and medieval literature to early modern romance. Sumptuous but less inclusive was Emily Underdown's *The Gateway to Spenser* (1911), illustrated by Frank C. Papé with extensive quotations from *The Faerie Queene*; it was reissued as *The Approach to Spenser: Prose Tales with Extracts* (1925). Two sections, without quoted passages, became *Stories from Spenser: Retold from "The Faerie Queene"* (1912) in Nelson's Golden River Series.

The Red Cross Knight, patron Saint George, was always Spenser's favored chivalric hero; only one collection did not feature him. W. T. Stead's Books for the Bairns #53 and 54, *The Red Cross Knight I and II* (1900) was two books. R. W. Grace's *Tales from Spenser* (1909) were all from Book I. In N. G. Royde-Smith's *Una and the Red Cross Knight and Other Tales from Spenser's Faery Queene* (1905), a large volume enhanced by T. H. Robinson's illustrations, "other" was a small section about Sir Guyon.

Mary Macleod, Stories from the Faerie Queene *(1897)*, The Red Cross Knight and Sir Guyon *(1908)*

Clarity, narrative control, and effective juxtaposition of allegory with chivalry distinguished Mary Macleod's *Stories from the Faerie Queene* (1897), a remarkably skilled rendering.[2] Macleod (d.1914) published several books of retold traditional literature with Wells Gardner, Darton— *The Shakespeare Story-Book* (1902), *Book of Ballad Stories* (1906), *The Book of King Arthur* (1900), and *Honour and Arms: Tales from Froissart* (1910)— with numerous editions in England and the United States. Generous illustrations and introductions by distinguished scholars / critics enhanced volumes where quality publishing supported excellent writing. Although identified as "sculptor," A(rthur) G(eorge) Walker (1861–1939) was also a painter, designer in mosaics, and illustrator; he followed *Stories from the Faerie Queene* with Macleod's *The Book of King Arthur* and F. J. Harvey Darton's *The Wonder Book of Old Romance* (1907). John W. Hales (1836–1914), who co-edited *Bishop Percy's Folio Manuscript* (1867) with Frederick J. Furnivall, provided a memoir to *Works of Edmund Spenser* (1897), the Globe edition by R. Morris, and wrote books about Shakespeare and Milton.

Hales's Introduction identified the discrepancy between poets and sophisticated readers

Extravagant covers were characteristic of Edwardian prize / reward books. *The Faery Queen and Her Knights* (1910), with its display of gold and red against a dark blue cloth cover, was especially handsome. Noteworthy was the depiction of the Red Cross Knight (Holiness) and Prince Arthur (Magnificence), principal English heroes. A. J. Church, who wrote many books to retell literary masterpieces, began with classical texts, then medieval, and finally Spenser's early modern romance.

who admired *The Faerie Queene* and a paucity of other readers; he recommended Macleod's *Stories* as helpful to children and adults. Having cited Milton's praise of Spenser as comparable to Aquinas and listed many so inspired that Spenser was called "the poets' poet" (viii), Hales quoted Macaulay's famous essay declaring how few reach even the end of Book I—and pointed out that this popular author, a voracious reader, had himself not read the whole (x-xi)! I remember my graduate seminar in which one student always began with a need to "get the story straight"; the professor promised admission to the select "Faerie Queene Club"—if we read the whole. Hales, who began with an impression of "a certain artificiality and elaborateness," further suggested Spenser would be more read if he had controlled the "very opulence of his genius ... the redundant stream of his poetry ... readers are overpowered and bewildered by the immense flood ... amazing overflow" (xiv-xv). Spenser, who admired Chaucer but did not imitate his self-restraint, was not comparable to "the masterly tale-teller" unequalled in all English poetry and matched only by Shakespeare in drama. Complications were worse in Books III and IV; even Spenser acknowledged he did not proceed directly to his destination (VI.xii.1-2). Hales expected Macleod's book would be "truly serviceable in preparing them [children] for the study of the poem itself" and nourished a "fain hope" older readers would find "a hearty welcome, as providing them with a clue to what seems an intricate maze" (xx).

Macleod, like Towry, divided *Stories from Spenser* into six major sections that did not exactly correspond to Spenser's six books. Aids to reading were large type, short, titled subsections, and facing running titles—the knight's name and a note of action. Captions for full-page illustrations were Spenser's lines (two or four, printed in Gothic), while a list identified all characters and actions. Eighty-five black-and-white pictures varied in size and placement: forty-two full pages, seventeen three-quarter pages, sixteen half-pages, ten quarter-pages, for a total of eighty-five, plus four small devices. Partial-page pictures added variety. Macleod's clear sentence structure, accessible vocabulary, simple dialogue, italics for allegorical names / meaning, and restrained use of adjectives and adverbs were a far cry from Spenser's archaisms and sixteenth-century convolutions. Her set piece descriptions closely turned Spenser's verse into clear prose. She kept allegorical names, but overt didactic commentary was rare and introduced with comparison to modern times.

The opening, which combined fairy tale and chivalry, established long ago:

> Once upon a time, in the days when there were still such things as giants and dragons, there lived a great Queen. She reigned over a rich and beautiful country, and because she was

good and noble every one loved her, and tried also to be good. Her court was the most splendid one in the world, for all her knights were brave and gallant, and each one thought only of what heroic things he could do, and how best he could serve his royal lady.

The name of the Queen was Gloriana, and each of her twelve knights was known as the Champion of some virtue. Thus Sir Guyon was the representative of *Temperance*, Sir Artegall of *Justice*, Sir Calidore of *Courtesy*, and others took up the cause of *Friendship*, *Constancy*, and so on [3].

The Red Cross Knight's "real name was *Holiness*, and the name of the lady for whom he was to do battle was *Truth*"; *Prudence* was their faithful attendant (4). Children, accustomed to Victorian didacticism and familiar with *The Pilgrim's Progress* and retold medieval romances, would be encouraged by Walker's iconic frontispiece: from a hill a lady waves to a knight with raised sword; he stands with one foot on the slain dragon.

Prince Arthur, who gave affinity with the Round Table, wears "glittering armour" and a jeweled belt. His shield made "of one perfect and entire diamond ... hewn out of the adamant rock with mighty engines" is impervious to spear or sword, to "magic arts" or "enchanter's spell.... Everything that was not exactly what it seemed to be faded before it and fell to ruin" (52). Prince Arthur, "type of all Virtue and Magnificence, and pattern of all true Knighthood," greets Una courteously and "with gentle and kindly words" encourages her to tell her story: "Misfortunes may be overcome with good advice, and wise counsel will lessen the worst injury" (53).

Contrast with Red Cross Knight was palpable; a didactic passage glossed how difficult and universal is the struggle to be good. Macleod unsparingly analyzed failings:

> Now the Red Cross Knight, because of his lack of loyalty to Una, fell into much danger and difficulty. His first fault was in believing evil of her so readily, and leaving her forlorn; after that he was too easily beguiled by the pretended goodness and beauty of Duessa. All who fight in a good cause must beware of errors such as these. If matters do not go exactly as we wish, we must not lose heart and get impatient; even if we cannot understand what is happening, we must trust that all will be well. We must keep steadily to the one true aim set before us, or else, like the Red Cross Knight, we may be led astray by false things that are only pleasant in appearance, and have no real goodness [26–27].

Application to readers' behavior established the cogency of chivalric stories. It also heightened Macleod's favoring of Una, heralded by the cover, where Walker depicted her with the Lion, and by a decorated page with a watchful lion (like C. S. Lewis's Aslan) guarding a sleeping maiden, as her donkey feeds at a distance (19). Prudence, servant who observed Red Cross Knight's fall, "sorrowfully collected his forsaken possessions—his mighty armour, missing when most needed, his silver shield, now idle and masterless, his sharp spear that had done good service in many a fray." When battling giant Orgoglio, "[d]isarmed, disgraced, inwardly dismayed, and faint in every limb, he could scarcely wield even his useless blade" (50–51). A didactic passage encouraged:

> Badly indeed would it now have fared with the Red Cross Knight had it not been for the Lady Una. Even good people daily fall into sin and temptation, but as often as their own foolish pride or weakness leads them astray, so often will Divine love and care rescue them, if only they repent of their misdoings. Thus we see how Holiness, in the guise of the Red Cross Knight, was for a while cast down and defeated; yet in the end, because he truly repented, help was given him to fight again and conquer [54].

After Prince Arthur releases the captive knight, he urges not recrimination but care, "'perfect happiness can never be lasting while we still live on earth'" (62). This prepares for further faltering in the Cave of Despair where Una first strikes the dagger from her knight's hand and then chides his faintheartedness (73). Macleod distinguished between physical and moral courage: "The bravest man who boasts of bodily strength may often find his moral courage fail in the hour of temptation. If he gain the victory, let him not ascribe it to his own skill, but rather to the grace of God" (73–74). In the House of Holiness *Contemplation* leads the Red Cross Knight to a vision of the New Jerusalem. Walker's old pilgrim with staff and young knight with sword stand on a cliff and gaze at a faint and glowing city on the horizon (81). Explaining Gloriana's kingdom is the fairest on earth, but Heaven awaits, the pilgrim promises, "'Amongst the saints you shall be a saint, the friend and patron of your own nation. Saint George you shall be called—'Saint George for merry England, the sign of Victory'" (84).

Preparation for "The Last Fight" was long and hard; even so "The strength of the Red Cross Knight alone would never have been sufficient to overcome the terrible Dragon of Sin, but the water of the Well of Life, and the balm from the Tree of Life, gave him a power that nothing could resist" (86). In a final illustration he kneels with Una before her parents; the Queen is seated, while the King stands to bless the betrothal; an observant page provides the child's point of view (87). While the marriage must be delayed for six years of service vowed to Gloriana, Macleod deleted Archimago's final challenge and stressed future happiness.

"The Good Sir Guyon" promised a knight less problematic. *Temperance*, supported by a Palmer, *Conscience*, early defined the virtue that "raging passion" can destroy through fury or despair: "Temperance with a golden rule can measure out a medium between the two, neither to be overcome by pleasure, nor to give way to despair. Thrice happy man who can tread evenly between them!" (102). Sir Guyon, having recognized Red Cross Knight and broken off the fight urged by Duessa, hears Sir Mordant's grieving, suicidal wife; he buries both honorably before setting out to destroy the Bower of Bliss. Bragadocchio—

"puffed up with self-conceit ... never trained in chivalry" (109)—stole Guyon's horse. Knight, in gleaming armor, and Palmer, in dark robe and hat with St. Jacques's shell, approach the castle of *Medina* (Golden Mean) on foot (105). Trompart (*Deceit*) is a fitting squire for the fearful braggart, whom "the wicked magician, Archimago (*Hypocrisy*)" urges to fight Prince Arthur. Further con-

A. G. Walker's black-and-white illustrations for Mary Macleod's *Stories from the Faerie Queene* (1897) matched the excellence of her verbal text. His attention to details, shining armor and varied landscapes, as well as lively action provided parallel storytelling. Here the Palmer leads Sir Guyon (Temperance) to the castle of Medina (Golden Mean).

nections follow. *Strife*, servant of Pyrocles (*the Anger of Fire*), brother of Cymocles (*the Anger of the Sea-Waves*), sons of *Malice* and *Intemperance*, seeks *Occasion*. When Pyrocles attacks, Sir Guyon defeats him, but courteously honors his wish to release *Occasion* and her son *Fury*; he accepts the Palmer's advice to leave Pyrocles, whose "folly and wilfulness" led him to fight Fury (121).

Opposite to "adventures of a stern and painful kind" were "sloth and luxury," alternative destroyers of temperance, faced on "The Idle Lake," an

With the Palmer's help in casting a net over Acrasia, Sir Guyon can proceed to destroy the Bower of Bliss so that knights, like the one fallen under her charms, will no longer be entrapped. A. G. Walker demonstrated skill in illustrating Mary Macleod's *Stories from the Faerie Queene* (1897) with subtle contrasts between solid armor and delicate lines to indicate mesh. Acrasia's voluptuous beauty makes clear how she entrapped men.

anticipation of the Bower of Bliss (122). A beautiful lady misleads Sir Guyon, only to be firmly rejected. Walton pictured them standing beside her moored gondola (123). Sir Guyon departs alone in response to Phaedria, Acrasia's servant, who asks him to desist from fighting Cymocles. In "The Realm of Pluto" Sir Guyon rejects all Mammon's "idle offers, whether Riches, Ambition, or Love of Honour." These efforts exhaust "The Champion of Chivalry"; the Palmer finds him "Watched over by a beautiful angel," a compelling image with affinity to G. F. Watts's mystical happy warrior (140). When Pyrocles and Cymocles attempt to despoil Sir Guyon of his armor, Prince Arthur dispatches both. Magnificence expects no thanks, "'Are not all knights bound by oath to withstand the power of the oppressor? It is sufficient that I have done my duty properly.'" Macleod commented, "So they both found that a good deed is made gracious by kindness and courtesy" (144).

Traveling together, they disperse knights attacking "The House of Temperance"—a castle in Walker's subtle picture; knights in armor scatter with swords "idle shades; / For though they bodies seem, yet substaunce from them fades" (147). Alma, whose house is an allegory of the body, leads Arthur and Guyon through its parts to three increasingly older counsellors: Imagination, Judgment, and Memory. Thus strengthened, Sir Guyon sails with the Palmer, past the Rock of Reproach and the Wandering Isles toward the Bower of Bliss. They evade Quicksand of Unthriftiness, Whirlpool of Decay, Sea Monsters and Land Monsters—all made by enchanters—and mermaids. The rigor of the oarsman's efforts in choppy seas is evident as he steers them past a huge rock (153). Macleod described the beauty of the Bower of Bliss, where Guyon refuses the cup of *Excess*. In two pictures the Palmer acts while Sir Guyon merely stands beside him. The Palmer raises his staff when transformed knights, "A pack of wild beasts rushed forward" (159); he casts his net over the temptress in "Acrasia tried to set herself free" (164). Delicate contrasting textures for net, armor, black robe, gossamer gown, bush, and trees were among Walker's most skillful.

The third part, "The Legend of Britomart," began with affirmation of chivalry: "many perilous adventures, which won them [Sir Guyon and Prince Arthur] great glory and honour, for their aim was always to relieve the weak and oppressed, and to recover right for those who had suffered wrong" (167). Although "Hurled from his horse" (illustration 169), the fault was not Sir Guyon's: "The spear that brought him to the ground was enchanted, and no one could resist it" (168). Such encounters inspired another of Macleod's explanations and urgings of chivalry's idealism:

> In those days, when knights fought together, it was often not at all in malice, but only to test their strength and manliness. The one who conquered won much renown, but the van-

quished felt no spite or envy. It is a great thing to be able to lose with a good grace, without becoming sulky and disagreeable. Later ages might do well in this respect to learn a lesson from the days of chivalry [171].

Warnings against "sulky and disagreeable" behavior apply to children. Arthur and Guyon pursue the "rough, clownish woodman" chasing Florimell. Britomart, who neither intends nor fears evil, rides alone and aids a knight attacked by six because he would not be disloyal to his lady. At Castle Joyous, reminiscent of the Bower of Bliss, "wasteful luxury" displeases Britomart. Macleod wryly noted Britomart's womanly response to Malecasta (Lady of Delight)—"a sudden affection for a wandering guest could not be worth very much" (178).

Illustrations of the woman warrior were carefully sequenced. The heading pictured a woman (narrow waist, breasts) dressed as a youth—like Shakespeare's Rosalind—with bare legs and holding a staff; beside her is an old woman in a long mantle (167). At Merlin's cave they face away from the viewer (189). Britomart is slender with breasts and abundant hair—her armor removed in Castle Joyous—when she faces six knights summoned by Malecasta; one draws an arrow (179). Only later does Britomart gaze into the mirror (184). Then in a splendid Romanesque church "Glaucé, taking down the armour, dressed her in it" (193). Thus pictures revealed physical features—long hair, breasts, and slender leg—before explanation of how the Magic Mirror inspired a woman to don armor. As a youthful knight—a gentle face under her helmet—Britomart lacked a typical nineteenth-century moustache (169,172)

After Merlin identified Sir Artegall (*Justice*) and prophesied Britomart's future, Macleod summarized ideal male characteristics, "in her fancy everything that was noble and lovable—'wise, warlike, handsome, courteous, and kind'" (196). But Britomart's experience makes clear her disguise and pursuit of chivalry were long anticipated:

> "I have been trained up in warlike ways, to toss spear and shield, to meet and overthrow warrior knights. I loathe to lead the lazy life of pleasure that most ladies do, fingering the needle and fancy thread; I would rather die at the point of a foeman's spear. All my delight is set on deeds of arms, to hunt out perils and adventures wherever they may be met by sea or land, not for riches nor for reward, but only for glory and honour" [181–182].

The fascination of Spenser's Book III is gender, well explored by Macleod and Walker, in the age of the New Woman. A rare interior scene depicts, with Pre-Raphaelite characteristics, how "Britomart looked well at the figure of this Knight" (184). In this lone depiction of Britomart dressed as a woman she sits pensively, chin on hands before a large round globe placed on a table, suggestive of Tennyson's musing heroine and John William Waterhouse's painting, *Lady of Shalott Looking at Lancelot* (1894). More than pictures, Macleod's words described feminine beauty (198). At Malbecco's castle Britomart and fellow knights remove armor to dry before the fire:

> When she lifted her helmet, and her golden locks fell like a cloud of light to the ground, they were all amazed to find the valiant stranger was a beautiful maiden. They stood gazing at her, silent with astonishment, for eye had never seen a fairer woman, but chiefly they marveled at her chivalry and noble daring [199].

This passage established the inferiority of the distaff to chivalry and foreshadowed the ignominy of Sir Artegall's bondage to Radigund, Queen of the Amazons. The warrior maiden's uneasiness with her attraction to "a gallant knight [whose] face ... showed forth like the sun, to terrify his foes and make glad his friends ... heroic grace and noble bearing added to the grandeur of his figure" (185) was an important theme. At their climactic meeting during Sir Satyrane's tournament the Knight of the Ebony Spear charged against the Savage Knight, "in the midst of his pride," and "smote him sorely on the visor" (237). This jousting had no hint of gender.

Yet Macleod affirmed traditional roles and their interdependence:

> Through all ages it has been the custom that the prize of Beauty has been joined with the praise of arms and Chivalry. And there are special reasons for this, for each relies much on the other; that Knight who can best defend a fair Lady from harm, is surely the most fitting to serve her; and that Lady who is fairest and who will never swerve from her faith, is the most fitting to deserve his service [236].

Sir Satyrane holds his tournament to honor Florimell, believed dead since he saw a hyena-like creature devouring her palfrey on the beach (picture 225). Britomart does not compete to be the fairest lady. This episode, from Spenser's Book IV, showed the folly and pretention of claims for the fairest through Braggadochio's antics and illusion of the false Florimell, the Snowy Lady. Britomart again fights Sir Artegall because the Savage Knight wanted to recover "the honour of the game" lost at the tourney when the Knight with the Ebony Spear shamed him. In contrast to this simple directness Macleod retained Spenser's elaborate language (IV.vi.19–22), albeit turning verse into prose, to describe revelation of Britomart's gender (253). Artegall shears her helmet's vizor. Angry Britomart, who orders him to rise, does not forbear after Sir Scudamour pleads—until he too becomes terrified by "this peerless image of perfection." However, after Glaucé asks a truce, the warrior maiden recognizes the knight seen in the enchanted mirror: "her heart leaped and trembled with sudden joy and secret fear. She flushed deeply, and thought to hide her agitation by again feigning her former angry mood" (255–256). Although Britomart persists in this mode through wooing, she marries Artegall, only to become "poor Britomart [who] would scarcely let him go" to

Vigorous action provides much of children's delight in chivalric story. Sir Satyrane, lying in the foreground after being unhorsed by Britomart, watches as the Savage Knight (Artegal) meets a similar fate from the Knight of the Ebony Spear. Gender was not recognized when the warrior princess jousted. This, one of several chivalric encounters depicted by A. G. Walker in Mary Macleod's *Stories from the Faerie Queene* (1897), shows his precision.

resume his quest (258). Walker's last picture reaffirmed her identity as knight. Although their stance is intimate, man and woman wear matching armor; astride his charger, he bows to kiss her raised left hand, while her right hand rests on his greave (258).

Like other knights Britomart had many adventures—notably rescue of Amoret, wife of Sir Scudamour, from enchanter giant Busirane's castle, where she carefully observed a formidable procession of allegorical conflicting emotions (illustration 209). With resolute determination Britomart overwhelms the enchanter and releases the lady (illustration 214), only to discover Sir Scudamour and Glaucé gone. The two young women ride together (illustration 219) and relate their stories of love, "girl talk."

After three parts with intricacies, interlacing of episodes, and shifting locations, "The Squire of Lowe Degree" was refreshingly brief. As Britomart and Amoret ride through a forest, "a huge, hideous savage" seizes Amoret, who wandered off while Britomart rested (260). In his cave Amoret meets Emilia, another captive lady, taken when she sought the squire of low degree her father deemed too inferior to marry. Plucky Amoret slips past when the villain removes the entry stone:

> Fast she fled, but he followed as swiftly. She did not feel the thorns and thickets prick her tender feet; neither hedge, nor ditch, nor hill, nor dale could stop her; she overleaped them all like a deer, and made her way through the thickest brushwood. ... Long she fled thus, and long he followed, and it seemed as if there were no living aid for her on earth [261-262].

At this moment of crisis "the glorious Huntress-Queen, Belphoebe" and her companions ride up. Although a squire initiates the attack, Belphoebe pursues and slays "the grizzly monster." Triumphs by other women reinforced Britomart's. Night leads to refuge in the cottage of a hag (*Slander*), poor accommodation but accepted: "It was an age which despised luxury. People were accustomed to hardness and homely fare, which trained them to warlike discipline, and to endure carelessly any hard fortunes or luckless mishaps which might befall them." Macleod glossed earlier ages; "they mildly and patiently endured it all" (264) to imply late Victorians and Edwardians were effete.

Walker's three illustrations were distinctive. "A mighty man, riding on a dromedary" pursues a Squire holding a dwarf before him as he gallops through an opening (264). Prince Arthur slays this Pagan and then hears the story of the Squire (Placidas), who, "For his Friend's sake," took the place of Amyas, the Squire of Low Degree who loves Emilia. *Corflambo* (the Giant with Flaming Eyes) captured and imprisoned him and thus thwarted the elopement. Next a dwarf discovered Placidas in the garden, mistook him for Amyas, returned him to prison, and showed prisoners to the giant's daughter Poena. One friend persuades the other to let him substitute; Placidas woos Poena—as Amyas, true to Emilia, had not; given increased liberty he seizes the dwarf and flees. Macleod praised a key virtue: "Of all human affection the love of one friend for another is surely the noblest and most unselfish;

and this true friendship Amyas and Placidas had for each other—not even their affection for kindred or fairest lady could shake their loyalty" (274). Child readers thus encountered a dimension of chivalry closer to their own experiences than the ubiquitous vagaries of wooing and marriages. The happy ending was easily achieved. Arthur ties the giant's corpse on the dromedary, and the Squire sits before him like a captive; thus they gain entry and release all prisoners, so that Amyas can wed Emilia. Arthur shares the castle's treasure, releases Poena, and "with his accustomed grace, charmed her to mild behaviour from the sullen rudeness that spoilt her." He also urges Placidas to requite the love Poena transferred to him.

"The Adventures of Sir Artegall" for which the knight left his bride Britomart, began with identification as *Justice*, called to succor Irene (*Peace*) from the tyrant Grantorto (*Great Wrong*). Typically many adventures preceded fulfillment of a primary quest. Artegall's childhood was recounted. Astrea, who trained the little boy, pointed to wild beasts in the woods as examples of "wrongfull power oppressing others of their kind"—Walker's rare depiction of a child (283). A pretty little boy stands beside a lovely lady seated outside a cave as they observe two stags fighting. After Astrea returns to live among the stars, Artegall is looked after by her servant Talus, "made of iron mould, immovable, irresistible, unchanging: he held in his hand an iron flail, with which he threshed out falsehood and unfolded the truth" (282). Talus, Iron Man, is Spenser's most distinctive knight's companion, an extension who metes out justice defined by Artegall. Saracen Pollenté guards a bridge and demands a toll to cross. Those who do not pay die: first they fall through one of the traps into the river; then the Pagan, a good swimmer, kills them. In Artegall Pollenté met his better, because Artegall "was skilful in swimming and dared venture in any depth of water" (287). Walker distinguished combatants—the Saracen's helmet has a sharp spike, not a decorative feather—as they struggle below the bridge's large arches (288). Although Pollenté's daughter Lady Munera tries to stay Talus by tossing riches from the parapets, he batters down the door to allow Artegall to enter the castle. The knight is moved by pity, but the Iron Man punishes relentlessly: he throws Munera into the water, burns treasures, and pours the ashes into the river; then he tears down the castle beyond repair. Similarly, Talus overwhelms "The Giant with the Scales," who claims he can weigh the world, and the foolish mob that listen to him.

The earlier story of Florimell and Marinell resumed at a tournament following their bridal ceremony. The groom wins for two days, then ventures too far and is captured. Artegal, who borrowed Bragadocchio's shield, rescues Marinell. Boasting, "bragging and unseemly speeches," provoke only contempt from all knights; Bragadocchio is justly punished, but not before he proclaimed his "Snowy Lady" fairest. Set against the true Florimell, "Straightway the enchanted damsel vanished into nothing," (illustration 299). Artegall gives the golden belt, true Florimell's girdle, to its rightful possessor. Bragadocchio's final punishment comes after Sir Guyon's horse, which he stole, responds to its name "Brigadore" and stands quietly by its proper master. Artegal (Justice) would slay Bragadocchio, but Sir Guyon (Temperance) dissuades him. Talus has no qualms; he drags Bragadocchio from the hall, shaves off his beard, blots the device on his shield, breaks his sword, scatters his armor, and scourges him from the court (picture 303). Rigorous punishment abates when Artegall arbitrates a case: brothers dispute ownership of a treasure coffer thrown on shore. Lawyerlike questions force a just resolution, even though not all are pleased.

Conflict involving chivalry, justice, and gender characterized Artegall's facing Radigund, Queen of Amazons: as was evident with Britomart, a knight should not fight women, even those who treat them shamefully (illustration 312). Instead Artegal sends Talus to disperse a troop with his iron flail. Radigund "looking half like a man," arrays her fighters, orders the gates open, and attacks when knights press forward. Invincible Talus "chased and outran them, and broke their bows, and spoilt their shooting, so that not one of them all dared to go near him" (316). This provokes Radigund to propose single combat with Artegall. Macleod closely followed Spenser's description (V.iv.2–3) of this "stately and magnificent" woman warrior:

> She wore a light loose robe of purple silk, woven with silver, quilted with white satin, and plentifully trimmed with ribbons; not to hinder her movements it was tucked up to her knee, but could when she liked be lowered to her heel. Over that her legs wore for defence a small coat of mail. On her legs were painted buskins, laced with bands of gold; her scimitar was lashed at her thigh in an embroidered belt; and on her shoulder hung her shield, decked with glittering stones, so that it shone like the full moon [318].

Sir Artegall, "dazzled with astonishment" at beauty, spares his fallen foe (320). When Radigund revives and resumes the fight, "by abandoning his sword, he willfully lost that which before he had attained" (322). Talus does not intervene; Artegal becomes Radigund's vassal, a humiliated knight in women's clothes and assigned to the distaff.

Britomart, told by Talus of Artegall's fate, sets out to rescue him and kills Radigund. As always the journey involved circumventing challenges, notably escaping Dolan (*Guile*) that offers hospitality (a bed above a trapdoor to capture visiting knights) and a vision at the Temple of Isis, long ago devoted to worship of justice. Walker juxtaposed western armor with Egyptian architecture and costume (333). Released and with vitality restored, Artegall resumed his quest to free Lady Irene. Another fight against a Pagan, albeit undertaken by Prince Arthur, expanded Orientalism. In an extraordinary encounter between mounted knight and chariot "The Sultan's horses, like hungry hounds, cruelly chased him" (illustration 342). Because Arthur unveils his shield, its dazzling light spooks the horses that ignore commands: the wheels tear their master. The Sultan's wife, Lady Adicia, rushes out and tries to kill Samient, who brought Artegall and Arthur to the castle. After Artegall deflects her knife she dashes into the wild wood—and is transformed into a tiger. Samient and the knights proceed through the Den of *Deceit* where Talus pursues this shape-shifting villain—fox, bird, stone, and hedgehog—and thrashes him with his flail. Finally they reach Queen Mercilla's palace guarded by *Awe*; *Order* is the marshal. At a trial all judge Duessa guilty of heinous crimes and doom her to death; Mercilla weeps with compassion.

In the final section Artegal arrives in time to be Lady Irene's champion and restore her kingdom. Sir Burbon, who failed to rescue his lady, also abandoned his shield. Because it was Red Cross Knight's gift and "traced his dear Redeemer's badge," Artegall chides such loss of honor: "'All peril and all pain should be accounted less than loss of fame. Die rather than do aught that yields dishonour.'" When Sir Burbon argues the efficacy of temporizing, Artegall exclaims, "'Fie on such forgery! ... Knights should be true, and truth is one in all. Down with all dissembling'" (354–355). Talus and Artegall disperse the rabble and rescue the lady. They sail to Grantorto's island, where Artegall issues a challenge to single combat. After the tyrant's poleaxe sticks in Artegall's shield, he executes a grizzly end: "Artegall, with his sword Crysaor, swiftly cut off his head" (symbolic castration). He rests a foot on the corpse and lifts the head; in the distance Irene clasps her hands together, as the tyrant's men turn to run (359).

While courtesy is expected of all, "Sir Calidore, Knight of Courtesy" excelled in this virtue. His mission was to pursue the Blatant Beast, "a hideous monster of evil race, born and brought up in dark and noisome places, whence he issues forth to be the plague and scourge of wretched men. ... with his venomous nature and vile tongue he wounds sorely, and bites, and cruelly torments" (361–362). First, Sir Calidore releases a Squire bound to a tree (illustration 363). The squire describes how Lady Briana's servants mistreat all who come by: "'they shave away the lady's locks and the knight's beard to pay toll for the passage'" (365). Crudor wants a cloak of cut hair. When a churl rushes past dragging a maiden by her golden hair, Artegall pursues him into Briana's castle and kills him. She entertains Calidore but sends for Crudor, whose pleas for mercy prompt Calidore's exposition of courtesy:

However strong and fortunate he may be in fight, nothing is more blameful to a knight, who professes courtesy as well as arms, than the reproach of pride and cruelty. In vain he seeks to suppress others who has not learned first to subdue himself. All flesh is frail and full of fickleness, subject to the chance of ever-changing fortune: what happens to me to-day may happen to you to-morrow. He who will not show mercy to others, how can he ever hope to obtain mercy? To pay each in his own coin is right and just [368].

The second, more exacting encounter involved class. Tristram, a youth in Lincoln green, slays a knight. Challenged by Sir Calidore that chivalry forbids anyone not a knight to slay a knight, Tristram argues he was loath to break the law of chivalry; however, the Knight "'assailed me first, regardless of what belongs to chivalry'" (370). Tristram, of course, precipitated the blow by faulting the knight's discourtesy to a lady—he rode, while she walked and was chided for lagging. Calidore, impressed by Tristram's heritage and training, makes him his squire and the lady's escort before proceeding alone.

A pastoral interlude provided respite. Seeking the Blatant Beast in a remote place, Calidore meets shepherds and shepherdesses. All love Pastorella, especially shepherd Coridon. Calidore, smitten by one who seems nobler than her present station, complicates the situation. After Old Melibee invites him to his cottage and extols joys of pastoral life, Calidore lives as a rustic; he sets aside his armor, tends Pastorella's flock, and makes Coridon jealous. When Calidore bests Coridon at wrestling, he courteously gives him the crown and is loved, "for courtesy breeds goodwill and favour even amongst the rudest" (379). This euphoric existence ends while Calidore is away hunting and brigands capture all. Because the captain claims Pastorella for himself, other bandits attack him; he dies defending her. Coridon escapes, meets Calidore, and reports events. Calidore reassures him, and they return to the thieves' den. Calidore releases Pastorella and kills or terrifies the brigands as they approach the entry. He gives recovered booty to Coridon, along with flocks stolen from Melibee. Class difference is resolved when Calidore takes Pastorella to the castle of Belgard, where Sir Bellamour and Claribel recover their child, born in prison and placed in a field to escape a tyrant's wrath. Melibee found the infant; "a little purple mark, like a rose unfolding its silken leaves" on Pastorella's breast identifies her (390).

Meanwhile Sir Calidore pursued the Blatant Beast that charged him

with open mouth, huge and horrible; it was all set with a double row of iron teeth, and in it were a thousand tongues of every kind and quality—some were of dogs, that barked day and night; some of cats that yawled; some of bears that growled continually; some of tigers that seemed to grin and snarl at all who passed by; and among them were mingled here and there the tongues of serpents, with three-forked stings, that spat out poison at all who came within reach, speaking hateful things of good and bad alike, of high and low, not even sparing kings or kaisers, but either blotting them with infamy or biting them with their baneful teeth [393].

This was another closely rendered description (VI.xii.26–28). Sir Calidore presses down his shield to subdue Walker's Blatant Beast—less extraordinarily endowed—in a narrow place below high cliffs (391). After he muzzles this beast, for a time it seems to have learned obedience. Nevertheless, *Stories from Spenser* ended on a disturbing note; the Blatant Beast breaks its chains and returns to the world: "and here he still ranges, barking and biting, sparing no one in his malice, and doing an infinite deal of mischief wherever he goes; and ... no man has ever been able to master him" (394). Although the present world lacks chivalric knights comparable to those who served the Faerie Queene, the story teaches children greater courtesy.

Macleod adapted two stories for younger readers. *Stories* was in a fifth edition when Wells Gardner, Darton issued *The Red Cross Knight and Sir Guyon* (1908).[3] This little book—4½ by 6¼ inches—had 128 pages instead of 395 and only six of Walker's illustrations: however, three were color plates. There was no introductory material, and text was simplified. Twenty sections for Red Cross Knight became fifteen, and fifteen for Sir Guyon became nine. Many were unchanged, a few completely omitted, and portions (dialogue and description as well as more difficult subject matter) were cut. Occasionally sections were combined and / or titles simplified: "The Knight Deceived by the Magician" and "The Knight Forsakes Una" became "The Bad Magician" to focus on evil character and mitigate the knight's lapses. Some of Una's needed encouragement was also left out. Loss of details like Duessa's urging of *Lawless* and the Knight of the Hempen Rope, protected younger children from unsuitable material; cutting Guyon's moralization of the Knight killed by Acrasia and his wife's suicide was similarly discreet. However, the color frontispiece, "The coach was drawn by an ugly team," showed the Seven Deadly Sins. Symbolic animals and grotesque men who ride them would fascinate and inspire questions, not least because in an English landscape.

In contrast, loss of courteous exchange between Arthur and Guyon merely simplified and speeded action, as did abbreviation of Guyon's tale in "The Three Sisters." Several sections—"Bragadocchio," "Fury's Captive," "The Anger of Fire"—were reduced to two transitional paragraphs to begin "The Idle Lake" and a return to "The Realm of Pluto" and "The Cave of Mammon." "Lady, you have not done right to mislead me like this," featured a knight in armor, a pretty lady, and a gondola, with Guyon alert to Phædria's deception (97). On the cover was "Behold what living eye has never seen," a dark cavern lighted by distant flames. Mammon shows Guyon "a hundred furnaces burn-

Temptation by Mammon was a severe test for Sir Guyon. A. G. Walker made a dramatic scene, not of counting gold pieces, but showing those who labor to produce Mammon's wealth. This was the cover picture in Mary Macleod's *The Red Cross Knight and Sir Guyon* (1908), somewhat simplified and selected from the original volume to suit younger children. Color greatly enhanced the effect, glowing yellows and reds from the fire and a green devil lurking on the left.

ing fiercely," stoked by "many evil spirits horrible to see"; a remarkable green devil hovers by the knight (108). A major cut eliminated "The Champion of Chivalry," Prince Arthur's adventure against Pyrocles and Cymocles. Younger children were reassured "before long the Knight [Guyon] awoke from his trance well and strong" (113). With no need to remain in "The House of Temperance" Guyon and Palmer proceeded to "The Rock of Reproach and the Wandering Islands," pictured as "A perilous passage lies before us" (117). Three final sections were unaltered. Arthur is a splendid figure in shining blue-gray armor, his helmet topped by a large dove, in "The Prince carried him out of the Castle" (68). Red Cross Knight, pitifully weak and in rags, slumps against him, while Una, with golden hair and an orange dress, glows as she extends her arms to receive her knight.

E. Edwardson, The Courteous Knight and Other Tales *(1899)*

Exquisite Art Nouveau decoration marked E. Edwardson's *The Courteous Knight and Other Tales Borrowed from Spenser and Malory* (1899). On a golden cloth cover with gilt title and brown stamping a knight in armor, lance in hand, rides his charger through interlaced vines and flowers.[4] Illustrations, all black-and-white–with some red lettering on the title page—were by Robert Hope (1869–1936?). Edwardson's one-page introduction admitted inexactness: "The additions, alterations, and omissions that I have ventured, or found myself obliged, to make are perhaps too numerous to render it quite justifiable to describe these stories as adaptations" (5). He claimed only that readers of Spenser and Malory would recognize his sources; the intent was to tell exciting stories, not to create a child's version of *The Faerie Queene* or *Le Morte D'Arthur*. A page with Art Nouveau frame, quoted three stanzas from Longfellow's *Prelude to Translations*, recognition of the American poet's popularity and contributions to making older European literature accessible (3). Combination of medieval and early modern authors argued continuity. Edwardson justified changing obscure names (Blatant Beast becomes Beast of the Thousand Tongues) because "of my preference as a child for stories into which only 'easy' names were introduced" (5).

Of seven items, three were "borrowed from" Malory and four from Spenser. Atypical was *The Sham King* from "Prosopoia: or Mother Hubbard's Tale," a satirical Reynard the Fox tale published in *Complaints* (1591).[5] *The Courteous Knight* "utilized parts of Books VI and VII of the 'The Faery Queen,'" while Books II and IV supplied matter for *The Treasure House of Mammon* and *The Wooing of Canace* (3). Running titles identifying characters or actions facilitated reading. *The Courteous Knight*, the featured item, had nine parts, each with explanatory title—"How Sir Calidore…." Italicized introductory paragraphs gave moral points with relevance in the story. Spenser's prefatory quatrain for each canto of *The Faerie Queene* suggested readers needed help to keep track of the action; Edwardson expanded such aids—not deemed necessary for other tales, whether from Malory or single episodes from Spenser.

Much of the appeal of *The Wooing of Canace* was the tournament. Spenser enhanced his completion of Chaucer's *The Squire's Tale* with "Cambina's Chariot," drawn by two lions (illustration 91). A peaceful resolution of competition with two weddings was a reassuring happy ending. Moreover, children who had read Chaucer would be delighted to know how the story ended. *The Treasure House of Mammon*, a representative episode of the recurrent theme of temptation, was readily understood.

Edwardson was the odd adaptor who did not include the Red Cross Knight / St. George. He featured Spenser's last knight, exemplar of good behavior who conquers the Beast of speaking ill, again a familiar experience of childhood. Substantial claims for courtesy extended beyond its origin in royal courts:

E. Edwardson's *The Courteous Knight and Other Tales Borrowed from Spenser and Malory* (1899) was distinctive because it combined medieval and early modern writers to illustrate courtesy. Thus Spenser's Sir Calidore was the chosen knight. Robert Hope's Art Nouveau decoration to frame the knight gave the extravagant yellow cover, which glowed with gold, distinction.

> No vices dishonour a knight more than pride and cruelty; nor can there be any folly greater than the folly of those cruel and proud men who show no mercy, forgetting that life is full of strange chances and vicissitudes, and that they themselves may some day fall into slavery and unspeakable misery, as has happened to many great kings and mighty lords: which things, as this story shows, Sir Calidore made plain to certain miscreants [14].

This didactic statement introduced Chapter 2 in which Calidore defeats Briana and Sir Crudor, guilty of "unknightly deeds." However, even Sir Calidore, "gracious in his speech, ... comely in appearance, ... gentle in thought and deed, ... dauntless and stout-hearted," falters before he becomes "a happy knight" whose task is over (9–10). Chapter 5 warned against distraction:

> Let all who read this story note what great mischances fall upon men when they are least upon their guard; for just as fair Serena, while she busied herself with nothing but gathering flowers for a garland, was carried off by the Beast of the Thousand Tongues, so while Sir Calidore thought but to rest himself a while in the company of shepherds, he was lured away from the task in which no dangers had availed to hinder him [28].

Hope's "The Fair Pastorella" pointed a sharp contrast. In a bucolic landscape with sheep, trees, and cliff, two shepherdesses listen to a shepherd playing his pipe (31).

Yet there was an argument that respite from striving can be beneficial. Chapter 7 "How Sir Calidore Acomplished his Task" began with Spenser's metaphor of the vagaries of winds and currents that determine sailing and apply to his hero:

> For of the adventures which befell that brave and courteous knight, and for a while withheld him from his task, he made use to display the shining virtues of which the fruit and the reward was that he brought his perilous undertaking to a safe end [42].

In a terrifying illustration The Beast is winged and fork-tailed like other drag-

Layout of pages in E. Edwardson's *The Courteous Knight and Other Tales Borrowed from Malory and Spenser* (1899) fulfilled the promise of Robert Hope's decorative cover. Interlace and roses in the heading were typical of Glasgow style, and the gently curling folds of a tall and slender maiden's dress typified his Art Nouveau.

ons, but projects multiple tongues from its gaping mouth (45). Sir Calidore, with sword poised to strike, moves his shield toward them. He does not slay the monster; he muzzles it.

A final chapter "How Sir Tristram Saw a Vision" related how Sir Calidore's squire spoke with a hermit who wept because the Beast of the Thousand Tongues had reappeared. Edwardson suggested this hermit might have been Sir Calidore, who died that day, and noted Sir Tristram was never able to overcome the Beast. Edwardson's prefatory note quoted Shakespeare and defined chivalry:

> The saying, "The evil that men do lives after them, the good is oft interred with their bones," is both true and untrue; for though an evil custom may spring up again when the good knight that overthrew it is dead, yet he has left an example that shall never die, showing how all good knights may in their time fight such fights as Sir Calidore fought against the Beast of the Thousand Tongues; and this story shows that those who would win such fame as Sir Calidore won, must make themselves in all things as worthy of fame as was Sir Calidore [53].

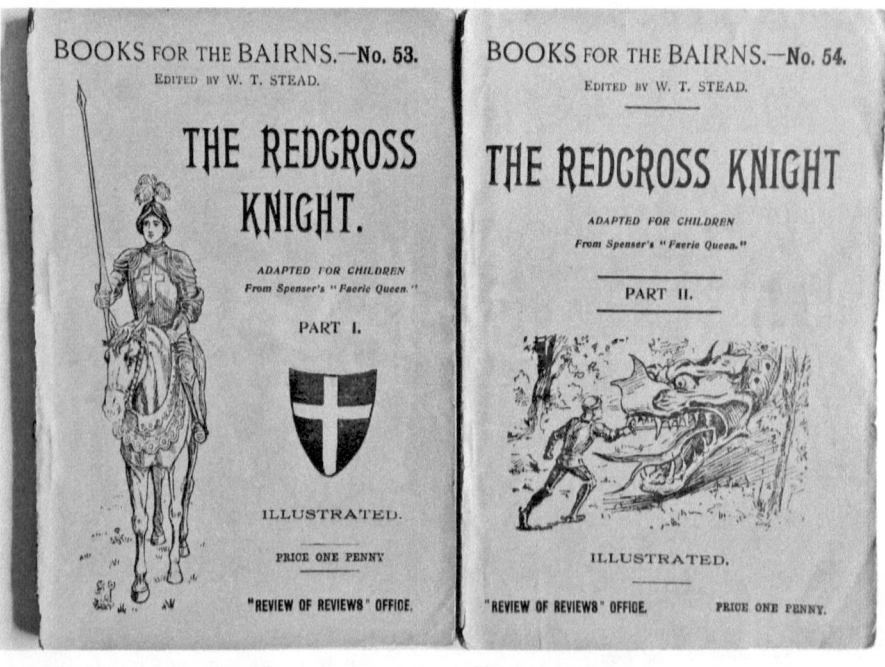

W. T. Stead's Books for the Bairns was a substantial publishing achievement that brought Spenser to a wide audience, especially those who could not afford extravagant reward / prize books. Pink paper wrappers, inexpensive paper, and abundant illustration by Brinsley Le Fanu marked affinity with chapbooks—all for a penny. Stead sufficiently admired Book I of *The Faerie Queene* to devote two issues to it, coverage given only to master works esteemed for children.

W. T. Stead, The Red Cross Knight, Books for the Bairns (1900)

W. T. Stead published *The Red Cross Knight* (1900) in two parts, Books for the Bairns #53 and #54, each with sixty pages of text plus two pages and covers with advertisements.[6] Since the series began in March 1896, *The Faerie Queene* was among the earliest "Classics of the Nursery" priced at one penny. Stead's preface to "My dear Bairns" lauded Spenser's *The Faerie Queene* by placing it in traditions of English literature and among children's books for uplifting (Christian) reading on Sundays:

> ... one of the best books in the whole world. It is a lovely Sunday book, for it is a story, or allegory, like "Pilgrim's Progress." The hero, the Redcross Knight, is St. George of Merry England, who represents Holiness. His adventures are those which all must go through in one shape or another if they would be true to the Cross—the Redcross—on which Christ died for men [I: 2].

Stead also recommended Penny Poets #18—although it had no pictures—for extracts from the poem, if readers were too impatient for the second part of *The Red Cross Knight*. Part I ended with a half-page illustration of a fairy paddling a leaf boat; on its sail in large letters was "To Be Continued" (60); Part II devoted a page to information about how to obtain Part I. Skilled marketing (advertisements) and pricing, as well as quality storytelling underlay Stead's success.

Books for the Bairns, pink paper-covered pamphlets, resembled chapbooks in price and profusion of illustration: in Part I, eight full-pages, thirty-nine half-pages, and three small devices; in Part II, seven full-pages and thirty-eight half-pages. Thus almost every opening had a picture, frequently two facing ones. Positions—top or bottom horizontal, left or right vertical—diversified interest, an advantage of double columns. Brinsley Le Fanu (1854–1929), principal illustrator of Books for the Bairns, created formal scenes, lively action, and distinctive monsters. Oddly costumes were of different periods. Christian knights wear plate armor, pagans wear chain mail, and enchanters long, medieval garments (I: 10–12, 22–23, 35). Men and women often were in Renaissance style (I: 3, 4, 5, 46; II, 9, 37–39). Una's dress fused Elizabethan (cap, ruff, and waist) and Victorian (skirt). Although only full-pages had captions, subjects were usually self-explanatory.

The Red Cross Knight had twelve chapters, six in each part. Although this suggests correspondence to Spenser's cantos, conformity was problematic in a simplified and abbreviated narrative—few classical allusions, elaborate metaphors, or allegorical complexities. Chapters usually focused on a vividly illustrated main event and finished on a note of expectation. The best example in Part I Chapter 4 was the House of Pride:

> No greater shame can attach to a knight than that he should be guilty of inconstancy. Far too easily had the Redcross Knight permitted himself to be deluded; far too readily had he doubted the loyalty of his most faithful lady; and by exchanging her companionship for that of the false Duessa, who now called herself Fidessa, he brought terrible trouble, not only upon Una, but upon himself [I: 33].

A vertical half-page picture showed a splendid castle, observed by a mounted knight (I: 33); he kneels in "At the Court of Queen Lucifera" (full-page I: 35) that paralled the initial "Una and her Unknown Champion" (I: 5). Decadent medieval opulence (decorated Romanesque arch and tapestry) have replaced severe elegance for Gloriana and her court—depicted as Queen Elizabeth I, Cecil, and so on (I: 5). More compelling was "The Six Counsellors of Queen Lucifera"; they ride allegorically significant mounts that draw her chariot, decorated with a skull and driven by a black devil that could be in a medieval manuscript (I: 37). Redcross's combat starts when "'Joyless' Appears on the Scene," and two knights struggle for the shield of "Faithless" (I: 39). The defeated Saracen begs pardon and pleads treachery against his brother; the Christian makes a chivalric challenge: "The Redcross Knight would not condescend to answer these reproaches, but threw down his gauntlet as a sacred pledge that he would defend his cause in combat the next day, and resolved that his sword, and not his tongue, should plead for him" (I: 40).

Chapter 5 opened with a sleepless night to devise strategy: "When a noble heart harbours a great and glorious purpose, it cannot rest until the purpose has been accomplished" (I: 42). Three pictures chronicled action. In "The Contest Between the Redcross Knight and the Saracen" they face each other with swords and heraldic shields (cross and "Joyless"), before two pavilions and a standing crowd (I: 43). The next opening was particularly engaging (I: 44–45). At top left Joyless strikes Redcross's helmet, a blow that inspires Duessa's praise and provokes a knight whose "faith had grown weak. … Anger, also, and shame nerved him to be avenged." At bottom right, Redcross, with sword and shield raised, leans toward a mysterious "dark cloud" after "the infernal powers had interposed, and had carried his foe away with the cloud." The next contrasting pictures were at the bottom (I: 46–47). On the left, Elizabethan courtiers listen to a messenger. On the right, Duessa meets Night, a figure in black; behind them is the mysterious cloud. A full-page showed consequences. In "'Night' Driving Duessa to Æsculapius" she stands in a chariot behind a crescent (Saracen) guardrail holding a long whip poised to strike three galloping black horses (I: 49). Last pictures had more contrast (I: 50–51). At top left two women stand at the entrance of a cave, where "the great physician" sits, imprisoned and bound in chains. The right vertical is Redcross in shining armor, lance in hand, a poised knight on his charger—the cover image.

Nevertheless, Chapter 6 explained how Red Cross Knight's stay in the House of Pride, "that dreadful place," weakened him; he needs the dwarf's help to escape. Una, rescued by satyrs—amusingly illustrated as they worship her donkey, after she rejected their homage (I: 55)—continues vulnerable. Although Satyrane accompanies her, she flees in fear while he fights the Saracen and is followed by "the false pilgrim ... old Archimago ... [who] now hoped to bring her to the last extremity of woe" (I: 60). Like Victorian serial novels, Part I ended with suspense.

Part II, Chapter 7 opened with explanation of human limitation:

> Many perils encompass the man who is not armed against the wiles that Falsehood employs to betray the unwary. And even if he is on his guard against them, yet no man is wise enough to detect and avoid all the snares that Falsehood can invent. Duessa was a perfect mistress of her art [II: 3].

When Duessa finds Redcross resting by a stream, she beguiles him. After a drink at a fountain deprives him of "his manly courage ... a curdling cold ... a fever ... faintness," he is "careless alike of his health and of his fame" (II: 4). Having destroyed dragon Error and Saracen knights in Part I, he now faces a giant. "The Redcross Knight attacked by the Giant Orgoglio" is tiny; the huge giant dominates the center and faces the viewer (II: 5). Such a foe could be defeated only by something beyond the human:

> Perils encompass the righteous man on every side; continually would he fall if he were not continually upheld by Divine Grace. And even when through foolish pride, or through weakness, he has fallen—when the power of evil has prevailed, and got the better of him—still, so firm is Divine Love, so constant in its care, that a way of escape is always provided, by which he may become free [II: 15].

Parallel to threat was resolution, "The Prince Attacks the Giant" (II: 17). Arthur, a small knight in full armor, faces Orgoglio, whose blood drips from the stump of his left arm that lies at his feet. He grimaces and grasps his head, his tree / club now rests against the bridge leading to his castle, where a three-headed monster watches at the gate. The earlier portion of Part II featured Arthur, whose role changes from fighting to liberating in "Rescue of the Redcross Knight by the Strange Knight" (II: 23). Before a portal, still wearing armor, he assists a "poor prisoner ... most pitiable" (II: 22). "The Prince's Vision" happens in a forest; a large figure kneels above a recumbent knight, whose horse waits in the background (II: 29). Prince Arthur tells Una his story, attributes his succor of her to "Eternal Providence," and identifies the "Queen of Fairies," the love that inspired him to chivalric pursuits. This followed a statement of the story's ethos:

> In the days of chivalry, men of noble mind were agreed in the pursuit of brave and generous enterprise. None envied the good fortune of others, or grudged aid to him who needed it. Each was the friend of all, and all sought how best to advance the praise of each [II: 26].

Giant killing was at least as archetypal as dragon slaying for champions like Guy and Bevis, and quintessentially English Jack the Giant Killer and Tom Hickathrift. Brinsley Le Fanu's Red Cross Knight is identified by his surcoat and shield in the corner; Orgoglio (Pride), whose club is a tree, dwarfs him. Most openings of *The Red Cross Knight* in Books for the Bairns Series included such exciting pictures.

Facing half-page illustrations were didactic pedagogy. At upper left Una listens attentively to Prince Arthur; on the lower right, a boy stands before seated Merlin (II: 26–27). The child gave young readers a point of entry and a model for attention to lessons.

The central portion of Part II detailed Redcross Knight's education after Una took him to the House of Celia. In this most thoroughly allegorical section, familiar terms ("hospital" and "matron") made the idea of a "cure" accessible. A picture, closely matched to the verbal text, featured Charissa

> in the prime of womanhood; she possessed great beauty, and was full of wonderful love. A multitude of babes, engaged in their sports, surrounded her, rejoicing in her presence. She wore a tyre of gold upon her head, adorned with precious gems of surpassing value. She was seated on an ivory chair, and a pair of turtle doves were by her side [II: 38–39].

Reassuring maternal love fostered confident empathy in an episode that culminates when Heavenly Contemplation shows Redcross Knight the New Jerusalem (illustration 44) and augurs the future: "'thou, fair knight, sprung from the English race—although accounted a fairy's son ... shalt be a saint and England's friend and patron. 'St. George of Merry England' shalt thou be!'" Contemplation also advises him to hang up his shield and "shun the pursuit of earthly conquest; wash thy hands from the guilt of blood, for blood yields sin, and war yields sorrow" (II: 45). There is poignancy: Stead, a pacifist, died on his way to a peace conference when the *Titanic* sank; legions of his readers died in the Great War.

Few illustrations were more compelling than those in Chapter 11. In a vertical one the dragon crawls down toward mounted Redcross Knight (II: 47); in the next opening a fearsome "St. George and the Dragon" (II: 49) rivaled verbal description:

> wings like two windmill sails ... tail ... nearly three furlongs in length, and two stings of deadly sharpness ... cruel rending claws ... head most hideous of all ... devouring jaws gaped like a deep abyss, with long ranges of iron teeth ... a cloud of sulphur steamed from his throat, filling the air with a dreadful stench ... blazing eyes ... like two bright shields, but full of rage and fury [II: 48].

As the battle rages, danger grows with "The Knight's First Defeat" (II: 51). The monstrous dragon breathes fire upon hapless Redcross, an ungainly figure in armor, tossed head first into a pool. Yet the text reassured; this "clear spring of water" is "The Well of Life" that restores life and washes away sin, cures diseases, and renews the decay of old age. Reference to Victorian habits of "taking the waters," like "hospital" and "matron," added immediacy: "No English bath or German water could match this well for healing power" (II: 50). Una kneeling in prayer (II: 52) preceded the final image, first seen on the cover—the knight thrusts his sword through dragon's gaping mouth (II: 54).

Numerous illustrations in *The Red Cross Knight*, Part II (1900) allowed Brinsley Le Fanu to introduce a variety of moods, including the fierce dragon's overthrow during the early stage of the combat. Certain effects—bulging eyes in a grotesque head and the knight's undignified fall—were somewhat comic. Yet children would discover the significance of the pool into which he fell, the Well of Life.

Chapter 12 celebrated family, Una's return to her parents and betrothal, and a fleeting threat before Archimago's final deception is exposed and he is imprisoned. However, chivalric duty led to six years of "many mighty deeds in the service of his queen, before Redcross Knight returned to marry Una and reign, "loved and admired by all men" (II: 60).

Books for the Bairns, outstandingly comprehensive and engagingly illustrated, were an impressive collection modestly priced. Children with more pocket money could collect them, while the poorer would treasure a volume or two; some titles became schoolbooks. In September 1918 the price per volume had increased to three pence, and an advertisement listed titles as "The Classics of the Nursery." There were special offers:

> For the small sum of **5/-** you may give a boy or girl a little library of 20 vols. of Fairy Tales or other suitable literature of a pleasing and seasonable kind, profusely illustrated and neatly bound in cloth. For **10/-** you may send a collection of 40 volumes; and for **20/-** you may give your little friends a positively wonderful collection—80 of the Classics of the Nursery. Such a library contains nearly 5,000 pages with about as many original sketches.[7]

N. G. Royde-Smith, Una and the Red Cross Knight and Other Tales from Spenser's Fairy Queene *(1905)*

N(aomi) G. Royde-Smith's *Una and the Red Cross Knight and Other Tales from Spenser's Fairy Queene* (1905) featured Red Cross Knight. Published by J. M. Dent in England and E. P. Dutton in the United States, it was uniform with other handsome volumes of chivalry: Cervantes's *The Adventures of Don Quixote* (1902), illustrated by W. Heath Robinson; a condensed *Froissart's Chronicles* and *The Story of Bayard* (1911), both illustrated by Herbert Cole. Books were uniform in format, 6 × 7¾ inches, but varied greatly in number of pages and size of print. *Una and the Red Cross Knight* with 264 pages and large print on heavy paper was designed for children.[8] Illustrations by T(homas) H(eath) Robinson (1869–1950) exhibited his characteristic attention to factual detail and historical accuracy. On the decorated blue cloth cover are cropped figures: a knight in silvery blue armor with heraldic shield (red cross on white) rides a white horse. Trees support a banner with title and author's name, gold letters with red initials. On the spine Una—in a plain white gown, her hair loose under a simple band—rests her hand on a brown lion. Pink roses were in Glasgow style. Banners with title and author added the illustrator. Una's circular portrait, framed by Art Nouveau foliage, decorated the back. Iconography, like the title, gave Una parity with Red Cross

Knight; end papers had ladies, not knights. My copy was "Prize Awarded by the London County Council."

Royde-Smith (1875–1964), for some years a literary editor of *Saturday Westminster Gazette*, had a long career; she reviewed and supported leading writers—Rupert Brooke, D. H. Lawrence, Graham Greene, Walter de la Mare, and Rose Macaulay. She also wrote novels of which *The Tortoiseshell Cat* (1925) is best known. Royde-Smith's short introduction included comment on religious conflict between Catholics and Protestants, biographical details, and observations about retelling for children "one of the finest books in English literature." She distinguished between "many stories ... all part of one great and very wonderful story" and "special meaning which grown-up people can see behind the tales.... Allegories" (xviii). Spenser's representations were: Gloriana for Queen Elizabeth and Prince Arthur as an Ideal Man. Red Cross Knight stands for Holiness and Una for Truth; their greatest enemies were magician Archimago—the Pope or Philip of Spain—and Duessa—Falsehood or Mary Queen of Scots, while Lucifera and Orgoglio were "two different kinds of Pride"; "all the other characters in the story represent either virtues or vices or else people who lived in those days. ... Sir Guyon or Temperance, and Acrasia is the spirit of Self-Indulgence against whom he has to fight" (xix).

Children, Royde-Smith hoped, would read additional stories "some day ... in the wonderful verses of the real book" (xx). To advance this commonplace expectation she interlaced stanzas of verse. Although spelling was modernized, many unusual words remained, explained with numbered references at the bottom of the page:

> [M]any quaint and old-fashioned words are used, but they are not difficult to understand, because Spenser was such a great poet, that, many parts of the poem he wrote more than three hundred years ago can be understood by children to-day if they will read slowly and carefully [xx].

Typical examples were:

> [1] *Silly*—This word used to mean harmless or simple[2]; *humblesse*=humility[3]; *Weeds*=clothes[4]; *Much rueth me*=fills me with grief [35]
>
> [1] *wist*=thought; *fearful* was used in Spenser's time in its simple meaning, timid or full of fear [97]
>
> [1] *That to the rest more able he might be.* That he might be better able to accomplish his work which lay before him [173].

Una and the Red Cross Knight finely balanced exciting stories with the appeal of verse. Chosen passages, often a single stanza but up to several pages (sometimes with a few lines of prose interlaced), included: Archimago's Hermitage (15) and wicked dream (23–24), warning against Fickleness (47), tournament with Sansjoy and Red Cross Knight (69–70), of Pity (86–87), the Lion (88–90), Arthur's armor (124–127), advice against grief (142), vision of Gloriana (149–150), Fidelia (163–164), the Dragon (183–187), celebration of victory (196–200), Fidessa's letter (201–202), Sir Guyon's palmer (213), dismay at failed knighthood (214), questing (218), the Bloody-handed Babe (226–227), Mammon (243) and his domain (246–248, 249), and the Bower of Bliss (258, 261–262). To vivid descriptions of characters' appearance and dramatic actions was added the delight of new words—helpful when playing knights and ladies.

Each of twelve self-contained tales had a descriptive title and short running titles with numbered titled sections to guide young readers. A color frontispiece, "Gloriana," promised the magic of fairy tales. In a wood a red-haired Queen (Celtic), wearing a pale green dress with a purple border, stands surrounded by elfin creatures that wear garlands of leaves, sing, and play pipes. Red lettering and small pictures of Red Cross Knight and of Una with her lion decorated the title page. Fifty-five bordered black-and-white pictures lacked captions, but were identified in List of Illustrations. Half-page headings introduced eleven tales. The Seventh Tale had a full-page Prince Arthur on a white charger and wearing shining armor, embossed and radiant (121). Arthur's squire, in armor and surcoat with heraldic Welsh dragon, is poised to sound a horn at Orgoglio's castle (half-page 129). Robinson's twenty-three full pages, sixteen half-pages, five one-third-pages, and six footers (unlisted) were bold and arresting.

Archetypal dragon slaying was first achieved against Error; a cowed figure, "She crept into the shadow," behind a proud, stiff, young knight in armor (9). Red Cross stands and points his sword down, undeterred by the hideous beast's gaping mouth and curled tail, or a skull and bone on the rocks. More terrifying was the hovering dragon ready to strike (189). With huge sail-like wings, close-lying scales, and curled claws, it fills three-fourths of the space and dwarfs the knight, trees, and castle in the background. "The Common people and the dead dragon" pictured awed response (197). The body lies across the center, but Robinson's interest was the people. Filling the left side a boy hides behind an old man; a man at the center has his back to the viewer; on the right, facing the viewer, a fat man with a turban looks down as another bends low for a closer look; behind them many, more faintly drawn, peer anxiously. Bragadocchio is "An uncouth, savage and uncivil wight," riding Guyon's horse and threatening a kneeling man with a spear (235). Realism informed Robinson's non-chivalric figures. In a cottage interior—rough-hewn timbers and rushes on the ground—are peasants—plain clothes and bare feet (93). A kneeling daughter clutches her mother, who sits with her beads; a pot

Imaginative drawings of dragons were a salient appeal of romances retold for children. "Then rising in the air with his great wings spread abroad" was T. H. Robinson's monster that inspired terror and awe in N(aomi) G. Royde-Smith's *Una and the Red Cross Knight and Other Tales from Spenser's Faery Queene* (1905). A huge serpentine creature fills most of the space as it flies above tiny brave Red Cross Knight, poised to destroy evil.

T. Heath Robinson gave a very human dimension to N(aomi) G. Royde-Smith's *Una and the Red Cross Knight and Other Tales* (1905) with "The Common people and the dead dragon." Here he depicted Spenser's account of response to being saved from oppression; he also showed ordinary dress instead of finery and armor. The frightened boy stares to engage the viewer.

suspended on boughs, a knife and flat bowls suggest robber's gifts. Una and lion stand at the entry.

Robinson imagined Oriental otherness. "At his haughty helmet making mark" pictured opulent Sarazin armor—point on helmet, patterned surcoat over mail, circular chest guard, scimitar; Sansfoy, a cropped figure close to the viewer, looks more formidable than young Red Cross Knight behind him (33). Sansfoy's Sarazin armor also added to a woodland scene when he rides with false Duessa—here a lovely lady (29). A mounted Sarazin sentinel introduced the Fourth Tale (63). In "The Paynim bore her away" an elaborately caparisoned horse gallops through open country; Una's large mantle flies above their heads into the border (101).

Red Cross Knight was impressively formal as "St. George for Merry England" (177). Robinson's youthful knight in plate armor stands very

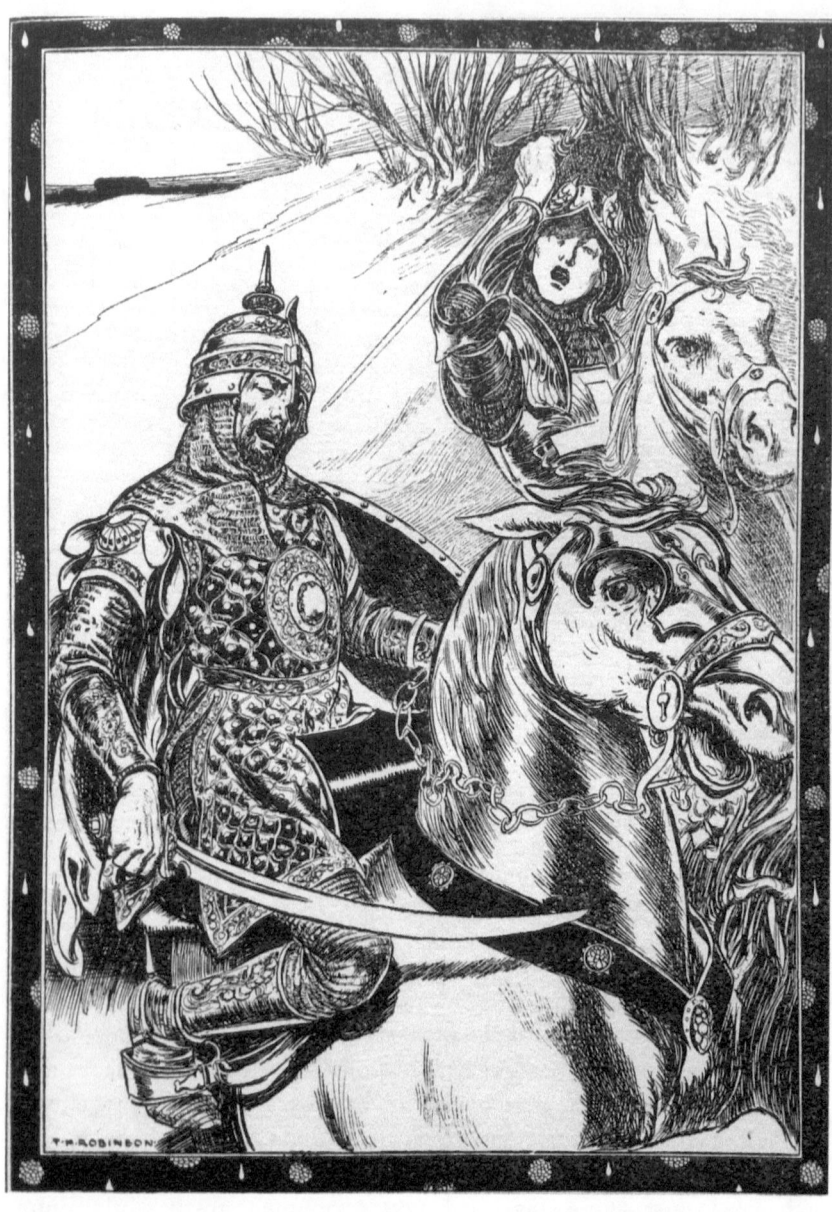

Opponents of knights were frequently Saracens. In N(aomi) G. Royde-Smith's *Una and the Red Cross Knight and Other Tales from Spenser's Faery Queene* (1905) T. H. Robinson's Red Cross Knight opposes Sansfoy, "At his haughty helmet making mark." Opulent armour and a bearded face distinguish an Oriental other from a modest and beardless Christian youth.

3. Edwardian Extravagance

straight, his arms crossed on his chest, holding a great banner. Like Galahad, he has a visionary's expression; with the aged holy man, he looks at "the City of the Great King ... wherein eternal peace and happiness doth dwell" (176). In contrast, "Sir Guyon following the way in which the Palmer directed him" expressed dour perseverance (219). Cropped figures in this heavily textured picture showed determination and strength, but not joy.

Robinson, who celebrated manliness, also drew ladies resembling Pre-Raphaelite stunners in decorative gowns enhanced by Art Nouveau patterns. Luxurious clothes suggested temptation. Red Cross Knight, entranced by Fidessa (false Duessa), kneels beside her as she sits and stares at the viewer (39). His armor gleams, yet her fair face, bare shoulders, and strands of pearls about hair and throat, are brighter; her gown, with folds that draw attention to the patterned fabric, fills half the picture. "The Wounded Knight," a rich interior, had similar effects; only the Paynim's head shows beneath a black coverlet (73). Interest centered on three stunners; two play lutes, while Duessa sat weeping. "The Maiden Queen" Lucifera, enthroned amidst wealth (a statue, goblets, jewel box), rests her feet on a dragon (51). Hearts are the pattern on her dress, and ropes of pearls restrain her hair. The mirror she holds signals vanity, as does the upward glance of a creature too proud to look down at the minstrel (Robinson's addition to the text) who plays a lute and sings. Utter decadence informed Acrasia's portrait: "a comely dame clad in flowing garments and holding in her left hand a golden cup while with her right hand she pressed out the juice from the ripe fruit which grew around her" (258 and 261). Robinson went further (259). Acrasia sits with her back—enticingly bare, like her arms—to the viewer, yet turns her head to show her seductive face—lips parted—in profile (259). Flowers festoon her hair. Grapes hang in clusters from a column. Robinson's usual black frame was broader and displayed thin fronds with open grains.

Although comparable details were in Arthur's dream of Gloriana, they suggested royal richness rather than luxury (147). The bejeweled Fairy Queen's sumptuous gown has Art Nouveau pattern, yet her gaze is modest as she gathers her skirt to avoid touching the youthful knight whose head rests against a tree where hangs his shield with heraldic pendragon. The vision is in a natural setting; a crescent moon and a lily were emblems of the Virgin. A different quality, sweet and gentle devotion to innocence, conveyed images of maternity. "Charissa" (the only picture with a caption) sits with four small nude children; she looks lovingly at the youngest cradled on her lap; one stands with hand on her leg, and two sit beside her (168). Charissa's gown, like Una's, is plain, albeit fully cut; a simple crown tops her flowing hair. The other mother, Amavia, is amidst vegetation with dark poppies in

T. Heath Robinson was one of the most distinguished illustrators for Edwardian children. Indeed his pictures were at least as significant as N(aomi) G. Royde-Smith's words to encourage thoughtful responses from readers of *Una and the Red Cross Knight and Other Tales from Spenser's Faery Queene* (1905). Robinson showed Archimago (Deceit, the Pope) surrounded by signs of his magician's practice and skill—books, lamp, skull, jugs, brazier, and wand. Here "So bold was he that he dared to awaken Queen Persephone." Black framing intensified and focused the viewer.

the foreground; her child, the Bloody-handed Babe, sits on her lap and looks at a flower, not understanding his mother's death (223). This Eleventh Tale's heading anticipated loss of parents and promised manly care: a mounted knight in armor cradles a naked babe against his chest (209).

Enchanters appeared in various guises: Archimago, a hermit magician with objects of his trade (books, cauldron, flasks, lamp, and skull), enjoyed a moment of success, "So bold was he that he dared to awaken Queen Persephone" (19). A lovely pensive face shows through swirling pale lines, a conjuration contrasting with dark solid forms. In "Archimago was bound and cast into prison" he is subdued, with only a simple flask and bowl (205). Here Robinson's style resembled Dürer with spare details, severe lines, light and shadow. Duessa, often a lovely lady, was debauched when perched on her beast, poised above Arthur's squire with her golden cup spilling magic wine (133). Moreover, a monstrous claw holding the youth down emerges from her skirts. That claw was a detail in "Fled to the wasteful wilderness apace," a small picture of a witch—hag's face and plain robe—who flies across the sky (143). Openings usually had one picture. A dramatic exception was Duessa as beautiful lady facing a hideous hag (44–45); another partial page made the same comment on appearance by pairing a lovely lady with an aged witch (76). Pictures, the work of a distincuished artist, were at least as significant as words by an influential writer.

Jeanie Lang, Stories from the Faerie Queene *(1906)*

Jack's Told to the Children Series was an impressive series of simplified major works, "nursery" books for "very little children." Jeanie Lang's *Stories from the Faerie Queene* (1906) was fourth in the series, after Robin Hood, Arthur, and Chaucer. Lang recognized Spenser as a poet, "brave and true and gentle ... he loved so dearly all things that are beautiful and all things that are good, that his eyes could see Fairyland more clearly than the eyes of other men ever could."[9] Eight stories, chosen and ordered at random, were fairy tales where evil is dispatched not delineated. Titles and opening paragraphs announced:

I. Una and the Lion
    Once upon a time, in a country not far from Fairyland, there lived a king and queen and their daughter, whose name was Una [1].
II. St. George and the Dragon
    Long, long ago, before the things that happened were written down in history books, a spiteful fairy came into the castle of an English king. She saw a beautiful baby-boy, the king's little son, lying asleep, and, out of mischief, she ran away with him and left her own ugly little fairy baby there instead [15].

III. Britomart and the Magic Mirror
   Long years ago there lived a beautiful princess whose name was Britomart [32].
IV. The Quest of Sir Guyon
   Long ago, on the first day of every year, the Queen of the Fairies used to give a great feast.
   On that day all the bravest of her knights came to her court, and when people wanted help to slay a dragon or a savage beast, or to drive away a witch or wicked fairy, they also came and told their stories [45].
V. Pastorella
   Long, long ago, in a far-away land, there lived a great noble, called the Lord of Many Islands.
   He had a beautiful daughter named Claribel, and he wished her to marry a rich prince [60].
VI. Cambell and Triamond
   Once upon a time a fairy had a lovely daughter called Cambina, and three sons who were born on the same day.
   The eldest son she named Priamond, the second Diamond, and the third Triamond [79].
VII. Marinell, the Sea-Nymph's Son
   ...Long, long ago, one of these nymphs became the wife of a brave knight, who found her sleeping amongst the rocks and loved her for her beauty. Cymoënt was her name [90].
VIII. Florimell and the Witch
   In Fairyland, where all the knights are brave, and all the ladies beautiful, the lady who was once the most beautiful of all was called Florimell [101].

Formulaic openings—delayed in VII—were reassuringly familiar.

As titles promised, girls could expect as much attention as boys; six of eight color pictures by Rose le Quesne featured female characters. "Britomart and the Magic Mirrror" depicted a Pre-Raphaelite stunner—long auburn hair and yearning expression—who declares, "I should like the crystal ball to show me what my husband will be like" (frontispiece). Only she was pictured twice. In "But the knight was Britomart, the fair lady with a man's armour and a man's heart" she stands by a blue-gray sea and faces the viewer with sword and shield lowered; Marinell lies behind her on the sands (92). Both wear silvery plate armor; however, Britomart's figure and sweet face indicate her gender. St. George is a manly knight in shining armour in "The dragon was dead" (30). In "Great heaps of gold lay about him on every side" a large Mammon wears short brown skins, while Sir Guyon is tiny, obscure in a verdant wood (48). Rejection of riches not destruction of the Bower of Bliss suited young readers who need not read of seduction. Pretty young women were appealing. Una walks through a wood (golden leaves, red berries, and dark tree trunks) with the lion, "He followed her like a faithful dog" (6). "In the middle of the ring of girls sat Pastorella" golden-haired and seated on a small mound beneath trees with pink blossoms, as four listen attentively (65). All wear pretty pastel frocks and flower garlands; light shepherd's crooks suggest their work.

Rose Le Quesne, like several other artists, made Britomart a stunning pre-Raphaelite beauty with auburn hair and soulful expression, as she reacts to the magic mirror, "I should like the crystal ball to shew me what my husband will be like." Jeanie Lang's *Stories from The Faerie Queene* (1906) was a nursery book in Jack's Told to the Children Series that provided early introduction to major works of European literature.

These were rather simpering and static images; two were dramatic. In "Cambell and Triamond" a mother's concern inspired "She asked the Fates to let her sons have long, long lives" (80). In "a dark place underground" three witches, clad in brown, spin white threads on a central bobbin. The

Spenser used the classical idea of the Fates, three crones who measure out the length of lives, in his story of a fairy mother who asked the witches that her sons Priamond, Diamond, and Triamond have long lives. In Rose le Quesne's illustration for Jeanie Lang's *Stories from the Faerie Queene* (1906) she holds a flaming torch, yet her white dress gives more light in the dark cave where witches sit measuring threads on a bobbin. One holds a knife. Their decision was that as one son died his strength would pass to the next brother. Triamond, the survivor, becomes Cambell's friend after his sister Cambina intervened in the lists.

nearest is poised to cut with a knife. The "fairy mother," draped in white, holds aloft a great torch, whose yellow and red flames light the foreground. Witches, as in Shakespeare's *Macbeth*, were mysterious and fearsome creatures. "Florimell's golden hair flew behind her," a startling last picture, conveyed courage and determination (102). As her white horse gallops through a dark wood, she stares at the viewer.

Lang replicated neither Spenser's interlacing nor subsidiary episodes. She began, "his name was George" but people called him the Red Cross Knight because of a red cross painted on his silver shield (3). Disregarding Una's fear and warning, he kills a "hideous monster." "Una and the Lion" relates her adventures after "the wicked magician" separated them (4–5). She flees in terror when knights engage: "Blood poured from their wounds, the earth was trampled by their feet, and the sound of their fierce blows rang through the air" (13). This story ended with Red Cross Knight in "a dreary dungeon" after "a giant had caught him" (14).

"St. George and the Dragon" was archetypal, with fairy tale motifs of the stolen prince and the boy who does not want to follow his foster father's work (ploughman) but become a knight. The Faerie Queen, who readily accepts the youth, Anglicizes his name from "Georgos" to "George" (15). Rural naiveté—"too simple and too true to think that beautiful Fidessa could be so wicked"—leads George to help a witch. Moreover, he "was very sorry for having hurt the tree-man, and with some earth plastered up the place that bled." He and Fidessa enter "a gorgeous palace where only bad people stayed" (18–19). Although the dwarf almost managed Red Cross's escape, Fidessa "cunningly" flatters and persuades him to drink from a magic fountain that takes away his strength. A giant captures him, imprisons him in "a gloomy dungeon," and weds Fidessa. In due course, Prince Arthur arrives and cuts off the giant's head. Una takes Red Cross to the House of Holiness, whose good and beautiful ladies teach him:

> He learned to be more gentle than he had been before, and never to be proud or boastful, and to love nothing that was not wholly good. He learned, too, not to hate any one, nor to be angry or revengeful, and always to be as generous and as merciful as he was brave [23].

High sentiment epitomized chivalric knights and conduct for good little children.

Equally pertinent was a child's longing to know his parents. A hermit explained a bad fairy stole the baby from his father's castle: "And although George loved his Faerie Queen and the fairy knights and ladies, he was glad to think that he was the son of an English king" (23). Rank and nation please, but there was greater promise—if he is always true, brave, merciful, and good.

George will be "the saint who belonged especially to all Englishmen and Englishwomen, and to English boys and girls."

> Saint George shalt thou called be,
> Saint George of Merry England, the sign of victory [24].

Strengthened and challenged George fights the dragon, the longest episode, retold with much of Spenser's description (25–30). Le Quesne's green dragon is small, but red blood gushes from its mouth and drips from George's sword (30). George, in plate armor, keeps his foot on the dragon's neck, the greatest victory among fairyland's fights and adventures (46).

In "Britomart and the Magic Mirror" she sees her future husband, is a lovesick maiden for a time, but then behaves like a male fairy knight. Britomart unhorses Sir Guyon, rides with him companionably, enters the tournament, and fells the "Savage Knight." Artegall in disguise little resembles the knight in the crystal: "His armour did not shine with silver and gold like those of the other knights, but looked like an old tree overgrown with moss. His horse was decked with oak-leaves, and he carried a battered old shield" (40). Nevertheless, he was a king's son stolen by fairies when a baby (36). Resting during a second fiercer encounter, Britomart sees "his face, so handsome and so brave" and recognizes "the gallant knight of the Magic Mirror" (44). Her gaze parallels Artegall's at "the loveliest face he had ever seen" (43). In Lang's fairyland Artegall did not need Talus, or indeed promote justice.

Calidore's quest for "the monster that he was pursuing when he first met Pastorella" warranted a single paragraph; Blatant Beast was not specified (76). Lang's pastoral idyll described happy life of shepherds, where Calidore's courtesy and love flourish. After a tiger seizes Pastorella while many gather strawberries (67) and robbers make all but Calidore and Corydon captives, the knight rescues his lady. The story began with Claribel's marriage to the Lord of Many Islands and ended with recovery of their lost daughter. Calidore marries "Pastorella, the simplest and sweetest bride that any knight brought to the court of the Faerie Queen" (78).

Two stories centered on Marinell and Florimell. Britomart returned to defeat challenger Marinell in a final display of excellence by a woman knight. Equally significant was the sea, vital to British identity. Lang delayed a "Once upon a time" opening to eulogize seascapes, fantasies, and creativity:

> Sometimes when the sun is rising on the sea and making the waves all pink and gold, the sailors whose boats are sailing out of the grey night fancy that they see fair ladies floating on the white crests of the waves, or drying their long yellow hair in the warm sunshine.
> Sometimes poets who wander on the beach at night, or sit on high cliffs where the seapinks grow, see those beautiful ladies playing in the silver moonlight.

And musicians hear them singing, singing, singing, ... The sailors tell stories of them, and the musicians put their songs into their hearts. But the poets write poems about them [89–90].

Edwardian children probably knew Hans Christian Andersen's "Little Mermaid." A rare address to readers was the conclusion:

> And if you listen some night when the stars are out, and the moon has made a silver path on the sea, you will hear the little waves that swish on the shore softly murmuring a little song. And perhaps, if your ears are very quick, and the big waves' thunder does not drown out the sound of their melody, you may hear them whispering the names of two happy lovers, Florimell and Marinell [100].

This invitation to imagine in the natural world a magical place peopled by lovely creatures, addressed childhood longing to go beyond confines of the mundane. Moreover, "the fairest lady in all Fairyland, lived happily ever after with her gallant husband" (115). Alternatives for older children were more challenging.

R. W. Grace, Tales from Spenser (1909)

R(obert) W. Grace's objective in *Tales from Spenser* (1909) differed from all others: to analyze Spenser's allegory and apply it to contemporary life.[10] Prologue invited: "Come with me to listen to that sweetest of English Tale-tellers, the poet Spenser, and let us hear again from his lips quaint talks of Ladies and Knights, of Castles and Dragons" (13). However, Grace immediately pointed to difference in the twentieth century; "we" will not encounter his champions or their foes. "Yet even in itself the old-time simplicity has a refreshing charm, and it rests eyes weary of tall chimneys and warehouses and engines to look on a world where these are not" [13]. He expected readers to "hear more than the tales of the dainty doings of high-born maidens, of the daring deeds of their faithful knights," and urged literature's universality, "brotherhood."

Although far removed, Spenser's subject—"the old, old fight between Right and Wrong"—has immediacy (13–14); we are indeed poor without the "friendship" of those who lived in the past.

> Come with me, then, not to gaze with incredulous eyes on impossible armour, but to discover how that chivalry grew amongst these men and women—which awoke the nations of Northern Europe out of their long sleep, and planted deep in them the conviction that Strength should be the servant of Beauty.
>
> For the fight is not finished: only the battle-ground is changed, and the sorest lack of these later days is of the heroism which they learned and taught.
>
> For the days of chivalry are never past while there remains on this earth a wrong to be righted, and a man—or a woman—who will say, "I will right that wrong, God helping me, or die in the attempt" [14–15].

Appropriation of the past was rarely more overt; chivalry remained the base of Eurocentric identity. Given this didactic objective, the Red Cross Knight / St. George was the best—only—exemplar. While Epilogue expressed hope that readers would "steal away again from the hard lesson-books and busy play-times" to read of Spenser's other knights and ladies, the essential lesson was "Spenser thinks we all should be Red Cross Knights" (243–244).

Tales from Spenser provided preparation for that role; in clear and familiar style Grace retold stories, but interlaced explanations to make allegory accessible and to inspire emulation. His didactic book was a psychological analysis suitable for children and Christian apologetics. Allegory and quest were understandable because of Bunyan's *Pilgrim's Progress*, second only to the Bible as popular reading and analog to Red Cross Knight's spiritual journey. Thirteen chapters, titled to epitomize action (a title page preceded each), presented a biography from callow youth to saint. Twelve black-and-white drawings by Helen S. Kück allowed scope for independent, freer responses; more female images somewhat balanced qualities of "boy's book."

"Chapter I. How Red Cross Became a Knight" began "There came to the Court of the Fairy Queen a loutish-looking Youth, big-boned and strong. ... country-made, ill-fitting clothes, ... arms and legs seemed too long to be controlled" (19). He is clumsy, embarrassed—he steps on a courtier's foot—but earnest and determined—an adolescent. Courtiers are derisive, yet the Queen sees something in him, and armor brought by Una fits him (23–24). His physique is the result of training, "manly bodily exercise"—fundamental to Muscular Christianity—while his aspiration made him persevere. Grace questioned, "Did the Queen make him a knight, or had he already made himself a knight, in practiced strength, by noble aim?" and answered no king or queen can make a *knight*; such exalted persons merely bestow a name. Resonating throughout *Tales from Spenser* was Samuel Smiles's belief in *Self-Help* (1859), an inspiring biography to "increase a man's self-reliance by demonstrating what men can be, and what they can do; fortifying his hopes and elevating his aims in life."[11] Grace shared Smiles's object "to re-inculcate these old-fashioned but wholesome lessons which perhaps cannot be too often urged,—that youth must work in order to enjoy" (vii). Red Cross "had much training in soul, where all true knightliness begins" (26). Robert Baden-Powell's concurrent founding of the Boy Scouts embraced and urged the same chivalric ideals.

Although the knight was new, his armor was dented and bloodstained, proven before given him. Red Cross easily rides his impatient horse, a skill—urged by "that far-seeing Englishman, John Ruskin," who recognized every boy should learn riding a horse or sailing a boat perfectly—that is a "complete mastery of some strong force outside himself" (32). Grace reminded readers the Cross is a symbol of Christ's death, "a vision always of his Radiant Leader," and defined national character: "we English people are born fighters, and it would be hard to keep religious thoughts out of the feelings in us that make us love fighting" (34). Red Cross's impetuous entry into Error's cave would have proved fatal but for Una's encouragement: "You see it is not muscle which wins fights—it is will" (40).

Having described the knight's sickening disgust, Grace addressed the issue of what is suitable: "What is the use of painting a picture so full of horrors as the one we have been looking at, you want to know?" (41). As in present day England, foul and ugly things, Error and Sin, are real and must be fought and overcome. In Chapter VIII, when Lawless terrorizes Una, Grace pondered the reality of evil. "Why does God let such things happen? Oh, you tell me this is only a fairy tale; and Spenser made it up out of his own head! Yes, true, but how came it into his head?" (130). Citing Browning's tale of an Eastern tyrant, he argued God is always the other half of the picture.

"Chapter III Red Cross Forsakes Una" began with lines from Tennyson who compared how easy it is to fight that which is all lie and how hard to fight a lie that is part truth. Pleased by Una's praise and with manhood heightened by victory, Red Cross too quickly believes Archimago's deceptive dream; "rather conceited" (55), he cannot bear the thought that Una betrayed him with another—adolescent angry resentment. He is eager to fight Sans Foy and readily acquiesces to Saracen lady Fidessa. To rhetorical questioning how the knight could so change, Grace answered: "Oh, we do strange and cruel things when we let pride and anger rule and direct us" (60). Fidessa continues to amuse Red Cross, even "cunningly" pretending to faint after the talking tree (Fradubio) tells his story.

Kück depicted Una and the Lion reclining in a woody spot with many flowers, gentle creatures situated in nature (70). But black spaces, Art Nouveau swirls and patterns, and flamboyant design in a dramatic formal portrait of "Lucifera" (91) suggest Aubrey Beardsley. Enthroned, the haughty queen rests her feet on a dragon and looks into a mirror; on either side is a peacock, emblem of Pride. Impatient with Red Cross for not suspecting his companion who brought him to the House of Pride, Grace mused on Spenser's "quaint, picturesque way" of describing its flimsy construction and shaky foundation (on sand). The analogue was human character: "If a boy will build for strong and noble manhood, then he must lay solid and real and deep foundations in quietness and patience through the days of his boyhood" (95). In "Chapter VI Lucifera and Her Strange Creatures" Grace revised unsuitable "Lechery" to "Quackery." This rogue, half doctor and half magician, "persuaded people, especially women," they were ill in order to gain influence; "there were many wicked ways he practiced to get people into the dissolute life he lived" (102). Descriptions of counselors and their mounts were Spenserian, but to stress their role as *advisors* to Lucifera Grace imagined a meeting:

> [C]an you picture them, seated round a table, conferring together, planning, discussing, advising Lucifera? Planning what? What kind of counsel could come from such? What control of kingdom and people could theirs be? Let us try to imagine them in the council room. Idleness would speedily be asleep in his chair, and Gluttony must have food and wine in front of him on the table; and Quackery sits simpering, and ogling, and throwing loose glances out of half-shut eyes at the Queen; and Avarice is reckoning in a little book how much Gluttony owes him, and every now and then looking anxiously up to see if any one is touching the bag of money he brought with him; and Envy's eyes travel from one to another, hating all and grudging Idleness his sleep, and Gluttony his food, and Quackery the attention he got from the Queen, and Avarice his gold, ... and Wrath, perhaps the best of the crew (for he could be sorry for what he did in his rages), his white face getting red with anger till he can hardly splutter out what he wants to say. ...
> What would the consultations of your Football Committee be, if amongst you sat Envy, and Gluttony, and Idleness? Not those which would lead to victory of your team, because for that you want mutual admiration and careful training of body and the stuff that won't know when it's tired! So keep them all out of your counsel! [105–106].

After this inspired display of boy's experience Grace warned that sins develop over time. Gluttony was a nice baby, then a greedy boy, before having a swollen body. Satan "means 'The Adversary,' the foe, that is, to all true manhood and knightly chivalry. But these six counsellors are also foes to manhood and chivalry!" (109).

Red Cross's killing the last Saracen knight occasioned formal combat but also why Red Cross fought Godlessness, Lawlessness, and Joylessness. Spenser put into "his quaintly-drawn pictures a great truth; one of the greatest those old days of Chivalry taught the world" (123). Life without awareness of God is meaningless and without dignity; absolute, loyal obedience to laws is necessary to develop knightly power; a knightly life so governed brings a glad and gleeful life. "Why not? Should not a man, who in God's name passes along giving loyal response to every call for help, be indeed a Happy Warrior?" (125). The allusion was to Wordsworth's poem and to Watts's painting *The Happy Warrior*, found in nurseries and schools, conditioning for the Great War.[12]

Citing Victorian poets expanded awareness of literary tradition. Matthew Arnold's lines ("In the gloom of November we passed / Days not dark at thy side") introduced "Chapter IX Red Cross Made Captive" (145). Arnold was a great Englishman who wrote about another great Englishman, his friend but also his father, Dr. Arnold of Rugby. English men and boys understand dismal weather and "Providence of God (mark that!) that also made men able to dispel gloom"; Tennyson named it *light*. Those who would be "light-bearers" would pay "a great deal," and like the poets in Mrs. Browning's poem respond, "Content!" Red Cross's lowest point comes after Orgoglio, a "somewhat stupid giant," makes him captive. Kück's giant dwarfs knight, lady, and horse (150).

Then was realized the promise of Providence of God: "The Knight Magnificent." On a charger with decorated caparison he rides toward the viewer, followed by his modest squire (160). Chapter X began with Arnold's lines characterizing his father, "Cheerful and helpful and firm" in spirit, however tried. Effort and perseverance are the foundation on which to build achievement. An earlier account of Magnificent's shield explained he uncovered its "blinding ray" only when opposed by a whole army, monster, or giant (154). When Orgoglio's club tears "aside the skin covering ... a dazzling ray of white light shot from the naked shield" (169). Magnificent cuts off Orgoglio's leg and head: "Whereupon the monstrous corpse collapses like an immense air balloon, and lo! Of the Giant Pride nothing is left ... but (as it were) an empty bladder" (170–171). Search through the castle leads to Una's joyful recovery of her weakened knight. Fidessa (Duessa), stripped of fine clothes, jewels, and false hair, is "a foul, ugly witch, wrinkled and bald, her fan-like teeth protruding over her bloodless lips; so offensive and horrible that all turn from the sight in disgust" (177).

"Chapter XI Reflections and Despair" made thoughtful comment. Grace, who changed the order of Spenser's narrative, expected readers not to be "altogether sorry" Red Cross had to stop and think, suffer "vile durance"— but did not want them anxious:

> I purposely left it out till you had heard of his glorious rescue by Magnificence, so that you might be sure the dawn would come before you looked closely at the horrors of the night. For there is nothing surer than the coming of the dawn! Whether it be of the sun's light after the hours of darkness, or of dawn of hope after the blackness of despair, or of Heaven's Morning after the Night of Death [184].

Opening with lines from Psalm 185, Grace was here most theological. "Hell," derived from Scandinavian, is "an English word for a Hebrew thought" (186). Red Cross's lowest point was in the Cave of Despair, a chilling narrative ending with recognition that "till men cease to sin, Despair cannot die" (195). Nevertheless, there was light. In "The Vision of the Knight Magnificent," a picture to expand a brief story of his life, the viewer shares his gaze of wonder at a lady whose radiant nimbus ends in blossoms (190).

Three lines from Lowell's *Twilight* introduced a riff on Rachmaninoff's *Prelude*; one from Browning further glossed Spenser's dominant theme, "The knightly life must be holy" (201), subject of "Chapter XII Dame Celia and Her Home." What Spenser needed to express still needs to be said:

> For sometimes we think that a holy man cannot be a fighter, and that fighters are generally unholy men. Whereas, the truth for boys and girls, as well as for men and women, is that if we would be good we *must* be fighters, and if we are to fight well and to good purpose, we *must* be holy [201].

In this haunt of Peace Dame Celia's daughter Fidelia is Red Cross's teacher; Patience is the doctor that cures his sickness before he meets Charissa and her friend Mercy and is taken to the Hospice where the brothers serve mankind. Finally in an inner cell, "a wonderful place where a good man meets God in solitary prayer," Red Cross kneels with Contemplation. In "Red Cross Sees the Glorious City" a serene old man in black habit points the way, while the mature knight in armor emblazoned with a cross, shades his eyes to gaze: "Too beautiful the sight was for human words to describe, and the Knight stands enraptured at the wonderful vision!" (213). Red Cross's goal "to be a soldier, strong, fearless, finding work for his good blade" was now something greater. He must be a soldier-saint before he enters the city Celestial: "having won to saintliness through knightly deeds, and men shall name you—"Saint George, of Merrie England" (216).

"Chapter XIII Red Cross Wins" left the metaphysical and used sport to explain change in Red Cross: how boys sometimes on the way to football or cricket say, "I feel jolly fit this afternoon!" (221). Another observation about English character—"somewhat afraid of wearing a Cross as they wore it in those days, saying it savours of superstition and the like"—expressed regret and longing. Recapitulating the arc of Red Cross's adventures and misadventures, Grace exhorted his boy readers:

> Ah, young Red Cross Knights, it is good to dream of high enterprise, and deeds of glory and renown, when strength surges through every limb, and life seems ablaze with Beauty and Truth! Believe in the dream, and dedicate yourself and your strength to the task. But its doing will not come in the way you expect! Nor will the path which leads to its accomplishment be what you would have chosen! You shall have the boon you pray for; the task of fighting for sweet Truth against all Injustice and Cruelty and Falsehood shall be yours. But you must not shrink from strange and painful preparation, often very difficult and hard to bear [225].

Before fighting the dragon Red Cross leads Una to safety—a manifestation of "careful thought." Courage is "not absence of fear, but control of oneself when things make one afraid" (228). This statement, with pragmatic application to childhood, reassured throughout exciting description of the dragon's strength and strategies; Red Cross perseveres when victory is not always certain. In many ways, *Tales from Spenser* was an impressive achievement. Grace made his didactic book appealing by conversational style, frequent use of questions to engage, pointing of chivalry as universal ideal, and confident affirmation of human possibility to follow Christ.[13]

Illustrations of R(obert) W. Grace's *Tales from Spenser* (1909) showed the influence of Art Nouveau with a sylvan setting festooned with flowers and attention on a beautiful lady who resembles many in posters made by Alphonse Mucha, a Czech artist who worked in Paris. Viewers shared the gaze of Prince Arthur in Helen S. Kück's "The Vision of the Knight Magnificence," an unusual attempt to depict the Faery Queen.

Lawrence H. Dawson, Stories from The Faerie Queene Retold from Spenser *(1909)*

Lawrence H. Dawson's *Stories from the Faerie Queene Retold from Spenser* (1909) was an extravagant volume in Harrap's Romance Series—uniform with books by M. I. Ebbutt and H. A. Guerber—and a modest edition in Told Through the Ages Series. Dawson (b.1880), who had previously published *A Book of the Saints* (1908), later edited Routledge's *Universal Encyclopedia* (1923) and *Rhyming Dictionary of the English Language* (1924), revised Ebenezer Brewer's *Dictionary of Phrase and Fable* (1923) and *Hoyle's Games Modernized* (1923).

Although he acknowledged Spenser's every tale and adventure had a moral, Dawson eschewed "exposition of moral lessons to be found in Spenser's great allegory" to write a book of stories.[14] He assumed: "If I have been faithful to my great original, the stories will be interesting for themselves alone, but the morals will be sufficiently obvious for you to discern for yourself" (v). There was a House of Holiness, where "a wise old Matron and her three daughters, with many helpers and retainers" heal Red Cross Knight's "inner wounds"—but no allegorical names (42). Identification of the Blatant Beast as "fit symbol of Slander, Calumny, and Evil-speaking" was an afterthought (233). Dawson named some historical personages; however, Spenser "went to many sources for his legends; brought heroes from the Arthurian romances, giants from the Charlemagne Cycle, imported whole episodes from the Italian of Ariosto, and ransacked the stories of travellers' tales brought from the far and newly discovered West; but all were transplanted and successfully acclimatized on Irish soil" that provided the locale and "rabble rout" (vi). Any who doubted were reassured "there *is* such a place as the Faery Land here described"—the first three stanzas of Book II, Spenser's address to the Sovereign that spoke of exploration and unknown regions (vi).

Stories from The Faerie Queene was a continuous narrative featuring five knights: Red Cross, I-XI; Guyon, XII-XIX; Britomart, XX-XXVII; Artegall, XXVIII-XXXV; and Calidore, XXVI-XLII. Convenient division of 234 pages into 42 precisely titled chapters, usually 4 to 5 pages, encouraged young readers, while gentle reminders helped them through a plot in which stories continually break off. Gertrude Demain Hammond (1862–1934), a painter and illustrator who worked in oil and watercolor, was especially praised for female figures and historical costumes. She illustrated other Told Through the Ages volumes, Thomas Carter's *Stories from Shakespeare* (1910) and *Shakespeare's Stories of the English Kings* (1912).

Lawrence W. Dawson's *Stories from The Faerie Queene* (1909) was a title in Harrap's Told through the Ages Series intended for older children and often read by adults. Gertrude Demain Hammond's "The Red Cross Knight was completely overcome" went far to explain his succumbing to the charms of Duessa. Hammond, known for accuracy in costume, imagined Duessa as a black-haired Oriental beauty, with white dress, red mantle, and extraordinary crown and jewels. Red Cross Knight, in gleaming armor, reaches out to raise her from her knees, a guileful posture to engage his sympathy.

In sixteen color pages strong and exotic women outnumbered knights in armor. Hammond, who avoided monsters and giants, expanded Spenser's romantic love of knight and lady, the virtue of good women, and the dangers of false women. The frontispiece, "Georgos claimed that Adventure" was a court scene; four ladies attend an enthroned young queen in Elizabethan costume. Hammond also contrasted field and court when the old woman's rustic son kneels and offers "forest wildings" to Fair Florimell in Elizabethan dress (116). In "The Satyrs danced round her in glee" Una, with flowing golden hair, wearing white and a black mantle, stands in a brightly lighted spot in a forest (30). Yet "The Red Cross Knight was completely overcome" by an alluring Oriental beauty with black hair (12). Hammond repeated her attire in "Duessa dispelled the Enchanted Cloud" (20). Her elegant hands magically raise a cloud above fallen Sansjoy, whose chain mail, gold helmet, and gauntlets indicate Saracen. Behind them are heraldic flags and lists. The last picture, "In a furrowed field the Ploughman found thee," harkened back to the first; the common man holds foundling baby St. George in an English countryside (44).

Hammond varied styles for the maiden warrior. "Britomart espies the mirror" was opulently Pre Raphaelite: a Rossetti "stunner" with abundant auburn hair in a green gown with slashed sleeves to reveal a white embroidered inner sleeve, brooches and a mantle (102). Seated, she stares at a globe that reflects the interior. "Britomart and Artegall" showed the moment of recognition; he kneels before her beauty, shown full-face (158). Still holding her shield, Britomart stands with lowered sword. Her armor—that of the captured Saxon queen—was mail. A gold breastplate with narrow panels below covered Artegall's mail; he has raised his golden helmet's visor. Hammond repeated this classical armor in "The Judgment of Artegall" on the seashore where two vie for a chest (190). Iron Man Talus, rarely depicted by others, wears mail and a plain helmet.

"Behold this heavy sight, thou reverend sire!" was inspirational (76). In a wood Sir Guyon lies exhausted and weak but not alone (76). An angel—glowing nimbus, golden hair, diaphanous wings, and thin white robe—sits on a rock above the recumbent knight in shining armor; his round golden shield lies on the grass. The Palmer—white beard, black robe with cowl, large cockleshell, rosary, and small pots of balm—leans on a long staff. Boldly different, "The Wanton Lady" has a voluptuous figure scarcely concealed by sheer drapery (96). She cradles a supine knight's head as they clasp hands while resting on a luxurious bed of pink roses. His armor hangs on a tree.

In another forest "Belphoebe succours Timias" (164). The knight in plate armor tries to rise, as Amoret's twin with flowing golden hair looks at him kindly. In "And ever when she nigh approached the dove would flit a little forward" the pretty huntress, wearing the same elegant but modest hunting dress, faces the viewer (170). "Fair Serena" stands in a field of wild flowers (202). She wears a long white gown with bordered wide sleeves and patterned purple shawl with a fringe, and a plain band holds her golden hair. Hammond pictured peasant attire and pastoral circumstances for "Calidore and Pastorella," shepherd and shepherdess, with sheep grazing in a sunny glen (222). A saucy hat and pink ribbon sash enhance a simple white gown; he wears a short blue tunic and pointed orange cap and holds a shepherd's crook. Pastorella is poised to play her pipe to accompany his horn.

Dawson judiciously cut much subsidiary material, appealed and recapitulated actions to offset Spenser's loss of continuity. This is crucial for framing chapters: "of which we shall tell anon" (23):

> Now return we to the Palmer, whom, you will remember, we left at the river-side when Phædria bore away Sir Guyon in her little painted shallop [75].
> Now for a while we must once again turn back to the time when on a day Prince Arthur and Sir Guyon, with whom was Britomart, were suddenly disturbed by a Damsel who came fleeing through the wood before a Forester [164].
> You will remember how that when Sir Calidore had rescued Serena from the fangs of the Blatant Beast he had rushed after the monster into the darksome woods [220].

Rhetorical questions, posed in conversational style, invited readers into a character's thoughts: "Where was Sir Artegall? she asked, and what was to be the end of her Quest? And those two watchers without, Glauce and Sir Scudamour? Were they still watching as she was, or had they, since she had passed through the fire, lost heart and hied them away?" (135). Britomart's queries are those children might pose to a storyteller. Other passages flattered their knowledge of chivalric stories. The lion becomes Una's "doughty guardian": "For you must know that in Faery and throughout all the ancient realm of Romance no lion would do the slightest harm to a King's daughter, if she were pure and good" (25). Sometimes Dawson reassured: "Fortunately the wound was but a small matter; and, indeed, so ordinary an incident in the course of a Knight's adventures would not be worth the telling were it not that this monster was, unknown to Sir Artegall, the Blatant Beast" (199). Archimago was occasion for surprise:

> No sooner were they sleeping than a change came over the old man. He threw off his Hermit's robe, the good, pious look on his kindly-seeming face left him, and he stood revealed as, what in truth he was, a wicked old magician. With crafty steps he stole to his little study, and there in the half darkness, fearful lest he should be observed, he opened his magic books and sat lost in thought, poring over their cabalistic writings, and ever and anon muttering dreadful incantations [9].

Although he described a monster ridden by Duessa—"Fearful was it to behold; seven great heads grew from its body on seven scaly necks; from each of the seven ghastly mouths large drops of blood, remnants of a recent gorge, fell streaming to the stones; its fourteen eyes glared green and yellow as it fiercely flew at Prince Arthur" (36)—Dawson acknowledged there could be a surfeit of such effects. When Red Cross faced the dragon, "Irksome it were, and well-nigh superfluous, methinks, to recite in detail the many horrors of this hideous Monster" (47).

Added explanations simultaneously enhanced excitement and plausibility. One, with sound effects, explained how Guyon found Mammon:

> He heard a tinkling that sounded strange and out of place in that pleasant woodland, where for so long he had heard naught but the songs of birds and the low call of beast to beast. He stopped and listened: *Clink, clink, clink; tinkle, tinkle, tinkle,* with every now and then a thud as of the heavy fall of something on soft and yielding mould. Could it be a Knight in full armour riding through the trees? But no, there was no noise of horse or breaking twigs; it was more like the sound of jingling coins than ever Knight on horseback made [67].

When Florimell the False vanished (V.iii.24), Dawson gave audience response: "All the Knights and all the Ladies gasped with astonishment, and never since that day has it been told how she vanished" (86). Authorial interventions reiterated the incompleteness of *The Faerie Queene*, necessary for children who always want to know how stories end. If keeping track was difficult, Dawson cut relentlessly:

> Bootless it were to follow this false Florimell through all her adventures, or to tell of the great troubles that she brought upon those gallant Knights of the Faery Court who were searching the wide world over for the true Florimell, all the time unknowing that there were two, and that—as often as not—she whom they were following was the wrong one; here it must suffice to say that all these things and many more happened, and that it was this false Florimell [142].

Lack of endings was disturbing. Dawson improvised: "Our Poet saith little concerning this, but we may be sure that not long time passed ere Timias was again the stout, well-favoured Squire that he had been of yore" (171). The tale of Arthur's squire and huntress Belphoebe must have a happy ending. Similarly,

> And we too take leave of Sir Artegall, for your great Spenser tells us no more of the Knight of Justice ... but we well know that had the poet lived to complete the magnificent fragment which at once outlives and enshrines him he would have told us that in the end Sir Artegall reached the Faery Court, and found his Britomart awaiting him after sore trials, and of the noble wedding and feasting that took place, and of the great happiness that remained with them, and still remains in that happy Land of Faery that lies not so far away, perhaps. All too early came Death and smiled with such sweetness on the great Poet that he might do naught but follow ... [200–201].

Dawson supplied the expected happy ending of romance / fairy tale: "We are not informed of all the rejoicings that befell this happy consummation of Sir

Calidore's Quest, but we may well imagine that they were great and glorious" (233).

His farewell to Arthur drew on legend and defined chivalry:

> Then did Prince Arthur once more press forward with his Savage attendant. No more shall we hear of them. The chivalrous Prince's part is still unfinished, for the great Poet tells us no more concerning him, and he fades from the story of Gloriana's Knights in like manner to Sir Artegall, and for like cause. Some there be who say that still he wanders to and fro between the Land of Faery and the world, succouring the distressed and righting wrongs wheresoever he may find them; while others hold that he at length reached the Court of his ideal and as yet unseen Queen, and there lived in happiness ever after [218–219].

Having restored Belgë's kingdom, Arthur resumed his Quest for Gloriana, "to deliver the afflicted from their enemies, and ever to succour the fatherless and weak (197)... But the Prince cared not overmuch for praise and thanks; when his work that he had set himself to do was accomplished he was fain to be away upon his long Quest, namely, the finding of distressed persons to succour" (198). Hammond matched Dawson's tribute; Arthur's stunning silver plate armor, decorated in gold, has exquisite simple lines (196).

Dawson's final statement was a coda, separated from the narrative by "* * * * *":

> Thus must we bid farewell to Spenser's "Faerie Queene," And leave the book—even as he left it—unfinished. Had he but lived we should have heard the end of this story ... and of many other unfinished stories we should have known the happy ending [233].

A perspective on critical fashions was Addison's "Account of the Greatest English Poets," addressed to Mr. Henry Sacheverel, 1694:

> Old Spenser next, warm'd with poetic rage,
> In ancient tales amused a barbarous age; ...
> But now the mystic tale that pleased of yore,
> Can charm an understanding age no more;
> The long-spun allegories fulsome grow,
> While the dull moral lies too plain below.
> We view well-pleased at distance all the sights
> Of arms and palfreys, battles, fields, and fights,
> And damsels in distress and courteous knights.
> But when we look too near, the shades decay,
> And all the pleasing landscape fades away [234].

Heeding this warning that interests / fashions in literary masterpieces change, Dawson retold the Spenser of "Knights and Squires, Witches and Magicians, Dragons, Dwarfs, Enchantments, and Monsters," confident Edwardian children would understand underlying "morals and allegories"; they read chivalric stories, as had knights of old:

> Among the treasures of this Castle, I should tell you, was a splendid library, and as Sir Guyon was looking through the great presses that contained the books he lighted on one which told him all about the deeds and adventures of brave Knights and Kings who had run their course long before he himself was born. Eagerly he lifted it from the shelf, and he spent days and days poring over the antique leaves, reading the wonderful histories that there he found and gaining much strength and encouragement from the marvelous tales of long ago [86].

Words and pictures (black-and-white on glossy paper) were the same in the frequently reprinted Told Through the Ages Series edition. World War II reaffirmed belief in the efficacy of Spenser's *Faerie Queene*, albeit as a severely modest book; March 1948, "This reprint is in conformity with the authorized economy standards."[15]

A. J. Church, The Faery Queen and Her Knights *(1910)*

The magisterial efforts of A(lfred) J. Church (1829–1912) to provide children with readable and attractive books of simplified great literature and history, beginning with Greek and Latin, culminated in *The Faery Queen and Her Knights: Stories Retold from Edmund Spenser* (1910). It followed *Heroes of Chivalry and Romance* (1898) and *Stories of Charlemagne and the Twelve Peers from the Old Romances* (1902).[16] Seeley listed Church's twenty-eight titles, including his historical novels. With its dark blue cover, gold stamping, red and white detailing *The Faery Queen and Her Knights* elegantly pictured Red Cross Knight and Arthur.[17] A border, white and red flowers amidst golden leaves, linked front and spine. Eight unsigned full-page color illustrations, rather child-like in style, used softer colors. They favored vivid knightly combat, especially appealing to boys, albeit my copy was a prize awarded to a girl—for arithmetic—by London County Council in 1920.

Church's narrative was comprehensive, 39 chapters in 309 pages: Chapters I-X, Red Cross Knight; XI-XIV, Sir Guyon; XV-XXXIV, Britomart and Artegall, with many subsidiary characters; and XXXV-XXXIX, Calidore. Arthur, one of three in his *Heroes of Chivalry and Romance*, was prominent. Church avoided Protestant polemic and eliminated seamy details yet discreetly included morals and stressed chivalry. With Red Cross Knight (Holiness) and Una (Truth), he retained religious details:

> ... the sturdy thief, by name Kirkrapine, that is to say, Robber of Churches, and this indeed was his trade. He was wont to steal away the ornaments of churches, and to strip off from the images of the saints the vestments with which they were clad, and to purloin the robes of the priests, and to break open the boxes in which were put the alms for the poor [18].

Una tries to teach Christian faith to satyrs—unsuccessfully since they want to worship her donkey, when she resists idolatry (37). However, Sir Satyrane, who finds Una with the forest folk, "teaching them holy things ... would fain be her disciple and learn the ways of righteousness and peace from her lips" (38). Red Cross's gift to Prince Arthur is "a book in which the Gospels were written in golden letters" (56); Spenser's complicated allegorical instructions were not included. When the aged sire pointed to the New Jerusalem, "as the knight gazed thereat, he saw angels ascending thereto and descending therefrom" (62). Destiny was clear; the ploughman "'called you George, which is by interpretation, 'worker of the earth'" (63). The Well of Life / Spring of Life restores the Red Cross Knight (67, 69), and the dragon's movements are prideful. The set piece was its fearsome appearance and the combat (65–69). When a pilgrim says, "God give you praise and peace," the Red Cross Knight replies, "His be the praise ... by whose grace I am what I am" (74).

Sir Guyon's resistance to Mammon's offer of all the wealth men love in the world was chivalric: "I do refuse your proffered grace. I seek not to be made happy in this fashion. I seek another end; I would spend my life in brave deeds" (83–84). His fame is acknowledged in the sweet, tempting song heard as he and the pilgrim sail: "O Guyon, ... flower of chivalry, most famous of all knights upon earth" (99). Prince Arthur replies "with due modesty" to Lady Belgé's exuberant thanks: "''Tis not the strength nor courage of the doer ... but the justice of the deed that should be looked to'" (260). When Pyrocles would despoil a dead knight of his armor, Prince Arthur accepts "evil lives after" the dead; "yet the knight who raises his hand against the dead, sins against his honour" (92). In dispute with Bragadochio over Guyon's horse, Sir Artegall cites "the law of knighthood, that if one man claim a thing and offer to make good his claim by might of arms, and the other will not, the judgment goes against the latter by default" (211–212). Single combats stressed individual over mass action. Britomart resists Radigund's claim of "perpetual service" if she loses: "'I will have no such conditions, no terms will I accept but such as are prescribed by the laws of chivalry!'" (238).

Those laws, demonstrated in several episodes, favored behavior that goes beyond expectation. Even though the lady does not ask for help with the wounded knight, Artegall has no hesitation: "'Fair lady, think not that I deem it a disgrace to carry this burden; gladly I will help you'" (284). Although knights of the Faery Queen sometimes faltered, the cause was usually naiveté. Red Cross is misled by Falsehood; and "force could not overcome him [Guyon], but he could be led astray by fraud" (77).

For Knights of the Faery Queen who fight monsters and Saracens, reli-

"Sir Guyon and the Men in Bestial Shapes," a colorful illustration in A. J. Church's *The Faery Queen and Her Knights* (1910), showed heroism as he warded off attack by those transformed into animals by Acrasia; it also provided an intriguing collection of animals for children to identify. Interestingly Guyon's shield bears the image of Queen Elizabeth I, while the building in the background is classical and the landscape Mediterranean.

gious faith was imperative. Britomart gives grieving Sir Scudamour temporal and spiritual advice:

> "Sir Knight, whose sorrow seems to overpass your patience, I would counsel you to submit your will to the providence of God. Remember, if you will, that virtue and faith are mightier than the very worst of sorrows. Surely he who cannot bear the burden of this world's distresses must not think to live, for life is a distressful thing. And now, tell me what this villain of whom you speak has done. Maybe this hand of mine may help you to win relief and redress" [128].

Although "torn asunder by anger and grief," she follows her own advice; nothing "would content her but that she must straightway put on her armour, mount her horse, and ride forth to deliver Sir Artegall" (235). Prowess and devotion, not gender, determine chivalry. Sir Artegall chides Fleur de Lys, once betrothed to Sir Burbon, who recovered her from Grantorto:

> "Fair lady, you cast a very great blemish on your beauty, if you change a plighted faith. Is there aught on earth so dear and so precious as faith and honour? Love surely is dearer than life, and fame is more to be desired than gold; but a plighted troth is more to be honoured than even love or fame" [266].

Attention to high sentiment did not inhibit thrilling accounts of foes and fighting that inspired six of eight illustrations. Exceptions were "The Lady Una and the Lion" (20) and "Agapé approaching the Dwelling of the Fates (142). Una, clothed like a nun sits in prayerful attitude as the watchful lion stretches beside her; tiny Red Cross Knight is approaching. More distinctive were three crones with distaff, scissors, and bobbin; beside them are tiny infants in fluid. Mounted, "The Red Cross Knight and Sansfoy" fight with swords after shattering their lances (10). The hero's breastplate has a red cross; the Saracen's shield is emblazoned "Sansfoy"; his lady, in scarlet, is just behind them. "Sir Scudamore overthrown by Britomart" was in similar forest glade, with a page and a knight as bystanders (184). His shield bears an image of Cupid, hers a red lion; her spear is ebony. "Prince Arthur slaying the Seneschal" showed the impact of lances; blood drops from the point where a lance pierced the Saracen's breastplate and knocked him back (256). The charge unfurled Arthur's short red mantle. His golden helmet has a winged dragon and red plume suggesting flame from its mouth. His round white shield is plain—the great diamond. They fight on a plain before a great walled city backed by mountains. 204). From a narrow bridge before a massive castle a lady looks down at "Sir Artegsll and the Saracen" struggling as their horses strike water. Vivid scenes of combat made Church's readily accessible text especially engaging for boys. "Sir Guyon and the Men in Bestial Shapes" was a warning against betrayal of chivalry (100).

Emily Underdown, The Gateway to Spenser *(1911)*

Among the finest Reward / Prize books were Nelson's series of major English poets. *The Gateway to Spenser: Tales Retold from "The Faerie Queene" of Edmund Spenser* (1911) was by Emily Underdown (1863–1947), who also wrote *The Gateway to Romance: Tales from "The Earthly Paradise" of William Morris* (1909) and *The Gateway to Chaucer* (1912). Mrs. Andrew Lang contributed *The Gateway to Shakespeare* (1908) and *The Gateway to Tennyson* (1910). Combined prose stories and modernized poetical extracts distinguished the series. Underdown (pseudonym Norley Chester), a graduate of University College London, first wrote *Stories from Dante* (1898) and a play *Dante and Beatrice* (1903). She contributed three volumes for Nelson's Golden River Series: *Stories from Spenser* (1912) and *Stories from Chaucer* (1913) selected from her *Gateway* volumes, plus an abridged *The Adventures of Don Quixote* (1910). Nelson reissued *The Gateway to Spenser* as *The Approach to Spenser*, Teaching of English Series #7 (1925). From Chester's *Knights of the Grail: Lohengrin, Galahad* (1907), *Lohengrin* was reprinted with stories by Richard Wilson in *Three Northern Romances: Siegfried—Lohengrin—Undine* (1925).

"Edmund Spenser," a brief introduction to *The Gateway* volume, acknowledged historical context—Gloriana as praise of Queen Elizabeth—but this was not significant "when we are enjoying the delightfully adventurous stories of knights and ladies, dragons and giants, sorcerers and witches, which make up the various books of *The Faerie Queene*."[18] Underdown recorded Spenser at Cambridge, court connections, and tragic circumstances that caused his return from Ireland "ruined and heart-broken, … a miserable ending for one of the greatest poets of all time; but the writer's work will live as long as the English tongue, and delight the hearts of all true lovers of adventure" (10). Featuring four knights she stressed adventure, pageantry, and ideals of chivalry, while avoiding excessive unpleasantness. Short parts with helpful titles eased access: "Una and the Red Cross Knight," seventeen, but "Sir Guyon" only five; "Britomart," nineteen, including Artegall and also Amoret and Florimell; "Sir Calidore and the Blatant Beast," eight. Similar emphasis marked poetical extracts, respectively three, one, three, and two. These filled 100 pages, each with two nine-line stanzas. Since verses came after each story and repeated events told in prose, young readers were eased into Spenserian stanzas—modern spelling but some archaisms. *The Gateway to Spenser* was large, 7¼ by 9½ inches, 397 pages, plus 16 color illustrations on glossy paper. Broad margins had 115 delightful small black-and-white drawings.

"The Quest" established context:

> In the far-away region of Fairyland there dwelt a great and wise queen called Gloriana. The time when she reigned was in those early days when the great Prince Arthur and other brave knights rode through the world in search of adventure, when fair ladies were imprisoned in lonely towers by cruel tyrants, when fierce dragons attacked and devastated whole countries, and when wild romantic events were of common everyday occurrence [11].

Moreover, heroes of chivalry and romance provided moral certainty. Red Cross Knight

> had within him that which was the best of all support, the knowledge that his quest was a true one, and that he had the right on his side; and he had a brave spirit which shrank from no danger, because he knew that what is true and good must in the end overcome all that is evil [15].

Allegory was not mentioned, and named virtues or vices appeared rarely.

"The Story of Sir Guyon" began with "The Orphan Babe" that taught, "how necessary a virtue is temperance or self-control"; because Mordant and Amavia lacked it, they lost their lives and deprived a "helpless infant of both motherly and fatherly care" (148). Guyon rejects Mammon's enticements: "'Ill it would beseem a worthy knight to care for such reward ...'" (157) and later expands the argument:

> "In truth, I do not choose to accept such happiness as you can offer. I seek another bliss than this, and my aim in life is quite different. Rather would I follow brave adventure, and spend my hours in the pursuit of arms, while keeping my soul free, than have the whole of these riches and be your slave" [161].

Prince Arthur defends chivalric integrity with due propriety when he discovers how Cymocles and Pyrocles took advantage of unconscious Guyon and tried to steal his armor: "The soul of the great Prince was kindled to just wrath at hearing of this ignoble deed." He is further stirred when Pyrocles "without waiting for a challenge or observing the usual courteous rules of knighthood" raises his sword in an "unprovoked attack and defiance of knightly rule" (169).

Not surprisingly Britomart, "brave and strong and true," whose "active nature found little enjoyment in the ordinary pursuits" of court ladies, wanted not to beguile the hours with embroidery and light conversation, but "longed to roam through the world in quest of manlike adventure, to meet and overcome dangers, and fight for some just cause, as ardently as any knight in the realm" (186–187). Underdown admitted Britomart's "somewhat restless, dissatisfied mood" (187) and "rather listless manner" when she gazes into the magic mirror; inevitably her thought is "of her future husband, as is wont to come to the minds of maidens" (188). A combination of adventures and love sickness was not limited to men.

More distinctive than dragons was Spenser's Blatant Beast, fought by Sir Calidore, whose story provided a warning against speaking ill, an elementary lesson for children. In Emily Underdown's *The Gateway to Spenser* (1911) Frank C. Papé's youthful knight presses down with his shield, but is unable to contain the creature's myriad forked tongues. The knight's plate armor includes a helmet with three extraordinary plumes (patriotic red, white, and blue).

A significant passage in "Sir Calidore and the Blatant Beast" was Serena's description "of how the savage had guarded and cared for her in as faithful and tender a fashion as any knight versed in all the laws of chivalry could have done." Just as many who are called "sir" are guilty of "unknightly" deeds, so a primitive man did all "right willingly" (342–343). Behavior, not class defines chivalry; peasants and hermits welcome as well as abuse strangers, and so do those who live in castles.

Unlike others, Underdown was very specific about the Blatant Beast. Calidore first sees the monster face to face in a church. The passage, immediately appealing with its list of animals, demonstrated Underdown's fluent style:

> very horrible was the sight ... the most terrible part of him was the great number of tongues which played to and fro within his mouth.
> Some were like dogs' tongues, and with these he barked, and some were like cats', and made a constant mewing; others were like bears' and tigers' tongues, and growled continuously; and others were like snakes', and these darted to and fro, spitting out deadly poison. But worse than all were the tongues which were like the tongues of men and women, for not even dogs' or cats' or bears' or serpents' tongues could do such deadly mischief as these [365].

Relevant stanzas from Spenser's poem were:

> And therein were a thousand tongues empight
> Of sundry kinds and sundry quality;
> Some were of dogs, that barked day and night;
> And some of cats, that wrawling still did cry;
> And some of bears, that groyn'd continually;
> And snarl at all that ever passèd by:
> But most of them were tongues of mortal men,
> Which spake reproachfully, not caring where nor when.
>
> And them amongst were mingled here and there
> The tongues of serpents, with three-forkèd stings,
> That spat out poison, and gore-bloody gear,
> At all that came within his ravenings;
> And spake licentious words and hateful things
> Of good and bad alike, of low and high,
> Ne kaisars sparèd he a whit nor kings;
> But either blotted them with infamy,
> Or bit them with his baneful teeth of injury [392].

Spenser's vocabulary might challenge children yet foster delight in words; marked accents prompted reading. Two significant modifications were: "tongues of mortal men" to "the tongues of men and women," and avoidance of "licentious."

Final stanzas described how the Blatant Beast "rangeth" and "rageth" through the world and expressed Spenser's hope his "rhymes," innocent of blame, would please. But Underdown concluded with a contemporary comparison to challenge readers and assert chivalry was not dead:

> His poisonous claws, and worse still, his thousand tongues, are a source of danger now as in the days of old. But now, as then, their evil attacks can be met unflinchingly by brave hearts, and those who are courteous and truthful and strong, even as was Sir Calidore, will share his quest and adventure, and help towards the capture once more of the Blatant Beast [367].

This reaffirmed verses at the top of endpapers: before Spenser's "melodius song" ended and angels took "this swan" to "caves where Fairies sing," he heard "how men lived of old." Within an Art Nouveau design flowers and vines extend upward in a scene where a lady holds a crown above the head of a champion whose lance is at rest. Below were "Honour and Victory" and "Virtue and Truth."

Indeed pictures for *The Gateway to Spenser* compel as much attention as words. F(rank) C(heyne) Papé (1878–1972), a prolific artist, was recognized for Art Nouveau style used for varied moods—grotesque, humorous, fantastic and horrific, as well as beautiful. His wife Agnes Stringer frequently colored his pictures. These characteristics were at play in *The Gateway to Spenser*. The frontispiece "Prince Arthur meets the Dwarf in the forest" established the central hero, a handsome knight in silver armor with golden details. Arthur holds his sword point down; his magnificent shield displays its diamond, surrounded by decorative vines. Outside the frame is a tree, bare but for a few leaves on thin branches that swirl to frame top and bottom. On the left a dwarf, with bushy red hair and beard and dressed in green, stares at the viewer.

More numerous and delightfully varied were "little Woodmen" who find Una resting in the enormous roots of a tree worthy of Arthur Rackham (64). Papé's satyrs have white beards and hair, pointed ears, small horns, wooly torsos, hooves—and gleeful expressions. Two examine the flowing yellow hair of beautiful blue-eyed Una in her plain white dress; gold bands encircle her hair, waist, and upper arms; her mantle is blue-black. The only young satyr rides on the back of the eldest; one satryr leaps over a large root, and another peers round the tree trunk. Several hurry from the background. Below the framed picture Papé added a bramble that rises into the foreground.

He showed knight in armor and beautiful lady in various circumstances, but always with nature (flowers, vines, birds) favored by Art Nouveau artists: "A Wood Nymph discovered the wounded Timias" (272), "Sir Calepine supports the wounded Serena upon his horse" (336), and "Sir Calidore woos the Shepherdess" (352).

More remarkable was Papé's vision of dragon slaying. Frequently the dragon dominates; Papé's did not. Observers, the viewer's perspective, are large figures in "Una and the Dwarf watch the encounter between the Red Cross Knight and the Dragon" (16). The dwarf, holding a lance with red pennant, looks away with a frightened expression, but kneeling Una leans forward to witness the encounter at the entry of a dark cave. Green dragon and shining knight, albeit at the center, were small. The dragon's tail encircles the knight's leg, but he forces its mouth open with his shield (heraldic redcross) and positions his sword. Fire from the dragon's mouth gives light; rising smoke with sparks brings the eye to background landscape. Papé's focus on those who behold dragon slaying was yet more striking in "The Watchman shows the King the vanquished Dragon" (96). A massive tower with an internal stair filled half the space. The king in an ermine-lined red cloak peers down as directed by the Watchman. Far below, tiny Red Cross Knight points upward with his sword. He stands triumphant on a green dragon with large purple wings. A thin trail of smoke from its mouth heightens the image's elongation; three birds flying before the tower give a sense of distance—they are larger than the dragon! Similarly unconventional was "Sir Calidor overthrows the Blatant Beast," again a narrow image (384). A knight in plate armor kneels and presses his shield on a monster that fills most of the space. Feathers (red, white, and blue) on the knight's helmet and a raft of forked orange tongues enlivened muted grays and browns.

    Dramatic and exotic effects characterized those who threaten. "Duessa visits Night to beg the life of Sanjoy" combined Orientalism and Symbolism as the beautiful witch rises to lift a slim arm in supplication (40). Exotic details were a gold breast cup, wide amulet and bracelet, several rings, jeweled girdle, and elaborate band holding her light auburn hair. She wears a thin white blouse, red skirt and bordered pale blue mantle. Night, a massive winged black figure with a pale face and bony hand that shades its eyes, recalls George Watts's Symbolist paintings. On the left is a chariot with red-eyed horses and flames snorting through bared teeth. "The Wicked Elf flies away with the Prince" above a moated castle lighted by a full moon (80). Although black-winged, she was beautiful with swirling light auburn hair, and blue drapery twirling around her body and outside the frame. This confident Elf holds the tiny blond infant in one raised hand.

    Papé contrasted East and West in "Britomart rescues Amoret from Busirane" (232). The magician's red shoes, patterned tunic, a multi-striped cummerbund, and a conical turban, signal Oriental (*Arabian Nights*) magician. Britomart in silver plate armor and winged helmet—like Wagnerian Brunhild—towers above. Fair-haired Amoret, in white, stands bound to a pillar, enveloped by wreaths of swirling pale smoke.

More problematic was "The Enchantress waits in her little painted shallop for Sir Guyon" (152). Her black hair neatly bound by a circle of red flowers, with a white veil behind, and an exotic fitted dress and red cloak held by brooches and chain were fit accompaniment to her seductive expression. The shallop, a white swan boat garlanded with flowers, is tied to another of Papé's picturesque trees with curved trunk and thin almost leafless branches. Feminine enticement was blatant in "The Mermaids discover Sir Guyon and the old Palmer in their boat"; seven grace the sea where a tiny boat rides undulating waves (176). Their long hair—whether black, brown, yellow, or auburn—was always garlanded—with flowers, seaweed, starfish, and shells. Silvery fish tails, marked with red circles, curve as do white arms to indicate swimming; orange fins extend up white backs. In a second underwater scene, "Florimell is held captive by the sea-god Proteus," seaweed—from the open mouth of a long green fish with reddish fins and markings—formed the Art Nouveau frame (280). Smaller fish and a jellyfish swim in the sea-green background. Proteus, the dark skinned captor / would-be lover with a crown of shells, has a flowing white beard and moustache. He looks longingly at a pale maiden, whose light brown hair floats in the water. Rigid, she is obviously frightened; her bare feet and a dress with tiers of thin blue fabric suggest vulnerability. "Florimell finds the cottage of the Witch in the gloomy glen" was a study of a rustic stone cottage with a thatched roof and low stonewall (208). Smoke rises from the chimney against a stormy sky streaked with rain; black birds fly into the frame. Florimell's long hair is obviously wet; her costume looks sodden, albeit still beautiful—a white dress with a pattern of four hearts, red like her long mantle.

Papé's engaging color pages are among the finest Spenser illustrations; moreover, frequent marginalia, carefully drawn and varied in subject matter, continually engaged readers of *The Gateway to Spenser*. Black-and-white drawings, varying in subject matter, size, and position on the page, accompanied prose tales, not poetical extracts. A fierce dragon encircled the lower right of the first page of "The Story of Una and the Red Cross Knight" (11). Its scales, fiery breath, and dominant position before a distant castle supplemented tiny dragons in color pages, as did a later fire-breathing head (92). The final marginal decoration paralleled the initial one: the Blatant Beast, muzzled and led by Sir Calidore toward a distant castle (367). Similarly large was Orgoglio, a primitive giant with raised club and shield (45); Prince Arthur is smaller than the severed arm he stands above (77) or a huge claw above him (78). Some figures were grotesque: Duessa as ugly hag (85), the witch met by Florimell (212), Mammon (157) and uncouth creatures who labor over his gold (161), a muzzled monster beneath a tree (223), satyrs (61 and 63).

There were lovely, often distressed, ladies (68, 72, 100, 104, 235, 240, 243, 257, 258, 265, 329, 334, 363) and gallant knights frequently challenged (99, 149, 168, 198, 208, 249, 262), huntress (186), Britomart as knight (204, 236, 239), hermits (19, 88, 142, 273, 344), peasants (12, 214, 267, 337, 350, 359). Simple sketches included: animals: Una's lion (52) and donkey (58), a horse's head (288), fish (278), the dove with Timias's ruby heart on a chain (274); objects— a jeweled casket (86), Merlin's mirror (190), girdle (244), lance (254), sword (268), knife (356); places—caves (158, 193), cottage/ huts (20, 91), castle (150), a door (82), landscape (154, 211, 217), seashore with boat (175), seascape with boat and birds (179); nature—flowers and butterflies (176), trees (29, 200), a mouse running from the old keeper of the keys (81); the supernatural, an angel (167).

Action marginalia were dynamic, exciting, sometimes frightening: Red Cross Knight demands surrender from the Saracen he felled (37), a dragon throws him and his horse to the ground (95), Prince Arthur lifts Pyrocles and crushes him (171), a knight charges with lance (250), the Savage Knight lies on the ground, under the leg of Britomart's horse (253). Una's lion flies through the air to fell Kirkrapaine (56) and a giantess throws a captive knight from her horse (220 were humorous. Several marginalia used faint lines: an attacking rabble (172), flames spiraling up to inhospitable Malbecco on his castle wall (226), Britomart with raised shield bravely plunging through a wall of fire (231), Florimell floating deep in the sea (287). Storytelling was well served by mini scenes: Merlin carries Arthur's shield (71), Sir Guyon leads his horse beside the Palmer (145) and an enchantress rows him in the shallop (153), Florimell rows herself (277), a savage priest in leopard skin stands with knife ready to sacrifice—only Serena's bound wrist is visible on the rock (347). Saracen details identified: a challenging knight's costume and scimitar (25), stealthy Fidessa with her lantern (34), and Sansjoy's seizure of his brother's shield from the dwarf (33).

From *The Gateway to Spenser* Underdown's first and last stories and eight of Papé's color pictures became *Stories from Spenser: Retold from "The Faerie Queene"* (1912) in the Golden River Series, price one shilling, not five.[19] This small book, 5 × 6⅜ inches, 155 pages, offered "The Story of Una and the Red Cross Knight," 102 pages and 7 pictures and "Sir Calidore and the Blatant Beast," 45 pages and 1 illustration. The cover picture was "Una and the Lion in the Desert" (48) and the frontispiece "Sir Calepine supports the wounded Serena upon his horse." Others in sequence were: "Una and the Dwarf watch the encounter between the Red Cross Knight and the Dragon" (16), "Duessa visits Night to beg the life of Sansjoy" (32), "Una is discovered by the Little Woodmen" (64), "Prince Arthur meets the Dwarf in the Forest" (80), "The

In Frank C. Papé's magical world Una watches Red Cross Knight fight dragon Error whose fire breath lights her cave, beneath a fanciful landscape. Fair-haired and wearing a white dress, Una kneels as she watches a small knight whose leg the monster has encircled. Her posture suggests prayer as well as observation that the viewer shares. Her dwarf stands loyally beside her but is too fearful to watch. As in most of his illustrations for Emily Underdown's *The Gateway to Spenser* (1911) Papé drew outside the frame to suggest breaking constraints.

Watchman shows the King the vanquished Dragon" (96), "Sir Calidore overthrows the Blatant Beast" (128). There were no marginalia or verse extracts in a book intended for younger children. Some in the series were schoolbooks and added questions.

Collections

Spenser was a canonical author in five mixed collections. Andrew Lang's *The Red Romance Book* (1905) placed *The Faerie Queene* as the culmination of a medieval tradition, while H. A. Guerber's *The Book of the Epic* (1919) recognized it in a context of world literature. Three very mixed collections were: W. J. Glover's *Tales from the Poets* (1915), Dorothy M. Belgrave and Hilda Hart's *Children's Stories from the Poets* (1915), and Christine Chaundler's *My Book of Stories from the Poets* (1919).

Andrew Lang, The Red Romance Book *(1905)*

Andrew Lang (1844–1912), Scots literary critic, poet, and novelist, is famous for collections of fairy tales in a rainbow of colors—largely written by Mrs. Andrew [Leonora] Lang—issued annually and distributed widely in the 1880s and 1890s. Two less known volumes were *The Book of Romance* (1902) and *The Red Romance Book* (1905), also enriched by many illustrations in color and black-and-white by Henry J. Ford (1860–1941); Longmans paid as much for pictures as for words.[20] *The Red Romance Book* placed early modern romances—two stories from *The Faerie Queene* and two from *Don Quixote*—amidst medieval examples.

Lang's Preface to *The Book of Romance* (1902) defined romances as:

> only fairy tales grown up ... a mixture of popular tales, of literary invention, and of history as transmitted in legend. To the charm of fairy tale they add the fascination of the age of chivalry, yet I am not sure that children will not prefer the fairy tale pure and simple, nor am I sure that their taste would be wrong, if they did.[21]

"What Romances Are (To Children and Others)," Preface to *The Red Romance Book* (1905), reassured boys they did not have to read items not of interest to them. Lang asserted male affinity to romances, superior understanding and gender difference:

> Now what are romances? They are grown-up people's fairy tales or story-books, but they are the kind of story-books that grown-up people read long ago, when there were castles and knights, and tournaments, and the chief business of gentlemen was to ride about in full

armour, fighting, while ladies sat at home doing embroidery work, or going to see the men tilt at tournaments, just as they go to see cricket matches now. But they liked tournaments better, because they understood the rules of the game. Anybody could see when one knight knocked another down, horse and all, but many ladies do not understand leg before wicket, or stumping.[22]

Then he quoted Mrs. Lang, who wrote all the romances. She cited not medieval but early modern exemplars Don Quixote, Una, and Bradamante. She acknowledged limited inclusion of adventures and hoped for future interest: "when you grow older, you can read them for yourselves, in the languages in which they were written." Andrew Lang's conclusion urged emulation of Sir Walter Scott, who read the old romances as a boy, and recommended *Ivanhoe* as "the best romance in the world" (viii).

Of 29 stories Mrs. Lang allotted *The Faerie Queene* two, 35 of 372 pages, "Una and the Lion" and "How the Red Cross Knight Slew the Dragon." The latter was St. George's archetypal triumph; the first embodied Mrs. Lang's decision to tell stories of women, "patient and true, in spite of fierce trials and temptations" (viii). The first lines were fairy tale: "Once upon a time there lived a king and queen who had only one child, a little girl, whom they named Una, and they all lived happily at home for many years till Una had grown into a woman" (93). Then a fearful dragon took her parents away as prisoners; Una, safe in a tower embroidering with her ladies, escapes. She needs a champion; however, no knight at court is suitable. Mrs. Lang identified three, all effete: "One spent his days in writing pretty verses to the ladies who were about the queen, another passed his time in putting on suits more brilliant than any worn by his friends, a third loved hawking, but did not welcome the rough life and hard living of real warfare" [93]. She eliminated Gloriana and her court; Una independently seeks the Red Cross Knight, whose fame she has heard, and finds him resting after a fight.

Relying on romance formula, "It were long to tell the adventures Una met with on the way" (94), Mrs. Lang recorded actions after lady meets knight. He enters the cave of a monster—with an ugly face, woman's torso, long arms, claw-like hands, and large serpentine lower parts (97). Ford's knight, with bold crosses on shield and breastplate, faces the viewer; Una and the dwarf, simple line drawing, wait outside. "In Archimago's Cell" the wizard, with pointed hat and book of spells, creates a magic dream to separate knight and lady (100). The Red Cross Knight slays Sansfoy but is not identified as Holiness: Mrs. Lang minimized: "either the Christian knight was the more skilful swordsman, or the cross [on his breastplate] lent new strength to his arm, for the fight was not a long one" (101). Wandering alone, Una meets a lion that "at the sight of her beauty" stops, kisses her feet, and licks her hands (101). Thus accompanied she rides a donkey and leads a lamb through Ford's detailed, colorful landscape, Pre-Raphaelite in style (102). During a night at a cottage the lion kills Kirkrapine before they resume Una's quest. Sadly the Red Cross Knight they encounter is disguised Archimago; he falls before Sansloy, but is recognized and spared. Sansloy kills the lion and rides away with Una.

"How the Red Cross Knight Slew the Dragon" began problematically; he "had given himself over to Duessa" (105). Outside a splendid palace he fights Sansjoy, whom Duessa saves with "thick Darkness" and takes to the Queen of Darkness. Duessa, "ever wont to take the side of him who wins," returns to ingratiate herself with Red Cross Knight, but the dwarf has warned him. Ford's "Una saved by the Wood-Folk" introduced a pastoral interlude; she teaches "many things," while they show her how to play on pipes and dance (109). With Satyrane, a knight eager to help her, Una resumes searching for the Red Cross Knight. However, she runs away when he fights Sansloy because a pilgrim (wizard Archimago again disguised) reported he killed Red Cross Knight. Actually "a hideous giant" made him prisoner and woos Duessa.

The faithful dwarf reports to Una, who seeks her champion. This time help comes from "a good knight" in very shining armor, welded by Merlin: "On the crest of his helmet a golden dragon spread his wings: and in the centre of his breast-plate a precious stone shone forth amidst a circle of smaller ones, 'like Hesperus among the lesser lights'" (111–112). Here Mrs. Lang echoed Spenser's language. Arthur calls forth the giant ("not the first to whom he had given battle"), accompanied by Duessa (112). In "Arthur fights the seven-headed serpent" Ford created a daunting complexity of hissing heads—and buxom Duessa (113). Below them lies the squire, whom Duessa sprinkled with "poisonous water" (112). Arthur faces woman and serpent with sword and shield; he has already struck off the giant's hand that lies at his feet. Inside the castle in a pit Arthur finds Red Cross Knight, "hollow-eyed, and thin as a skeleton" (117) and offers manly advice to Una: treat Red Cross Knight "carefully" and forbear asking about his suffering: "men love not to speak of their sorrows" (117). Arthur leaves Duessa's sentence to them: "the dazzling maiden" is exposed as "an old bald-headed shaking crone" (118).

After some weeks Red Cross Knight's strength was restored; however, he must survive another challenge. "In the Cave of Despair" a wretched figure, bearded and wearing only a short tattered garment, offers swords, rope, or fire as a means of death. Una struck the dagger from her knight's hand and broke the spell with her commanding cry (illustration 121). Recognizing Red Cross's weakness, she takes him to a nearby "house" where ladies give him "strength and counsel" until he is ready to fight the dragon (123). Again Mrs. Lang eliminated religious allegory. Ford's huge golden dragon portrayed the magnitude of the task; a small knight and lady look at the fallen creature (124). Here Mrs. Lang's Spenserian description was worthy of romance:

> Besides the brazen scales which thickly covered his body, his wings were like two sails, and at the tip of each huge feather was a many-pronged claw; while his back was hidden with the folds of his tail, which lay doubled in a hundred coils, and in his mouth were three rows of sharp-pointed teeth [124].

She also devoted two full pages to the fight before stating: "There is little more to be told of Una and the Red Cross knight" (126). In half a page they return to her parents, Duessa and Archimago's attempt to prevent the betrothal is thwarted, the king "performed the marriage rite," and a feast is held. Red Cross Knight's vow to serve the Faerie Queene for six years takes him "from Una's side, and, sad though the parting might be, both held their word too high ever to break it" (127). Thus Mrs. Lang ended with a principle for worthy behavior. Ford's pictures—two color, two half-, and five full-page black-and-white—were more memorable than her words.

W. J. Glover's Tales from the Poets *(1915)*

W(illiam) J(ohn) Glover's *Tales from the Poets* (1915) selected Spenser's continuation of Chaucer's *Squire's Tale* from Book IV of *The Faerie Queene*. "For Love of a Princess" described a tournament. Camballo fights three knights, Priamond, Diamond, and Triamond, who are brothers; since all were destined to die young, their fairy mother got the Fates to pass the life of each into the next. The last combat ends when both Camballo and Triamond are felled; however, they rise and continue fighting until a beautiful lady rides into the lists in a car of Persian design. She opens the rail of the lists with her wand, gives the two Nepenthe, "a celestial cordial ordained by the gods to heal all grief of the heart, and to chase away bitter strife and rage, and to establish a sweet peace."[23] Fury is transformed, as foes become friends—and relatives—when Canace weds Triamond and Camballo weds Triamond's sister, "all loved and ... beloved alike" (94). Spenser's tale, 9 of 280 pages, was not illustrated.

Dorothy M. Belgrave and Hilda Hart, Children's Stories from the Poets *(1915)*

Dorothy M. Belgrave and Hilda Hart's *Children's Stories from the Poets* (1915) chose "The Chase of the Blatant Beast," an adventure of Sir Calidore, the knight of courtesy in Book VI. Hart explained Faery was not "the ordinary

3. *Edwardian Extravagance* 129

M. Dorothy Belgrave and Hilda Hart's *Children's Stories from the Poets* (1915), a volume in The Raphael House Library of Gift Books, had only one story from *The Faerie Queene*, Hart's "The Chase of the Blatant Beast." However, pictures by Frank Adams gave it greatest prominence, including this black-and-white frontispiece, where the beast, a dog-like creature, faces the viewer.

Fairyland" but a place "full of noble knights in shining armour, and gentle fair ladies, and ... stirring deeds."[24] In a black-and-white picture preceding the color frontispiece and title page a strange dog-like monster with wide eyes, open mouth, and darting tongue faces the viewer; a knight stands poised to strike it with his triangular shield emblazoned with a fleur-de-lys. Frank

Adams (fl.1903–1944) also pictured Sir Calidore in a forest with autumnal leaves; he faces the viewer and points his spear at a brown monster held back so that its raised paw cannot strike. Calidore wears chain mail, greaves and plate coverings of arms and hands, white surcoat with a red fleur-de-lys; his scabbard and helmet's plume are also red. This beast was more startling than the tiger from which Sir Calidore rescues Pastorella (picture 39). Thus while Hart told of Melibee, Pastorella (picture 36), and shepherd Coridon, rivalry in love and fights against brigands (half-page picture 41), reunion of mother and lost daughter (half-page picture 43), the Blatant Beast was the compelling interest. "Tired of molesting knights and ladies, the monster had determined to plague the clergy for a change" and attack a monastery (45). Hart's tone, like Mrs. Lang's, was somewhat wry. Sir Calidore triumphantly cuts off the Beast's head: "But then what do you think happened now? Immediately a new and more horrible head sprang up to replace the old!" (45). Sir Calidore, riding a caparisoned horse, leads the muzzled Blatant Beast (black-and-white half-page 46). Hart recorded return to the Faery Queen, the wedding of Sir Calidore and Pastorella, and the Blatant Beast's escape: "The last I heard of him was that he was plaguing the inhabitants of Faeryland more than ever; and to this day they are waiting for another Calidore, who will not merely muzzle the Beast, but find some way of stopping his supply of heads!" (46).

Christine Chaundler, My Book of Stories from the Poets *(1919)*

Christine Chaundler's *My Book of Stories from the Poets* (1919) numbered 34 in 320 pages.[25] Many came from the Middle Ages—Chaucer's *Knight's Tale*, the ballad "Valentine and Ursine," five from Percy's *Reliques*—or Medievalism—Lord Byron, John Keats, Robert Browning, and Dante Gabriel Rossetti. Stories were often three or four pages, or seven to ten—encouraging lengths for child readers. "The Red Cross Knight," forty-five pages, was longest and most demanding. Chaundler (1887–1972) did not divide it into parts; she separated episodes with a sentence: "Meanwhile where was the Red Cross Knight?" (100), and "Now let us turn back to Una and see how her fortune fared" (112). She simplified and sanitized. Accompanied by Una the knight kills Error in her cave. "[A]n old man who appeared to be a hermit," actually "the terrible magician" Archimago, causes a "wicked dream" in which the loved lady does "something that was very wicked and wrong" (94). Thus Red Cross Knight abandons Una, who soon acquires a lion as faithful companion. It kills a robber at the cottage where they sheltered. Meanwhile, Red Cross

Deceptive appearances are a Spenserian commonplace. A. C. Michael's "They came in sight of a stately palace—the Palace of Pride" in Christine Chaundler's *My Book of Stories from the Poets* (1919) epitomized this. Lady, knight, and squire sounding a horn approach across rocky terrain, gazing up in anticipation. It could be read as ordinary seeking rest in a hospitable castle; however, the dash causes pause, and the name "Palace of Pride" should warn against entry.

Knight kills Saracen "Sans Foy," only to become involved with "a very good actress" (101) who pleads for his protection. Chaundler told readers: she is the enchantress Duessa.

A. C. Michael pictured quest, when lady, knight, and squire approach "a stately castle" (104). Red Cross Knight fights Sans Joy, whom Duessa saves with "a mist of blackness and darkness" (108). Inside the Palace of Pride giant Orgoglio defeats the Red Cross Knight and puts him in a dungeon to please vengeful Duessa. Concurrently the third Saracen brother Sans Loy, who fells the disguised Archimago, kills Una's lion, and rides away with her—"a terrible plight" (114) until satyrs in the forest rescue her and she meets Sir Satyrane, who accompanies her to search for the Red Cross Knight. Archimago, in pilgrim guise, reports him slain by Sans Loy; Sir Satyrane challenges the pagan, but frightened Una flees. After the dwarf's explanation of Archimago's deceptions, they seek the Red Cross Knight.

At the center was Arthur, "the bravest and strongest knight of all the knights of the Fairy Queen":

> He was arrayed in the most beautiful armour, ornamented with precious stones, which shone and sparkled and glittered in the sunlight. His sword was of burnished steel, so keen and powerful that it could pierce any mortal armour, and its hilt was richly encrusted with gems. His helmet was of gold, and his shield was made of one huge diamond cut out of solid rock. So bright was this shield that the Prince would never show it to mortal eye, for it would instantly kill whoever looked upon it. He always kept it closely covered, except when he was fighting some dreadful dragon or some other monster whom he could not subdue by the might of his arm alone. The dazzling light of this shield turned all who saw it into stone. Nothing that was not real and true could stand against it. Men were turned to stone, stones were turned to dust, and dust was turned to nothing at all [118].

Arthur, the quintessential knight, triumphs over mortal enemies through personal strength and over the unreal with a supernatural weapon. When Duessa protracts combat with Orgoglio—"spurring on her dragon she hurried to his aid" (119)—Prince Arthur and his squire "had no chance against such unequal odds" until he uncovered his shield. Orgoglio falls, the dragon flees, and Duessa is captured (120). The Prince frees the Red Cross Knight, Una weeps with joy at his recovery and distress at his weakened condition. She decides Duessa's fate: stripped of her "costly attire ... magic garment" to reveal "how old and ugly and hateful the wicked woman really was" (122). Arthur and his squire seek further adventures in one direction, while the Red Cross Knight and Una resume quest to slay the dragon that oppresses her parents.

A final obstacle was Despair; Red Cross Knight yields to his urgings. Una snatches away his dagger and upbraids, "'Faint-hearted knight!'" She takes him to the House of Holiness, where a wise lady's daughters—faith, hope, and charity—restore his strength. Thus Red Cross Knight is able to face the dragon, indeed a dreadful-looking creature. His body was covered with glistening scales like a thick coat of armour. He had two great wings with which he could fly, and his tail was almost three furlongs in length, with two terrible stings at the end. His claws were sharp and strong, and out of his mouth came clouds of smoke and flames of fire [128].

The stream and tree that refresh the Red Cross Knight were not given allegorical meanings. After "the quest of the Fairy Queen had been performed" Una takes her knight to meet her parents for great feasts; theirs is a long engagement, since he vowed to serve the Fairy Queen "for six years as a maiden knight" (131). Archimago and Duessa make a final false accusation of his betrothal to Fidessa. The Red Cross Knight admits his failings; after Una penetrates Archimago's disguise, the magician is cast into prison. A last paragraph asserted "patience and constancy" and "fresh honour and glory added to his name" will make separation seem brief before "happiness all through the rest of their lives" (132). Chaundler's comprehensive narrative was a solid introduction to Book I. An encyclopedic book defined *The Faerie Queene* as epic.

H(élenè) A(deline) Guerber, The Book of the Epic *(1919)*

H(élenè) A(deline) Guerber's *The Book of the Epic* (1919) was international in scope and suitable for older readers, a systematic introduction to epics from seventeen cultures / places.[26] Guerber (1859–1929) provided literary history and some analysis as well as summary. Six were "Epics of the British Isles": *Beowulf, The Arthurian Cycle, Robin Hood, The Faerie Queene, Paradise Lost,* and *Paradise Regained.* Since no other nation had more than two, English literary tradition dominated. Last was American *The Song of Hiawatha.* Thirty-two full-page illustrations, sixteen in color, were on glossy paper. A few were paintings; most were pictures from other books published by Harrap.

Guerber's review of *The Faerie Queene* filled 42 of 586 pages. She explained Spenser's poem "purposed to depict the twelve moral virtues in twelve successive books, each containing twelve cantos, written in stanzas of eight pentameters followed by a hexameter. But he completed only six books of his poem in the course of six years." It was: "not only an epic but a double allegory, for many of the characters represent both abstract virtues and the noted persons of Spenser's time" (313). Guerber's first example was "Gloriana, who personifies Elizabeth and is the champion of Protestantism" (313). The illustration was Gertrude Demain Hammond's "The Faerie Queene," Gloriana's court scene from Dawson's *Stories from The Faerie Queene* (1909).

Publishers like George G. Harrap often repeated illustrations in successive volumes. Gertrude Demain Hammond's "Georgos claimed that Adventure" was the first picture in Lawrence H. Dawson's *Stories from the Faerie Queene Retold from Spenser* (1909); it was repeated in H(elene) A. Guerber's *The Book of the Epic* (1919) as the only illustration for *The Faerie Queene*. Gloriana was a youthful Queen Elizabeth in a court scene with attendant ladies, amused by the peasant youth who asks for Una's adventure.

Titles identified allegorical meanings and protagonists:

Book I: The Legend of the Knight of the Red Cross, or of Holiness
Book II: The Legend of Sir Guyon, or of Temperance
Book III: The Story of Britomart, or of Chastity
Book IV: The Legend of Cambel and Triamond, or of Friendship
Book V: The Legend of Sir Artegall, or of Justice
Book VI: The Legend of Sir Calidore, or of Courtesy

Why male knights have "legends" and the female knight a "story" was not indicated.

Book I's extensive allegory required identifications. Una is Truth; Gloriana dubs Georgos (Holiness), "'Knight of the Red Cross' because the armour which Una has brought bears this device" (314). His first encounter is with a dragon (Heresy and Error) in a cave. Archimago personifies Hypocrisy; Duessa is Mary, Queen of Scots as well as Falsehood and Popery. Fidessa takes Georgos to the stronghold of Pride, where Queen Lucifera is attended by Idleness, Gluttony, Lechery, Envy, Avarice, and Wrath. Giant Orgoglio personifies Spiritual Pride. The old woman's cottage is the house of Superstition; her daughter is Stupidity. The Lion (Courage) does not devour Una because "in fairy-land, wild beasts cannot harm kings' daughters, provided they are pure" (318). Arthur is both Leicester and Chivalry (320). Una takes weakened Red Cross Knight to "a house, where the wise old matron Religion, Doctor Patience, and three handmaidens, Faith, Hope, and Charity, nurse him" (321). He "wanders to the top of the hill of Contemplation, whence he is vouchsafed a vision of the New Jerusalem." An old man prophesies that upon completing his quest Red Cross Knight "will be known as 'Saint George of mery England, the signe of victoree'" (321). Guerber told a story of quest, giant killing, and dragon slaying; however, explanations of personifications made clear that Book I was heavily didactic.

In Book II the adversary of Sir Guyon (Temperance), accompanied by "a black-garbed palmer (Prudence or Abstinence)," is Acrasia (Pleasure), an 'enchantress who detains her captives in the Bower of Bliss.' Guyon's challenges include the baby—"Ruddy Main, or the Red Handed" (323–324) and "the madman Furor." Guyon ill-advisedly leaps into the skiff of Phaedria (Mirth) who takes him over the Idle Sea to her magic realm where he meets jealous Cymochles (Deceit). When Phaedria intervenes, Guyon declares lack of interest in her and continues his quest for the Bower of Bliss, albeit without the palmer. He barely resists appeals of Mammon (God of Wealth)—in whose cave workmen are "oppressed by Care and driven by Force and Fraud, who keep them constantly at work and never allow Sleep to approach them" (326)—even marriage to his daughter. Guyon escapes to a garden and is reunited with the palmer, who discovers him watched over by an angel. Ruffians are stripping a still unconscious Guyon when Prince Arthur arrives to slay them.

As the two knights ride in the forest, "hungry barbarians" attack when they try to enter a castle. They "utterly annihilate their assailants" and release prisoners before spending days in rest and "perusing 'old records from auncient times,' where they learn the history of all the British kings." Then each goes his separate way. After the palmer forges "chains and a steel net" needed to "capture and hold the witch Acrasia," they sail "safely past the Magnetic Rock, over the Sea of Gluttony, etc.' to an island" (328). Avoiding 'delusions of mists and monsters' Guyon reaches the enchanted bower where Acrasia dwells with beasts, visitors she transformed. When he refuses a drink that would transform him, Phaedria tries to delay Guyon. With the palmer's aid he captures Acrasia in the steel net, binds her, and sends her to the Fairy Queen "to dispose of her according to her good pleasure" (329).

In Book III a woman personifies Chastity—but is also a knight. Britomart "had from earliest childhood so longed to be a boy that, instead of devoting her time to womanly occupations, she practiced manly sports until she became as expert a warrior as any squire in her father's court" (329). Although she fights knights and rescues ladies, Britomart's primary quest is to find "Sir Artegall, the Champion of Justice and proud possessor of Achilles' armour," seen in a magic mirror when she tried to discover "whom she should ultimately marry" (330). Book III has many links to Books I and II; Britomart meets heroes—Guyon, Arthur, and Red Cross Knight—and demonstrates comparable or greater prowess. She assists Red Cross Knight when he alone fights six. Although "a golden curl" revealed her sex, "he courteously ignored it"; yet as they left the castle "he courteously offered to serve as the lady's protector and escort." Exposure of Britomart's gender leads her to speak of her love "rather slightingly" to conceal her feelings. But after the Red Cross Knight "hotly protested that he [Sir Artegall] was the noblest and most courteous knight that had ever lived ... 'The royall Maid woxe wondrous glad'" (331).

Nevertheless, Britomart perseveres as knight; she alone goes through fire to rescue Amoret, Sir Scudamore's bride stolen by Busirane. Inside the castle she correctly responds to "'Be Bold'" and "'Be not too bold'" and observes "a strange procession of Fancy, Doubt, Desire, Danger, Fear, Hope, Dissemblance, Grief, Fury, and many others"—a plethora of personifications (335-336). Amoret dissuades Britomart from killing Busirane because the magician "must heal her wound and free the other inmates of the castle from magic thralldom" (336). The two women proceed together.

In Book IV the story shifted to the false Florimell and Sir Satyrane's tournament. In competition Britomart unhorses Sir Artegall and wins the girdle, which she presents to false Florimell. When it will not stay in place, ladies mock and try, but "none could wear it save Amoret, evidently the only perfectly faithful lady present" (338). Sir Scudamore, jealous of the knight who rescued Amoret, and Sir Artegall, defeated by the stranger knight, pursue Britomart. She unhorses and disarms Sir Scudamore; Sir Artegall tries to rescue him, but is also disarmed. Fortuitously, Britomart's helmet is knocked off. When men realize they have been fighting a woman, they humbly kneel and ask pardon. Sir Scudamore is delighted a woman rescued his wife; Glauce reveals Britomart's quest for Sir Artegall, and they are betrothed.

Meanwhile a forester wounds Arthur's squire Timias, who is found by nymph Belphebe—Amoret's twin. Timias duly falls in love, but regards himself as too lowly and spends his days "'in dolour and despaire'" (339). When he helps a damsel fleeing from a monster, Belphebe assists but becomes jealous because Timias kisses the lady—who is, of course, Belphobe's twin sister Amoret. Like Orlando in Shakespeare's *As You Like It*, Timias assuages his grief at losing Belphebe by carving her name on trees and kissing it. He also places a ruby heart—Belphebe's gift—round the neck of a dove that flies to her. She follows it, recognizes Timias's devotion, and resumes hunting activities until the Blatant Beast wounds Timias. Arthur rescues his squire, all are properly reunited, and weddings follow. Guerber's summary ended with the real Florimell, taken by sea-nymphs to Proteus's hall to witness the wedding of the Thames and Medway. Florimell discovers Marinell, cared for by his goddess mother; full recovery comes when the lovers wed.

In Book V Sir Artegall resumes questing; "the noble champion of Justice (the Lord Deputy of Ireland)" goes there to defend Irena. His companion is "Talus, an iron man, whose flail threshes out falsehood" (341). In several episodes Sir Artegall exemplifies justice. He makes "a Solomon-like judgment" when the true lover prefers loss of his lady to her death, slays a Saracen (who despoils those that pass over a bridge) and his daughter, and exposes a charlatan's trick scales "by weighing such intangible things as truth and falsehood, right and wrong" (342). Guerber abbreviated, "The poet now ably describes the wedding of Florimell and Marinell and the tournament celebrated in their honour" (343). There Braggadochio claims Sir Guyon's horse; Sir Artegall demands proof of "secret tokens the animal bears," and awards it to Sir Guyon. And he settles a dispute between twin brothers over a treasure chest washed ashore.

Guerber merely noted Spenser's "brilliant description of Radigone's appearance and of the duel." Sir Artegall fights this Amazon queen, but is enslaved by her blinding beauty. After Talus enlists Britomart to rescue Artegall, they have "extraordinary adventures by the way" (344). She fights Radigone, who flees into her castle; Britomart follows, frees her lover, and "bids him continue his adventurous quest." Knight and squire join Arthur to rescue a maiden servant of "Mercilla (another personification of Elizabeth)," from two pursuing Saracen knights (345). Artegall dons Saracen armor to enter the Soldan's court; Arthur follows, challenges, and kills the Soldan whose wife Adicia tries to kill the maid. But Artegall "drives the Soldan's wife into the forest, where she is transformed into a tiger." The maid warns against Guyle; "thanks to the bravery, strength, and agility of Arthur, Artegall, and Talus, Guyle's might is broken" (345). At Mercilla's court, Awe and Order usher them to the Queen enthroned with the English lion at her feet. Duessa (Mary Queen of Scots) is proved guilty of crimes; but Mercilla, "too merciful to condemn her, sets her free" (346). Guerber identified further allegory. A three-headed monster Gereones (Philip II of Spain) deprived Belge (Belgium) of her sons and delivered them to the Inquisition. Arthur volunteers to help, only to learn a faithless steward (Alba) has driven Belge from her home. Arthur battles and reinstates her, then defeats Gereones's assault, after Belge told him "to overthrow an idol in the neighboring church" (346).

Continuing on their way Artegall and Talus learn the knight can free Irena by becoming her champion against Grantoro. Before reaching Ireland Artegall pauses to rescue "a distressed knight (Henry IV of France) to whom he restores his lady Flourdelis." Grantoro's forces meet Artegall and Talus but are "soon scattered" by Talus's flail. Artegall forces Grantorto "to bite the dust"; they restore Irena to her throne (347). As he is returning, hags Envy and Detraction attack Artegall and release the Blatant Beast (Slander). He rejects Talus's offer to kill them and hurries to Britomart.

In Book VI Sir Artegall meets Sir Calidore, who "impersonates Courtesy (or Sir Philip Sidney)," sent by Gloriana to slay the Blatant Beast. Rushing away on his quest, Calidore defeats a villain who took hair from every woman and beard of every man that passed: his ladylove wanted "a cloak woven of female hair and adorned with a fringe of beards" (348). He next acquires a squire—Tristram of Lyonnesse—an unarmed youth who saved a lady from a brute. They meet a wounded knight whom they take, with his lady (Priscilla), to the castle of the knight's father.

Moments of male camaraderie—a long conversation of Calidore, his squire, and a knight—lead the latter's lady Serena to wander off to gather flowers. When the Blatant Beast tries to seize her, her cries alert the men. Sir Calespine cares for his wounded wife, while Sir Calidore pursues the monster. Seeing a bear carrying off an infant, Calespine rescues it and takes it to a nearby castle. Unfortunately he cannot locate Serena, found by "a gentle savage" (350). Fortunately Arthur and Timias come upon them and realize the man is kind. Because Serena and Timias "have both been poisoned by bites of the Blatant Beast, Arthur takes them to a hermit"; his healing arts fail, but his prayers cure them (350). Arthur and the wild man search for Sir Turpine, who escaped from Radigunde; at his castle they defeat him but spare his life at his wife's request. This clemency Arthur soon regrets: Turpine's knights attack them. Arthur lures and seizes Turpine, and hangs him to a tree. Timias and Serena meet "a lady and a fool (Disdain and Scorn), who are compelled by Cupid to wander through the world, rescuing as many people as they have made victims" (351). Again Arthur sets things right; he frees his squire and deems Cupid's penalty adequate. Concurrently Serena wandered off again; savages seized and would sacrifice her. Sir Calespine rescues her—but does not know the lady is his wife.

A pastoral idyll interrupted Sir Calidore's pursuit of the Blatant Beast. He sees beautiful Pastorella "dancing in the forest to the piping of Colin Clout (a personification of Spenser)" and has "the good fortune" to rescue her from a tiger, soon after her fearful suitor Coridon ran away (351). A band of brigands, who take Pastorella, Coridon, and Melibee (a helpful farmer) prisoner, plan to sell their captives to merchants. When the Captain wants to keep Pastorella, a fight ensues. Coridon escapes, the brigand Captain and Melibee are killed, and Pastorella faints. At this point Sir Calidore returns to set all right: he slays robbers and merchants, recovers stolen flocks and booty that he gives to Coridon as compensation for taking his love Pastorella. Still pursuing the Blatant Beast, Sir Calidore takes Pastorella to the castle of Belgard, whose wife discovers a birthmark. Pastorella is their lost child—abandoned by a handmaiden to whom they entrusted her to conceal their secret marriage. All enjoy happy reunion. Sir Calidore manages to overtake the Blatant Beast, muzzle it, and take it to Queen Gloriana. Sadly there is no permanent solution; the monster escapes because not well chained; it now roams the country, sparing none, not even poets.

Guerber did not tell stories; she identified allegory and summarized plot. *The Book of the Epic* was a guide to Spenser's Protestant references and tortuous episodes—helpful for students, teachers, and librarians.

4

American Difference

Since Americans, as well as Victorians and Edwardians, regarded American literature as a continuation of English literature, books read by children in the United States often originated in Britain. Publishers with main offices in London typically had ones in New York—and cities of the British Empire. A telling example of connection was *The Story of the Faerie Queene* (1902), edited by Edward Brooks. He merely added an introduction for the unchanged words of Mary Macleod's *Stories from The Faerie Queene* (1897); the publisher reduced the number of A. G. Walker's illustrations. Calvin Dill Wilson's *The Fairy Queen, First Book* (1906), a modest attempt, was thoroughly American. Later Grace Adele Pierce in a beautifully printed book marked social changes after World War I as well as evaluations of a literary masterpiece. She selected *The Red Cross Knight and The Legend of Britomart [The Lady Knight]* (1924), an overt declaration of parity in gender that paralleled emphases by English women.

Collections of chivalric stories retold for children by late Victorians and Edwardians typically favored medieval romances; however, as shown in Chapter 3, several included *The Faerie Queene* as an early modern culmination. Spenser's stories, notably of the Red Cross Knight, deployed the excellence of chivalric romance—including identity as St. George—and were deemed canonical. *The Faerie Queene* fared very differently in the United States. Among collections only Abbie Sage Richardson's *Stories from Old English Poetry* (1871) and Carolyn Sherwin Bailey's *Stories of Great Adventures* (1919) included *The Faerie Queene*.

More numerous were home libraries that at the start of the twentieth century made stories and history available, especially for readers without access to libraries or expensive books. They offered wide coverage and editorial comment about the significance of literature in children's lives. Editors' treatment of *The Faerie Queene* reflected interest and / or confidence that readers would find Spenser accessible and / or rewarding. *The Delphian Course* (1913), ten volumes suitable for older children and adults, aptly described the purpose of home libraries. The subtitle was: *A Systematic Plan of Education, Embracing the World's Progress and Development of the Liberal Arts*. Home libraries designed for children differed in emphases. *The Young Folks' Library* (1901–02) had twenty volumes, many devoted to history and travel, plus a separate guide. Three others had ten volumes and stressed literature: *The Children's Hour* (1907), *Journeys through Bookland* (1909), and *The Junior Classics* (1912); the first two had separate guide volumes. With somewhat less emphasis upon literature *Young Folks' Treasury* (1909) had twelve volumes, while *Young People's Home Library* (1910) was a single volume. Medieval romances, *Don Quixote*, and *The Pilgrim's Progress* were usually included, but not *The Faerie Queene*; canonical status was not widely urged in the United States. Yet *My Book House* (1920–21), originally six volumes, later divided into twelve, featured *The Faerie Queene*.

Professional advice about circumstances for learning from teachers and librarians were concurrent resources for understanding reception of *The Faerie Queene*. *The Book Lover* (1884/1902) by James Baldwin, a prolific writer for and about children, was influential for a long time. Mary E. Burt's *Literary Landmarks* (1897) and John Harrington Cox's *Literature in the Common Schools* (1909) drew upon classroom experiences. Books to be read were the subject of librarians' surveys: Montrose J. Moses's *Children's Books and Reading* (1907) and Frances Jenkins Olcott's *Children's Reading* (1912). Literary histories where evaluations *The Faerie Queene* by American and British writers often agreed, contained more critical analysis and are discussed in Chapter 6.

Books

Edward Brooks, ed., The Story of the Faerie Queene *(1902)*

The Story of The Faerie Queene, edited by Edward Brooks (1831–1912) in 1902, was a telling example of American dependence upon English books and of lax acknowledgment.[1] There was no indication this book, discussed in Chapter 3, reprinted Mary Macleod's *Stories from the Faerie Queene* (1897). The contribution of Brooks, Superintendent of Public Schools, Philadelphia, was an eight-page Introduction. While the verbal text was unchanged, some of A. G. Walker's illustrations were eliminated. Uniform with several other volumes of chivalric stories, the navy blue cloth cover had a cropped image of a knight charging with lance, stamped in four colors (white, yellow, brown, green). The title page, black letters with orange framing, was decorated with a sword. Compact volumes (5 × 7½ inches) printed on medium quality paper lacked the high finish of the British edition. This made somewhat smaller illustrations less sharp; but Gothic type for titles, subtitles, and verse quotations on illustrations, added some style.

Brooks's Introduction enthusiastically praised "One of the greatest poems in English literature," part of Elizabethan glorious achievement, with poetical merit ranked with Shakespeare, Chaucer, and Milton (9). Like Hales, Brooks recognized Spenser's "rich imagery and fertility of conception"; he referred to those who responded positively: "the delight of every accomplished gentleman, the model of every poet, the solace of every scholar," yet acknowledged regrettable present lack of audience (10). Archaic language, lack of unity and completeness—six independent poetic tales—meant only "men and women of high literary culture" read the poem. Having noted problems, Brooks urged reasons to read *The Faerie Queene*:

> so much that is delightful and elevating, so much that is sweet and noble, ... the moral tone ... so elevated and the sentiments set forth so full of refinement and beauty. ... allegorical in style ... designed to hold up for admiration and imitation the virtues of morality and religion. The book thus stands on the highest plane of moral thought and feeling, presenting a picture of the loftiest motives and actions; and it is adapted to hold before the mind the moral virtues in their most fascinating guise. It appeals to the young of both sexes, touching their imaginations by its heroic deeds and lifting their hearts in admiration of that which is pure and high and noble [11-12].

Puritan Spenser suited Puritan America; moreover, he was appropriate for boys and girls, a pedagogical advantage. In contrast to Hales's sophisticated analysis, Brooks gave a concise summary of contents for each book: names of knights, allegorical meaning, and general statement of action (13–16).

Brooks, writer of books of chivalric stories for children—Siegfried, King Arthur, Tristram—knew well their significance and that fairy tales occasioned parental concern and boys' indifference. He distinguished precisely:

> The Fairy Land of Spenser is really the land of chivalry rather than a real fairy land. It is a region in which heroic daring and ideal purity are the objects chiefly presented to our imaginations. The principal personages are knights bound on perilous adventures, ladies of rare virtues rescued from hideous monsters and miseries, and good and evil enchanters whose spells affect the destiny of those with whom they come in contact. The hero of the poem is said to be the chivalrous Arthur of the British legends [12].

Book IV The Squire of Lowe Degree, a tale of Friendship, was comparatively brief because "many incidents ... are unsuited to young people and cannot be so well told in a prose narrative" (14). Brooks ended with strong affirmation and high expectations:

> In its present form it is a book for youth, to whom tales of chivalry are especially fascinating. Its influence will be to develop in the mind of youth high ideals of courtesy and honor. It

holds forth to their youthful admiration sentiments of friendship, fidelity, justice, temperance, chastity, and holiness—the greatest Christian virtues—which, if early inculcated in the hearts of the young, lead to high ideals and noble thought and action. One of the highest objects of life is the development of character; and the books read in childhood, when full

Edward Brooks "edited" *The Story of the Faerie Queene* (1902) for readers in the United States. The book reprinted—without acknowledgment—Mary Macleod's *Stories from The Faerie Queene* (1897) and many of A. G. Walker's illustrations. His scene of a mother with several charming children, albeit he showed them receiving knight and lady, was a rare domestic scene and occasion to picture children.

of noble sentiments and actions, are among the surest means for the cultivation of those feelings and purposes that enrich the spiritual nature and result in a noble manhood and a beautiful womanhood [16].

High sentiments and pedagogy were in accord with Macleod's. The American edition eliminated some pictures that did not support chivalric manliness. Of the original eighty-five illustrations, fifty-four were included—thirty-two full and twenty-two partial pages. Loss of feminine images and scenes of male weakness suggest avoidance of negative reaction from boys. Missing full-pages were: the procession of Counselors (Seven Deadly Sins) and vision of the New Jerusalem shown to Red Cross Knight; Guyon with the lady and gondola at Idle Lake, the Palmer faces the beasts (transformed men), Guyon unhorsed by Prince Arthur; the arming of Britomart, and Artegal falling in a joust. Absent partial pages depicted: Britomart with the mirror, Pœana playing a harp, meeting of true Florimell and false Florimell, a lady seated at a window, Pastorella and shepherdesses, and Artegal muzzling the Blatant Beast. Here was unmitigated manly chivalry not feminization of America.

Calvin Dill Wilson, The Faery Queen, First Book *(1906)*

American educator Calvin Dill Wilson (b. 1857) first retold stories of Spain's chivalric heroes, *The Story of The Cid for Young Readers* (1901) and *The Child's Don Quixote* (1901). He then turned to England's great authors with *The Canterbury Tales: Prologue and Selections* (1906) and *The Faery Queen, First Book* (1906).[2] Wilson's foreword judged Spenser's work: "one of the most splendid long poems in the English language. It is also a wonderfully interesting story-book, containing all sorts of adventures. But not many children are likely to read this long poem in its original form." Recognizing "the whole set of tales" would make a "larger book than you would care for," he retold only Book I. Moreover, "as young people are usually more interested in story than in its meaning, we have not given an explanation of the allegory, believing that the story in itself is sufficiently pleasing, and that readers can find something of the meaning without help."[3] This supported the title page's reassuring "Rewritten in Simple Language." Concluding promises were introduction to "the world of fairies" and a lifetime of finding "references to famous scenes and people told of in the book" (vi). The first paragraph affirmed expectations of fairy tale and chivalric romance:

> Once upon a time the great Gloriana ruled as the Fairy Queen, and not only were the little fairies subject to her commands but many strong and great knights also obeyed her. And these were sent forth by her endowed with magical powers, so that they were able to do what no other knights could perform [3].

Absence of pedagogical apparatus left children free to enjoy without constraints.

One unusual feature was a separate title page to introduce each chapter with topical summary of action (all capital letters) and ornamental device of leaves and flowers. Like Spenser's introductory verse summaries, this guidance alleviated efforts needed to cope with narrative complexity; for example: "CHAPTER I. GLORIANA, THE FAIRY QUEEN.—HER YEARLY FEAST.—THE AWKWARD YOUTH AND HIS REQUEST.—THE LADY WHOSE PARENTS WERE SHUT UP" (1). Wilson's eleven chapters did not always correspond to Spenser's twelve cantos. Una meets Arthur in Chapter VIII not Canto VII, and Arthur's armor is more detailed (96–97) than his lineage and love (Canto IX). Yet Una's response is to character: courteous speech, "feeling words suited to her humor … goodly reason and his well-guided speech" (98)—a model to inspire careful speaking. Redcross Knight's time in the House of Holiness (Canto X) warranted less than a paragraph and lacked religious details: "In this house of Holiness they dwelt awhile. And there in quiet and in reading the Redcross Knight gained strength and was comforted" (118). Race, descent from Saxon kings, Saint George's path to heaven take only two paragraphs before Redcross Knight and Una return to her native land. More than the encounter with Error in Chapter II (13–15), Spenser's account of dragon slaying (Canto XI) was fully rendered in Chapter X (120–129). Repetition was effective: "So down he fell, … So down he fell, … So down he fell, … So down he fell, … The Knight himself even trembled at his fall, so huge and horrible a mass it seemed" (129).

Like attention was given to giants: Orgoglio's triumph over Redcross Knight in Chapter VIII (93–94) and Arthur's protracted engagement (104–109), ending with decapitation (the giant "wallowed in his own foul, bloody gore, which flowed from his wounds in wondrous streams"). Una's grateful eulogy, made with "sober gladness and mild modesty," recognized ideal chivalry: "'Fair branch of nobility, flower of chivalry, that have amazed the world with your worth, how shall I reward you for the pains you have suffered for my sake?'" (109).

Witches and magicians posed greater danger than giants, mental deception instead of physical strength. The Fradubio story, which is not about altruistic endeavor, led to Duessa's changing knight and lady into trees. He fought to vindicate beauty, "'in the prime of my years when hot courage was first kindled in my breast by the fire of love and joy of chivalry'" (32). Having won once, Fradubio competed again; then "the wicked witch ... by her magic raised a foggy mist" to obscure Fralissa's beauty ("'deformed wight'") and prompted Fradubio's disloyalty. Only a view of "the false witch" as "a filthy, foul old woman" restored Fradubio's judgment. Her "golden cup, which she carried filled with magic stuff, death and despair and secret poison" disables Arthur's squire (106). Archimago, who appears a holy man, told "of Saints and Popes and strewed his prayers through his talk," but in his study "amid books of magic and various arts ... sought out mighty charms ... horrible spells ... called up hundreds of Sprites" (18–19). Wilson associated deception with magic: "by his mighty art he [Archimago] could take many forms and shapes, sometimes like a fowl, sometimes like a fish, now like a fox, now like a dragon, so that he would often quake with fear of himself. Who can tell the power of magic?" (26).

Rhetorical questions engaged young readers. "And what do you think this youth asked for himself?" (4). After her Lion's death "Who now is left to guard the forlorn maiden?" (50). Encounters simply occur: "It happened one day that a noble, warlike knight (80); "At last she chanced by good fortune to meet a goodly knight" (96). Amusing passages enriched, like Chapter III's delightful evocation—"When the cheerful Chanticleer with his shrill note had warned them once that the Sun's fiery car was hastily climbing the eastern hill"—in which children could recognize Chaucer's *Canterbury Tales* (25). Avoiding description of the last feast could pleasingly mark an end or disappoint: "Why need I tell of this feast, in which there was nothing riotous? Why need I tell of the dainty dishes, of the courtly train? My pages cannot contain all" (137). Dame Pride's counselors numbered only six: Idleness, Gluttony, Riot, Avarice, Envy, Wrath; missing was Lechery that might encourage speculation (59–60).

A distinction of *The Faery Queen, First Book* was visual presentation. McClurg, a Chicago publisher that favored Arts and Crafts decorated pages reminiscent of medieval manuscripts, printed 143 pages of text within leaf and flower borders, the bottom enhanced by devices (flower, knight charging with lance opposite Una and Red Cross in armor, Red Cross with raised shield opposite dragon). It was not a strenuous read.

Grace Adele Pierce, The Red Cross Knight and The Legend of Britomart *(1924)*

The title of Grace Adele Pierce's *The Red Cross Knight and The Legend of Britomart (the Lady Knight): Being Tales from Spenser's "Faerie Queene"*

(1924) signaled gender parity. Nevertheless, the black cloth cover featured a paper picture of Red Cross Knight on his brown charger and holding a lance with pennon. His shield bears a Celtic red cross and his surcoat a simple red cross; a white nimbus encircles his plain helmet. The figure is within a red cross with distant fairy tale castles on left and right. Heraldic shields (light blue and yellow diagonals) emblazoned Truth, Chastity, Fidelity, and Justice in blue corners. While Redcross Knight or *Holiness* is "the hero of the first book," Britomart, "the lady knight representing *Chastity*" is "the adventurer of the third book."[4] Spenser's first stanza (I. i.1, modernized English) introduced "The Red Cross Knight; A Story of the Faerie Queene"; the heading for "The Legend of Britomart" claimed equivalence:

> In days of old when knights were bold,
>   The ladies, too, took part;
> And none sought right with greater might,
>   Than our Lady Britomart [I, 1].

Henry Pitz's frontispieces were amusingly contrasted. The first, black lines on white, showed an interior where men of the court gaze at a youth, holding sword and helmet: "The armour suited the youth so well that he seemed the goodliest man in all that company." The second was dramatic—white on black, with Art Nouveau foliage reminiscent of Walter Crane. A pretty young woman stands in the stirrups of a large richly caparisoned charger; she holds the reins in her left hand and a sword in her right: "Thus, in the armour of Angela, the Saxon queen, Lady Britomart rode forth to conquer."

Pierce (1858–1923), who wrote *The Silver Cord and the Golden Bowl* (1901) and *Child Study of the Classics* (1898), a collection of tales, included a one-page foreword. She placed Spenser, "The Poets' Poet," in the glorious reign of Queen Elizabeth. *The Faerie Queene,* an "allegorical romance of chivalry," is his best-known poem, "a pean of praise to England with the Redcross Knight as the idealized Englishman of Spenser's mind." Britomart, "a most virtuous and beautiful Lady," symbolized Elizabeth, as did Gloriana, a Queen. Other historical identifications were Mary, Queen of Scots as Duessa and Lord Grey as Artegall. Allegory is "a story about one thing which means quite another"; reference to *Pilgrim's Progress* indicated American children knew Bunyan's book. Nevertheless, allegory was for later learning: "Now we are interested in it only as a beautiful story of adventure and chivalry in which the right finally conquers evil." Emphasis was on high sentiment and elimination, or at least mitigation, of the unsavory. However, Pierce's disclaimer of allegory refers to political / historical equivalents; she used allegorical names for even minor characters and added frequent authorial explanations and interpretations. Her simple style avoided Spenser's protracted flourishes. Each part had twelve "adventures," four or five pages in length, for easier reading of 120 pages; additionally, a picture filled half of most pages. Red decorated capitals added variety, and larger size (7½ inches by 10¼ inches) resembled picture books. The style was Arts and Crafts, like Morris's Kelmscott Press, itself emulation of incunabula. Titles were in Gothic letters and illustrations black-and-white, and framing devices red. Like Edwardian volumes, Pierce's was elegant, albeit visually bolder.

Henry C. Pitz (1895–1976), then working mostly with children's books, provided pictures and decorations that exemplified his place in the Arts and Crafts movement of the United States; in later life he wrote *The Brandywine Tradition* (1969) and *Howard Pyle* (1975). Philadelphia born, Pitz, a professor at the Philadelphia Museum College of Art for many years, was a painter as well as an illustrator. Although only the two frontispieces were full-page illustrations, twenty-six memorable headings introduced adventures, and footers ended the two stories. Moreover, 73 pictures, one at almost every opening (52 half-page and 21 quarter-page), 115 red initials, and 17 small devices added color and variety. Pitz's illustrations, like Pyle's, were bold and celebratory depictions of chivalry. End papers, dark on light blue, depicted a marching army led by two mounted knights, but most illustrations had one or two figures, which reinforced Pierce's emphasis on individuals and their challenges Particularly effective was use of black backgrounds.

The Redcross Knight, young and vain, in his first adventure slays dragon Error; Pierce gave few details (nothing of Error's offspring, gore, papers), only that Una and the dwarf were apprehensive and the knight won by the power of God. The Second Adventure, which takes them to the hermitage of Archimago, occasioned Pierce's reflection that greatest danger is often not obvious; youthful folly—quick and intense reaction to the magician's vision of Una, "which made him very unhappy"—lead Redcross to abandon Truth [II, 5]. In his fourth adventure he kills Sansfoy, but becomes enthralled by Fidessa (Fidelity), who is really Duessa (Deceit). With knight and lady separated, two storylines alternated. Pierce always indicated what will happen in the next adventure:

> But where all this time was the lady Una? She, too, was meeting with strange adventures. Of these I will tell in our next story. This will tell of a thick wood and of a ramping lion (everyone knows of Una's Lion) and more about the poor deserted lady [III, 3].

The parentheses indicated a well-known episode, and a lion provided opportunity for didacticism. When the initial rage of "a most ferocious lion" becomes gentle catlike "licking her hands and feet," Pierce declared: "so wonderful is the influence of truth on the savage beasts of this world. Una, too, lost her fear and, trusting in Divine power, accepted the lion as her friend"

(IV, 1 and 2). Yet Una, weeping because Redcross (false Archimago) was defeated, forgets how the lion protected her: "so do we mortals forget our blessings and our friends" (V, 3). Saracen Sans-loy is on his charger (V, 2) and in a sword fight (V, 3). The adventure finished with Una his captive; a cliffhanger moment preceded the transition:

> What the real Redcross Knight with his false mistress, Duessa, was doing all this time of the lady Una's unfortunate adventure, you will learn in the next story—The Sixth Adventure of the Redcross Knight. You will also learn much about the palace of Pride and of many strange things that happened in this court of lawlessness [V, 4].

Quickly the reader was informed: "a place enticing at first sight, it was really very ruinous and old. ... But how could this be known by the Redcross Knight, who was really a rustic and knew little of the wicked ways of the world?" (VI, 1–2). Children could empathize with lack of experience.

Some transitional promises led to disappointment. "In the Seventh Adventure you will see a real tourney as it took place in the time of the Faery Queen" (VI, 5); however, the next line assessed "a story of the strange usages of knights and ladies in the days of Gloriana, queen of Faerie-land." Pierce described rich and colorful preparations and feasting, but added a disapproving reminder: "for was not Gluttony steward over the house of Pride?" (VII, 1). Pitz pictured fierce combat: the Saracen on one knee falters before forceful Redcross Knight; red swords with swirling bands make a partial frame (VII, 3); both knights are crouched, one warding off a sword blow with his shield, while ready to thrust (VII, 4).

Because Spenser's poem becomes increasingly complicated and confusing, Eighth Adventure started with a reminder of earlier adventure and a warning:

> But now we must go to quite another part in the realm of the Faerie Queen. For we will have many changes if we follow all the characters we have learned about in this strange tale.
> How fared the Lady Una on her way, the lady whose real name was Truth and who had been deserted by her rightful champion, the Redcross Knight or Holiness? For it is meet that Truth and Holiness should ever walk together [VIII, 1].

Authorial assistance and rhetorical question combined for characteristic reassurance and didactic statement. In contrast to focused "adventures" the eighth reported briefly: Una's time with the satyrs and setting out accompanied by Strength, Redcross's dallying with Fidessa and capture by a giant (Tyranny), and the arrival of Arthur (Purity), whose life and role Pierce altered somewhat.

Arthur's entrance was spectacular. Against the glory of a sunset on a hill

> a war-horse spurred. Nearer it came, and on its back they saw—a vision glorious—a knight shining against the sun. His shield was a diamond, his sword most wonderful, and all his

armour gold glinting in the light. It was King Arthur, he of the Round Table, most wondrous knight of all the world. ...
  In our next Adventure we shall learn more of King Arthur, the most glorious knight of all the realm in Britain [VIII, 5].

Pierce devoted two paragraphs to Arthur's story of his life—not Spenser's vision and love for the Faerie Queen, but details from Arthurian legends and Tennyson for moral chivalry. Cared for by Timon and taught by Merlin, Arthur grew from childhood

> unlike others who sported carelessly in play. With manhood, great aspirations dawned for me and longings for the good of man. Thus was my life one of ideals high, and I was made a Knight to strive for Truth and the greater things of life. ... [I acquired] my trusty blade Excalibur ... in a mysterious way. ... drew it with ease from its hard bed and claimed it as my own in the great cause of Purity. So was I made a King by great acclaim, and so I purposed me a Table Round, of twelve good Knights and true who should uphold my purpose in the world [IX, 5].

Purity was needed to help Truth free Holiness. Orgoglio, like Duessa, was made a captive—death by dismemberment was too horrible. Tyranny was cast into a dark dungeon, but Deceit stripped and sent to wander in the desert of Despair. In a formal three-quarter portrait "King Arthur"—rare use of title—holds his sword so that the hilt forms a cross; opposite, a mounted knight has lowered his lance; red panels with helmet, sword, and heraldic shields framed both (IX, 4 and 5). More dramatic were half-page illustrations in the previous opening: Arthur strikes with his sword through a throat of Duessa's many-headed beast and confronts the aged sire (Ignorance) with keys at his waist (IX, 2 and 3).

  In the Tenth Adventure in the House of Celia Redcross learned "his needed lessons for the Great Adventure ... pride is vain and trust in his own prowess but a broken reed" (X, 4). Although Contemplation does not show Redcross the New Jerusalem, he foretells a "famous victory" and advises: "after all thy painful pilgrimage, seek peace and follow in the footsteps of our great ensample, Christ. So shalt thou be a saint—Saint George of Merrie England, thy name of victory" (X, 5). Una and her Knight "set forth once more, equipped with holy panoply, to meet The Great Adventure" (X, 5).

  Pitz's dragon slaying was spectacular. In the Eleventh Adventure's heading Redcross Knight, with raised shield and sword, faces the dragon; its body stretches across the top, and it wraps its tail around both the knight's legs. That amazingly long tail filled the foreground of a second illustration, first of three with black backgrounds: the dragon alone (XI, 2), Redcross thrusts his sword through its neck (XI, 3), and an exhausted knight rests under a tree (XI, 4). Each carried two red medallions; the knight aims his lance at the dragon from opposite directions. Pierce, who used some of Spenser's description, added explanatory, allegorical detail. The dragon's "great wings spread out like the sails of some vast ship—so wide in girth is the dark power of evil" (XI, 2). Redcross does not stand next to the crystal spring by chance, "—so He, who made us all His children, cares for us—" (XI, 3). Mitigated chivalric display meant emphasis on God's help against Evil:

> Thus did the hour of the Great Adventure come. There was no blare of trumpets nor sound of cheering voices as in the House of Pride. All was silent save the Dragon's roar. The Field was rough, and only Una watched the conflict from afar. There was no prize for joust or tournament, but only promise of high Heaven's unseen reward [XI, 2].

Una, whose prayers are constant, beholds the victory and praises: "Thus with no pomp or vanity of Pride, The Great Adventure ended" (XI, 5). Predictably, when people beg to hear his tale and acclaim him, Holiness demurs: "the young knight would not accept the praise as for his own poor prowess, but for His sake whose humble follower he had been—our brother and our great example, Christ" (XI, 4). Pierce's happy ending is the wedding day of Truth and Holiness; she made no mention of Redcross's promise to return to the Faerie Queen.

"The Legend of Britomart" started with an address to readers:

> This time, little knights and ladies, we are to be followers of quite another leader. Her name is Britomartis and she is a lady knight known to all the world as Chastity. The wonder of it is, that every one supposes her to be a real knight, and she has many strange and perilous adventures—adventures which usually do not befall a lady. ...
> She was tall and slender with long yellow locks and skin as fair as lilies, and when she was dressed as a princess, she was very beautiful. But when she buckled on her armour and rode forth to her father's jousting field, she looked to be a brave and splendid knight. The meaning of her name was "Chastity: and, through all her life, she fought for purity and justice [I, 1].

Lonely and bored, Britomart, who "longed for some new adventure," ventured behind the closed door and discovered the magic mirror (I, 2). Although she is love-smitten, Merlin's tales "of Briton and of victories that must be won to save the country from traitors and defeat" awaken "high hopes and courage for her country" (I, 4). Her name "the Britoness" (XII, 3) indicated she is a female counterpart of England's patron saint. After Britomart's gaze falls upon Artegall—"a goodly knight, ... as if in answer to her maiden wish, most brave to look upon, all dressed in massive armour. Thus did the maiden learn that love is to be desired above all things" (I, 3)—she pines. Yet she transforms herself into a knight with alacrity. Accompanied by nurse Glaucé, she rides forth "in conquest for the right, in search of Justice" (I, 5). The Second Adventure opened with two of Pitz's best chivalric images. Britomart, a white knight on a white charger raises shield and sword, against a black background with white lines; her lance strikes the shield of Sir Guyon, who reels back, his own lance shattered (II, 1, 2). Pierce's gloss explained: the Palmer advised Guyon to desist; "this wise man knew that the lance of Chastity was charmed—so does a pure heart gain victory over worldly might" (II, 2). Pitz repeated cropping and black background for Redcross, who raises his sword and uses his shield (black cross on white) to guard against six thrusting swords (II, 3). Britomart's easy converse with male knights was an example of companionship not inhibited by gender. Her Third Adventure emphasized that Chastity's pursuit of Justice, however meet, is arduous: "But God never lets us see the path before us, and thus great tasks are accomplished by just living day by day" (III, 1). Britomart sits pensively beside a tree at the seashore (III, 2) before combat with Marinell, in full armor, the trident on his shield announcing his heritage (III, 3). "The Nereid," another titled illustration, exploited an exotic otherworldly creature—bare breasts, fish tail, and Art Nouveau swirls of flowing hair balanced by spirals of sea plants (III, 4).

These feminine images preceded the adventure at the Castle of Malbecco (Jealousy), where Britomart (Chastity) is protected by her magic spear (Virtue) and aided by Satyrane (Chivalry), who intervened after she unhorsed Paridell (Inconstancy)—Pierce's allegorical explanations. Once inside, Britomart, like other knights, cast off her armor; her golden hair and silken robes reveal her gender. Combination of Chastity and Chivalry was essential in the Fifth Adventure. When these knights meet Scudamore, whose lady is held by giant Ollyphant, he is fearful only because of Chastity, "for Chivalry alone had little power upon his sinful person" (V, 2). Britomart protects the youth, whose shield bears a picture of Cupid, "for Chastity is the chosen guardian of Love" (V, 4). She confidently promises help because "a Power above" can release Scudamore's love: "Submit you to God's power, for all sorrow in this world is less than Virtue's might" (V, 5). Confronted by flames outside Busirane's castle, Britomart will not falter: "'Much better try the extremities of change for noble cause than to give up God's goodly work for fear'" (VI, 3). This sound advice did not preclude stressing the maiden knight's fear as she proceeded alone through the castle and her thoughtful prudence to observe the Masque, subject of The Seventh Adventure. White on black pictures show posing Fancy and Desire (VII, 2) and a line of four dancers (VII, 5). With fortitude Britomart rescues Amoret, a lady more fearful than she. By giving comfort Britomart herself becomes braver: "So is it that thought of others' good more strengthens the brave heart than any selfish aim or personal desire" (VII, 6). Growing confidence develops with shared stories. At the next castle Britomart extends compassion to the youth she bested by insisting he too be admitted. Opposites were Duessa (Deceit) and A-te (Mischief), accompanied by Sir Blandamour, who charges knight Britomart but is unseated with the first blow. Thus he must rely upon Sir Paridel when they meet his enemy Scudamore. Scheming, evil women defame Amoret to gain mastery where unknightly men could not.

Headings for Adventures assigned them to Britomartis / Britomart, except the Ninth "which is of Sir Scudamore," a lover who travels with Glaucè to the cottage of blacksmith Care. Although Pierce did not elaborate, Pitz showed the bent creature observing the sleepless knight. Scudamore meets the Salvage Knight, who is similarly depressed and explains, a "'knight in open tourney wrested my honor from me and bore to ground the best of all the company'" (IX, 5). Both seek revenge, one from jealousy and one from shame. Pitz's knights wait beside a tree (X, 2). Pierce waited until The Tenth Adventure to identify Artegall, when Britomart again fights her love. A picture of combat with swords introduced the third description of how Britomart's gender was revealed. The Salvage Knight, "by fortune's change," struck a glancing blow to Britomart's crest: "Thus did it hap that to his gaze was bared a face that like an angel's seemed, and all about it, framing as in beaten gold, the hair unloosed and fell in locks most wonderful to see" (X, 4). Scudamore perceives his love's rescuer, while Glaucè takes command; faces are shown and events related. Chastity and Justice at last meet.

The Eleventh and Twelfth Adventures were markedly compressed: wooing and betrothal, Artegall's departure "on his great quest." Since Pierce's legend was of Britomart, she told little about Artegall. A paragraph explained "one sad day, Sir Artegall was overcome by treachery and held in thralldom by two wicked Amazons" (XI, 4); and Talus, "a man of iron will"—perhaps the most extraordinary transformation—heard his master moan "Britomart" and set out to find her. Because Dolon mistakes a knight accompanied by Talus to be Artegall who killed his son, two remaining sons challenge them at a bridge (illustration XII, 3), where Britomart "made a flying leap as on a winged horse—and pressed between the two, thus crowding them into the water below" (XII, 4). Since no episodes gave evidence of Justice in action, Artegall becomes only the object of love pursued by a female knight, an inversion of chivalric romance. Indeed Britomart rescues him from the Amazon's bondage and replaces his "womanish attire ... shining armour once more her own loved vision of a knight" (XII, 5–6). They tarry many days to regain strength, but then go their separate ways, confident of future union. Pierce's summation fused martial, marital, and didactic:

> And now, after long travel, we bring our journey to an end in Faerie-land where Gloriana reigns. And all the place is girt with bloom and flags of victory. And all the wide domain is filled with happy clamor and sound of marriage music. Shields and spears lie on the ground. And Britomart and Artegall stand together, crowned in the light of this great day of glory— the glory of this earth's most arduous tasks well done [XII, 6].

Two headings featured minstrels, The Sixth Adventure of Redcross Knight and The Fourth Adventure of Britomart. The first was a single figure, while the second included a lady as listener and a fairytale castle in the background, obvious signals of chivalric romance. Size, rich decoration, and profuse illustration of *The Red Cross Knight and the Legend of Britomart* anticipated books often more visual than verbal.

Collections and Home Libraries

Abbie Sage Richardson, Stories from Old English Poetry *(1871)*

Abbie Sage Richardson's *Stories from Old English Poetry* (1871) was idiosyncratic; sixteen stories emphasized drama, an expression of her experience as an actress.[5] In a short preface Richardson (1837–1900) described her childhood reading of books found in a garret—two small volumes of Shakespeare—treasure to add to three books she owned at age eight—the Bible, *Pilgrim's Progress,* and *Arabian Nights Entertainment.* Reading sophisticated literature at an early age was not uncommon in the nineteenth century and probably explains why Richardson retold Chaucer, Shakespeare, and Spenser. Distribution of chapters matched their conventional ranking, respectively five, eight, and two stories. Richardson favored the romance, including reference to oral tradition and chapbooks that inspired Shakespeare.[6] She retold Chaucer's romances told by the Knight, Man of Law, Wife, Clerk, and Squire.[7]

"The Story of Candace" defined the close relation between Chaucer, the only medieval writer, and Spenser, his avowed successor. *The Faerie Queene* (IV. ii) completed the *Squire's Tale,* left unfinished in *The Canterbury Tales.* Richardson explained, "I have taken some liberties with the two stories in order to unite them gracefully, but they are very slight and immaterial" (57). She told of Emperor Cambuscan's gifts, the tournament, and how lives of brothers Priamond and Dyamond passed into Triamond whose combat against Cambello warranted elaboration:

> Like two clouds charged with black thunderbolts, they meet each other, and are merged in dire conflict. Blow rang on blow, blood stained the fair sand, weapons were broken and thrown aside, and yet without stay, the battle waged, and each combatant seemed untiring and incapable of defeat. ... [until] Through the parting multitude drove a silver chariot,

drawn by four tawny lions, who moved obedient to the reins. In the chariot stood a lady, dazzlingly beautiful, who bore in one hand a wand twined with an olive wreath, and in the other a cup filled with a rare liquid called nepenthe, which none but brave warriors are able to quaff [63].

The "lovely fay" Candace, Cambello's sister, feared the outcome; fairy Cambina, Triamond's sister, stops the fight and administers the cup that ends all enmity. Two marriages follow and a friendship of knights so famous "that among all the knights of Faery their names stood for a sign of brotherly union, in arms and in love" (64).

This chapter was transitional. "Spenser" detailed the poet's poverty, patronage, and admiration of Sir Philip Sidney, "the very sound of whose name is as music in the ears of those who honor chivalrous manhood" (65). Richardson noted rivalries at Elizabeth's court and Spenser's time spent in Ireland, where Raleigh visited him and listened to *The Faery Queen*. Richardson, who did not identify Puritan Lord Grey and his murderous treatment of Irish Catholics, stressed the poet's suffering:

... in one of the insurrections of the ignorant and barbarous peasantry, who were constantly putting the English residents (whom they hated then, as now) to the fire and sword, they swept down upon the poet's castle, burnt and ravaged it, and drove out the inhabitants. In the haste and fear of the attack, a new-born baby was left in the castle, and perished in the flames [66–67].

The victim died "poor and broken-hearted, when hardly forty-eight years old" (67).

A paragraph introducing "his poem of poems," written in a measure called "Spenserian," raised the issue of reception:

By those who do not know its charm, the poem is called "stiff, pedantic, and unreadable." But there are those who find in its pages a subtle and pervading atmosphere like that which encompasses the Bower of Bliss, or breathes from the enchanted gardens of Amida; which throws the same spell over the maturer imagination that the quaint yet unequalled allegory of old John Bunyan still hold over the brains of childhood.

To the tender judgment of those who know the poet, and, knowing, love him, the little story which follows is intrusted [67].

Richardson flattered and encouraged young readers by recalling her own childhood reading and subsequent maturing; she also paralleled two great Puritan writers.

"Adventures of the Fair Florimel," which avoided religious issues and allegory, possessed many charms of fairy tale and placed women at the center of action. The opening line was rhetorical: "What voice shall do justice to the deeds of the renowned warrior-maiden, Britomart?" Richardson, who eliminated the magic mirror and feminine pining, concluded with a paean: "So many conquests had she won in tourney and in the field, that her fame almost equaled that of the peerless Arthur, Prince of the Round Table, a knight whose friendship held her in high esteem" (68).

Division into four parts encouraged reading. Part I opened with Britomart riding on the shore, seeking combat with scornful Prince Marinell, famed for his encounters with knights. She sought to "avenge the wrong done to beauty and chivalry by his scorn of the lovely Florimel" (71). Marinell despises women because his sea-nymph mother Cymoent so reared him in an effort to thwart a prophecy that a woman would give him a deathblow. Britomart's lance fells but does not kill Marinell, whose mother nurses him.

In Part II Britomart is riding with three knights of Faery—Arthur, Red Cross Knight, and Sir Guyon—when they see a forester pursuing a beautiful maiden. Relying on them to aid this distressed woman, she continues to seek Lady Amoret. Sir Guyon catches the forester and deals with him "according to his desserts." Arthur meets a dwarf, servant of Florimel, comforts him, and then leaves to "stir up the flower of knighthood to form a league that they might recover and bring back the lost damsel" (75). At this point Richardson identified the fleeing maiden as Florimel. She finds shelter in a rude cottage, where a witch welcomes her; however, the son, an "uncouth monster," frightens Florimel who flees. So great is the son's grief and rage that his mother uses her "black arts" to summon "a swift, horrible monster" to pursue Florimel to the shore. Since she escaped in an old fisherman's shallop, the monster claws her horse and feasts on "his mangled sides," until Sir Satyrane rides up (79). The witch's magic protects her monster, yet the brave knight sends it "howling back to his mistress" (80). He picks up Florimel's girdle.

In Part III the witch creates false Florimel to comfort her son; unfortunately Braggadochio challenges "the poor clown" and takes false Florimel to Sir Satyrane's tournament, where Florimel's girdle is to be the prize. Several encounters are reported. Braggadochio flees from Sir Blandamour, and the "wicked sprite" in the false Florimel stirs up quarrels among knights. The tournament was an occasion of chivalric display with contests and knights claiming 'my lady is fairest.' The crowd's enthusiasm for false Florimel inspired didactic observation: "Indeed so often does the vulgar mind prefer the false seeming to the simple truth, and permits itself to be deceived with glittering pretense" (86). Similarly vain women who try to put on the magic girdle— "the base Duessa, the witty Candace, the fairy Cambina, charming Lucinda, and many others"—provoked rebuke: "But alas, what shame and confusion ensued, when it was found that from every waist it slipped away, and refused to clasp itself!" (87). Amoret, whom the girdle fits and holds, offers it to false Florimel. Although she fails, knights are so besotted with her seeming beauty they disbelieve the girdle's charm. Having again sowed dissent, she chooses Braggadochio and rides away with him.

As is often the case in romance, an obvious statement shifted the narrative. Part IV began, "It becomes us now to return to the true Florimel, whom all this time we left in the little boat with the fisherman, afloat upon the bosom of the sea" (88). Stirred by "the black spirit of Avarice," he attempts to take Florimel's jewels. Her cry brings the enchanter Proteus, who takes her to his underwater palace. There the rescuer becomes the wooer; Proteus grows vengeful when Florimel, ever loving Marinell, refuses to be his bride. Marinell, of the earth and thus unable to attend the feast of sea-gods, waits outside and overhears Florimel's love lament from the dungeon. When he seeks Cymoent's help, his doting mother asks Neptune to order Proteus to release his prisoner. Following a time of recovery and wooing the nuptials of Florimel and Marinell are held with feast and tournament. Resolution comes with the arrival of Braggadochio and false Florimel, but not without a final dispute over who is fairest. Arthegall, Britomart's knight—unmentioned since the first paragraph—brings the two Florimels together. The true Florimel "they placed beside the waxen figure 'like a true saint beside an image set,' and all at once the enchanted damsel vanished, as a snow-wreath melteth into air." The girdle is restored to its true wearer. "And thus, as glorious day succeeds thick and gloomy night, did the troubled fortunes of Florimel give way to an unclouded wedded life whose happiness was unsurpassed in song or story" (44). For Richardson, who featured complicated love, knightly prowess at arms was incidental—and the greatest warrior was a woman.[8]

Carolyn Sherwin Bailey, Stories of Great Adventures *(1919)*

Carolyn Sherwin Bailey (1875–1961) offered a traditional selection in *Stories of Great Adventures* (1919): Arthurian, Beowulf, Chaucer, Robin Hood, other ballads, Roland, and Frithiof. "Una and the Red Cross Knight" and "The Red Cross Knight's Last Battle" from Book I and "Sir Guyon's Great Adventure" (Cave of Mammon, Bower of Bliss) from Book II were from Spenser's "Faery Queen." Bailey, whose critical note urged the poem's greatness and use of allegory, voiced a moral point of view:

> The Fairy Queen is one of the greatest pieces of English literature and is read by boys and girls, and even adults, long after they have grown away from the world of fairyland. That was Spenser's greatness, that he could see goodness personified in a queen who ruled a fairy

court, wickedness and falsehood as having the bodies of dragons, hypocrisy in human dress, and temptation clothed as a sorceress. ...

The Fairy Queen is a very long poem, and it is written in the original in such strange old English words that it is difficult to read. The stories of Una, of the brave Red Cross Knight, and Sir Guyon are told here for you in prose, and they will give you a glimpse of a magical world that may be yours even after you have decided not to believe in fairies.[9]

She retained allegory. The Red Cross Knight, whose dwarf servant is Prudence, is lost in the Wood of Error with Una (Truth); they meet Falsehood, "a horrible monster, half dragon and half snake" (185). The Magician who deceives them is Hypocrisy. After they are reunited they meet Lawless. Prince Arthur accompanies Una, kills Giant Pride, and rescues Red Cross Knight, who slays the dragon. Sir Guyon sails on the Idle Lake, but returns ashore and encounters Great Mammon and accepts his offer since "the ancient pilgrim who had accompanied and guided Sir Guyon on his many former adventures" was not with him (205). Sir Guyon and Mammon pass Vengeance, Fear, Horror before they reach "a huge, gloomy cave" (205). When the pilgrim (Conscience, 212) rejoins Sir Guyon they cross the Gulf of Greediness, the quicksands of Unthriftiness, and then meet a lady who takes them to the Bower of Bliss, which "the Fairy Queen's Knight of Temperance" destroys. Bailey simplified Spenser.

Home Libraries

Charles William Eliot (1834–1926), academic reformer, advocate of liberal education, and President of Harvard, encouraged a vogue for encyclopedic collections of primary texts. With William A. Neilson he created *Harvard Classics* (1909–1914), fifty-one volumes, first known as Dr. Eliot's "Five Foot Shelf. Spenser's "Letter to Raleigh" was in *Prefaces and Prologues*, Volume 39; Spenser's lyric poems were in *English Poetry I: From Chaucer to Gray*, Volume 40, 72–82. Part One of *The Delphian Course* cited Eliot's case for training from childhood with reading as the foundation that adults would extend by using "the brief periods of freedom for self-improvement."[10] A comprehensive course, presenting "the wisdom of the past" (ix) could serve the many who read only "the lightest and most transient literature" (x).

The Delphian Course: A Systematic Plan for Education, Embracing the World's Progress and Development of the Liberal Arts (1913), ten parts, was designed by The Delphian Society, a national organization founded in Chicago to advance women and foster life long learning. Seventeen persons from various universities were Council of Review. Part Eight privileged English literature. Of 500 pages, 423 were: Résumé of English History, Chapters I-VI; English Poetry, Chapters VII-XXI—XX and XXI were Prose. In contrast Western Europe, I, General Survey; Résumé of French History, Chapters II-VII; and Germany, Chapters VIII-IX—German Unity, Modern Literature in Germany filled 76 pages, 424–500.

Chapter X Spenser gave most attention to *The Faerie Queene*. A critical Introduction acclaimed Spenser but recognized limitations:

> England's golden age of poetry began with Spenser, first and fairest of Elizabeth's choir of true singers, then and still honored as "the poet's poet," and rightly so, as few but poets can claim any knowledge of his work. It ranks above the heights scaled by the every-day reader for pleasure. His master-work lacks popular attractiveness in being an allegory and not a dramatic story. Its music is the subtle Æolian harmony of sounds that most delight the delicate ear. And with the unfamiliar look of that somewhat grotesque English, ruffled with archaisms and starched with stiff Italian forms, counts substantially among the apologies for modern readers whose taste is moulded by the fashion of their own century.[11]

Nevertheless, Elizabethan literature cannot be "properly understood without a passing study of Spenser, who was a very great poet and more besides" (106). That he was being introduced to women—"ruffled" and "starched" referenced gender—recognized their circumstances. Without exoneration, biography stressed Spenser's experience of Ireland and characterized him as allied with "young bloods of the aristocracy" that conducted "a raid of suppression, to be rewarded with the spoils of war. Gentle spirit though the poet had, his other self shared the romantic love for adventure and for sordid gain, so characteristic of the time." Spenser served Lord-Deputy Grey and "bore his part in the terrible suppression of the uprising, and shared in the division of the Earl of Desmond's forfeited estates" (107). Contradiction in creating *The Faerie Queene* was startling: "How Spenser had managed to build up this monument of faery verse, instinct with serenest beauty of thought and form, amid the turbulent scenes of his life in Ireland, is a mystery of the craft" (107–108). Poems with special appeal for women were "Alcyon's Lament for Daphne" and "The Epithalamion."

A critical introduction to *The Faerie Queene* declared it "transcends all other allegories" as the first "pure English poem, since Chaucer's day," and

> marks the new departure from medievalism through the renaissance to the strong intellectualism which took its second impetus from the Reformation, and wrought our later civil and religious liberties. In this poem Spenser bridges the gap between the old mythology and poetic romanticism of the past, and the prophetic anticipation of great realities to come from the opening of mental and material activities already at work [116].

This combined literary with intellectual history; moreover, it urged advantages of the Reformation that resonated in Protestant America. Characters in Book I that "allegorizes Religion, tightly robed in the bigotries of the time" were then specified. The argument was briefly stated. Books II, III, and IV treat of Love in all its manifestations, with Sir Guyon as the personification of Temperance, and Britomart, the most charming heroine of the whole poem, representing Chastity. Book V is devoted to Justice, and in the sixth and seventh, ... the minor virtues, Courtesy and Constancy, are shown in their relation with Love and Justice. In Prince Arthur is typified Magnificence, an idealized conception of the secondary Glory of God [116].

Readers were then reassured: "Leaving the ethical significance of the poem, though Spenser puts it well in the fore-front of his work, the 'Faerie Queene' can be read at random for its poetical beauties without loss, probably with more pleasure than as a whole. The chivalric romance was the favorite reading of the people" (116). There was a contradiction: recognition of poetic beauty and reputation versus admitted tediousness and no longer relevant allegory. Yet *The Delphian Course* urged necessary acquaintance to be educated. Even though heavily allegorical, Book I, Canto 1 was quoted—perhaps to encourage further reading or because it was most widely known and likely met in conversation. Home libraries for children expressed similar judgments, but introduced *The Faerie Queene* in simpler form. A Delphian goal "to develop our insight into the mystery of life; to gain an individual viewpoint; to establish our standards of conduct and modify our judgment" (1: xiii) survives in Great Books programs.

Young Folks' Library *(1901–02, revised 1910)*

Thomas Bailey Aldrich (1836–1907) was editor-in-chief of *Young Folks' Library* (1901–02, revised 1910), comprehensive resource for American youth in twenty volumes, with different editors, reprinted in various editions for many years. A prolific writer and editor of *The Atlantic Monthly* (1881–1890), Aldrich early made significant contributions to children's literature. His somewhat autobiographical novel *The Story of a Bad Boy* (1870) gave a realistic picture that anticipated Mark Twain. Aldrich, who was an early reader of Keats, Tennyson, and Longfellow and himself a poet, edited *Famous Poems*, Volume XX—without examples from Spenser.

Prefatory material in Volume I *The Story Teller* provided context for home libraries at the start of the twentieth century in the United States. In "On the Influence of Books" Aldrich asserted, "Books read in youth leave an indelible impression. ... The period of childhood is the most sensitive and receptive in life. The books read exert directly or indirectly a great influence in molding thought and character."[12] He noted Keats was inspired by reading Chapman's Homer and Spenser's *Faerie Queene*, and recognized children's ease in learning foreign languages and inspiration for career choice. Aldrich concluded:

> I fancy that old-time books have frequently an unsuspected complicity in coloring even our maturer thoughts and actions. What impulses may not occasionally be prompted in us by the perhaps half-unconscious reminiscence of some record of daring, or generosity, or self-sacrifice that moved our hearts in the days of youth! [xiv].

From high praise of "the beneficent influence of books" he turned to negative consequences of choosing from "a vast quantity of tempting and poisonous food within easy reach ... lurid juvenile dramas in which the glamour of romance is thrown over the adventures of personages who in real life generally find their apotheosis in the prisoner's dock." Aldrich, who was not a didactic Victorian moralist, judged "the well-meant mawkish story only a few degrees less hurtful" (xv). Exemplars were English *Sandford and Merton* (1783, 1786, 1789) and American cousin *Elsie Dinsmore* (1867)—who inspired his strongest denunciation:

> [S]he sedately pirouettes through a seemingly endless succession of girls' books. I came across fifteen of them the other day. This impossible female is carried from infancy up to grand-motherhood, and is, I believe, still leisurely pursuing her way down to the tomb in an ecstatic state of uninterrupted didacticism. [xvi].

These remarks explain why girls read boys' books, but boys did not read girls' books.

Aldrich viewed as inadequate "the local library ... a republic of good, bad, and indifferent literature, the greater part of which should not be read by anybody. The duty of selection remains." Moreover, this process required "exceptional familiarity with many branches of letters ... [that] involves conditions of leisure and study not compatible with the usual affairs of life" (xvi). The *Young Folks' Library* was designed so that "each volume deals with a distinct department of letters ... has a special character ... a book for almost every mood and hour—narratives of adventure and exploration by land and sea; fairy tales; bird and animal studies; folk-lore and legend; episodes of boy and girl life at home and at school; poetry, biography, history, science, etc. etc." Aldrich claimed a broad audience—"readers of all ages" for "a choice library brought to your hearth-side" (xvii).

Charles Eliot Norton (1827–1908) edited *The Story Teller*, Volume I. He was the first professor of art history at Harvard, wrote *Historical Studies of Church Building in the Middle Ages* (1880), and arranged exhibitions of J. M. W. Turner (1874) and John Ruskin (1871). Norton translated Dante's *Divine Comedy*, wrote a biographical sketch of Longfellow, edited his letters and those of James Russell Lowell. Charles Welsh's *The Key to the Treasure House: A Book of Reference* (1902) provided indexes, pronouncing vocabulary, sources, allusions, and maps to accompany volumes in *Young Folks' Library*. Perhaps as a mark of democratic support of the common man *The Story Teller* presented traditional early literature popular through chapbooks, not canonical writers. Welsh's note gave a brief history of chapbooks, intended for less well educated adults but appropriated by children because of delight in stories.[13] He recognized nearly all the stories in volume one as "Chap Book Literature" (1). Significantly in this first volume of stories that readily engage children, the early modern romance was Richard Johnson's *The Seven Champions of Christendom*, published the same year as *The Faerie Queene*, which was not included; nor was Chaucer. Sophisticated, difficult texts, "higher branches of literature," especially earlier English literature, were not included in this home library that favored history, American writers and experience.

The Children's Hour *(1907)*

Eva March Tappan's *The Children's Hour* (1907) had a different design and objectives. *Stories of Legendary Heroes*, Volume IV were all medieval and placed geographically. Heroes of the British Isles were Beowulf, Arthurian, Robin Hood, and Welsh (Mabinogion), while Havelok and Frithiof were Scandinavian and Danish. Ralph the Charcoal Burner and Charlemagne, Fierabras, and Roland were Heroes of France. The German Hero was Siegfried, and The Spanish Hero was The Cid. Rustem, The Persian Hero, was the only non–European, albeit frequently appropriated because of Matthew Arnold's poem about the tragic father-son relationship. Early modern English romances did not provide stories of legendary heroes perhaps because Tappan (1854–1930), a teacher and prolific writer of books for children, was such a strong advocate of medieval literature. Robert Newton Linscott's *A Guide to Good Reading with Practical Directions for the Use of The Children's Hour in the Home* (1912) relegated Spenser's *Faerie Queene* to "Suggestions for Further Reading." Linscott recommended two Spenser titles— under "Stories from Medieval Literature."[14] A(lfred) J. Church's *The Faerie Queene and Her Knights: Stories Retold from Spenser* (1910) was "Retold from Edmund Spenser's great romantic poem '"The Faerie Queene,'" while Mary McLeod's *Stories from the Faerie Queene* (1897) promised "Adventures of the Red Cross Knight, the perilous voyages of Sir Guyon in search of the Bower of Bliss, the Quest of Britomart, the warrior princes and other tales of brave knights and fair ladies" (20). Just as Tappan included no story from *The Faerie Queene* in her home library, she omitted reference to it in *A Short History of England's Literature* (1905/1933) that identified his succession from Chaucer, but as author of *The Shepherd's Calendar*, first of a long tradition of pastoral in "Shakespeare's Century."[15] The Protestant text favored over Spenser, John

Bunyan's *Pilgrim's Progress*, was in *Stories from Seven Old Favorites*, Volume V along with *Robinson Crusoe, Gulliver's Travels, Arabian Nights, The Travels and Surprising Adventures of Baron Munchausen, Don Quixote*, and Lamb's *Tales from Shakespeare*.

Journeys Through Bookland *(1907)*

Charles Sylvester's *Journeys through Bookland* (1907) was deliberately intended not to resemble others in design or intent and did not privilege English literature. Sylvester omitted *The Faerie Queene* but made selections from its Protestant successor, Bunyan's *Pilgrim's Progress* in volumes IV and V.

The Junior Classics *(1912)*

William Patten's *The Junior Classics* (1912) devoted a volume to *Heroes and Heroines of Chivalry*, a compendium of stories from distinguished collections of canonical literature retold for children. *Don Quixote*, not *The Faerie Queene*, exemplified early modern romance. The Preface explained chivalry, a word "taken from the French cheval, a horse."[16] Patten summarized stages through which a boy became a knight and the culminating ceremony that "was almost as solemn an affair as it was to become a priest." After fasting, vigil, confession, prayer, receiving the Holy Sacrament, and having the priest bless the sword suspended from his neck, the youth knelt before the presiding knight: "touching him three times on the shoulder with the flat of his sword, he pronounced the words that received him into the company of worthy knights: 'In the name of God, of St. Michael, and St. George, I make thee knight: be valiant, courteous, and loyal!'" The knight's "real work. And greatest joy, was fighting for someone who needed his help" (10). Chivalric ideals applied to "a manful fighter," then and now: "to speak the truth, to perform a promise to the utmost, to reverence all women, to be constant in love, to despise luxury, to be simple and modest and gentle in heart, to help the weak and take no unfair advantage of an inferior" (11). Patten's canonical choices for *Stories That Never Grow Old*, Volume V were the same as Tappan's: Bunyan's Protestant *Pilgrim's Progress* rather than Spenser's religious allegory. Different were E. Nesbit instead of Lamb for Shakespeare's *Tales*, and Sir Walter Scott's *Ivanhoe* and *Guy Mannering* instead of *Don Quixote*, which Patten placed with *Heroes and Heroines of Chivalry*.

Our Wonder World *(1914)*

In *Our Wonder World: A Library of Knowledge* (1914) only two of ten volumes had literary interest. *Every Child's Story Book*, Volume V contained "selections from traditional literature."[17] The first "Every Child's Story Book" had six sections; five, 273 pages, were: Fairy Stories and Fables, The Folk Tale of Many Lands, Stories and Plays of Knights and Yeomen, Some of the Great Works of Literature, and A Group of Favorites. The sixth, Pictures That Are Good to Live With, had only 32 pages. Evelyn C. Johnson wrote the second part, "Child Life in Many Lands," which tells of an imaginative world journey in an air ship "Sea Gull" that took "little lads and lassies of America" through seventeen places before returning to New York at Christmas. This was a kind of cultural history / geography with stops in China, Japan, Russia, India, Persia, and Africa as well as Europe, locus for folk tales. Nevertheless, British and American writers and their stories were dominant.

The embossed dark blue cloth cover of a fine edition printed in 1929 has a cropped picture of a knight in shining plate armor; his shield has a red fleur de lys and a blue rampant lion. The horse, with similar armor and golden caparison, rears in excitement. The title page included a promise: "Happy the child whose pathway to the realities of life lies through the enchanted realm of Storyland." A brief introduction established expectations:

> Every child loves a story, and in this matter there is no age limit—we are all "only children of a larger growth." What an undying fascination there is in fairy stories and legendary tales! We are sure of your interest, therefore, as you begin this volume, and find yourself in the romance fields of old England, slaying dragons with the noble knight Saint George, and passing through all sorts of interesting experiences with Dick Whittington, Tom Thumb, Jack the Giant Killer, King Arthur, Robin Hood, and the rest. Then fairyland is entered through the marvelous imagination of the Brothers Grimm and Hans Christian Andersen. Folk tales of various peoples are full of interest and add variety. Fables follow, with their quaint teaching; after which there are romance plays and a glance into the great works that have made our English literature renowned. ...
>
> So this volume opens the door into other worlds where you will be glad to enter. "They all lived happily ever after"—that is the way for stories to end, even if real life does sometimes make a slip in the last chapter. Through all the glamour and marvel, with princesses and dragons and talking beasts, you may always be sure that right will conquer wrong, and beauty and virtue find their satisfying reward. As for what we offer here you have nothing but the best. New tales may be written, and some good ones, but the stories you find in this book will never be out of date, any more than will the romances of Scott, the novels of Thackeray and Dickens, or the poetry of Browning and Tennyson. We shall not have another Gulliver or Robinson Crusoe, nor another Table Round of Knights, for their day has gone. But we shall enjoy the stories about them in the twentieth century as much as their first readers did in the nineteenth [1].

This specific summation, which urged the virtues of older stories for children, explained why it is essential that great literature be retold. Several critical points are significant. This home library, produced in and intended for use in the United States, claimed America's place within English literature, which provided the first, last, and most numerous stories. Those chosen are the best and will never go out of fashion, not least because they will not be excelled. Moreover, literature teaches as well as delights, since it distinguishes between right and wrong, and exalts beauty and virtue. Literature read as a child is the essential introduction to understanding the world.

Masterpieces of literature were not in *The Child's Story Book* but in *Story and History*, Volume VIII, with major authors, almost all English or American. "The Best of Good Reading" filled 308 pages, but history only 94, including lists of dates. Space for early modern romances differed markedly. Spenser was scantly recognized, while *Don Quixote* was emphasized as the final story.[18] A brief introductory note explained each selection chosen was "complete ... readable, and whets the appetite for more" (1). "The Best of Good Reading" began with Greece and Rome, ignored medieval writers, and included only Shakespeare (Lamb's story of *The Tempest*), Milton, and Bunyan from early modern. Other selections were English or American with three exceptions— *Swiss Family Robinson*, Baron Munchausen, and Cervantes. History followed story, "literally much was packed in little space, with our own American development filling the larger part, as it should" (1). Preceding History were four pages of bibliographical information, names and dates for: The Chief English Poets—24, The Chief English Dramatists—20, The Chief English Novelists—21, Twenty Great English Novels (305), The Chief English Historical, Scientific, and Philosophical Writers—17, The Chief English Essayists— 17, Good Books to read—100. Spenser was among the poets, and Mary Macleod's *Stories from The Faerie Queene* among the one hundred. Two final lists were Picture Books for Children and Public Libraries. That Library Commissions were listed for only thirty states suggests why home libraries were so important in the United States.

Young Folks' Treasury *(1919)*

Classic Tales and Legendary Stories was Volume III of *Young Folks' Treasury* (1909/1919), edited by Hamilton Wright Mabie, Edward Everett Hale, and William Byron Forbush. A brief Introduction by Forbush (1868–1927), founder of the Knights of King Arthur in 1893—inspiration for the Boy Scouts—and author of *The Boy Problem* (1907), explained a design to entice children to read. Of "really two volumes in one," he began with the second: "STORIES OF PLAY AND ATHLETICS, STORIES OF ADVENTURE, STO-

RIES OF HEROISM, and STORIES OF HUMAN LOVE," intended for "the big boys and girls who are in what we used to call 'the grammar grades' and high school."[19] OLD-FASHIONED STORIES "quaint and funny ... all have a sweet flavor and savor" (v); Forbush did not mention Funny Stories and Everyday Stories—presumably considered accessible. Most significant to a study of canonical literature retold for children was the second part:

> The CLASSIC TALES in the first part of the book may look a bit alarming at first. They are placed here so that the names of Homer, Shakespeare, Chaucer, Cervantes, and Lamb may become as familiar as "Cinderella" and "The Three Bears." Really read them through and you will be spellbound. You will find something more than a silly old man in noble Don Quixote, and you will see the fun that Swift was having in Gulliver's adventures, you will lose your way in magical Bagdad during fascinating Arabian Nights. Those daring mariners, Ulysses and Robinson Crusoe, will make you forget your home for a while. Chaucer will take you on a journey that you will never wish to end and Bunyan on a pilgrimage that closes with the Celestial City; Charles and Mary Lamb will carry you to Fairyland and Prospero's isle of magic. We want you through these CLASSIC TALES to get acquainted with some of the world's greatest writers, so that when you are older they will be lifelong friends [v].

Forbush also edited *Myths and Legendary Heroes*, Volume II. Contents of both volumes were comprehensive and wide-ranging. Nevertheless, they ignored *The Faerie Queene*.

My Book House *(1920/21)*

Olive Beaupré Miller's *My Book House* (1920/21) both resembled and differed from earlier home libraries. It was very much the work of Miller (1863–1968), a Christian Scientist and a Mid-Westerner from a distinguished family that supported learning; she wrote the stories and edited the series.[20] As a graduate of Smith College in 1904 Miller exemplified Edwardian ambitions and opportunities for women; indeed production and sales of *My Book House* were carried out almost entirely by women—including door-to-door sales in the 1930s during the Depression—though her husband Henry Miller managed business aspects until their divorce in 1935. Educators and religious leaders, who praised their "broad concept for social living," deemed Miller's stories "one of the greatest things you could provide a home or church or school library" (67). In 1931 a mother whose daughters attended university recorded the influence of *My Book House*: "In addition to supplying beloved stories, it built character. Truth, honesty, generosity, persistence, these are abstractions beyond the concept of small children except in story form with a moral in terms they can understand" (51).

Olive Beaupré Miller's *My Book House* (1920–1921) was an eminently successful home library that stressed literature. The Romantic image of knight and lady riding in the forest promised that *From the Tower Window* would provide chivalric stories to excite and delight. Home libraries were especially important in the United States, where fewer extravagant books and schoolbooks presented *The Faerie Queene*.

The cardboard box in which the first edition was packaged explained the title. There were no paper jackets; Miller's desire was "to arouse in the child a deep love for his book—and anything that separates the hand of the child from the beloved possession—his book—defeats the purpose" (94). The publisher, The Bookhouse for Children, continued Edwardian practice of pasting a color illustration on the cover, originally black cloth, but also a handsome whitewashed green "Fabrikoid"; blue cloth began with the seventeenth edition. Titles were stamped in gold. End papers originally pictured children moving toward a magical castle on a cliff—an image of romance and fairy tale—later revised to show knights in armor facing a Viking ship with a castle in the background. Colors were originally subtle, reminiscent of Randolph Caldecott; later editions had bold lines and bright colors in Art Deco style. Countless editions over many years provide a record of changing expectations and values.

Large volumes (7 × 9¼ inches) featured big print and frequent illustrations, both color and black-and-white. The first edition's format, six volumes, I– IV (1920) and V–VI (1921), remained unchanged until the seventeenth edition (1932–1933) that had twelve instead of six volumes, about 216–240 pages instead of the original 448. From 1937, The Rainbow Edition, there were alterations in contents and updating. This history reflected some developments in expectations but continuing success of an essentially Edwardian home library. My discussion is based on the 1920–21 volumes, but notes differences in later editions. What did not change was Miller's emphasis upon literature, principally English and American, but also major non-English writers. Her other works advanced additional subjects: *My Book of History: A Picturesque Tale of Progress*, four volumes (1929–1933), reissued as *A Picturesque Tale of Progress* (1935) in eight volumes; *Heroes of the Bible* (1940).

The Latchkey, Volume VI was a literary history, biographical stories about authors, several critical essays, as well as various indexes and a pronunciation guide.[21] In revised editions the title was *Halls of Fame*, Volume XII.[22] Change epitomized difference in values, as did elimination of a charming pictorial title page that preceded "Childhood Biographies of Authors." John Dryden's "What the child admired, / The youth endeavored and the man acquired" defined "Ideals"—beside a knight in shining armor who rides toward a castle of romance (11). Seated before a fireplace a mother reads to three children: a boy, the oldest, listens attentively, sitting on the edge of his chair, his elbows on her knee; a little girl, equally enthralled, sits demurely on the floor beside her mother; the toddler pets a cat licking its paw (ii).

In the first edition four essays surveyed essential types of children's literature: "The Interesting History of Old Mother Goose" (nursery rhymes),

"The Origin of Folk Tales," "What Is a Myth?" and "The World's Great Epics." *Halls of Fame* repeated only essays about Mother Goose and Epics. Similarly later editions offered significantly different indexes, lessening ways to encourage understanding of contexts; "General Index of Authors, Titles and Leading Characters" was continued as was "Special Subjects Index" with "Geographical Index" added as "Countries of the World"; however, "Historical References" was eliminated. Moreover, "Character Building Index A Guide for Parents" replaced "Ethical Theme Index." Gone were topics like Chivalry, Compassion, False Pride, Pluck, Religious Feeling, Vision, and Words without Deeds. Nevertheless, in a preface to *Halls of Fame* Miller expressed a desire to give "a large view of the sweep of English and American literature … to bring out definitely the character of the contribution of each author to the whole development of literature … to give a comprehensive picture of literature as a whole by including the lives of the most outstanding from foreign countries" (5). She identified English authors from Chaucer to the Victorians, then American (including contemporary writers), and finally "world-famous authors from foreign countries (7). While the principal ordering of entries in *The Latchkey* was idiosyncratic—"The Circus Man" (Phineas T. Barnum) was first and "The Young Quaker (John Greenleaf Whittier) last—that in *Halls of Fame* was chronological.[23]

Miller's final paragraph reiterated the case for literature:

> It touches off the creative fire of fancy, it enriches our lives with a fund of beauty, humor, truth, and ever expanding knowledge. Above all, it is always molding and reshaping our concepts of what is good and what is not good, not only presenting a wider and truer understanding of life but stirring in our hearts a strong emotional reaction to that understanding … it is this *feeling* rather than knowledge of facts alone, it is this drive of the emotions behind the intellect, which becomes the dynamo, the motive power for action—the *do-*something behind the *know-*something. Thus MY BOOK HOUSE not only enlarges the child's knowledge and understanding of life but helps to plant within his heart and spirit that dynamo which impels him to live life fully, wisely and well [7].

Her use of "dynamo" recalled a distinction between medieval and modern—"The Virgin and the Dynamo"—made by Henry Adams (1838–1918) in *Mont Saint Michel and Chartres* (1904) and the prediction of Matthew Arnold (1865–1888) in "The Study of Poetry" (1880) that literature was increasingly replacing religion as the source of moral values.

"Kilcolman Castle: Edmund Spenser (1552–1599)" stressed the Irish estate the poet received when secretary to the Lord Deputy in 1580. Miller contrasted situations of court and province. Being away from Queen Elizabeth's court was "no small sacrifice…. No more to see Sir Philip Sidney, Spenser's true ideal of knighthood! To be parted from that brilliant young dramatist, William Shakespeare! To hear of the defeat of the Spanish Armada, and the exploits of Drake and Hawkins and Frobisher, only as a distant echo!" Although advocacy of Protestantism was essential in *The Faerie Queene*, Miller evaded comment about religious differences, conflicts and factions. Spenser was "all unconscious of the hatred that was smouldering round about him, like a seething volcano in the hearts of the Irish people" and lived in the world of his imagination (318). A visit from Sir Walter Raleigh led to a return to court with the first three books of *The Faerie Queene*; his friend presented Spenser to Elizabeth, who granted him "a little pension." His poem inspired "delight and admiration. How sweet was its melody, how abundant its fancy! For two hundred years there had been no great poem written in the English language. *The Faerie Queene* was the first great work since the days of Geoffrey Chaucer." "Nevertheless," Miller noted Spenser's pleasure in returning to Ireland (*Colin Clout's Come home againe*), meeting and marrying Elizabeth, living happily with her and their children, and publishing three more books of his great poem. Then the Irish "volcano" erupted; peasants attacked and burned Kilcolman Castle, the Spenser family fled to London, where the poet soon died, leaving his "beautiful *Faerie Queene*" unfinished (319). Miller offered little critical analysis but declared Spenser a major author.

In *From the Tower Window*, Volume V (1921) "Una and the Red Cross Knight Retold from Book I of The Faery Queen" was the first item. This book featured medieval heroes of literature and history, but also stories from the United States, including Israel Zangwill's "The Melting Pot," James Russell Lowell's "Stanzas on Freedom," and Woodrow Wilson's "An Address to New-Made Citizens." Just as Spenser used an archaic style for *The Faerie Queene*, so syntax and vocabulary in "Una and the Red Cross Knight" suggested medieval romances. Seventeen verse quotations—with modern spelling—provided examples of Spenser's poetic skill. Proper names were printed syllabically with accents—Glo-ri-an'a, Ar-chi-ma'go, Fi-des'sa, Du-es'sa, Lu-ci-fer'a, Fi-del'i-a, Sper-an'za, Cha-ris'sa, Sa'tyrs, and so on. The narrative effectively related principal adventures of Book I with enhanced romantic ending: "And so the King gave Una to her Knight and thus happiness did end that long and toilsome quest."[24] Avoidance of separation was in keeping with M. D. Charleson's Romantic cover with a youthful knight and lady riding through a forest. Similarly, Donn P. Crane's title page had a framed image of a knight in plate armor who sounds a horn as he and the lady who rides behind him approach a picturesque castle on a cliff high above a river; beside it were lines of Alfred Tennyson's "The Bugle Song" (11).

Donn P. Crane (1878–1944), who was self-taught, was the primary artist of *My Book House*.[25] He worked with pen and ink, using three colors with various shading, to create subtle illustrations. A few were full pages, but usually smaller pictures were combined with words. Una in black mantle and white veil reaches out to the Red Cross Knight in full armor (15). The lamb is beside her, and a bearded dwarf walks a little behind. Una's modest attire contrasted with Duessa's patterned gold dress. She watches the Red Cross Knight fight Sansfoy, in Saracen armor and riding a black charger (19). Red Cross Knight and Duessa pause on a hilltop, as she points out their destination across the plain where crowds of people come and go in a large landscape with a splendid, fanciful castle; those approaching are richly attired, while those departing are beggars (bottom 23). While the verbal text described them as "counsellor," it did not specify the Seven Deadly Sins. In Crane's most startling picture Lucifera gazes into her mirror as she rides in an ornate chariot, driven by Satan whose whip extends across pages (26–27). Each counsellor was characterized by a symbol of vice and the mount described by Spenser. Then visual interest shifted to Una: the lion offers homage (30), and happy Fauns and Satyrs surround her in a wood by a stream (31). Orgoglio uses a tree as club to face a tiny figure, with shield and sword but not armor (34); opposite is a smaller portrait of Prince Arthur in armor (35). Especially charming was Charissa, "a woman in her freshest age, of wondrous beauty and rare bounty.... Upon her head she wore a tire of gold adorned with richest gems, and she was sitting in an ivory chair, a pair of turtle doves perched by her side. About her arms, her breast, her chair there hung a multitude of babes, playing their sports that filled her full of joy to see ... (42). Crane's eleven nude babes, some fair and others dark haired, play quietly, climb a wall, stand to watch, and fall backward (43). Although Crane consistently adhered to verbal descriptions, pictures had their own imaginative vitality. In the final opening the dragon, golden scales with black highlights, stretches across the top and down to accommodate its tail (47). Opposite at the bottom is Red Cross Knight, a small picture; with shield raised and lance poised he looks up to this formidable monster; tiny Una watches from a distant hill.

When the six volumes of *My Book House* became twelve, *From the Tower Window*, Volume V was divided into *From the Tower Window*, Volume X and *In Shining Armour*, Volume XI. Absence of a preface in the first edition suggested young readers attuned to appreciate the material included, but later editions explained:

> "From the Tower Window" is primarily the book of romantic as well as heroic adventure, ... all the great national epics. ... the highest, loftiest, noblest, most stirring and deeply moving thoughts of the people expressed in their various long epic poems. From generation to generation these tales were told or sung by wandering bards in hall and castle or to a crowd on the street, until at last some poet appeared, of sufficient genius to write down the tale and give it permanent form in the peculiar style and rhythm of his own country. In these massive old epics, with their splendid seriousness and dignity, their rousing stir of

Lucifera (Pride) rides in her chariot, drawn by "counsellors"—euphemism for the Seven Deadly Sins so often found in Catholic iconography. Donn P. Crane, illustrator of *My Book House*, followed Spenser's descriptions of physical characteristics and mounts for each counsellor. By making the procession cross two pages he conveyed their dominance, an inversion of Chaucer's pilgrims.

activity, their rhythmic flow of line, their numberless passages of great and lofty beauty, we find the finest literature of each country.[26]

Most were anonymous medieval works; thus Spenser was *In Shining Armour*, Volume XI that "continues and completes the romantic and epic tales."[27] Not acknowledged were changed expectations and an aesthetic removed from the first edition's Edwardian manners. Many illustrations were repeated, sometimes in different positions and now with bright orange and turquoise green of Art Deco. Lucifera's expansive progress with her "counsellors" was reduced to a single small black-and-white picture (16); Charissa and her babes were also black-and-white, and there was no little portrait of Prince Arthur. On the title page the added small picture of the Red Cross Knight and Duessa under trees increased recognition of Spenser's story, but this cropped version eliminated the soulful faces of Fraelissa and Fradubio inside the tree (14).

Changes in words were even more drastic and extensive. Verse quotations were reduced from sixteen to nine. The longest, enough to communicate Spenser's poetic brilliance—eighteen lines describing Lucifera's palace (24)—

4. American Difference

was eliminated, and several longer quotations shortened to two or four lines. Anxiety about reading capacity and response also explains why the style of "Una and the Red Cross Knight" was modified to eliminate words and simplify syntax that suggested an older time. Two examples illustrate difference, Una's first appearance and the slaying of the dragon.

> Soon after, entered a fair lady in mourning weeds, riding on a white ass, with a dwarf behind her leading a warlike steed and bearing the arms and spear of a knight. The lady, falling before the Queen of Faeries, complained that her father and mother, an ancient King and Queen, had been by an huge dragon many years shut up in a brazen castle, who thence suffered them not to issue; and therefore besought the Faery Queen to assign her some one of her knights to take on him the deliverance of these twain. Presently that clownish person, upstarting, desired that adventure; whereat the Queen much wondering, and the Lady much gainsaying, yet he earnestly importuned his desire. In the end the Lady told him that unless that armour that she brought would serve him, he could not succeed in that enterprise; for that armour was of such a sort as would fit him only who had great courage and faith, great uprightness and truth; which armour being forthwith put upon the youth with due furnitures thereunto, he seemed the goodliest man in all the company and was well liked of the Lady.
>
> And eftsoons, taking on him knighthood, and mounting on that strange courser, he went forth with her on that adventure. Right faithful and true he proved, and on his breast and shield he wore a blood-red cross in dear remembrance of his dying Lord and to make known to all the world that he would give battle only in the cause of righteousness and truth [12].

This was revised to:

> Soon came a lady fair in mourning weeds. She rode a snow-white ass, and with her came a dwarf who led a warlike steed and bore the arms and armour of a knight. The Lady, falling prone before the Queen, made sad complaint how that a fearful dragon kept her father and mother shut up within a castle whence he suffered them not to issue. Weeping, she besought the Queen to give her some good knight to work deliverance for these twain. That clownish person, then upstarting, desired that he be given this adventure. The Queen much wondered and the Lady much gainsayed; yet did he press his case, full earnest in desire. Then cried the Lady: "This armour which my servant bears will fit no man save one of the greatest faith and courage, uprightness and truth. If it fits I will accept you as my knight."
>
> The armour then was put upon the youth. It fit him perfectly and in it now he seemed the goodliest man in all that company. The lady Una liked him well. Eftsoons, he took the vows of knighthood and departed by her side, wearing on breast and shield, a blood-red cross in memory of his dying Lord and likewise to declare that he would battle only in the cause of right and truth [8–9].

Sentences were significantly shorter—one divided with part made direct speech—and paragraph division altered. Una's parents were not identified as "an ancient King and Queen," and their castle is no longer "brazen" (brass, not bold); "furnitures" (technical term for armor) was also eliminated. Una asks that the Queen (not Faery Queen) "give" not "assign" her a knight. Some changes in vocabulary clarified meaning: "complained" became "made sad complaint," while the youth that originally "earnestly importuned his desire" became "did press his case, full earnest in desire." However, a few unchanged words—"eftsoons," "upstarting," and "gainsaying / gainsayed"—preserved an older flavor. The dragon became "fearful" instead of "huge," perhaps to anticipate a less thrilling revised account of the meeting of knight and monstrous foe.

The longest episode, dragon slaying, was similarly modified. The original (45–46) echoed the complexity of Spenser's Elizabethan style yet also recalled thrilling descriptions of dragons in popular chapbooks; the revision (26–27) lacked that vitality because it eliminated much detail, and short sentences lost the cumulative building of action. A few archaic words remained, but the text was easier for American children to read. It could, of course, inspire less imaginative responses. Although neither version retained Spenser's extensive allegory, "the well of life with wondrous virtue to recover health and strength" suggested religion while "that magic well with life and strength renewed" evoked fairy tale. The distinctive history of *My Book House* is a gloss on changing views of how to attract young readers to retold English masterpieces. Concurrent were books of pedagogy and advice from librarians.

American Pedagogy and Librarians' Advice

Evaluations of *The Faerie Queene* as children's literature differed greatly in Britain and the United States. This was evident in books that retold its stories, but even clearer in books of pedagogy and advice from librarians in the United States, where there was less commitment.

James Baldwin, The Book Lover *(1884/1902)*

James Baldwin (1841–1925) was an American educator whose children's books—*Fifty Famous Stories Retold* (1896), *The Story of Siegfried* (1882), and *The Story of Roland* (1883)—were widely disseminated. While he recognized how Victorians in England valued Spenser, Baldwin was not confident about the appeal of *The Faerie Queene*. His audience for *The Book Lover: A Guide to the Best Reading* (1884, 14th edition 1902) was "persons charged with the education of youth, no less than to that considerable class of men and women who seek self-culture through the aid of books."[28] Coupling these sets of readers glossed current circumstances. Later editions recognized vast changes in schools: most now had well equipped libraries, reference supplemented textbooks; "right habits of reading has become one of the most important duties of teachers" (5). Patriotism informed Baldwin's passion: "You only, O books, are liberal and independent. You give to all who ask, and enfranchise all who serve you assiduously" (13).

Like many others he recognized some writers were difficult to understand. "A beginner will be likely to find but little comfort in Chaucer or Spenser, or even in Emerson; but after he has worked up to them he may study them with unbounded delight" (246). *The Faerie Queene* was not on Baldwin's list of twenty-five famous "books fashioned by the intellect of godlike men" that included translations of six classical writers, one medieval (Dante by Longfellow), seven novels (Scott's *Ivanhoe* exemplified Medievalism) and three poets of the nineteenth-century, five essayists, Shakespeare's Works, Goethe's *Faust*, Milton's *Paradise Lost*, and Cervantes's *Don Quixote de la Mancha* (53). "Chapter V What Books Shall Children Read" recognized medieval chivalric literature for children, but not early modern romances.

Baldwin quoted English writers to recognize a canon. John Ruskin named Spenser on a short list: of "some books which we all need, and assuredly if you read Homer, Plato, Æschylus, Herodotus, Dante, Shakespeare and Spenser as much as you ought, you will not require wide enlargement of your shelves to right and left of them for purposes of perpetual study" (49). Sir John Lubbock in an address to the Workingmen's College, London in January 1886 included *The Faerie Queene* in a list of "The Hundred Best Books"— across cultures and periods but no living writers.

"Chapter IV Books of Power" contained Baldwin's most informative list, one in which critical observations from distinguished literary figures accompanied names and titles. Baldwin chose

> the works which embody the best thoughts of the noblest thinkers of all countries and ages.... Such books are for the building up of a lofty character, for the turning of the soul inward upon itself and the fitting of it for greater, stronger, worthier achievement. ... words of eternal truth and beauty, instructing, uplifting, and delighting generation after generation of mankind [95–96, 106].

On this list there was a place, albeit qualified, for

> SPENSER'S Faerie Queene, not to be read through, but in selections. "We can scarcely comprehend how a perusal of the Faerie Queene can fail to insure to the true believer a succession of halcyon days."—HAZLITT [105].

Typically Baldwin's annotations identified translations; the only other qualification was for Chaucer: "If not the complete works, at least the Canterbury Tales" (98). Cervantes's *Don Quixote* and Bunyan's *The Pilgrim's Progress* were in this list of seventy-five.

Mary E. Burt, Literary Landmarks *(1897)*

Like Baldwin, Mary E. Burt (1850–1918) was acutely aware of educational conditions in the United States. Based on twenty years of experience in the classroom and writing for the Chicago Board of Education, she recognized that fifty per cent of children who attended school left at age ten. This made the curriculum of *Literary Landmarks: A Guide to Good Reading for Young People, and Teachers' Assistant* (1897) all the more remarkable for its sophistication and high expectation.[29] Burt vigorously opposed current children's books: "The truth is that the classics are simpler by far than the great mass of modern reading. They are nearer to children and the childhood of the race" (24). She rejected pedagogical emphasis on "external forms instead of ideas [that] has led on to distaste for good reading ... the theory that reading should be very simple and monosyllabic ... has done much to expel good literature from school-readers and substitute weak and pointless studies. ... a child does not dread hard words so much as insipid thought" (28–29). Burt epitomized such schoolbooks as "My Nag can run" (109). While she stressed the role of fairy tales and chivalric stories as children's literature, she did not mention Spenser's *Faerie Queene*; his name was not among those clustered for the Age of Shakespeare, which came between the Age of Dante and Chaucer and the Age of Goethe. In her comprehensive chart with a cross to mark the Age of Christ as a major division she placed writers from classical / Biblical times through the nineteenth century. Immediately under Shakespeare the name was Marlowe, with Cervantes and Milton on either side. Many were English writers (Ben Jonson, Sidney, Raleigh, Lyly, Chapman, Bacon, Herbert, Herrick), but also present were Tasso and Lope de Vega. Since Burt included a sweep of world literature, Spenser's absence was telling. She made diagrammed grade plans with specified ages from First, age six years, through Eighth, average age fourteen or fifteen years. Although Spenser was not in charts, he was in Book Lists: Riverside editions of British Poets (116) and a ten cents edition of *The Fairy Queen* (146). Also listed, and published by Houghton Mifflin, was Abbey Sage Richardson's *Stories from Old English Poetry* (1871/1891), discussed above. Burt described it as "highly recommended to me" (100). A description of this volume, 291 pages and cost 60 cents, was in the list of The Riverside School Library Series, "Prepared with Special Regard for American Schools." The recommendation was a bit uncertain: "A group of stories after the manner of Lamb's Tales from Shakespeare, drawn from Chaucer, Spenser, Shakespeare, and some of the lesser poets, not now generally read; stories of great beauty in themselves, and illuminated by the genius of the poet who used them" (8–9).

John Harrington Cox, Literature in the Common Schools *(1909)*

John Harrington Cox (1863–1945), professor of English philology in West Virginia University, was a devotee of medieval chivalric stories; for older children he retold in close translations *Beowulf* and *Sir Gawain and the Green Knight* in *Knighthood in Germ and Flower* (1910), the *Song of Roland* in *A Hero of Old France* (1913), and *Siegfried* (1915). *Literature in the Common Schools* (1909) was based on "five years experience with teachers in the Summer School of the West Virginia University and in teachers' institutes in several States."[30] It combined a philosophy of learning with specific pedagogy: detailed study plans for eight grades, distinguished as primary—relying mostly on oral presentation and drawing—and upper—making sophisticated analyses of books. Cox, who included a topical outline of his book to help teachers, described "A Model Lesson" and specified "Course of Study" with lists of works, supplemented by "Extended List for Substitution, Leisure Hours, and Home Reading."

Cox urged reading is the most important subject and literature is essential to life:

> The hunger to know the meaning of life is almost as primal as the hunger for food. It is the function of the seers of this world to satisfy this hunger. The wisdom which the race has acquired is for the most part locked up in those books we call literature. In them the meaning of life has found a permanent expression. Out of the Bible, Shakespeare, and the rest, come the issues of life [2].

He enthusiastically declared, "The primary object is pleasure, the ultimate objective assimilation. Thus to approach the great works of art is both a joy and a duty" (8). Cox insisted upon "the best" and defined the results possible with such reading:

> It awakens and stirs the emotions; it exercises the imagination and the fancy; it trains the æsthetic faculty by developing a sense of beauty in form and diction; it cultivates the moral and religious sentiment through ideal representation; it creates a taste for what is clean and healthy and enlarges the appreciation of what is choice and best [9].

He identified "five tributaries of the literary stream": the King James Bible, folklore and fairy tales, myths, chivalric, and Shakespeare. Writing for schools in the United States, Cox stressed American literature, especially Longfellow's *Hiawatha*. Spenser was in the chivalric tributary "of wondrous beauty and great volume," mostly medieval romances that informed early modern romances: "Here Spenser found his great inspiration and gave it back to us in 'The Fairy Queen'" (86). However, absence from a course of study or extended list meant Cox did not find *The Faerie Queene* suitable for American schools. Two librarians made contrasting evaluations.

Montrose J. Moses, Children's Books and Reading *(1907)*

Montrose J. Moses (1878-1934) worked in the New York City Public Library and consulted librarians at Columbia University, Hartford, Pittsburg, and Cleveland. *Children's Books and Reading* (1907) provided a history of children's literature, including changes from Sunday-school literature to public-school systems that over produced for an "enormous average taste" (156), a current account of developments like children's reading rooms, and skepticism about sociological surveys to gauge "the child."[31] Moses's message was the same as teachers': traditional literature is superior to "inane fiction," the dime-novel vogue, the sensationalism of books like "Ragged Dick" (171). He stressed the mass of books available and urged careful selection. He eschewed obvious didacticism, yet emphasized the relation of literature to life and the moral structure of romance. Perhaps because of New York's immigrant population, Moses offered separate lists of books in French and German. He was also more forthright in declaring the affinity of American and English literature and the superior quality of English books over schoolbooks.

Lists made up about a fourth of *Children's Books and Reading*. Under several types Moses presented titles with publisher and price. "Classics" had eleven items, and early modern romances framed the alphabetical list. First was Cervantes's *Don Quixote of the Mancha*, retold by Judge Parry, and last was M. H. Towry's *Spenser for Children* (220-221). Others were Chaucer's *Canterbury Tales*, Lamb's *Tales from Shakespeare* and Mary Cowden Clarke's *Girlhood of Shakespeare's Heroines*, Swift's *Gulliver's Travels*, and five retold classics of Greece and Rome.

Frances Jenkins Olcott, The Children's Reading *(1912)*

Frances Jenkins Olcott (1872?-1963) prefaced *The Children's Reading* (1912) with a double page, "A Table of Classics and Notable Persons Influenced by Them."[32] Twelve classics were arranged in columns, four by three: The Bible, *Faerie Queene, Odyssey, Robinson Crusoe; Arabian Nights,* Fairy Tales,

Pilgrim's Progress, Scott's Novels and Poems; *Don Quixote*, *Gulliver's Travels*, Plutarch, Shakespeare. Olcott explained this list was selective, but derived from numerous biographies that recorded reading before age sixteen and many before twelve years old.

Under each classic were listed four influenced by it; for *The Faerie Queene*: Lowell, Milton, Hawthorne, and Keats. Noteworthy were the unusually small number of ancient classics, only two, as compared with the Bible and three English authors whose works were overtly informed by the Reformation—Spenser, Bunyan, and Milton. Olcott's chapter "Ballads, Epics, and Romances" quoted Cervantes for the defense of "romantic writings" that at their best seek to combine instruction and pleasure (103). She judged early romances "the product of the sentimental side of medieval chivalry," yet "they have great value in the education of young people ... appeal to budding sentiments and the awakening enthusiasms ... imbued with charming fancy and tenderness ... deal less with the depth of life and more with its emotions ... draw youthful altruistic aspirations towards an ideal goal." Olcott, who quoted Milton's "Apology for Smectymnuus" for the esteem in which he held knights, noted that chivalry and romance were part of story hours in libraries. She described William Forbush's "Knights of King Arthur" that sought to rekindle ideals of chivalry and Christian daring (105–106).

In contrast to brief references by others, Olcott gave pride of place to *The Faerie Queene* in the context of chivalric romances; she offered analysis of its moral quality, expected it to be read by all children, and provided a program of study:

> Spenser's "Faërie Queene," although not a part of folk-literature, but an original metrical romance, may be made the next link in the progressive reading that will lead young people to an appreciation of other fine things. Richly imaginative, full of wonder incidents, romantic, and above all allegorical, the "Faërie Queene" may well form part of the mental diet on which every child is brought up. The poem teaches holiness, truthfulness, prudence, justice, fortitude, and temperance. It instills its lessons through beautiful allegory making the good lovely and the bad gross. Milton, speaking of "our sage and serious poet Spenser," writes that he "describing true temperance under the person of Guyon, brings him in with his palmer through the Cave of Mammon and the Bower of Earthly Bliss, that he might see and know yet abstain. Since, therefore, the knowledge and survey of vice is in this world so necessary to the constitution of human virtue and the scanning of error to the confirmation of truth." This mysterious inner significance, mingled with a romantic plot and the relation of many wonders, both softens and enthralls the imagination of a growing boy or girl.
>
> A programme of stories from the "Faërie Queene" may include "The Quest of the Red Cross Knight," "Una and the Lion," "The Red Cross Knight and the Dragon," "Sir Guyon's Search for the Bower of Earthly Bliss," "The Adventures of Britomart," "Britomart and Artegall," and "The Quest for the Blatant Beast" [110–111].

As previously discussed, several who retold Spenser's stories eschewed allegory for adventures or poetic beauty. Olcott valued the poem for its use of allegory and Protestant message. Thus she privileged it as the quintessential epic / romance. Having indicated ballads as the initial progression from fairy tales, she identified mythic legends of Siegfried and Beowulf, but did not proceed with medieval romances. Only after her encomium of Spenser's *Faerie Queene* did Olcott introduce Chaucer, Carolingean and Arthurian romances, followed by Homeric poetry and Shakespeare, and Cervantes.

In the list of books discussed Olcott recommended two versions of Spenser: Macleod's *Stories from the Faërie Queene*—"A close rendering of the original poem. Illustrated and attractive. Less expensive than 'Una and the Red Cross Knight,' and Royde-Smith's *Una and the Red Cross Knight*—Retold in charming prose. Bits of the original poem are woven into the stories. Illustrated gift-book" (124). In a final long (thirty-six pages in small type) "Purchase List of Children's Books for Children and Young People from One to Sixteen Years of Age" she added the edition in Everyman's Library, two volumes, published by Dutton in leather for seventy cents.

Collections, home libraries, pedagogy and librarians' advice in the United States showed significant differences from British tradition that schoolbooks advanced.

5

Schoolbooks

Elegant books of *The Faerie Queene* served as gifts and reward / prizes, but schoolbooks—single texts and portions of graded readers—assured wide experience of Spenser as a major author, storyteller, and promoter of nation and religion. Advocacy for his place in the English literary tradition vied with recognition of difficulty. Henry Newbolt's *The Teaching of English in England* (1924), completed in 1921, included a "Memorandum by Mr. A. E. Palfery on the Scheme for the Circulation of Books in London Elementary Schools," based on two million volumes. In a list of fifty titles (many of which were novels) in greatest demand, *Stories from Spenser* was forty-six; Shakespeare was number one and Chaucer was twenty-nine.[1] Relative positions in the canon have not changed.

Although markedly less expensive than elegant storybooks, readers were attractive, and even presented as rewards / prizes. Some books not originally so intended became school readers; two examples have already been discussed. Modest in price (1d. and later 3d.) was *The Red Cross Knight, Part I and II* (1900), W. T. Stead's Books for the Bairns, #53 and #54. Macmillan published *Tales from Spenser: Chosen from The Faerie Queene* (1889) by Sophia H. Maclehose as a school edition with introduction and notes in 1905. Romance Readers, usually five or six titles in a series, supplemented graded schoolbooks that provided wide coverage for each year. In Longmans' Continuous Story Readers Junior Series *Tales from The Faerie Queene* (1910) was "adapted from the Christmas Books edited by Andrew Lang"—*The Red Romance Book* (1905) with illustrations by H. J. Ford.

Horace Marshall published Clara L. Thomson's *Tales from the Faerie Queene* (1902)—Red Cross Knight and Sir Guyon—and *Spenser: The Faerie Queene, Book I* (1905). In Arnold's Tales of Old Romance Series *Stories from "The Faerie Queene"* (1902) was one of six titles. Alfonzo Gardiner's *St George of Merry England retold from Spenser's "Faerie Queene"* (c. 1908) was in Edward Arnold's The "A. L." Bright Story Readers, which numbered in the hundreds; it was combined with other titles for a larger volume in The "A. L." Welcome Readers.

Alternatives to books of prose stories were selections in modernized verse. Mary E. Litchfield's *Spenser's Britomart: From Books III, IV, and V* (1896) was an attempt to address failure to recognize a singular woman knight; Ginn published it in the United States. *Selections from The Faerie Queene* (1914), English Literature for Schools Series, edited by Arthur Burrell, was published by J. M. Dent in London and E. P. Dutton in New York. Both provided older students with the original text, modernized when necessary. Cambridge University Press reissued Minna Steele Smith's *Stories from Spenser* (1919) in 2014. M(ary) Sturt and E(llen) C. Oaken's *The Knights of The Faerie Queene* (1924), The Kings Treasuries of Literature Series, #115, which served the general reader and schools, was reissued in 1936.

While readers devoted entirely to Spenser gave a greater sense of his romance / epic, anthologies more frequently provided first encounters. Large single volumes were Henrietta C. Wright's *Children's Stories in English Literature* (1891) and C. Linklater Thomson's *A First Book in English Literature* (1906). More characteristic were series with books for each form / grade. E. Arnold's *Literary Reading Books for Junior Forms* (1902–08) included *The Faerie Queene* in two volumes. *In Golden Realms* told of Princess Una and the Red Cross Knight, while *Chips from a Bookshelf* offered a brief quotation. Arnold's *Steps to Literature* (1905) included "St. George and the Dragon" and "Princess Una and the Red Cross Knight" in Book II *Tales of Many Lands*; "Story of Britomart" in Book IIIA *Stories from the Literature of the British Isles*, and the opening four stanzas of *The Faerie Queene* in Book VI *Glimpses of World Literature*. Thomas Nelson's *Tales that Are Told*, Book VI in *The Royal Treasury of Story and Song*, gave opening stanzas about the Red Cross Knight in modernized language. *Highroads of Literature*, which allotted more space, placed *The Faerie Queene* in the spectrum of English literature as the last work in Book III *The Morning Star*, which began with Chaucer and stressed a tradition of English romance.[2]

In the United States, as Chapter 4 showed, *The Faerie Queene* fared less well in schools. James Baldwin (1841–1925), a prolific writer for children whose books enjoyed world circulation, did not include *The Faerie Queene*—or other early romances—in either *Fifty Famous Stories Retold* (1896/1917) or *Thirty More Famous Stories Retold* (1905). Spenser was also absent from Marion Lansing's *The Open Road Library*, an attractive series that favored medieval stories. *Page, Esquire and Knight* (1910) told "Order of St. George" (2nd and 14th century) rather than Spenser.[3] The exception was Hubert M. Skinner, who featured *The Faerie Queene* in *Readings in Folk-lore* (1893) a reader inspired by nineteenth-century development of an academic study.[4] Skinner (1855–1916) considered folklore the "same as myths of legend and pure fable" (4) but "far more comprehensive than mythology" (8). Diversity included Native American, Oriental /

Eastern stories, and more European. Welcoming study beyond Greek and Latin, Skinner found English literature that encompassed several lands, especially rich.

An introduction "British Folk-lore" provided names and descriptions of major figures—ancient Britons and Celts, principal Arthurian characters, Welsh Maeldune, Saxon Beowulf and Wiglaf—but no texts.

> A break came in the sixteenth century when "the genius of Edmund Spenser introduced into English letters a new class of imaginary personages in his great work *The Faerie Queene*. These differ from other British myths in that they are not derived from ancient popular tradition, but were created to serve the purposes of the poem. They are allegorical characters, representing abstract virtues and vices; but Spenser has interwoven with his narrative some very ancient legends" [48].

A note contextualized:

> This was the last great work of chivalry. Awakening from the gloom of the theological contests of Edward and Mary, the court of the Maiden Queen, from state policy and her own disposition, had been transformed into a court of romance. ... Elizabeth, stately and tender, was herself the Faerie Queene, without even the poet's flattery ...—*Isaac Disraeli* [48].

One list defined characters: Gloriana, Una, The Red-Cross Knight, Acrasia, Sir Guyon, Amoret, Britomartis, Duessa, Orgoglio. Another gave allegorical equivalents for characters from Books I and II but no historical identifications.

After a brief note about Shakespeare's use of fairy lore in *A Midsummer Night's Dream*, Skinner provided "Notes of Literature Relating to British Folklore"; it too began with *The Faerie Queene*, which "contains a succinct account of all the legendary kings of England down to Uther, the father of King Arthur." Skinner ranked Spenser

> among the great four masters of English verse, and his *Faerie Queene* is one of the greatest classics in the language. Later poets have generally acknowledged their indebtedness to him for much of their inspiration. The measure in which he wrote is known as the Spenserian stanza. The *Faerie Queene* is the repository of the Spenserian myths. One of the most familiar cantos of the poem is that which describes the slaying of the dragon [50].

This episode (I. xi.50–55) was quoted (79–90). However, the first quotation (54–78) was Spenser's chronicle of British kings (II. x.5–62), appropriate for folklore.

Romance Readers

Clara L. Thomson, Tales from the Faerie Queene *(1902)*

Few rival Clara L. Thomson's pedagogical contributions to the study of literature and history by Edwardian children. *Tales from The Faerie Queene*

(1902), an early modern romance, extended her retold medieval stories—Beowulf, Malory, and *Tales of the Middle Ages*, 5 in The Romance Readers Series that Thomson edited for Horace Marshall. She drew upon extensive experience in the classroom to produce readable and accurate versions. Her preface reported "great interest and enthusiasm" as the response of children between ages nine and thirteen who were told the first two books of *The Faerie Queene*; thus she wrote a reader for additional individual work.[5] Her "paraphrase" differed from several "adaptations," for she told the "story as simply as is compatible with a close adherence to Spenser's narrative ... frequent quotations from the original will lead some, at least, of the pupils to a first-hand acquaintance with the original" (v). Thomson's books were praised for simple, clear style and skill in engaging children.

Her introduction admitted some loss of the beauty of Spenser's poetry; however, Thomson was hopeful and pragmatic. Her analysis is worth quoting at length because it exemplified how skillfully a perceptive Edwardian teacher used Spenser's stories to entertain and subtly advocate moral values.

> I think you will enjoy these stories of knights and giants and lovely ladies, and all the adventures they went through; and perhaps it will not make them less interesting to know that Spenser was all the time preaching a sermon as well as telling a story. That was his way of teaching his readers, and he made it so delightful that many people who do not care for ordinary sermons read his over and over again. His subject throughout is the struggle between good and evil—that struggle which is always going on and seems never to be finished. Thus when he tells of the Red Cross Knight destroying the dragon, he is really describing how a good man sets out to overcome the evil in the world; and how he sometimes conquers and sometimes fails, but is helped by Truth (Una) and the Love of God (Prince Arthur). You will see how St George falls a victim to deceit (Archimago and Duessa) and is led astray into the House of Pride, and conquers Unbelief (Sansfoy); and how, when he lays aside his armour, he is taken prisoner by the giant Orgoglio, and languishes in a dungeon, until he is delivered by Truth and the Love of God. Then he is so much ashamed of his sin, that he nearly gives way to Despair, who persuades him to kill himself; but Una rescues him once more, and takes him to the House of Holiness. There he is taught how to grow strong and brave again, till at last, restored to all his former health, he attacks and vanquishes the dragon.
>
> In the second book the story is rather different. Here Spenser tries especially to show how wrong extremes are, and how every thing that is good in itself may become bad by being carried to excess. Amavia, who killed herself for grief, and left her little baby all alone, proves the evil of indulging too much in sorrow even for our lost friends; while the story of Furor teaches how wrong it is to be too angry and impatient; and that of Mammon the troubles that may arise from having too much money. It is true that Guyon, who is the hero of this second book, withstands the temptation of Mammon, but he is so worn out with the effort that he becomes unconscious, and would fall a victim to his foes if Divine Love in the shape of Prince Arthur did not come to his aid. It is also told in this book how Prince Arthur defends the Castle of the Soul (Alma) from siege, and slays Maleger, the Prince of Evil. Lastly, Guyon is tempted by ease and pleasure; all beautiful things that can lead a man astray are shown him in Acrasia's bower; but this temptation he also withstands, and takes captive the beautiful sorceress who has beguiled so many men by the same enchantments [vi-vii].

Having given "the inner meaning of the story," Thomson recognized young readers may perceive only fairy tale and miss the moral, although the moral level does not make stories worse. Pedagogy favored Books I and II where lessons of fighting for good and avoiding excess are readily understood because close to children's experience; they also are most like medieval epics / romances, literature of choice for ages nine to thirteen.

Thomson praised Spenser—"so earnest in the cause of righteousness ... his ideal of conduct so high ... he hated falsehood and cowardice and churlishness, and ... loved 'truth and honour, freedom and courtesy.'" She introduced history by placing Spenser in Queen Elizabeth's reign, a time with many great men. She professed an analogy between knight and gentleman that pervaded nineteenth-century ideas of chivalry: "St George and Sir Guyon and Prince Arthur are all model gentlemen, brave and unselfish, tender to the weak and helpless, and furious at the sight of tyranny and cowardice or disloyalty." While this epitomized the English public school, pupils in humbler schools also read *Tales from The Faerie Queene*. Thomson defended "a great deal of fighting in this book—perhaps too much" (viii). Spenser stressed fighting because of violence in the sixteenth century, when taking up arms was a part of education; now "fortunately" gentlemen no longer have to fight so often and do so only reluctantly. This opinion, perhaps a response to the end of the Boer War, was ironic and poignant. She foresaw only a personal contest, the battle between Good and Evil, a war that never ceases and in which all must be ready to engage.

> For as long as the monsters of pride and untruth and selfishness exist in ourselves or other people, we, like the Red Cross Knight, must go forth against them; and if, like him, we often fail and are often disappointed, yet in the end, like him, we hope to slay the dragon and set the castle free [viii].

Schoolboys who read Thomson's books fought in the Great War, initially inspired by chivalric idealism.[6]

Paraphrase removed whatever Thomson deemed unsuitable. Red Cross slays dragon Error, but Thomson eliminated Spenser's specified filth and progeny (8). Yet she kept violence typical in medieval romance. Sir George—title for English identity—deals "such a mighty blow that the steel of Sansloy's helmet was riven in twain, and his head was cleft asunder" (15); the lion tore the robber and left his body in "a thousand fragments" (23); slaying the dragon was the climax (81–88). While violence—in a good, heroic cause—was essential, sex was a topic best left to adults. In the House of Pride Lucifera has only five evil counselors (Idleness, Gluttony, Avarice, Envy, and Wrath); Thomson elided Lechery. When Guyon encounters mermaids, he is "allured with their ditties" (a stanza is quoted); children were alerted: "once fair ladies famed for their beauty and their lovely lays; but because they had been too vain of their sweet faces they had been transformed to fish from the waist downwards" (175). Thomson fully delineated Furor and Occasion; anger and self-control are everyday issues for children (123–126).

Pedagogical information was "a short bibliography for the use of the teacher" (v, 182), but no notes. Mantegna's painting *Saint George* established youth, chivalry, patriotism, and the sacred (frontispiece). Inside an interlaced square were a donkey, lion, lamb, and satyr—iconic for Una's adventures (title page). Spenser's portrait faced Book I's title page. "List of Illustrations and Decorated Pages" linked supplementary material to pictures. Sixteen decorated pages framed quotations that distinguished this reader. Five constituted a mini survey of literary responses: Kingsley, Milton, and Hazlitt (xiii); "On Spenser," from W. Browne's "Britannia's Pastorals" (36); Samuel Taylor Coleridge and Leigh Hunt, "On Spenser" (48); Raleigh's "A Vision upon the Conceit of the Faerie Queene" (96); James Russell Lowell and Edward Dowden, "On Spenser" (106). Eleven pages quoted Spenser's verse, usually two stanzas: dedicatory sonnet to Raleigh (2), "In Pity of Una," I. iii (12); "The House of Pride," I. iv (28); "Weary Wandering," I. ix (64); "Saint George," I. x (74); "The Haven," I. xii (80); "Belphoebe," II. iii (112); "From 'The Passionate Pilgrim'" (122); "Phaedria's Isle," II. vi (128); "Heavenly Love" (156); "The Mermaids' Song," II. xii (170).

Helen Stratton (fl.1891–1925), who was influenced by the Pre Raphaelites and Art Nouveau, specialized in fairy tales and children's books. Her grisaille drawings detailed Thomson's words. Adolescent figures inspired empathy. The first of seven full-pages for Book I was "Una and the Red Cross Knight"; the lady, rides sidesaddle on a charming donkey whose neck she pats, while she draws a lamb (not a simple task with these frisky animals) toward her (6). Her expression is rueful, while Red Cross Knight, heraldic shield on his back and helmet off, has halted his massive charger and turned to see the cause of delay. In the distance the dwarf lags behind, cleverly shown by cropping and a curve in the road. In "Una and the Lion" she sits in a forest glade, and the huge animal lolls beside her and licks her hand, but her cautious donkey and the lamb wait in the background (20). Watched by a bevy of child-faced satyrs Una stands anxiously with arms crossed (42). Disheveled hair and sad expression indicate a low point, when she cradles Red Cross's helmet and touches his shield (52). "In the Cave of Despair" Una, who has cast down a dagger, stands between a ragged threatening figure and seated Sir George (70). In these six illustrations Una was the dominant character. In "Sir George and the Dragon" she was scarcely visible; a slim curling dragon with large wings and snarling mouth dwarfed even the mounted knight (85).

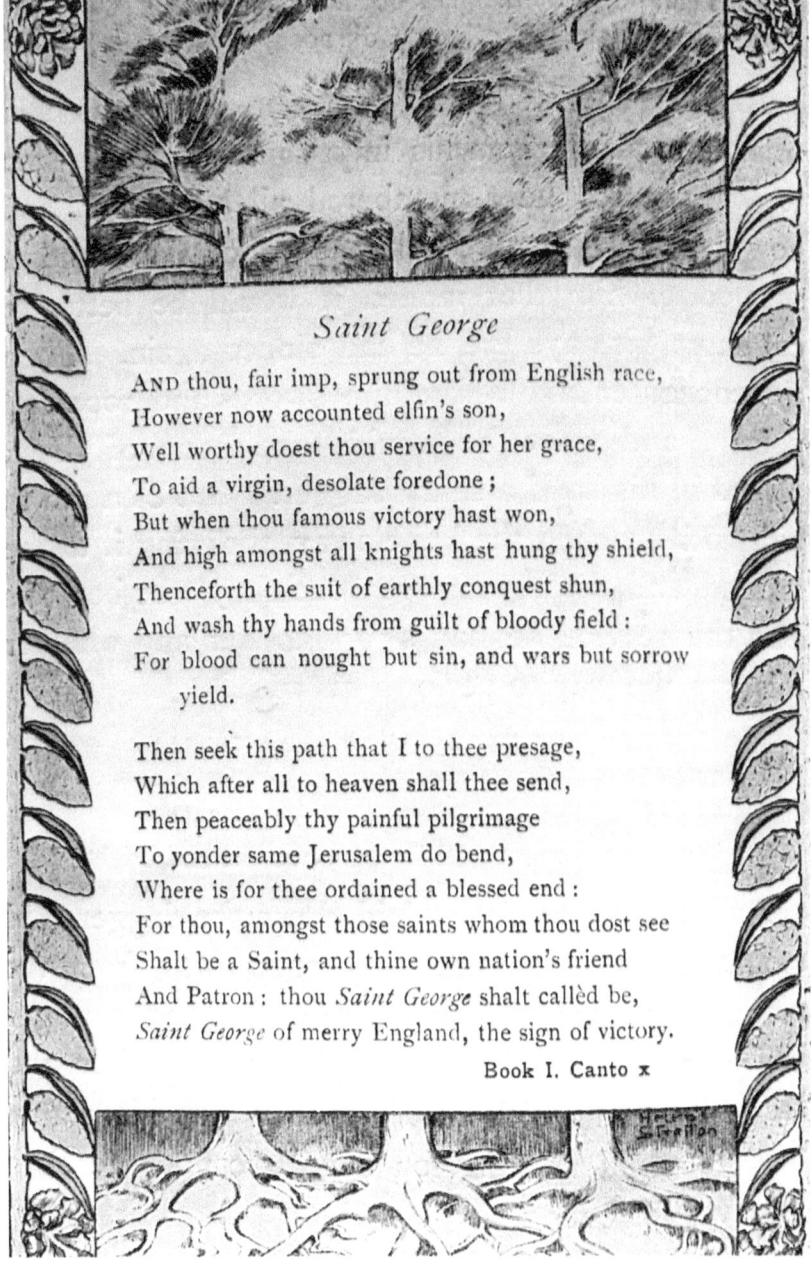

Saint George

AND thou, fair imp, sprung out from English race,
However now accounted elfin's son,
Well worthy doest thou service for her grace,
To aid a virgin, desolate foredone;
But when thou famous victory hast won,
And high amongst all knights hast hung thy shield,
Thenceforth the suit of earthly conquest shun,
And wash thy hands from guilt of bloody field:
For blood can nought but sin, and wars but sorrow yield.

Then seek this path that I to thee presage,
Which after all to heaven shall thee send,
Then peaceably thy painful pilgrimage
To yonder same Jerusalem do bend,
Where is for thee ordained a blessed end:
For thou, amongst those saints whom thou dost see
Shalt be a Saint, and thine own nation's friend
And Patron: thou *Saint George* shalt callèd be,
Saint George of merry England, the sign of victory.

Book I. Canto x

Those who retold *The Faerie Queene* for children frequently expressed a fond hope that as adults those who had read the stories would read Spenser's poetry. To encourage this, books like Clara L. Thomson's *Tales from The Faerie Queene* (1902) introduced quotations from the poem, in modernized language, at intervals within prose stories. Helen Stratton's decorative borders framed each selection of two stanzas, a tactfully gauged length to encourage interest in poetry.

Pictures for "The Story of Sir Guyon" also featured women. "Sir Guyon finds Sir Mordaunt and His Lady" as he advances through trees; a kneeling lady kisses the corpse's hand, indifferent to the toddler who sits amidst her dress's abundant folds (101). "Belphoebe and Braggadochio" shows a slender dynamic huntress, with a man that looks a bit stupid (118). Appealing and uncertain, was "Sir Guyon and Phaedria" (136). The enchantress, leaning luxuriously in her little boat, smiles enticingly; the knight sits stoically, his sword with hilt as a cross between his legs. Stratton here gave fuller play to Art Nouveau style with a canopy of leaves and darker trees. Guyon, sheltered by the Palmer's restraining hand, sits pensively in a dragon ship to hear "The Mermaid's Song" (174). Five mermaids, faint lines, yet displaying flowing hair and delicate breasts, fill two-thirds of the space. With hands extended "Alma Greets Prince Arthur and Guyon"; a wide-eyed boy with a torch watches, the child's gaze (159). "Mammon" warns against excess as he kneels amidst piles of coins (142).

Small figures sustained interest. Each section began with a Roman numeral in dark gray superimposed on a line figure—satyr (I), mermaid (II), lady (III), winged creature (IV), lion (V), donkey (VI), lamb (VII), dragon with human face (VIII), stag (IX), dragon (X), werewolf (XI), eagle? (XII). Because numerals were used for both stories, images did not always correspond. Footers were clearer, often amusing commentary: a coiled dragon's body with a rueful woman's face (11), two trees, one with Fradubio's head just discernible (18), Una's donkey turns its head (27), a swimmer below large tree trunks (56), an old man with large keys for Orgoglio's castle (63), girlish Una clasps her hands (88), a child reaches to touch the dragon's huge claw (94); Guyon washes the Bloody Babe's hands (110); unskilled Braggadochio tries to mount Guyon's horse (121); a page has an arrow in each hand and a shield on his back (127); a knight charges with spear and raised shield (132); "Philotime" holds a massive chain pulled by many hands (150); an angel cradles exhausted Sir Guyon (155); a man with a dog's head (169); Acrasia peers through the entrapping net (181). Stratton's pictures, like Thomson's words, set a high standard.

Stories from "The Faerie Queene" *(1902)*, Arnold's Tales of Old Romance

Six volumes in Arnold's Tales of Old Romance Series offered classical (*The Wanderings of Ulysses* and *Jason and the Golden Fleece*) and Northern (*The Story of Siegfried* and *Baldur the Beautiful and Other Tales*) as well as

English (*Stories from Chaucer* and *Stories from "The Faerie Queene"*). Price for a paper cover was four pence, cloth six pence. Division into titled parts facilitated reading and lessons, but there was no pedagogical material. *Stories from "The Faerie Queene"* (1902) retold four books.[7] The only picture was "Sir Guyon meets with Mammon" (frontispiece); a knight in plate armor and a giant in chain mail seated amidst coins.

Titles indicate how Spenser's long allegorical poem was adapted. Parts for "Una and the Red Cross Knight" (5–20) were "St George," "Una and the Lion," and "The Slaying of the Dragon." Children read of the beginning of the quest, separation through Archimago's deception and the giant's imprisoning the knight, Arthur's rescue and Una's taking her champion to the House of Holiness before he fights and defeats the monster. "The Story of Sir Guyon" also had three parts: "The Quest," "The Cave of Mammon," and "The Bower of Bliss" (20–36). Meeting the baby whose parents were murdered occasioned a special message to children: "Fairies, you know, like all wise people, are very fond of babies, and think them the most interesting beings in the world. And they are quite right" (20–21). Arthur and friendship were inspiring:

> His vizor was up, and framed in the shining steel, Guyon saw the noble face, the grey eyes beneath the broad white brow, firm in their glance, yet gentle as a woman's ... [the two knights grasp hands] There was no need to speak. Each looked at the other, and from that time forward there was a tie between them stronger than that of brothers [30–31].

Although male bonding appealed especially to boys, they were left in suspense. Arthur fights; however, "If you wish to know how the besiegers were driven back and the lady delivered, you must read "The Faerie Queene" for yourselves. That story is too long to tell here" (31). The Palmer who remains with Guyon warns against drinking and a witch.

"Britomart and the Magic Mirror," seven parts, was more extended and gave girls parity (36–61): "The Picture in the Mirror," "The Sorrowful Knight," "The Palace of Enchantment," "The Mask," "The Rescue," "The Tournament," and "Sir Artegall." Pageantry marked the tournament:

> It was a gay scene. The sun flashed on the shining steel of weapons and armour. Silken flags, richly embroidered with the devices of various knights, fluttered in the breeze. Gaily dressed squires and pages hurried hither and thither, laughing and talking. Trumpets blared, horses pranced, the people cheered [55–56].

Similarly, the happy ending was of romance and fairy tale: "In a short time he asked her to be his bride. Of course, Britomart said 'Yes,' and they lived happily ever after" (61). Proper gender roles were made clear.

Spenser's multiple threads required yet greater adaptation in "Florimell and the Sea-Nymph's Son" (62–96), with eight parts: "The Rich Strand," "Marinell," "Cymoeth's Grief," "Florimell's Journey," "The Spotted Beast," "The

False Florimell," "Florimell's Adventures," and "The Happy End." Young readers met extraordinary characters and situations unburdened by allegory.

Alfonzo Gardiner, ed., St. George of Merry England, "A. L." Bright Story Readers #32 (c. 1908)

"A. L." Bright Story Readers, edited by Alfonzo Gardiner and published by Edward Arnold, was the largest series; titles listed on covers numbered over five hundred. Books were easy to handle, 5½ × 7¼ inches, large print, and line drawings for amusement. In paper covers the original price was 1½d., cloth 2½d. Prices increased; my eleventh edition in paper sold for 3d. The number of pages varied: levels P, I, and II had 48; Grades III, 64; Grades IV-VI, 94; S (Supplementary Classes), 128. Edwardian editions, usually numbered, had soft green covers with floral design. Later reprints had stronger card covers, bright red or green with linear design—an Art Deco look.

Blurbs described objectives and listed "Books for the Lower Classes":

> The books in this Series are all Classics and may be used as Additional Readers. They consist of Fairy Tales, Tales of Valour and Chivalry, and Moral Stories. Special care has been taken that the language shall be quite within the capacity of pupils of the ages stated below.[8]

Since *St. George of Merry England* (c. 1908) was #32, *The Faerie Queene* was one of the earliest titles. Gardiner prepared the text. Assignment to Grade III, suitable for ages 8 to 10, placed it in a context of chivalric romance and fairy tale. Of six titles for Grade P, ages 5 to 7, two were *The Knights of King Arthur* and *Old English Tales* (*Bevis the Strong* and *Guy of Warwick*, both influences on Spenser). Grade I, ages 6 to 8, with thirteen titles featured fairy tales (Perrault, Grimm, Andersen) as did Grade II, ages 7 to 9, expanding with Norwegian, Indian, and *Arabian Nights*. *St. George of Merry England* was the "Tale of Valour and Chivalry" for Grade III, with two added tales from *Arabian Nights* and recent authors (Kingsley, Maria Edgeworth). *The Faerie Queene* preceded Chaucer's *Canterbury Tales* that was for Grade IV, ages 9 to 11. "A. L." Bright Welcome Readers combined several titles. Special attention was given to Tales of Valour and Chivalry. Pa, 76 pages combined *Old English Tales*, *The Knights of the Round Table*, and *Tales of the Northmen*; Book IIIA, 200 pages, contained *St. George of Merry England*, *Sindbad the Sailor*, and *The Blue Bird*.

Of fifteen chapters in *St. George of Merry England* fourteen told parts of *The Faerie Queene*. "St. George of Merry England" acknowledged Spenser's poem in two paragraphs, while thirteen explained the heroic tale is more legend

Alfonzo Gardiner, editor of The "A.L." Bright Story Readers, a series with hundreds of titles, engaged children with the large title *St. George of Merry England*; in smaller print was *from Spenser's "Faerie Queene."* Children in Grade III would be more interested in England's patron saint than an Elizabethan poet. Nevertheless, they would have an early and simple introduction to a demanding canonical work.

than history. St. George "was a very good Christian man, and was always ready to help those who were in trouble, especially Christians," so that churches were named to honor him (60). Gardiner cited two English precedents: "in the sixth century, King Arthur of Britain put a picture of St. George on his banner, to show his soldiers that they were to follow the example of this great and good man" and King Henry V in 1413 established April 23rd as St. George's Day (61). A picture of a five-shilling piece, dated 1901, merited three paragraphs to describe "St. George, seated on horseback, in the act of slaying the Dragon" before stating the meaning: "It tells us that he fought against sin and wickedness, and that we are to follow his example" (62). Following this moral lesson was a patriotic one, centered on "The Union Jack" ... 'our National flag known by every boy and girl'" (62). Opposite were four drawings, crosses of St. George, St. Andrew, St. Patrick, and the Union Jack that combined the three and dated from 1801. Particular context was for "the flag of 'St. George of Merry England,'" the red cross on a white ground, used by Edward III during wars against France in the fourteenth century and worn by English Crusaders.

The final page and a quarter, printed in small type, were Notes by the Editor of the Series. Gardiner surveyed "the story of St. George, who is the special Patron of Chivalry, and the 'tutelary' or protecting Saint of England," albeit East and West Europe also venerate him (63). He cited the *Acta Sanctorum*, begun in 1643 by John Bolland, a Jesuit priest, for basic "facts" about the "distinguished soldier" martyred on April 23, 303, in the time of Diocletian. St. George's fight with the dragon was traced to the *Legenda Aurea* of Jacob of Voraigne (1230–89), translated and printed by Caxton in 1413. Gardiner summarized the ballad preserved by Bishop Thomas Percy (1729–1811) in his *Reliques*: signs at birth, rescue of Sabra from the dragon, Saracen attempts to prevent their marriage, imprisonment, escape, and return to England. Children, having read deeds of Bevis and Guy in *Old English Tales* would be delighted to discover a connection with these Middle English romances. In Grade IV *The Seven Champions of Christendom* gave St. George's story from Richard Johnson's popular early modern romance.

Notes challenged. Spenser's *Faerie Queene* differed from other versions of St. George's story; it was an allegory, explained by the poet in a letter to Sir Walter Raleigh—a knight whose story was often told to children:

> The Red Cross Knight expresses *holiness*; Una, *truth*; the Dwarf, *patience*; Archimago, *hypocrisy*; Sans-Foy, *faithlessness*; Duessa, *false religion*; the Blind Woman, *superstition*; Sans-Loy, *lawlessness*; the Lion, *honour*; Price Arthur, *virtue*, the pattern of Knighthood; and Gloriana, *glory*, as set forth in Queen Elizabeth. The Dragon is regarded in most Christian countries as symbolical of evil in an active form [64].

Final aids identified editions and exact source for the parts of Book I of *The Faerie Queene* retold "in this little book": "Our Chaps. I., II. and III. in Canto I; Chap. IV—Canto 2; Chaps. V. and VI.—Canto 3; Chaps VII. and VIII—Canto 6; Chap. IX—Canto 7; Chaps. X., XI. and XII.—Cantos 8 and 10; Chap. XIII—Cantos 11 and 12" (64).[9] Two editions of *The Faerie Queene* were recommended. Since books for lower grades did not include such elaborate Notes, it seems Gardiner wanted to assure approbation and continued interest in Spenser's great patriotic Protestant romance.[10]

Tales from the Faerie Queene *(1910), Longmans' Continuous Story Readers*

Few books for Edwardian children exceeded the success of Andrew Lang's fairy books; their popularity led to *The Red Romance Book* (1905), discussed in Chapter 3. From it two stories became the main part of *Tales from the Faerie Queene* (1910) in *Longmans' Continuous Story Readers*.[11] The title page identified *Tales* as "Adapted from The Christmas Books edited by Andrew Lang." The Junior Series, published in limp red cloth covers, were at four levels, with increasing size and price. Two Story Books for Little Folks had 32 pages at 2d. Immediately following was Junior Series, 64 pages, price 4d. Somewhat unexpectedly this was the level for *Tales from The Faerie Queene* along with *Stories from Hans Andersen*—an obvious affinity of fairy tale. *Fairy Tales from Grimm* and *Old Tales of the Homeland* were Intermediate Series, ninety-six pages, price 6d. Progression was from Andersen to Grimm and from Spenser to medieval antecedents. In the Senior Series, 144 pages, price 8d., *Stories from the Arabian Nights* furthered Orientalism, while *A Book of Heroes* and *Two Heroines* distinguished gender.

Comparison of *The Red Romance Book* and *Tales from The Faerie Queene* shows changes made for school use.[12] In *The Red Book* "Una and the Lion" and "How the Red Cross Knight Slew the Dragon" took twenty-seven pages with small print; in *Tales*, they filled forty-six pages of large print. Adaptation was dividing long paragraphs into several short ones, and occasional changes in grammar or vocabulary. Typical were revisions in the opening episodes:

"Let us go forth at once," she cried gaily, and sprang into her saddle. The knight hastily fastened on his armour, and placing a blood-red cross upon his breast, swung himself on to his horse's back. And so they rode over the plain, a trusty dwarf following far behind, and a snow-white lamb, held by a golden cord, trotting by Una's side [94–95].

"Let us go forth at once," she cried gaily, springing into her saddle. The knight hastily fastened on his armour, and placing a blood-red cross upon his breast, swung himself on to his horse's back.

> And so they rode over the plain. Behind them rode a trusty dwarf, and a snow-white lamb, held by a golden cord, trotted by Una's side [7–8].

Abbreviations were elementary: "the beauty of the flowers and the sweet scent of the fruit" (95) became "the beauty of the sweet-smelling flowers" (8); the knight fought "bravely" rather than "valiantly" (96). Names were modified: Sansjoy was "Saracen" (22), not "Paynim" (105), while "the cursed wight" Despair (120) became "a wretch" (42). Often word order was simplified: "The perils of this place I better know than you" (95) was changed to "'I know the perils of this place better than you,'" and five verse lines of description were dropped (9). "Fain would they now leave the dreadful wood ..." (96) became "Both Una and the knight now longed to leave the dreadful wood ..." (10). Archaic syntax and language were changed: from "The maiden was herself wandering distraught, seated on her 'unhastie beast,' when with a fearful roar a lion rushed out from a thicket with eyes glaring and teeth gleaming, seeking to devour his prey" (101) to "Poor Una was wandering along, seated on her 'unhastie beast,' when with fearful roar, a lion with glaring eyes and gleaming teeth, rushed from a thicket upon her" (16).

Elaborations were deleted; for example, "Archimago, the professor of lore which could read the secrets of men's hearts" (96). When Una meets the Red Cross Knight, released from the giant's prison by Arthur, the original gave her dialogue: "'Welcome,' she said, 'welcome in weal or woe. Your presence I have lacked for many a day'" (117). The junior reader minimized the cost of a knight's misadventures: "She welcomed him warmly, and told him how much she had missed his company" (37). That "men love not to speak of their sorrows" (117) was softened to "men do not like to speak of their sorrows" (37). Changes to the dragon slaying were minor: "instantly" (124) became "at once" (47); the dragon swooped down "suddenly" as well as "swiftly" (125 and 47). There was no final plot to prevent betrothal of the hero and heroine.

This reader expanded romance as love story with J. C. Allen's "The Story of Britomart and Artegal," 13½ pages, another balancing of gender. Although a first description indicated physical beauty, attention quickly went to moral character:

> Her golden hair reached down to her feet, and her brow was as white as snow. Yet this maiden's mind was so full of high, chivalrous thoughts, that she did not even know that she was beautiful, or if she knew, she never thought very much about it. She spent her time engaged in duties that she set herself. These duties were often the care of those who were weak or sick or in trouble [51–52].

When Artegal stripped off "his adversary's face-piece" and exposed Britomart's face, "he beheld, not what he expected to see, the lined, scarred visage of a warrior—but the delicate features of a maiden whose countenance shone like the ruddy morn. Around her, her hair, loosened from its band, fell like a golden shower upon her armour" (61). Both passages stressed flowing golden hair—'woman's crowning glory.' Particularly intense was Britomart's cumulative reaction: she was "thoroughly vexed" and would continue fighting. However, when meeting "her worst trial ... in a moment her courage failed her" (62). Then "to hide her confusion ... she strove to speak harsh, imperious words, but her lips refused to utter them" (62–63). Old Glaucé's "outspoken" intervention "caused greater discomfort to Britomart than ever. Nothing could ever enable her to overcome her feelings of shame and confusion" (63). This depicted maidenly modesty and cautioned against speaking too boldly— it may resolve a quandary, but not without causing distress.

Allen recounted Britomart's chivalric successes, but repeatedly attributed them to her "magic" spear. Moreover, he made perfectly clear what a young woman most desires. Looking at the knight in the mirror the worthy maiden is led "to wonder who will come to claim her as his wife. For, you see, the fair Britomart, in her inmost secret heart, did hope that some day she should have a gallant knight to care for her; one whom she could look up to, and in her turn take care of, as good wives do their husbands" (52). Along with such stereotyping Allen identified Britomart's "task in life to *rescue* Artegal from Faerieland," where he dwelt even though he was not a fairy but "stolen from his cradle when a child" (italics mine 54). Later in the recognition scene she acknowledges he is "the very knight whom she has loved, and set out to *rescue* from Faerieland" (italics mine 62). Offsetting this emphasis were familiar references: "Riding about from place to place, as knights did in those days, Britomart was not long in meeting adventures. Helped by her magic spear, she performed many doughty deeds" (56); "Many were the wounds given that day, and many were the shivered spears, broken swords, and riderless horses upon the field" (58). Here was stirring chivalry. Allen distinguished qualities by describing their deficit. Sir Scudamour failed because "he spoke arrogantly to the flames, and they burned the more fiercely and scorched him instead of letting him through. Thus did his own proud passions prevent the knight from vanquishing them" (57). Yet more indefensible was his ingratitude—and paranoia. Impatience not only leads him to forget "what a chivalrous act it was of Britomart's to offer her services at all, he let the idea run away with him that Britomart had run off with his wife" (57).

Allen's final judgment was a paean to marriage. For Britomart and Artegal Merlin's prophecy proved true:

> but we do not know the remainder of the story, because the poet Spenser died before he finished the poem that would have told us. No doubt, though, Britomart and Argegal, and the faithful though outspoken Glaucé, returned to Cambria, where Britomart and Artegal

were married, because Merlin prophesied they would. Whether they became King and Queen of Cambria and Cornwall or not does not matter so much. Their being married would have made them as happy as it is possible for human beings to be [64].

Allen answered the child's ubiquitous question "What happened next?" but added wryly: "For the same reason we do not know if the headstrong knight, Sir Scudamour, ever found the Lady Amoret. Perhaps Britomart and Artegal advised him to go and see Merlin" (64).

Although the title page did not identify H. J. Ford, Longmans' Continuous Reader included his signed illustrations from *The Red Romance Book*. All black-and-white pictures were repeated, two half-pages and four full-pages. The color frontispiece was not "The End of the Dragon" but "Una and the Lion" that featured a woman and a landscape with appealing animals (lion, (donkey, and lamb). Curiously the last picture "In the Cave of Despair" was frightening, not the inspiring victory of England's patron saint.

While the typical way to introduce *The Faerie Queene* to children was prose stories with engaging pictures, presenting his poetry—albeit modern-

H(enry) J. Ford famously illustrated Andrew Lang's books, collections of fairy tales and also romances. Ford's pre–Raphaelite use of brilliant color and attention to details of nature made his picture of Una unforgettable. She rides her donkey and leads her lamb, as the faithful lion walks beside them. First seen in *The Red Romance Book* (1905) the illustration was the frontispiece of a schoolbook *Tales from the Fairy Queen* (1910) in Longmans' Continuous Story Readers. The landscape is inviting, albeit twisted trees introduce some stress. The viewer shares the child's gaze at this extraordinary group.

ized—was desirable. Two significant samplings were the work of editors with different points of view, an American woman and a British man.

Mary E. Litchfield, Spenser's Britomart: From Books III, IV, and V *(1896)*

Mary E. Litchfield retold *Nine Stories from Norse Mythology* (1890) before editing a number of books for children. Much of her attention was to eighteenth-century English writers: *Sir Roger de Coverley Papers from The Spectator* (1899) and *Selections from English Poets* (1901). Recognizing poetry was closely related to music, she directed attention to Spenser, esteemed for the musicality of his verse. *Spenser's Britomart: From Books III, IV, and V* (1896) required careful selection.[13] That a woman was the unifying and honored knight, corrected the traditional emphasis in Spenser readers.

> Except to the special student of literature, Britomart, the most charming of Spenser's heroines, is almost unknown. Indeed, she has for long years been wandering in the mazes of the poet's fairy-land, well-nigh lost to view. And yet no story in the Faery Queene is so romantic and none has such a strong human interest as that which tells of the "lady knight." As we read of her adventures we are reminded of Rosalind in the forest of Arden. In this little book the scattered portions of Spenser's interesting narrative have been taken out and re-united [iii].

Reference to *As You Like It* linked Spenser with Shakespeare as champions of women, although he lacked Shakespeare's dramatic power, passion, and capacity to "touch those chords that awaken an echo in the deepest recesses of the human heart." Spenser was a "genius," yet he "has, with the exception of Britomart, created no living character; and on occasions Britomart, even, becomes shadowy, unsubstantial" (xx).

Litchfield defended her approach: "to take out and re-unite scattered portions would be an evident impertinence" for Dante and Milton, but was "justifiable" for Spenser, "a genius whose constructive ability did not enable him to make of a large poem an artistic whole" (iii). She used the best editions and authorities to create one with modern spelling yet always sensitive to Spenser's language. One pedagogical decision was to place needed notes at the bottom of the page to make study "a delight rather than a task." Another reassured: "Except for a few suggestions, there has been no attempt at tracing the allegory" (iv). Again a book for young people was a pleasing narrative, not religious argument.

Nevertheless, in her substantial Introduction Litchfield stressed the significance of religion in the sixteenth century, particularly translation of the Bible:

> In the province of religion old barriers were swept aside and new forces were given full play. ... developing the moral and religious sentiment of the nation. ... In a few years the Bible, known already through the teachings of the clergy, became the one book of the mass of the people; ... More than Homer to the Greek was the Bible to the Englishman; for from it he gained that moral strength, that realization of his individual worth as the child of God, which made him battle with a stout heart against the dreaded power of Catholic Spain [vi–vii].

The Bible's language, an English readily understood, made possible Elizabethan literature "not of a class, but of a nation" (vii). Litchfield contextualized religion in "an age of inquiry" in science, classical learning, and exploration. She also noted that in the New World England's power of conquest and colonization was an awakening of "the spirit of the Vikings" (viii). While Spenser sometimes used language arbitrarily, his vocabulary was "more Germanic than that of any other great English poet" (xxv). This affirmed Victorian and Edwardian claims for a Northern heritage.

Litchfield imagined the variety of Spenser's boyhood experiences in a vibrant "strange London of the 16th century, with its filth and its splendor, its Puritanism and its license, its hatred of popery and its staunch loyalty to the queen,—above all, with its daring hopes and its worldwide interests" (xi). Among a variety of encounters, including plays, she identified "above all, the shows!—processions, pageants, masks, mummeries, morality plays; every kind of spectacle that could delight. ... *Mask of Cupid* that Britomart witnesses in Busirane's castle is only a court mask of Spenser's time that has found its way into fairy-land" (xii). Recognizing public encounters along with the influence of books, Litchfield named Greek, "Italian poems, French romances, and Spanish tales," as well as Geoffrey of Monmouth and *Morte d'Arthur*." Nevertheless,

> With these romantic tales were mingled Scripture narratives; and back of all,—a dark, deep undercurrent,—whispers of popish plots and stories of Spanish cruelty. It is no wonder that the *Faery Queene* is at the first glance a strange medley; that Christian knights and fair ladies as they wander in Spenser's fairy-land meet with sorcerers and dragons, with Saracens and Amazons; while the vices and virtues personified live on terms of intimacy with the thinly disguised characters of the poet's own time [xii–xiii].

Its complex and rich diversity was analogous to the age, a mixture of great learning and daily struggles. Litchfield, who cited the view that Spenser was, after Milton, the most learned of English poets, judged him "peculiarly representative of his own age in its higher aspects" (xxi), the poet of beauty with artistic style and an inventive stanza.

Her view of Ireland was complicated: "peopled by a barbarous, turbulent people—Catholics for the most part—who were, for sufficiently good reasons, bitterly opposed to English rule" (xvi). Exile was painful; nevertheless, Ireland suited Spenser's genius as a place where he "could transform the scenes of violence and disorder, whose echoes reached him, into glorious knightly achievements, and could people the wild solitude of Kilcolman with the varied creations of his fertile imagination" (xvii). Although Lord Grey was an over zealous civil servant, commendation of him (Artegall and in *View of the Present State of Ireland*) validated Spenser's "most admirable trait ... his chivalric constancy in friendship" (xviii). Litchfield quoted his letter to Raleigh, a further mark of friendship and essential to understanding *The Faerie Queene*. Her incisive criticism enlivened biography, lists of works read and written, and bibliography.

Confident that the "careful student" would read the whole *Faerie Queene*, she directed her book to

> the general student of English literature ... especially calculated to arouse his interest and to stimulate him to further study of the poet. The poem has a peculiar value in connection with the study of the institutions of Chivalry: and on this account it may be classed with Chaucer's *Knightes Tale*, with Scott's romantic poems, and with Tennyson's *Idylls of the King*" [xxiv].

Reading *The Faerie Queene* in the tradition of great romances, Litchfield placed it in context of the Reformation without urging Puritanism or allegory.

Arthur Burrell, ed. Selections from The Faerie Queene *(1914)*

Selections from The Faerie Queene (1914), English Literature for Schools Series, edited by Arthur Burrell, was one of fifty volumes intended for junior and senior forms. The introduction acknowledged Spenser's poem "for some reason, is not a favourite with the young." Burrell, who compared Spenser with Chaucer, found the former wrote "more difficult stories ... infinitely more learned and academic."[14] Professing not to understand why Spenser is called the Poets' poet, he preferred "the painters' poet" and quoted a few lines "chosen almost haphazard" that showed a "picturing-power" deemed superior to Chaucer and Tennyson (5–6). Moreover, Spenser's poetry was accompanied by "a consistent melody ... the music of earth" in the "great, rolling, thunderous stanza" he invented. Burrell, who noted Spenser's wisdom and complicated allegory that selections do not show, wanted boys and girls to feel an aesthetic response to image and sound even if unable to express it in words. Of fourteen selections, nine came from Book I; Guyon, Britomart, and Calidore each had one, and two were about nature.

Minna Steele Smith, Stories from Spenser *(1919)*

Intended for older children, Minna Steele Smith's *Stories from Spenser* (1919) combined prose paraphrase with quoted verse and pedagogical material.[15] Smith, a Fellow of Newnham College, translated Friedrich Kauffman's *Northern Mythology* (1903) and Goethe's *Poetry and Truth from My Own Life* (1908). Her preface to *Stories from Spenser* compared him with Chaucer, contrasting her efforts with those of Miss Macaulay's *Stories from Chaucer* in the series and defining her own process. *The Faerie Queene* was

> too long for one volume, and lacks the unity of structure which the drama of the pilgrimage gives to *The Canterbury Tales*, but language in modernized spelling and with occasional notes offers little difficulty to readers to-day. Short passages of Spenser's verse have, therefore, been inserted at frequent intervals in the prose paraphrase in order that young readers may be made familiar with the music and cadences of Spenser's poetry. Much, too, of Spenser's vocabulary and diction has been retained with a view to preserving as many characteristics of his style as was compatible with an abbreviated prose rendering of the stories. It is hoped that this little book may prove attractive to make its readers wish one day to read the original [v].

Acknowledging limitations of Spenser's narrative, Smith stressed his verse. Pedagogical aids were a List of Proper Names (182), Notes to explain words and allegory (183–202), and two appendices. "Appendix I The Legend of St. George" contained a summary and a quotation from Caxton's translation of *The Golden Legend* (179–181). "Appendix II Prince Arthur" defined him as a "living prototype"—sometimes Leicester and sometimes Sidney, both friends and patrons of Spenser. Yet Arthur as embodiment of all virtues was less real than characters as a single virtue (181).

A sample of Smith's style was the introduction of Sir Guyon:

> Sir Guyon was an elfin knight, held in high repute in his native Fairyland for deeds of valour. He was clad in armour from head to foot; in bearing he was comely and upright; his looks were modest and temperate, yet so stern as to strike terror to the heart of any foe. The aged palmer by his side was robed in black and steadied his faltering steps with a staff. Yet it was he who led the way, while the rider curbed his steed and taught it to match its pace to that of his venerable guide [81].

Although spare in description, Smith contrasted physical strength and beauty of a knight in shining armor with the physically feeble but morally strong palmer. Sir Guyon's deference is courteous but also humble.

Smith managed Spenser's diffuseness with transitions typical of romances: "Now it chanced one day" (84); "One night she was overtaken by a heavy storm of rain and hail not far from a castle" (149); "One day as Sir Scudamour was riding on his way he espied an armed knight …" (172). Or summary preceded an encounter:

Prince Arthur and Sir Guyon, accompanied by his palmer, were traveling together through many countries, seeking to win glory. On their way they achieved many hard adventures in which they gave aid to the weak and redressed the wrongs of such as were oppressed. At last as they rode across an open plain they spied a knight pricking toward them [131–132].

Stories from Spenser were: "The Story of the Knight of the Red Cross or Holiness" (11–80), "The Story of Sir Guyon or Temperance" (81–130), and "The Story of Britomart" (131–178), which paraphrased Book III and Satyrane's tournament in Book IV. Smith ended with Spenser's ship imagery that acknowledged incompleteness: "Were long to tell; therefore I here will stay / Until another tide that I it finish may" (178).

Eight illustrations were on glossy paper. Three were contemporary: Spenser's portrait at Pembroke College, Cambridge (frontispiece), a print of Pembroke College (facing 7), and a woodcut of St. George and the Dragon from *The Faerie Queene* (1596), one of four pictures for the most famous episode. Two were English paintings. *Una and the Red Cross Knight* by G. F. Watts (1877–1904) had fullest gloss: "one of the greatest Victorian painters, some 250 pictures, mostly given to native portraits and allegorical pictures. He also selected a limited number of subjects from Tennyson, Shakespeare, Dante, and Spenser. Pictures that owed their origin to *The Faerie Queene* are *Una and the Red Cross Knight* and *Britomart*." While today honored for his Symbolist paintings, Watts also practiced nineteenth-century painting as storytelling. Very different was No. XXXVI. *Liber Studium* by J. M. W. Turner (1775–1831), from *The Faerie Queene,* though the episode was not obvious; Smith thought the scene was the cave of Despair. Continental artists contributed: *St. George's Fight with the Dragon* by Carpaccio (c.1450–1522), an Italian Renaissance painter; and French illuminated manuscripts, "A Medieval Garden" from *Roman de la Rose*, dating from c. 1500 (facing 125) and "A Tournament" (fifteenth-century). A woodcut and illuminations could prompt lessons about making of the book, from scribe to printer; and a Cambridge college might lead to a lesson about attending university—both topics found in Edwardian schoolbooks.

M(ary) Sturt and E(llen) C. Oaken, The Knights of The Faerie Queene *(1924)*

Sir A. T. Quiller Couch (1863–1944) edited The Kings Treasuries of Literature Series as one of his diverse efforts to further English Studies and inspire patriotism informed by Liberalism. M(ary) Sturt (b.1896) and E(llen) C(atherine) Oakden co-authored three collections: #94 *The Canterbury Pil-*

grims: *Being Chaucer's Canterbury Tales Retold for Children* (1923), #115 *The Knights of The Faerie Queene: Tales Retold from Spenser* (1924), and #159 *Minstrel Tales* (1928).[16] A brief introduction to *The Knights* noted *The Faerie Queene* was an allegory and gave a few political identifications, less crucial than "lessons in morals." The letter to Raleigh explained purpose, virtues represented by knights who are tested and Arthur as ideal knight:

> We must therefore read the *Faerie Queene* with two things in mind—the story that Spenser tells, and the meaning he hides under his fictions of brave knights and lovely ladies who roam the enchanting valleys and woods of Faerie Land.[17]

"Edmund Spenser," the frontispiece, was a sketch framed like the facing title page with swirling leaves interspersed with flowers; outer borders included a sword; below a chalice was set against a heart and flames with a dove in radiance above it.

The Knights of the Faerie Queene had four parts, with titled sections: "Sir George, The Knight of Holiness and the Red Cross," twelve sections; "Sir Guyon, The Knight of Temperance," ten; "Britomart and Sir Artegal, The Champions of Chastity and Justice," nine; and "Sir Calidore, The Knight of Courtesy," five. "The Feast at the Court of Gloriana, the Faerie Queene" established context and balanced an imaginative speculation of "How the 'Faerie Queene' Might Have Ended." Sturt and Oakden's opening combined chivalry and fairy tale:

> Long, long ago, the Realm of Faerie was ruled by Gloriana, the most beautiful queen the world has ever known. Her hair was golden, like the sun's rays, and glowed with light as she moved. Her limbs were white and of perfect form, her bearing proclaimed her queenliness of soul and her power to command men's love and devotion. She was served by the bravest knights that legend and history can tell of. Throughout her realm her name was reverenced. Many were the deeds of chivalry done in her honour, for there were many enemies to fight. The Queen desired that her land should be freed from all evil monsters which attacked men's bodies and sullied their souls, and at the time of which I write, these monsters still flourished and caused great suffering [9].

Elimination of classical allusions and chronicles of British ancestry fostered fairy tale.

Depiction of evil was graphic, with details added. Archimago, "strong in evil and eager to destroy men's souls," draws a magic circle on the ground with his wand and summons evil spirits "by every dreadful name of hell.... God and heaven he cursed" (19-20). In Lucifera's pageant of six chief servants Lechery is Uncleanness (25); Orgoglio is Giant Proud-heart (36). The dragon's flames scorch Sir George:

> His armour grew red-hot. He gasped for air. Faint and weary, almost hopeless, with strength spent, he prayed for death. The dragon saw his chance. He raised his tail and, striking with all his might, he felled Sir George to the ground.

> Now, by the greatest good fortune, and the infinite mercy of God, it befell that behind the knight there sprang a magic fountain, called the Well of Life [57].

Simple sentence structure and spare language heightened the moment. An added reference to God's mercy pointed moral meaning. Una praises and would thank her knight. "But Sir George was too amazed to answer. To him it seemed that power other than his own had worked there, and strength greater than man's had achieved the victory" (60). Spenser's Una's praised God (I.xi.55), an example of Sturt and Oakden's mitigating women's role.

"Sir Guyon, the Knight of Temperance" began on the second day of Gloriana's feast, when the Palmer requested a knight to destroy Acrasia. The queen responds it is harder to overcome that which is attractive than horrible monsters, a point reiterated after Guyon destroyed the Bower of Bliss: "His task was achieved, but who can tell whether his heart was altogether joyful that he had been called upon to destroy so much beauty?" (110). Since children can be put out by difficult names, Pyrocles and Cymocles were renamed Firebrand and Whirlwind (76). Guyon is merciful to the former, but his Saracen brother refuses Arthur's "bounteous thought." Offered pardon and life if he will renounce his false faith, the pagan answers, "'Fool, ... I refuse thy grace. Use thy good fortune. I am tired of life. Come, Death'" (93–94). Here "grace"— Arthur's word to denote religion—replaced "gift" (II.viii.52). Instead of protracted references to classical figures in hell there was Pilate, "the falsest judge on earth, who by unrighteous judgment delivered up to death the Lord of Truth" and tried unsuccessfully to wash his hands (87).

"Britomart & Artegall, the Champions of Chastity and Justice" simplified and combined parts of Books III, IV, and V. Much was eliminated, most obviously Amoret and Florimell and Marinell. Britomart's story began with a paraphrase (III.ii.1–3) to explain female prowess:

> Do not wonder that a maiden was able to perform such deeds as did Britomart. I find it written in antique history that women long ago were wont to hold sway in martial exploits, and in every contest bore away the garland, until men growing jealous of their sway, made laws to curb their liberty. Then women gave their thought to politics, in which they excel now as they did in arms before. Of war-like women Britomart was the chief, among statesmen our Queen Elizabeth stands foremost [116].

Sturt and Oakden's Britomart is more a woman in love than a bored young woman who enjoys adventure and action as much as seeking her love. There was no tourney in which Sir Artegall and Britomart first fight; furthermore, recognition was briefly told, as was their betrothal (124–126). The ending commented on Talus's "strange looks and armour ... made of iron, and none may wound nor dismay him. With that iron flail he bears on his shoulder he can winnow to chaff all wrong-doers" (127).

More space went to Sir Artegall's deeds of arms. Destruction of Tyranny, a Saracen knight, on the bridge was a thrilling, gory episode: "As the Saracen climbed up on the land Sir Artegall from behind with a single sweep of his sword cut off his head. The head fell and the teeth gnashed at the ground, but the body slipped back into the river and was carried away" (129). Talus inside the castle "cut off her [Bribery] hands and feet and cast her body into the river to be borne away to sea. ... broke down all the castle and burnt up the riches in it" (131). Difference came in confronting the charlatan giant who dupes the mob with his scales. Sir Artegall reasons against such folly, but Talus casts down the giant who tried to drive out Truth. When the people rush Sir Artegall, he deliberates; unhesitatingly Talus uses his flail. Justice prevailed through skilled argument to settle brothers' dispute over land and treasure.

Britomart reentered after Radigund, queen of the Amazons, made Artegall prisoner because in pity he ceased their combat—a costly adherence to chivalric ideals of gender. Britomart avows, "I fight but by the rules of chivalry," denies Radigund's conditions, fights bravely, and kills this captor of men (143). Rescued and refreshed, Sir Artegall resumes his quest to save Irena. With Arthur he dispatches two Saracens, enlists Mercilla's help to draw Guile from his cave, and relies on Talus to destroy the shape-changing creature. Duessa's trial at Mercilla's court exemplified "mercy cannot stay justice" (150-151). A single paragraph explained Prince Arthur undertakes restoration of Belge's throne. Finally Sir Artegall faced giant Grantorto, who "bore a poleaxe heavy and strong, and on his head was a cap of rusty iron, while a stout suit of iron plate encompassed his body" (154). Returning home, he meets hags, Envy and Slander, and is bitten by the Blatant Beast, but hurries to lady Britomart.

"Sir Calidore, The Knight of Courtesy" most resembled the modern gentleman:

> courteous ... beloved by all for his gentleness of spirit: his charming manners and gracious speech stole all hearts away. Yet he was no carpet knight, but a man robust and tall, and renowned in fight. He loathed all deceit and flattery, and long had loved and practiced steadfast truth and simple honesty [157].

He displays these qualities in several episodes—challenge and correction of Sir Crudor, acceptance of youth Tristram as squire, defense of Priscilla ("'No true knight hesitates to guard a woman who needs his help,'" 168)—before encountering the Blatant Beast that seized Serena. Although Sir Calidore knows the "loathsome beast" is the object of his quest, he is attracted to shepherds' life and beautiful Pastorella and "enchanted" by Melibee's anti-court sentiments and contentment (173). In fact, nowhere is safe: Coridon is jealous, and brigands capture and kill those who live a pastoral life. Sir Calidore ensures its survival by providing resources to Corridon. Yet Pastorella is restored to the courtly position of her birth.

Still disturbing was the Blatant Beast:

> ... in every land ruin and misery told of the monster's passage. Sir Calidore's heart grew fierce at what he saw. Monasteries had been despoiled, cloisters broken down and books destroyed. The beast had not spared the most sacred objects. In the churches it had befouled the altars, broken windows and images, torn up the chancel pavements, and thrown down desks and pulpits. All beautiful things bore the mark of this most vile monster [185].

This paraphrase (VI.xii.23–25) returned attention to religion. Unique combat followed; Sir Calidore can only muzzle the beast. After his death, "alas, it broke its chain and roamed the world again, wreaking even more mischief among men than it had done before." Courtesy is necessary if children are to be educated; their animal spirits are hard to muzzle. Sturt and Oakden's "How the 'Faerie Queene' Might Have Ended" provided a happy conclusion; knights return to Gloriana's court with their ladies and stories of chivalric achievement. Sir George brings Prince Arthur, who is overcome with joy to be enthroned beside the lady of his dreams: "Thus in joy and mirth ends the Faerie Queene, and so should all stories end in which men and women strive truly for the right" (191).

Graded Schoolbooks

Henrietta Christian Wright, Children's Stories in English Literature *(1890)*

Thomas Nelson listed Henrietta Christian Wright's comprehensive *Children's Stories in English Literature* (1890) with "Classic Stories Simply Told"— Mary Seymour's *Chaucer's Stories Simply Told* and Charles Henry Hanson's *The Siege of Troy and the Wanderings of Ulysses, The Wanderings of Æneas and the Founding of Rome*, and *Stories of the Days of King Arthur*. English writers ranked with classical Homer and Virgil. Chapters were arranged chronologically from "I. The Old British Songs" to "XV. The Rise of the Drama."[18] Wright (1854–1899) provided historical contexts and biographical information but gave greater space to stories. The only illustration was a frontispiece engraving—three Viking ships with a caption from Longfellow. Although "The Rise of the Drama" discussed pre-Shakespearean, with Christopher Marlowe as a "not unworthy name near Shakespeare" (345), medieval literature was most apposite. Old British and Saxon songs (Taliesin, Beowulf) presented imaginative adventures; other Anglo-Saxon writers established a religious context, furthered by Langland and Wickliffe, when romances flourished. Early modern Spenser (263–298) and Sidney (299–320) were a culmination of medieval traditions of romance and chivalry. "At his own request he [Spenser] was buried in Westminster, near Chaucer" (249).

In "XIII. Edmund Spenser and The Faery Queene" Wright's measured view of Elizabethan England explained inspiring contexts:

> During all these changes Spenser had been studying the condition of England, its glory and its shame, and forming a plan of a great work which should contain some remedy for the evils that beset his country, and made it, even in that time of power and success, deserving of the reproach of earnest men. Thinking that there is no teacher so powerful as a good example, he resolved to write a poem in which the hero should be a pattern of Englishmen, possessed of courage, courtesy, honour, and all true manliness: and his story, he thought, might influence his readers to strive for noble things, and not to be content with ignoble aims. Spenser thought it wise to put his message to his fellow-men in the form of a fairy tale, for, however men may be occupied, they are always ready to listen to fairy tales. The poem was called *The Faëry Queene*, and this is the story:—[228].

Spenser's inspiration was highly moral, his purpose to change men's attitudes and behavior. Wright declared the efficacy of fairy tales; archetypal story is more effective than didactic assertions.

Book I included allegorical names and statement of moral purpose—"teach men to be faithful to their trust and to live righteously" (272–285). Yet story was thrilling: "a dreadful roaring ... the dragon, stretched along the side of a hill, his scaly form glittering in the sun, and his eyes gleaming with the horrid light of hate; and in a few moments he spread his wings and came swiftly ... (232). A paragraph reported how a "magic well" and "stream of healing balm" restored St. George after the first and second days. With strength recovered on the third day he

> beset the dragon so vigorously and courageously that the monster thought it best to end the fray at once, and opening his horrid jaws, advanced toward the Red-Cross Knight, intending to swallow him. But St. George took advantage of the manner of attack to thrust his faithful sword into the dragon's mouth with such might that the life-blood came rushing out in deadly streams, and sinking back, the monster soon breathed his last [238].

One paragraph reported rejoicing and betrothal.

Book II offered several memorable moments like Sir Guyon with the dead mother and her bloody babe (240). Predictably a children's story handled human desires discreetly: "In his journey he also met with many temptations. Once he was taken to the centre of the earth, where dwelt the god Mammon" (241). Arthur rescues Guyon in a single sentence. Furthermore, children did not read of Lucifera's chariot pulled by the Seven Deadly Sins. As a corollary "after a visit to the Castle of Temperance, Sir Guyon with the palmer parted from Prince Arthur." A paragraph enumerated their journey on the "Idle Lake" past the "Wandering Island," threatening creatures ("hydras and sea satyrs and other dreadful monsters"), and enticing songs at the "Bay of Mermaids" (241). Acrasia is bound and her palace left desolate. "And then Sir Guyon departed, having achieved his adventure gloriously, as became such a noble knight" (242).

The final adventure required most selection: "In the third book we have the story of the beautiful heroine Britomart" (242-243). Wright described the vision of Artegal in Merlin's magic mirror; even in childhood his "face was of noble purpose." While her nurse Glauce becomes Britomart's squire, Artegal is better equipped. Astrea provided "Chrysaor, the most perfect sword in the world, garnished with gold, and of such temper that it could cleave any armour. And she gave him as his companion the sturdy Talus who carried an iron brand, and was often called the Lion-man" (246). Summaries enhanced: "Artegal and Britomart had many strange adventures before they met, but they both came at last to a grand tournament.... Here were all the most famous knights of Fairy Land, who all did such wondrous deeds" (247); recognition and betrothal were quick. "The story of Britomart and Artegal, with many other incidents thrown in, occupies the third, fourth, and fifth books of *The Faëry Queene*, and shows the triumph of Purity, Friendship, and Justice" (249).

Spenser "is sometimes called the 'poets' poet' because his works are more cared for by poets than by the general reader. He has been the inspiration for some of the greatest writing in English literature, and the greatest poets of succeeding ages have delighted in calling him master" (249). Wright knew *The Faërie Queene* was not an easy read but urged Spenser's rank in the literary canon chosen by adults made him worthy of children's efforts. Sidney— who "performed such acts of bravery and heroism as to well sustain his reputation as the finest knight in England" admired even by the enemy— gave credence to Gloriana's admirable chivalric knights (313).

C. Linklater Thomson, A First Book in English Literature *(1906)*

In addition to *Tales from The Faerie Queene* (1902) discussed above, C(lara) Linklater Thomson also wrote *A First Book in English Literature* (1906); Spenser was in *Part III Lyndsay to Bacon*.[19] Thomson kept a high standard; She apologized for the delay of *Part III*: to condense large works and to write gracefully took time. Lack of space even though Part III was larger meant no book lists and questions. "Chapter VIII Edmund Spenser" was one of the longest (169–202). Evaluations were measured, full of praise but discriminating and arguing vast difference in effectiveness between Books I and II and later ones. Opening praise, perhaps the fullest advocacy of Protestantism, united religion and patriotism:

> In the great house of Elizabethan literature there are many mansions, and the one ruled by Edmund Spenser is, in some respects, the most exquisite of all. No Englishman of his time appreciated more keenly the fair and lovely things of other lands, yet none could be more patriotic or more characteristically English both in sentiment and idea. Possessing to the full the intense delight in beauty which was stimulated by the Renaissance, and with a joy in physical perfection that in another man might have developed into sensuousness, he had the self-control of the Puritan, the burning enthusiasm for righteousness of a Latimer, and to him good art and good morality were one and indivisible. "Our sage and serious poet Spenser," said Milton, "whom I dare to be known to think a better teacher than Socrates or Aquinas, describing true temptation under the person of Guyon, brings him in with his Palmer through the Cave of Mammon and the Bower of Earthly Bliss, that he might see and know and yet abstain" [169].

Thomson identified the challenge facing an English Protestant poet who favored native romances but needed to avoid Catholic associations—Italian expansions by Ariosto and Tasso as well as English medieval—to create an early modern romance. Citing Milton's praise supported Puritanism not as didactic repression but as vibrant experience informed by refined morality.

After a brief biographical survey, Thomson described *The Shepheardes Calendar* as quintessentially English "in subject matter, as well as language," sharing "the moralizing tendency of so much of our poetry" (171). Shepherds lament and tell edifying stories, including three that discuss "some of the burning religious questions of the day" (172). Spenser's role as advocate for Protestantism was well established before *The Faerie Queene*. Acknowledging the first three books depended upon Sir Walter Raleigh's advice and sympathy, she indicated the magnitude of Spenser's scheme: twelve books to be followed by an additional twelve but only six finished, a fourth of the projected plan. There was a paradox in reception: "Never was any book more enthusiastically received," yet Spenser received only fifty pounds (176).

Thomson clarified success and limitations: "the first two books are well planned, and present a connected and easily intelligible allegory, although both narratives proceed rather too slowly, and are delayed by minute descriptions of fights similar to those which are familiar in the 'Morte d'Arthur'" (178). Using the letter to Raleigh, she summarized Book I before judging:

> The second book, which tells the story of Sir Guyon, is less well constructed than the first, and the narrative is interrupted by episodes (such as that of Belphoebe, given on p. 103)

which has no direct bearing on the main story. But in some respects it excels the first, and some magnificent descriptions, among which may be mentioned those of the Cave of Mammon and the Bower of Bliss, are among the most famous passages in Spenser's works [180].

Thomson made incisive critical distinctions. Allegory was "well carried out" in Book I and Book II, but Book I was much preferred with Red Cross Knight / St. George who represented Holiness. Yet Thomson praised Sir Guyon's Temperance more, Book II's "strife of man with temptations of excess" rather than Book I's "struggle of the human soul" (180–181). Evaluation of subsequent books was stringent: "But after this both the allegory and the narrative languish; the story is difficult to follow, the interest is not sustained, and though the latter part of the poem contains many fine isolated passages, it cannot compare in beauty with the first two books" (181). Yet Thomson generously suggested this change was a result of Spenser's having less leisure to refine his poem.

A strong case for Spenser's poetic language—"the poets' poet"—was coupled with difficulty of keeping the story straight. Thomson tried to resolve the dilemma:

> The success of "The Faerie Queene" is easily explained. In the first place, the story itself is interesting. Spenser, though a child of the Renaissance, was yet sufficiently in touch with the medieval world to treat seriously the old stories of knight errantry, which, even if they went out of fashion for a time, never quite lost their popularity with the general public. But perhaps even he would not have rendered them attractive to the educated English men of his time had he not made them the vehicle of an allegory on some of the most interesting questions of his days. For, besides the religious allegory, which appealed so strongly to men absorbed in theological disputes, there is a less clearly defined political allegory.
>
> Then the poem is steeped in the learning of the Renaissance, and Spenser's familiarity with Greek, Latin, Italian, and French authors is shown on every page [181–182].

The vogue for medieval romances was changing, but they still inspired Spenser, albeit learning informed moral virtue as the salient quality.

What chiefly endeared *The Faerie Queene* "to later readers was its beauty of both the subject and expression." Thomson lauded the role of literature to inspire:

> Its high moral tone, its appeal to the better side of human nature, and the lofty ideal of conduct which it holds up, have been a support and stimulant to many thousands of men and women in their journey through the perils and difficulties of life; no one can rise from studying it without being better for the task [182].

The Spenserian stanza was invented to "enhance the romantic effect" of a poem that Coleridge described as a domain "in which everything seems to occur in a kind of charmed sleep" (183). Style supported rather than being an end in itself. Thomson eschewed Spenser's use of obsolete words—homage to Chaucer but a barrier. She modernized language in three quoted passages:

I.i, Una and the Red Cross Knight; II.iii, Belphoebe and Braggadocio—with some cuts. From *Mother Hubberd's Tale* was "The Perfect Courtier," Sir Philip Sidney who reaffirmed high sentiment.

Edward Arnold

Edward Arnold marketed with exact descriptions. *Literary Reading Books for Junior Forms* numbered seven. *In Golden Realms* (1902), An English Reading Book for Junior Forms, 224 pages, price ⅓d., was

> Designed to form an introduction to the study of English literature. Containing folk-tales from various sources, stories from Homer, Virgil, the Beowulf poem, Chaucer, Malory, Froissart, Spenser, Shakespeare, Barbour, Scott, Lamb, and Washington Irving, and a large number of extracts from the works of the best poets. Illustrated with beautiful reproductions of twelve famous painting, including "Sir Galahad," by G. F. Watts, R. A.

This rooted English literature in the classics and extended with American writers. Specifying Watts's *Sir Galahad* emphasized chivalric content; it was the frontispiece.

A later expanded description added a statement of objectives and quoted reviews:

> The first aim of the editor of this little volume has been to please the young reader; the second, to make the readings as suggestive as possible to the teacher of literature and history, and to the educator generally.[20]

Three reviews came from different parts of the English-speaking world:

> **The Times.**—"Since the writing of books for children became a popular and remunerative branch of literature, these classic stories have run no little danger of neglect; and boys and girls who are made early familiar with the deeds of Beowulf, Roland, Una, and can be tempted to read for themselves Froissart, Malory, or Mandeville, will have gained more than any modern tales, too often somewhat invertebrate, can ever give."
>
> **The Saturday Review.**—"'In Golden Realms' is a successful attempt to utilize the fairy-story and legend as a stepping-stone to literature."
>
> **South African Educator.**—"A liberal representation of fairy-tale and legend, all of sterling merit as literature, and genuinely interesting."

The Times reviewer's case for retold great literature over new, written-to-order children's books urged preserving the great and timeless tradition, while *The Saturday Review* affirmed a place in forming appreciation of literature. A response from South Africa documented broad response to English schoolbooks.

In Golden Realms placed "Stories from Spenser's *Fairy Queen*" between Malory's "Arthur, Flower of Kings" and Shakespeare's *The Tempest* and *Mac-*

beth (from Lamb's *Tales*). The last half-page of "The Princess Una and the Red Cross Knight" printed five lines from Shakespeare's *King John* ("This England never did, nor never shall, / Lie at the proud foot of a conqueror" and eleven from *King Richard II* ("This royal throne of Kings, this scepter'd isle."[21] Patriotic nationalism was a primary theme. Book I, seven parts, retold key adventures: securing the quest, deception and separations; combats against Sansfoy, Sansloy and Sansjoy; Una protected by the lion, satyrs, and Sir Satyrane; intervention by Arthur, who dismembers Orgoglio and releases St. George; after Una's careful tending, the knight destroys the dragon, and a summary happy ending. Allegory was light, but good (Fidelia, Speranza, and Charissa, daughters of Caelia at the House of Holiness) versus evil (Duessa and Archimago) was an obvious theme.

"The Princess Una and the Red Cross Knight" used phrases from fairy tale: "In the land of the fairies.... Once upon a time." Characters were archetypal: Queen Gloriana was "as good and gracious as she was lovely to behold"; Una is "a fair maiden": the dwarf led "a warlike steed, which bore the armour of a knight" (131); the hero is "a clownish young man," who quickly fights and kills "a deadly misshapen thing ... horrid monster" (132–133). Patriotic interest—"Saint George, for that was the name of the Red Cross Knight"—came early (133). Una as a "princess" and Arthur as a "prince" were young protagonists, readily empathized with. Luxuriant descriptions were simplified, yet deftly suggested. Since schoolbooks for junior forms favored chivalric romances, pupils were familiar with combats and armor. Arthur, known from Malory, Tennyson, and Victorian historical paintings, was dazzling:

> glittering armour shone from far away. His name was Prince Arthur, and he was glorious to behold. His shield was one massive diamond; his helmet all of gold, with a golden-winged dragon as a crest; his breastplate shone with precious stones, like twinkling stars; his sword hung in an ivory sheath, and had a hilt of burnished gold. No magician had power over him, for shield and sword had been wrought for him by the enchanter Merlin, of world-wide fame [140].

The House of Holiness inspired:

> Here the Red Cross Knight was healed of his wounds, both of body and mind; here he gathered strength and power for his coming conflict with the dragon; here, too, he learnt that he was sprung from an ancient race of Saxon kings, and that in days to come men of England should fight and conquer, crying the war-cry of "Saint George for Merry England!" [143].

Religion and patriotism informed the history, past and future, of mythical England.

Students read more of the *Fairy Queen* in *In the World of Books*, 6 (1902), An English Reading Book for Middle Forms, 256 pages, priced 1/6d. A page in *The Greenwood Tree* defined purpose:

> The extracts do not pretend to represent the best work done by each writer whose work is laid under contribution. The aim of the compiler has been rather to arouse interest—romantic, historical, literary—and to introduce the reader to some of those great books which he is able to appreciate. As in the Junior Book, an attempt has been made to supply readings as suggestive as possible to the teacher of literature and general history.

Recognition of the necessity to engage / amuse students was again given priority. A second long paragraph, which reiterated children learn from a combination of verbal and visual texts, listed "beautiful black-and-white reproductions of pictures." Arnold quoted evaluations from a variety of journals: *The Guardian, The Saturday Review,* and *Indian Education.*

Nine lines of (modernized) verse in *In Golden Realms* described action between Saracen and Christian knights after "a thrilling trumpet gave the signal and the combat began" (138). An extract, "The Red Cross Knight and Sansjoy," from Book I, Canto 5 in *In the World of Books* was a reminder of prior reading and a completion.[22] Another Arnold series stressed this pedagogy of cumulative learning.

Steps to Literature: A Graduated Series of Literary Reading Books (1905), seven volumes, combined English and world literature. Book I *Tales of the Homeland*, 112 pages, price 10d., presented folk and fairy tales of the children's native land and simple rhymes. Stories from *The Faerie Queene* were in two of four books for Junior Forms. Book II *Tales of Many Lands*, 144 pages, price 1/, was largely folk and fairy tales of foreign lands, with England's champion and patron saint well represented. The frontispiece was Raphael's *St. George and the Dragon*, from the National Gallery. The first story related how he rides out to a marsh to rescue a maiden about to be sacrificed to a fearsome dragon: "a long body, on which were scales as hard as iron ... wings on which it could lift itself up into the air. Its eyes shone like balls of fire, and its breath was full of poison."[23] St. George has the Princess tie her belt around the dragon's neck: "Then, all at once, the dragon lost its fierce anger, and became very quiet. And St. George killed it, and cut off its head." The people offer gold.

> "It will please me best," he said, "if you will teach the men of your city to be brave and good."
> Now, this good deed of St. George was in time told in all lands. And the people of our own land took him for a pattern. They made up their minds to try and be as brave and good as he was.
> So when they went to fight their foes they would cry, "Saint George for Merry England."
> There is a picture of St. George killing the dragon on some of our gold pieces. Ask someone whom you know to show it to you [11].

This legend was England's exemplar in "many lands," an inspiration to be "good and brave"; it provided context for Spenser.

In graded series Book III was the locus of chivalry; *Steps to Literature* had two, each with stories from *The Faerie Queene*. Book III *Stories from English and Welsh Literature*, 192 pages price ⅓d., 17 prose stories and 22 poetical items arranged chronologically, was described as "Stories from the works of great writers, with simple Poems of the first rank. A charming introduction to literature of the best kind."[24] Stories were: Bede, Beowulf's fight with Grendel, Caedmon's dream, Chaucer's pilgrims and the *Knight's Tale*, Spenser's "Princess Una and the Red Cross Knight" and two stories form *The Shepherd's Calendar*, Shakespeare's *Cymbeline* (relevant for England and Wales), and Malory's Balin and Balan. Interlaced were Nennius's Vortigern and the Red Dragon of Wales, and three from *The Mabinogion*. Longfellow's lyric "Twilight" represented the United States.

"Princess Una and the Red Cross Knight," seven parts, told of the feast at Gloriana's court, St. George's quest, temporarily foiled by Duessa, Prince Arthur's intervention, time at the House of Holiness, and the Red Cross Knight cuts off the dragon's head. Paragraphs began like fairy tales: "In the land of the fairies…. The fairy Queen was…. Once upon a time …"[25] Patriotism was established: "Saint George, for that was the name of the Red Cross Knight" (65); both were used.

There was much to excite: "an ugly monster, half serpent, half woman" (64); "the hermit who seemed so kindly was really a wicked wizard" (66). Children were reminded of magical shape shifting and delight in evil: "the old pilgrim, who was none other than the wicked wizard, stood in hiding, laughing at the mischief he had made" (77). Readers even had the thrill of knowledge denied the hero: "But he knew not that Fidessa, who seemed so fair, was a wicked old witch named Duessa, who had taken the form of a beautiful lady to lead knights astray" (68).

Inevitably the schoolbook limited episodes and shifting focus. Una was significantly less prominent in this version—there was no Lion. Two final parts were thrilling giant killing and dragon slaying. Arthur battles the giant, cutting off its left arm; but the witch guides the giant's "many-headed beast … with cruel claws," so that Arthur's squire intervenes, only to fall before her spells (79). Then "Prince Arthur ran to the rescue. Lifting high his blade, he struck off one of the dragon's heads." A blow from the giant's club fells Arthur. However, when his shield's veil falls away, "its blazing brightness" strikes the beast "stark blind," and its dismemberment proceeds—"left leg by the knee" and "his head at a blow."

After such excitement, calm rejoicing was only noted: "We cannot here tell in full of the joy of the Red Cross Knight and the Princess Una, nor of the praise which they gave to Prince Arthur" for freeing him (81). The House of Holiness specified national glory:

Here dwelt a lady and her three fair daughters—Faith, Hope, and Charity.
Here the Red Cross Knight was healed of his wounds; here he gathered strength and power for his coming fight with the dragon; here, too, he learnt that he was sprung from the race of Saxon Kings: and that in days to come men of England should fight and conquer, crying the war-cry of "Saint George for Merry England!" [82].

An initial description of the dragon referred to failure by "many a brave warrior" against a monster with "brazen scales ... great jaws, each set with three ranks of iron teeth" but quickly became a report of blows and swift movement, including the dragon's swooping up horse and man. Like Arthur's giant killing St. George's dragon slaying was incremental, blows delivered over three days. The end comes quickly when the monster charges with open jaws: "With one last strong stroke the Knight ran his bright blade through its mouth, and drew the life-blood. Down fell the dragon, so that the earth shook, and lay like a heaped-up mountain. So the Red Cross Knight won the victory." Una praises God and thanks "her faithful champion" (84) before a brief final paragraph records report to the King and Queen, people rejoice and praise, the wedded pair "lived in joy and peace for many happy year" (85).

This book relied upon words to bring *The Faerie Queene* to children; two full-page illustrations (72–73) did not tell the story but pictured eight young children seated on a bench at school. In *The Smile* they are relaxed, most face the viewer, a boy and younger friend look at each other, one eats an apple. Accompanying lines were: "Full well they laughed with counterfeited glee, / At all his jokes, for many a joke had he." *The Frown* was captioned: "Full well the busy whisper circling round, / Conveyed the dismal tidings when he frowned." Children hold up their books, several read, one peers anxiously over his book, and another completely covers his face. Thomas Webster (1800–1886), a distinguished genre painter of school and village life, was a Royal Academician whose works were widely known through prints. That his pictures were positioned with Spenser was suggestive: *The Faerie Queene* is a very difficult work, and children must respond properly or face the teacher's wrath? The preface of *Stories from English and Welsh Literature* explained the parity of verbal and visual art:

> The pictures in this volume consist of reproductions of paintings by British artists of repute. They appeal to the imagination and to the aesthetic faculty in the same way as a true poem or a well-told story ought to do; and many of them might as fitly be made the subject of lessons as any of the stories or poems in the book. In the cultivation of taste it is surely a mistake to introduce our pupils to some of the masterpieces of Literature and neglect those of Painting [vi].

Book IIIA *Stories from the Literature of the British Isles*, 244 pages price 1/6d., 64 items, contained "Stories from Literature and Folk-Lore of England,

Wales, Scotland, and Ireland. Poems of the various countries by leading poets."[26] Nearly a hundred pages were Highland and folk tales of Celtic tradition, frequently retold by early Romantics. In chronological order, alternating prose and poetry, some English items harkened back to earlier volumes: Geoffrey of Monmouth's founding tale of Brutus and "Beowulf and Grendel's Mother." "The Story of Britomart," introduced a new character, "a beautiful and brave daughter," whose knightly adventures culminated in union with Artegall (26–45). The illustration was Dante Gabriel Rossetti's *Day Dreams* (1880), a memorable oil painting of Jane Morris, his most famous "stunner," now in Tate Britain. Evoking Britomart's gazing into Merlin's magic mirror and seeing a handsome knight, an exotic woman gazes toward the viewer. Merlin defines her quest: "to bring him back to his own country to fight the heathen … become his wife… from your children shall spring a famous line of kings." Glaucé suggests disguise "as man-at-arms" for "tall and strong" Britomart who will be able to fight "bravely against noble knights" as "other maids" have (28). Britomart takes the ebony spear and a shield made by magician Bladud.

Adventures were told in three parts. Part I established Britomart's quest and venture to Castle Joyous, where "lords and ladies spent their whole life in idleness and feasting. Britomart had no mind to stay in this place" (30). She encounters a giant, but the main action is seeking Sir Scudamore's love Amoret imprisoned in a castle isolated by fire and sulphur fumes. In Part II Britomart fearlessly enters, but fumes stop Sir Scudamore. She properly responds to BE BOLD and BE NOT TOO BOLD and sees a picturesque procession. Ease leads a band of minstrels and singers, while other allegorical figures convey threats and emotions: Fancy, Danger, Fear, Hope, Make-believe and Suspicion, Grief and Fury, Pleasure and Anger. Amoret is dragged along. Britomart discerns how to get through, patiently waits and then finds Amoret bound by Busyrane whose wooing she resisted. Britomart quickly fells Busyrane, but at Amoret's request binds the enchanter who alone can set her free. Fearless, brave, and temperate, Britomart refuses a reward, "'It is enough that I have been able to set you free'" (37).

In Part III Britomart overthrows a knight that claims Amoret as his lady: "Then the victor unlaced her glittering helmet, and her golden locks fell about her like a silken veil, low to her very feet" (38). All are surprised. Amoret and Britomart wander before reaching a tournament, where Britomart unhorses a knight with a shield disguised with moss and oak leaves. Alert children might surmise this is Artegall. After further wandering and separation all characters come together. Sir Scudamore and Glaucé spend a night at the cottage of a blacksmith (Care) before meeting Sir Artegall. Britomart fells in turn two knights that seek the Knight with the Ebony Spear. In a longer fight against the Savage Knight, on foot with swords, her helmet falls. When Artegall beholds "the beautiful face and golden hair of the Princess," he kneels (43). Glaucé pleads, and Britomart complies after Artegall raises his visor: "Her heart beat furiously, and she shrank back, full of gentle modesty and secret fear lest Artegall should think lightly of her for her manly deeds" (44). Women respond differently when gender is acknowledged. "It is too long to tell of the wonderful adventures which befell them all before" (45); a story that began "Once upon a time" (26) had a happy ending. This school reader, which balanced genders, gave Spenser parity with Shakespeare. *The Winter's Tale* stressed Perdita's festival, and the longest quotation was the statue scene. Four titles were Arthurian, Tennyson in prose, Geoffrey of Monmouth, and lines from Tennyson's *Lancelot and Elaine*. Robert the Bruce was Scotland's hero, represented by Scott's *Tales of a Grandfather*, Barbour's *The Bruce*, and Robert Burns.

Book IV *Literary Readings Relating to Empire*, 244 pages price 1/6d., broadened study—"Legends and Myths of the Native races of the Empire. Travel Tales of Empire pioneers. Literary extracts describing great events in the history of the Empire. Poems relating to the same subject—" outside the canon.

Book V, *Literary Readings Relating to Europe*, also 244 pages priced at 1/6d., returned to "Tales from the Greek and Latin Classics, the Song of Roland, the Nibelungen Lied, the Heimskringla Saga, and later Romances. Literary Extracts from English and American writers relating to the people or countries of Europe, and introducing great names in European literature. Poems from English literature with a European background."[27] This asserted the role of the Middle Ages in the history of English literature, furthered by later authors Longfellow and Thomas de Quincy. "The Spanish Knight" was Cervantes's Don Quixote; Americans William Prescott and Washington Irving also provided Spanish stories. "The Defender of the Holy Sepulchre" was from Tasso's *Jerusalem Delivered*.

Wide but brief coverage defined Book VI *Glimpses of World Literature*, "Extracts from the works of some of the greatest poets and prose writers of the world, from Homer to Tennyson. Arranged roughly in chronological order." Seven were Greek, six Latin, one each from the Koran and Omar Khayham, thirteen British, many from medieval stories introduced in earlier books. The initial four stanzas of *The Faerie Queene* began early modern examples; "A Knightly Encounter" of Don Quixote and Shakespeare followed, then selections from Corneille's *The Cid* and Goethe. Nineteenth- and twentieth-century British and American authors filled the final half (172–

256). *Steps to Literature* asserted British dominance of world literature and celebrated Chaucer, Spenser, and Shakespeare as canonical. Arnold's *Sesame Readers* (1908), less concerned with a canon, did not include Spenser.

Thomas Nelson Schoolbooks

Thomas Nelson published elegant reward / prize books discussed in earlier chapters. Their distinguished schoolbooks began with Royal School Series in 1856. Three Edwardian series had different emphases: *The Royal Prince Readers* (1902–1903), *The Royal Treasury of Story and Song* (1907–1909) and *Highroads of Literature* (1913–1920).

The Royal Prince Readers were named for the current Prince of Wales, who became King George V (1910–1936). During World War I he changed the family name to Windsor to avoid anti–German sentiments. King Edward VII chose naval training for his son's preparation to rule as King of the United Kingdom and of British Dominions. *The Royal Prince Readers* series combined literature and history so that lessons were mutually reinforced. *The Faerie Queene* was part of instruction in Third Book (1903).

The Royal Treasury of Story and Song, seven parts, was an inviting introduction to literature, but Spenser was not as prominent as in Arnold's series. While earlier books contained stories and poems celebrating chivalric knights, none were from *The Faerie Queene. Tales That Are Told* Part VI gave two quotations from Book I in modernized language.[28] The six opening stanzas described the Red Cross Knight ("pricking on the plain") accompanied by Una and her dwarf, and seven stanzas told of their meeting with "an aged sire" who takes them to his hermitage. "He told them of Saints and Popes, and evermore / He strow'd an Ave Mary after and before."* The note explained, "The rest of the surprising adventures of Una and the Red-Cross Knight are told in Book I, of Spenser's Faerie Queen" (19).

A painting and a portrait enriched the selections. G. F. Watts's *The Red Cross Knight*, in plate armor with lance and shield, rides a large charger (15). He towers above Una, in white dress and black cloak, riding her small donkey. Both are bare headed and gaze down; he at her and she at the ground. Watts's painting (4'5" × 4'11"), the first he registered for copyright (1869), continued a Spenserian theme, explored in his fresco in the Palace of Westminster (Parliament), *The Red Cross Knight Overcoming the Dragon* (1853). Arthur Prinsep and Mary Jackson were the models.[29] In my copy someone—a student?— made a critical comment on the small picture of Spenser; a pencil added a high pointed cap with "DUNCE" written just above the poet's head.

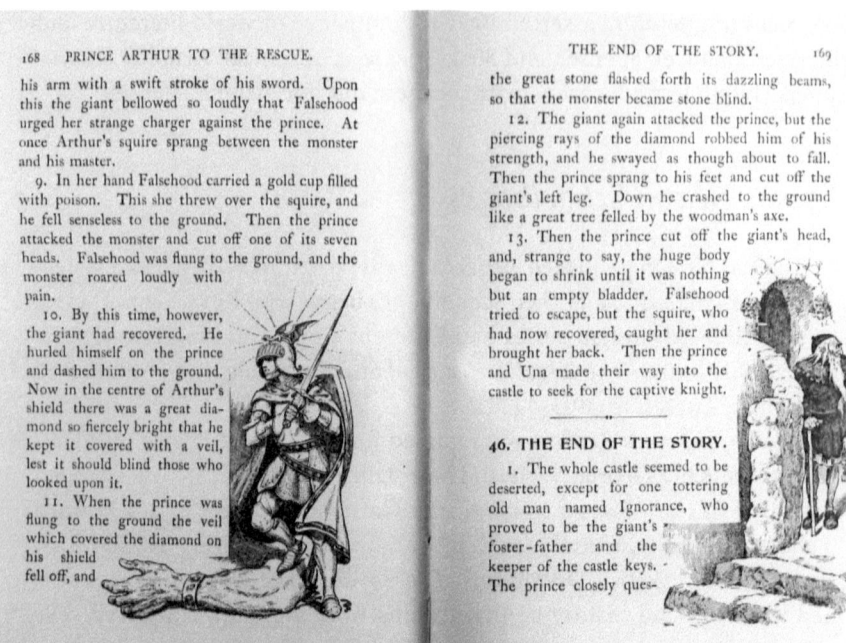

Thomas Nelson's Highroads of Literature Series (1913–1920) was distinguished in many ways, especially with its emphasis upon visual learning. This opening shows how pages of verbal text, made more accessible with running titles, also featured compelling pictures. On the left Arthur, in resplendent armor, places one foot on the severed arm of the giant that he killed by gradual dismemberment. On the right, a vague old man, Spenser's Ignorance, carries keys to parts of the castle. The marginalia were repeated from Emily Underdown's *The Gateway to Spenser* (1911).

Highroads of Literature recognized *The Faerie Queene* earlier and more fully. It provided the last story in *The Morning Star*, Third Book, which began with "Poets' Corner," a lesson to establish the significance of literature as a monument of civilization and a record that survives.

> Here we do not find memorials of kings, warriors, and statesmen, but of men who have served their country nobly by writing noble books in the mother-tongue. You must not forget that one of the chief glories of our land is the great mass of writings which gifted Britons have produced. In Poets' Corner you will read the names of many of those who have made our language glorious for all time.[30]

Shelley's "Ozymandias" inspired a final comparison:

> Think of the countless cities, temples, palaces, and statues which kings and warriors and statesmen have set up in the ages of long ago. They have all crumbled to dust; we can scarcely find a trace of them. At the same time, we have books which were written by humble men more than two thousand years ago. These are the monuments which never decay. They live on from age to age and never lose their freshness and beauty [11].

Victorian historical paintings were a splendid resource to increase understanding of literary texts. Spenser was the final author retold in *The Morning Star* (1915), Grade III, which began with and emphasized Chaucer. Primary in John Gilbert's painting *St. George and Una* are the romantically young and attractive knight and princess. Only the dragon's head at the lower right is a reminder of threat.

Third Book told the story of the emergence of English as fit language for books (lesson 2) and described physical processes to make books (Lessons 23, 27 to 31). Chaucer was the major author (Lessons 4 to 6 and 10 to 18), and *The Fairy Queen* (Lessons 40 to 46) was the culmination. Lessons were sophisticated, but not intimidating:

> 1. It is an allegory. The persons in the poem represent such qualities as Holiness, Truth, Falsehood, and Justice, but they also stand for men and women who were then living.
> 2. When we read the "Fairy Queen" we care very little about the persons in the poem, or the qualities which they represent. We read the "Fairy Queen" for its sweet and musical verse.
> 3. Let me tell you the story of Una and the Red Cross Knight, which we find in the first book of the "Fairy Queen." Una stands for snow-white Truth, and the Red Cross Knight represents Holiness [145–146].

Allegorical meanings were perhaps to be remembered years later and verses to please, but storytelling ranked first. "George" when he arrived at Gloriana's court in Fairyland, was in "peasant's dress, but there was something both brave and noble in his bearing" (146). The queen immediately names him knight; armed he sets out with Una and her dwarf. In Lesson 40 he enters a cave and, encouraged by Una, destroys "a horrible and fierce monster Error. … an enormous snake … terrible to behold … its huge coils almost filled the cave" (148). Opposite was *St. George and Una*, a Victorian painting by Sir John Gilbert (1817–1897). Seventeen of Papé's marginalia from Underdown's *The Gateway to Spenser* (1911) made this schoolbook as engaging as Nelson's reward / prize.

In "41. The Red Cross Knight and Falsehood" circumstances and behavior became more complicated. Disguised magician Archimago gives shelter, tells stories of saints, and uses deception to separate knight and lady. Red Cross Knight kills Saracen Faithless, but his lady in scarlet, calling herself Faith, dupes him. Possible confusion was eliminated in "42. The Palace of Pride" and "43. The Red Cross Knight and the Giant." The knight accompanies "Falsehood—for we will now call her by her right name—" (155). The Queen of Pride, "scornful and vain," kept "a hideous dragon at her feet" (155), and called "for her coach so that she might take the air." Details were specific:

> First came Idleness, clad in black and riding an ass. Then followed Gluttony, a huge fat man who bestrode a pig. After him came False Love dressed in green and riding a goat. The other three attendants were Greed, Envy, and Wrath. Greed was in rags, and was mounted on a camel loaded with bags of gold. Envy was seated on a wolf, and clasped a deadly snake to his bosom; while Wrath rode a lion and bore a burning brand in his hand [156].

While there was no picture, these words discouraged bad behavior. Red Cross Knight triumphs against Joyless, but again succumbs to the magic arts of

Falsehood, a long draught from a stream; he cannot resist "the huge giant ... so big he seemed almost to reach the sky. His name was Sin" (161). When Falsehood pleads, his life is spared—he becomes a slave. A sentence offered some reassurance—"How he [the dwarf] found it [aid] and how his master was set free we shall learn in a later lesson" (162)—before shifting the narrative to Una.

Lesson 44 began with her "sorrow" at being deserted. The lion's entry fulfilled expectation of danger, alleviated when it became her guardian. Episodes were selective: "I cannot tell you all the maiden's adventures, but I must tell you of a cruel trick that was played upon her by the magician Archimago" (163). Una thinks a mounted knight is the Red Cross Knight; a picture shows a Saracen charging with lance (163). On the next page, children learn he is Lawless, who fells Una's "knight" and thus exposes Archimago. She flees, the Saracen pursues, kills the lion, and seizes her; but "the little wild men of the woods" rescue her (165).

"45. Prince Arthur to the Rescue" introduced "the most gallant knight in all the world. His armour shone like sunlight, and he carried his magic sword and shield with him" (166). Falsehood diverts Arthur by charging his squire and throwing poison over him, yet Arthur dismembers the monster after the diamond in his shield is exposed.

Atypically Arthur's lesson was more thrilling than "46. The End of the Story"—dragon slaying and wedding. Papé's Ignorance (169) and old Despair (171) made pedagogical points visually. Una takes Red Cross Knight to "a beautiful, peaceful house, where three maidens named Faith, Hope, and Charity, and a skilled doctor named Patience" help him recover his strength. On the way to complete his quest the Red Cross Knight met an old man that "told him that he was the son of a British king and that, in after days, he would become the guardian saint of his native land, and be known to all future ages as St. George of Merry England" (172). The iconic fight required only three paragraphs; two told how Una and Red Cross Knight went to her parents, feasted, and married before he left to serve Gloriana for six years; then "he returned to his beloved wife and lived happily with her to the end of his days" (174). *St. George and the Dragon* (1908-09), a painting by Briton Rivière (1840-1920), anticipated this muted version. The champion killed a huge monster, whose coiled greenish brown body fills much of the painting (152). However, St. George lies on the barren ground.

"Exercises (To be worked under the direction of the teacher)" mirror Edwardian expectations. Every lesson had a list of "words to put into sentences." As passages quoted above make clear, vocabulary was mature. Other exercises developed grammar: make nouns of verbs, correct agreements of

In Briton Rivière's *St. George and the Dragon*, also reproduced in Nelson's *The Morning Star* (1915), the slain monster, dark and serpentine, fills the dominant foreground. The exhausted champion, who lies at the dragon's head, marked the effort to defeat evil. Presenting students with the two paintings, one Victorian and one Edwardian, could prompt lively discussion.

subject and verb, correct verb tenses, identify parts of speech and comparatives. Some combined visual and verbal work: Lesson 40, "Turn to the coloured picture on page 149 and study it carefully. Then describe it" (189); Lesson 46, "Turn to the coloured picture on page 152 and describe it" (191).

Non-verbal exercises were copying drawings: the Palace of Pride (189), the dwarf (190), the giant's arm (191), and Una (191). Essays were: "Write a letter to your aunt telling her about your school" (189) and "tell in your own words the story of Una and the Lion" (190). Ten "Additional Exercises" (191) indicated flexibility in assignments and a wish to demand more advanced work from very young children. The first five asked for a judgment—"Which story [or ballad, picture, man, woman] do you like best in this book? Say why." Three were comparisons: Constance with Una, Chaucer with Sir Philip Sidney, Sir Thomas More with Sir Walter Raleigh. Exercise 9 referred back to opening lessons that argued the role of literature: "Which man mentioned in this book did the greatest work for his land? Give reasons for your answer." The last repeated an exercise similar to one for the first Spenser lesson: "Write a letter to a friend telling him or her about this book." My copy of *Highroads of Literature* was a prize, "Presented to Amy Lowe for neatness in work and good conduct during school year 1920–21." Historical information and criticism accompanied stories in schoolbooks; literary histories surveyed and expanded such evaluation.

6

Literary Histories

British schoolbooks put Edmund Spenser's *The Faerie Queene* in the canon of major authors. Edwardian literary histories supported this view; Americans, although they claimed concomitant history, often did not. Public lectures in the United States and England, Abby Sage Richardson's *Familiar Talks on English Literature* (1881/1892) and Dorothea Beale's *Literary Studies of Poems Old and New* (1902), addressed women's current educational development. Multiple editions of Eva March Tappan's *A Brief History of English Literature* (1905/1914 and 1920/1932) chronicled changing views of national literatures in the United States. In 1909 Nelson published two literary histories—by a woman and by a man—with alternative views: H(enrietta) E. Marshall's *English Literature for Boys and Girls* and Edward Parrott's *The Pageant of English Literature*. C. L. Thomson's *Our Inheritance* (1910) was a brief statement. Two surveys published in 1912, Andrew Lang's *History of English Literature* and W(illiam) H(enry) Hudson's *An Outline History of English Literature*, made divergent estimates of *The Faerie Queene*. Henry Gilbert's eight *Stories of Great Writers* (1914) did not include Spenser.[1] Shakespeare was the early modern writer; four were medieval, and Sir Walter Scott the latest. Amy Cruse recorded evolving judgments of texts and critical approaches in *English Literature through the Ages* (1914) and *The Shaping of English Literature* (1927). In the midst of World War I American William J. Long's *Outlines of English and American Literature* (1917) and English Herbert Bates's *English Literature* (1918/1923) advanced opposing evaluations.

Abby Sage Richardson, Familiar Talks on English Literature *(1881/1894)*

Abby Sage Richardson's *Familiar Talks on English Literature* (1881/1894) was not formal literary history. She chose a "colloquial tone" to avoid the fault of typical handbooks that "made the study of literature uninteresting ... too much like graveyards, where a series of stones record the life, death, and principal events relating to an author, ending with a few lines from his work as a sort of epitaph."[2] Richardson (1837–1900), who had talked about literature with "classes, principally of young women" for many years, hoped "my book may be read largely by young people" (v, vii). As in *Stories from Old English Poetry* (1871), discussed in Chapter 4, she made distinctive choices. Few exceeded her claim for American and English affinity. Insisting on "*our* literature" and "*our* English authors," she urged on young Americans "a pride in the works written in their language" as though their grandfathers had not settled in Massachusetts and Virginia: "English literature to the year 1800 is as much our literature as it is that of any girl or boy born in London or in Yorkshire. Let us lay hold of and claim this grand inheritance" (vii). Richardson divided 433 pages into 6 parts, with major authors and dates: "I. English Literature before Chaucer. 449 to 1350; II. From Chaucer to Spenser. 1350–1550; III. From Spenser and Shakespeare to Milton. 1550–1608; IV. The Civil War and the Restoration. Milton and Dryden. 1608 to 1700; V. From Pope to Wordsworth. 1700 to 1790; VI. The Lake School and its Contemporaries. 1790 to 1832." The terminal date supported Richardson's *our*.

In Part III "Introductory" claimed the most great names for "The Golden Age of English Poetry." Elizabeth was a "fitting central figure ... young ... beautiful... ideal sovereign [who] inspired the poet's pen," highly educated, fluent in languages, interested in current poetry, and "luxury of living and all kinds of elegancies in dress and manners," especially extravagant clothes— an appeal for gender. Influences of Italian literature, "a flood of romances, in prose and verse," were noted (96–97). There was the Spenser circle and Shakespeare "towering like a Colossus above the crowd of dramatic poets that surround him," Lord Bacon was between them (97).

Chapter XVI named Spenser "the second great English poet in the line which begins with Geoffrey Chaucer." Richardson resisted "tiresome researches into family history, without much result. Evidently Genius is quite independent of genealogies" (98). She gave a gender perspective to a Romantic view of the poet. For *The Shepherd's Calendar*, "Let us be grateful to the fair Rosalinde that she was indifferent to the poet, since we reap the benefit of her indifference" (98). Richardson marked Spenser's friendship with Sidney and Raleigh and expressions of gratitude to these patrons. She lauded Spenser's time at Kilcolman, where "he lived happily, working on his greatest of poems *The Fairy Queen* ... more fortunate in a second love ... married to a lovely wife, to whom he wrote an *Epithalamion*" (98). In "his beautiful retirement" she imagined Raleigh's visit: "two friends lying at ease on the green banks under the trees that bordered the Mulla" while he read his poem and discussed London friends and gossip (99). Life in Ireland ended with another rebellion, burning, and flight, followed soon by Spenser's death in London.

Critical evaluation and quotation concluded this chapter:

> His poem of poems, *The Fairy Queen*, stands as one of the monuments of literature. There are few persons who have read it through, and their number is likely to grow less as the years go by. It is useless for anyone to read poetry merely for the sake of saying he has read it, and I certainly should advise no one to take up this poem unless he reads it purely for the enjoyment of it. To those who do enjoy it, there is no need to say anything in its praise. To whose who would find the entire poem tedious,—and I think perhaps these will form the larger number,—I will briefly tell its plan, and give a few extracts as illustration of the style [99–100].

In successive paragraphs Richardson cited Raleigh's letter, named knights, and described the Spenserian stanza, before asserting, "For my part, I prefer to read Spenser for his poetry, and not for his allegory, and therefore I attempt no explanation of it here." After describing Book I's opening, she praised, "Una, one of the most beautiful figures in the poem" and the gentle knight "pricking on the plain" (101). Five quoted stanzas told of Una's search after Red Cross Knight leaves and meeting with the lion, while another described her beauty on "a happy wedding day" (101–102).

"Chapter XVII. On Spenser's 'Fairy Queen'" told two stories. A summary of Florimel, featured in Richardson's *Stories from Old English Poetry*, included quoted stanzas for Britomart's battle against Marinell (103–104). Gender was key:

> The women in Spenser's poem are a constant delight to the imagination. They live in his pages like creatures in some land of enchantment, and while they are not like real women in a real world, they are so natural to their surroundings that we cannot help believing in them as much as if they had actually existed [103].

A second issue was aesthetic, Book II's contrasts of "Spenser's grandest style to his most beautiful and poetic" (105, as in Guyon's visit to Mammon's cave and the Bower of Bliss, five stanzas describing Acrasia's gateway, although such extracts did not give "any full idea of the riches of *The Fairy Queen*." Richardson named a few "graceful, chivalrous, fascinating creatures of our poet's unwearied fancy"; "elfin creatures conjured by his magic pen"; and scenery—"the fair green woods, the sea grottoes, the noble castles, the subterranean caves, the fairy gardens" that will lead readers "just to begin to fathom the inexhaustible depths of his fancy." His "exuberant" imagination inspired "young versifiers" (107). Richardson's "familiar" approach advocated pleasure and excluded religious controversy, moral purpose, and Puritan belief.

Dorothea Beale, Literary Studies of Poems Old and New *(1902)*

Dorothea Beale (1831–1906), an educational reformer and suffragist, was Principal of Cheltenham Ladies' College; she established a residence for teacher training in Oxford that became St. Hilda's College in 1893. *Literary Studies of Poems, New and Old* (1902) were papers written for students, ranging from "Dante and Beatrice" to "A Vision of Many Dimensions: An Allegory." "Britomart, or Spenser's Ideal Woman" united Beale's High Church belief and commitment to the advancement of women.

A brief preface explained allusions "to stained glass windows representing six episodes in the story: "(1) Britomart looking into the magic mirror. (2) She is clothing herself in armour in the Church. (3) She is defending the Red-cross Knight. (4) She is passing through the fire. (5) She meets Sir Artegall. (6) She sends him out to accomplish his work."³ Beale, who quoted stanzas that inspired the windows, told Spenser's story, interlaced with questions and critical responses. "Specially interesting for us is the story of the Lady Knight. We know what was Spenser's general design, 'to fashion a gentleman or noble person in virtuous and gentle discipline.' I think by the story of Britomart he sought to fashion a true woman" (17). Beale's conclusion was twelve items defining how the ideal woman learns and serves, faces and overcomes hardships in a context of gender parity / difference / mutual support within a life of service to others on earth and "perfect union which is to be realized only in the peace of heaven" (51).

Beale admired Spenser's beautiful imagery, feeling for nature, musical verse, lofty thoughts, high spiritual teaching (26). His storytelling was not so praiseworthy:

> I suppose that few, even of us who love the *Faery Queene*, have read it right through. We set out joyfully.... Delighted with the first book, we passed onwards: but, alas! in the second our interest began to flag. ... And as we went on the interest was less and less sustained—we seemed shut up in a labyrinthine forest, in which we were ever meeting knights and ladies, pursued or pursuing; the *dramatis personæ* became too numerous and too impersonal [25].

Eva March Tappan's A Brief History of English Literature *(1905/1914)*

Successful educator, editor and author of books of literature and history of the Middle Ages, Eva March Tappan (1854–1930) was well qualified to write *A Brief History of English Literature* (1904/1914), revised and reprinted several times. Originally she devoted two final chapters to American Literature; a later edition separated these to become *A Short History of American Literature* (1932) with additional chapters by Rose Adelaide Witham. *A Short History of England's Literature* (1920 and 1933) was reorganized with eight chapters.[4] Titles indicated periods and major authors: "I. The Early English Period, Centuries V-XI; II. The Norman-English Period, Centuries XII and XIII; III. Chaucer's Century, Century XIV; IV. The People's Century, Century XV; V. Shakespeare's Century, Century XVI; VI. Puritans and Royalists, Century XVII; VII. The Century of Prose, Century XVIII; VIII. The Century of the Novel, Century XIX." Numbered sections made reference easy. Chaucer and Shakespeare were singularly important; however, Spenser was only one of many in Chapter V.

Within a chronological survey, Tappan identified dominant genres. Thus Edmund Spenser, #50, was a writer of pastorals, *The Shepherd's Calendar*, dedicated to his friend Sir Philip Sidney. It initiated a claim for "the new poet," Chaucer's successor, and an appointment to Ireland. After sections about Sidney and Marlowe, Tappan returned to Spenser, #55. "*The Faerie Queene, Books I–III, 1590. Books IV–VI. 1596.*" He read the first books to Sir Walter Raleigh who visited him in Ireland. Tappan quoted the opening stanza and explained the "'gentle knight' represented Holiness, who was riding forth into the world to contest with Heresy." A small picture from the Elizabethan edition identified "The Red Cross Knight" (93). Tappan dealt briefly with the poem's plan and allegory—twelve books, each with 'some virtue's victory over its contrary vice' and King Arthur to embody all and marry the Queen of Faerie in the final book—before confronting the poem's difficulty:

> a very material allegory.... Elizabeth is the Queen of Faerie, Mary of Scotland is Error, etc. So far the double allegory is reasonably clear; but as the poem goes on, it wanders away and away, and is so mingled with other allegories and changes of characters that it is impossible to trace a connected story through even the six books that were written of the twelve that Spenser planned.
>
> Tracing the story is a small matter, however. One need not read an imaginative poem with a biographical dictionary and a gazetteer. The allegory of the struggle of evil with good is beautiful; but one need not trouble himself about the allegory. Read the poem simply for its exquisite and varied imagery, and the ever-changing music of its verse, and you will share in some degree the pleasure which for three hundred years Spenser has given true lovers of poetry [93–94].

Tappan said nothing of Spenser's effort to transform medieval romances and gave religion short shrift. Spenser's value was primarily aesthetic, yet Tappan did not declare him "the poets' poet." While others rationalized complexity and inaccessibility, few were quite so cursory or unenthusiastic.

H(enrietta) E. Marshall, English Literature for Boys and Girls *(1909)*

Henrietta E. Marshall (1867–1941), author of many books of stories from literature and history for children combined her interests and skills in *English Literature for Boys and Girls* (1905).[5] To Jack's Told to the Children Series she contributed stories of Robin Hood, Guy of Warwick, William Tell, and Roland. Marshall's most influential book was *Our Island Story* (1905), published in the United States as *An Island Story*; Edwardians often praised it, and thousands of copies were recently distributed to schoolchildren in Britain.[6] *Our Empire Story* (1908) and *Scotland's Story* (1906) were similar histories. Marshall's literary history was a companion volume, 6½ × 9½ inches, 687 pages with large type, twenty full-page color illustrations, an Index, and "Chronological List of Writers Included in this Volume." The original white cloth cover—suggesting vellum—bore portraits of five writers; Spenser was not one of them. Jack, subsequently Nelson, published Marshall's large volumes in uniform, rather academic covers—dark blue, with title stamped in gold and heraldic device in gold and red, price 7/6d. Stokes was the publisher in the United States. *Standard Catalog for High School Libraries* (1929) listed *English Literature for Boys and Girls*, price $5. *New York Best Books* rated it highly: "Tells the story of the development of literature from Caedmon to Tennyson, adapting with remarkable success both style and selection to children's interests and quoting freely. Attractively printed. Excellent colored plates."[7]

Eighty-five chapters spanned from "the dim, far-off times when our forefathers were wild, naked savages, they had no books" (1) through Tennyson. Marshall forthrightly issued "To Boys and Girls—An Apology"; this book was not one they asked for but the fulfillment of her "wish." "Long, long ago" a Magician made it possible by giving her two golden pennies to rub together with a promise her first wish would be granted. Marshall then asked children's help: "You know in fairy tales when people get their wishes they often find that instead of being made happy they are made unhappy by the fulfillment. But if you like my book, then I can truly say that my wish has brought only happiness in its fulfillment" (vii-viii). This personalized author-reader dialogue, more direct than typical Edwardian engagement, indicated uncertainty about literary histories for children.

A second preface "To 'The Olympians'—An Explanation" was for "those semi-fairy godmothers and godfathers whose purses ought to be bottomless as their kindness is limitless." Using Kenneth Grahame's identification, Marshall acknowledged adults choose and buy the books children read. She then claimed originality, a book unlike many others, "all written for use in schools, while my desire has been to produce a book which a boy or girl will read, not as a task, but as a pleasure" (ix). She boldly stated: "The object with which I write being to amuse and interest rather than to teach, a great deal has been left out which must of necessity have been included in a book meant for school use." Not all great names were included, but "the most representative writers in the various periods"; Marshall "tried to keep literature in touch with history, to show how the political development of our country influenced, and in turn was influenced by, the literary development." Special emphasis was upon early literature, "it being my belief that what was attractive to a youthful nation will be most attractive to the young of that nation" (x)—a widespread Victorian and Edwardian attitude.

Despite a declared intent to please, Marshall expressed didactic hope when she quoted early humanist John Colet (1467–1519), who modestly presented his "lytle boke" (Chaucer echo) not as something new, but as better ordered and considerate of "the tenderness and small capacyte of lytel myndes" (xi). Colet's pedagogy was explicit: "Wherfore I praye you, al lytel babys, al lytel children, lerne gladly this lytel treatyse, and commende it dylygently onto your memoryes. Trusting of this begynnynge that ye shal procede and growe to parfyt literature ..." (xii). Finally formulaic prayers asked for theirs and avowed his.

Colet's words provided context for *The Faerie Queene*, infused with learning and religious fervor. The historical moment from Henry VIII's death through Elizabeth's first twenty years "were years of struggle, during which England was swayed to and fro in the fight of religions. They were years during which the fury of the storm of the Reformation worked itself out" (247). Then came the extraordinary brilliance of Elizabethan authors, among whom Spenser was "foremost"—first in time and—perhaps—achievement (247). Distribution of chapters reflected the latter: three chapters to three authors (Chaucer, Spenser, and Shakespeare), two chapters to twelve, and one to the rest.

Marshall sustained her manner of storyteller and fairy tale, while recognizing its necessity with difficult writers. Her comparison of Spenser and Chaucer was incisive:

> If we could stand aside, as it were, and take a wide view of all our early literature, it would seem as if the names of Chaucer and Spenser stood out above all others like great mountains. The others are valleys between. They are pleasant fields in which to wander, in which to gather flowers, not landmarks for all the world like Chaucer and Spenser. And although it is easier and safer for children to wander in the meadows and gather meadow flowers, they still may look up to the mountains and hope to climb them some day [248].

A child could grasp that not all literature is of equal worth; even among the best qualitative differences gave English authors worldwide appeal. Having established this ranking, Marshall devoted the rest of "Chapter XLI Spenser—The 'Shepherd's Calendar'" to biography.

"Chapter XLII Spenser—'The Faery Queen'" reiterated succession from Chaucer, and Spenser's shift from pastoral to "'trumpets stern ... knights and ladies gentle deeds ... fierce wars and faithful loves'" (254). Marshall reported Spenser's ambitious plan and addressed the issue of allegory:

> The first three books tell the adventures of the Red Cross Knight St. George, or Holiness; of Sir Guyon, or Temperance; and of Lady Britomartis, or Chastity. The whole poem is an allegory. Everywhere we are meant to see a hidden meaning. But sometimes the allegory is very confused and hard to follow. So at first, in any case, it is best to enjoy the story and the beautiful poetry, and not trouble about the second meaning [254].

Later she returned to meanings beyond events of the story, its patriotism and religion:

> In it Spenser has made great use of the legend of St. George and the Dragon. The Red Cross of his Knight, "the dear remembrance of his dying Lord," was in those days the flag of England, and is still the Red Cross of our Union Jack. And besides the allegory the poem has something of history in it. The great people of Spenser's day play their parts there. Thus Duessa, sad to say, is meant to be the fair, unhappy Queen of Scots, the wicked magician is the Pope, and so on. But we need scarcely trouble about all that. I repeat that meantime it is enough for you to enjoy the story and the poetry [264].[8]

This acknowledged Spenser's Protestant advocacy, but did not dwell upon it.

True to her intentions, Marshall made no demands, yet hinted there was something more for young readers to understand when older. Her summary of Book I (255–263) included reassuring rationalizations for the hero's lapses. The first encounter with Archimago was typical. A single paragraph explained, "this seeming godly father was a wicked magician" who "wove evil spells" to create "the wicked dream" (two references) that makes "the Knight believe his Lady to be bad and false" and, "believing her to be unworthy," to ride away "sadly" (257). Similarly, the Red Cross Knight became Duessa's companion, for "he believed [her] to be good because he was 'too simple and too true' to know her wicked" (258).

Unlike other children's versions Marshall's paid scant attention to giant killing and dragon slaying, nor was there description of Prince Arthur. A single sentence told his triumph over Orgoglio: "Guided by the Dwarf they reached the castle of the Giant, and here a fearful fight took place in which Prince Arthur conquered Duessa's Dragon and killed the Giant" (262). The Red Cross Knight's triumph was equally abbreviated. After a paragraph explaining how Una helped him recover, they "reached her home where the dreadful Dragon raged. Here the most fierce fight of all takes place. Three days it was renewed, and on the third day the Dragon is conquered" (263). One stanza described the Dragon's fall, no greater emphasis than the one stanza about Error (256), or another for Christian and Saracen combat (260).

Instead of terrifying and exciting descriptions of dangers and dismemberments, Marshall sought lasting influence and explained her difference:

> There are so many books now published which tell stories of the *Faery Queen*, and tell them well, that you may think I hardly need have told one here. But few of these books give the poet's own words, and I have told the story here giving quotations from the poem in the hope that you will read them and learn from them to love Spenser's own words. I hope that long after you have forgotten my words you will remember Spenser's, that they will remain in your mind as glowing word-pictures, and make you anxious to read more of the poem from which they are taken [265].

Stanzas were at every opening, fifteen passages. Two established how Spenser began in the middle of the story and introduced a memorable knight (254–255); others described: characters—"an aged sire" (257), Duessa (257–258), fawns and satyrs (258), giant (261), old man who "cannot tell" (262)—and the house of Pride (259–260).

"Chapter XLIII Spenser—His Last Days" was incisive literary analysis. For the commonplace view of Spenser as "the poet's poet" Marshall cited Charles Lamb; then she added the case for "the painter's poet," word pictures:

> The whole poem blazes with colour, it glows and gleams with the glamour of fairyland. Spenser more than any other poet has the old Celtic love of beauty, ... He loved neither the Irishman nor Ireland. To him his life there was an exile, yet perhaps even in spite of himself he breathed in the land of fairies and of "little people" something of their magic ... [265].

This acknowledged Celtic influence on English literature espoused by Matthew Arnold and others in the nineteenth century.

Most interesting was further comparison with Chaucer:

> That it is a fairyland and no real world which Spenser opens to us is the great difference between Chaucer and him. Chaucer gives us real men and women who love and hate, who sin and sorrow. He is humorous, he is coarse, and he is real. Spenser has humour too, but we seldom see him smile. There are, we may be glad, few coarse lines in Spenser, but he is artificial. He took the tone of his time—the tone of pretence. It was the fashion to make-believe, yet, underneath all the make-believe, men were still men, not wholly good nor wholly bad. But underneath the brilliant trappings of Spenser's knights and ladies, shepherds and shepherdesses, there seldom beats a human heart. He takes us to dreamland, and when we lay down the book we wake up to real life. Beauty first and last is what holds us in Spenser's poems—beauty of description, beauty of thought, beauty of sound. As it has been said, "'A thing of beauty is a joy for ever,' and that is the secret of the enduring life of the *Faery Queen*" [266].

Having cited Courthorpe's *History of English Poetry* as summation of her critical judgment of Spenser's reputation, Marshall illustrated his "wonderful

6. Literary Histories 233

Every biographical account of Spenser stressed his friendship with Sir Walter Raleigh. J. R. Skelton's illustration in H(enrietta) E. Marshall's *English Literature for Boys and Girls* (1909) was a study of stylish Elizabethan costumes and opulent tapestries in a spacious room at Kilcolman, where the poet read *The Faerie Queene* to the friend who was to sponsor it at court.

power of using words and weaving them together" with a stanza describing sleep's abode, as example of how 'the glamour of words enchanted or lulled" readers (266-267). Style affected Spenser's reputation: general failure in his own time, yet admiration by fellow poets and burial "not far from Chaucer" in Westminster Abbey.

For Marshall the greatest writers were "storytellers" (4). Each chapter ended with "Books to Read," listing publishers' names and prices. Three children's versions were *Stories from the Faerie Queen* (Told to the Children Series), N. G. Royde-Smith's *Una and the Red Cross Knight* (many quotations), and C. L. Thomson's *Tales from the Faerie Queene* (prose); four editions of the poetry, designating spelling and selection. The list for Chaucer suggested further comparison with Spenser: "As there are so many books now published containing stories from Chaucer's *Canterbury Tales*, I feel it unnecessary to give any here in outline" (146). Early modern did not fare as well as medieval tales. Pictures reflected this difference. Three illustrations traced transmission of texts—a monk writes in a scriptorium (frontispiece), a minstrel sings of famous deeds in an Anglo-Saxon hall (28), and a happy crowd enjoys a medieval play (196)—all medieval experiences. Seventeen were portraits of writers by J(oseph) R(adcliffe) Skelton (fl.1888–1927), not their works. Several were scenes of conversation, like "Spenser read the first part of his book, 'The Faery Queen,' to Raleigh" (252).

Edward Parrott, The Pageant of English Literature *(1914)*

Marshall was a Scots woman who never married and supported herself by her writing, while Edward Parrott (1863–1921), an English man became Liberal MP for Edinburgh and was a teacher and administrator. Thomas Nelson, where Parrott was educational editor, published both. Just as Marshall's *Our Island Story* (1905) preceded *English Literature for Boys and Girls* (1909), so Parrott's *The Pageant of English Literature* (1914) followed his *The Pageant of British History* (1908). These sumptuous volumes furthered confidence in national / racial identity that preceded the Great War.

Paintings by major artists beautifully illustrated Parrott's book, 7¼ × 9¼ inches. In sepia end papers major authors stand on stairs rising to a wide ledge above an arch. On each side dates indicated the trajectory of history: 1300 on the left with Chaucer on the first step, and on the right 1900 with Tennyson. Portraits promised biographical emphasis. Alluding to the great popularity of civic historical pageants held in many cities in the opening decade of the twentieth century, Parrott explained their objective: "an opportunity of arousing a widespread interest in the great deeds and great personages of the past, and of stimulating a desire to become better acquainted with them."[9] In fifty-six chapters, beginning with "The Dim Primæval World," he tried to "compose a series of pen-pictures revealing, he would fain hope, the great masters of our Literature as living, breathing human beings arrayed in the appropriate trappings of their time and circumstance" (iii). While acknowledging improvements in education, Parrott still saw a need to inspire "joyous delight to browse on the 'fair and wholesome pasturage of good old English reading.'" He believed the way to interest young readers was to tell the life stories of authors that would furnish "a clue to interpretation" (iv).

"Chapter XIX. Two Noble Friends" introduced Spenser with Sidney, "the 'jewel' of Elizabeth's realm, the very mirror of knightly chivalry, courage, and grace" (143). Sidney was "the greatest personal influence that ever came into his life," since he encouraged Spenser to write *The Shepheardes Calender*. It established him as "a new Chaucer" and brought preferment as Lord Grey's private secretary and posting to Ireland. Parrott, who stressed Lord Grey's zealotry as a Puritan who thought "the Roman Catholics of Ireland were Amalekites, ripe for the sword" and whose rule was "a piteous record of massacre, scourging, hanging mutilation, and famine ... his blood-red harvest" of killings and executions," assumed Spenser was "an eye-witness of this reign of terror and that he endorsed Grey's policy" (148). For eight years service he received Kilcolman Castle and the leisure to complete the first three books of his great poem.

This biographical account established a religious context of Protestant advocacy for "Chapter XX. The Faery Queene." Parrott described Spenser's relationship with Sir Walter Raleigh in Macaulay's words, "the soldier, the sailor, the courtier, the orator, the poet, the historian, the philosopher ... the completest representative of the Elizabethan spirit" (150). Raleigh's visit to Kilcolman Castle inspired the illustration: John Claxton's *Edmund Spenser Reading "The Faery Queen" to Sir Walter Raleigh*. A lady in shimmering satin enhanced the moment; Elizabeth stands beside her husband and gazes at the manuscript. This domestic scene somewhat offset the account of Lord Grey. Although Parrott quoted the opening stanzas of Book I, he shifted biographical focus to Raleigh—his "romantic visions of El Dorado," imprisonment, and *History of the World* (152). Then he described Spenser's praise of Queen Elizabeth but disappointment in London, his return to Ireland, where he wrote before the Irish attack, return to London, and death in poverty. Parrott, who judged the *Epithalamion* and the *Prothalamion* alone warrant placing Spenser "the chief of English poets before Shakespeare" (155), described his burial in Westminster Abbey near Chaucer's tomb.

Two pages evaluated *The Faery Queene*: the letter to Raleigh for plan and moral allegory: Gloriana, "Queen of Fairyland" and "image of divine glory of God"; Prince Arthur, "the perfect man," who was to wed her; six completed books embodied virtues "Holiness, Temperance, Chastity, Friendship, Justice, and Courtesy," opposed by "such vices as Falsehood, Wrong, Self-indulgence, Despair, etc." (157). Then Parrott identified

> historical allegory: Gloriana is Elizabeth; Duessa, who typifies Falsehood, is Mary Queen of Scots; Prince Arthur is now Sidney and now Leicester; while Lord Grey, Raleigh, and Philip the Second are various other characters. Subsidiary allegories slip in, and the project becomes so confused and complicated and bewildering that the reader is forced to abandon all attempt to comprehend the purpose of the poet, and simply wander amidst the pictorial splendours of a world of dreams [157–158].

Further sharp criticism followed: "as the poem was intended to be narrative it must be confessed a failure." Yet Parrott discerned

> as a rich and glowing pageant, as a gallery of highly-wrought pictures, as a sensuous dream of beauty, it is a triumph, "not for an age but for all time." Scattered through it are noble passages that call like a clarion to high endeavour, lofty enthusiasm, and spiritual grandeur; but beauty of soul and body is his main theme, and the whole vision is suffused with colour, form, and music [158].

Some moderns have praised Spenser as "the poet's poet," admired for

> his music ... his magical word-painting, his love of loveliness, his delicate observation, his mastery of simple emotions, and his own unique and graceful personality appeal unerringly to those who love poetry for its own sake. There are spots on the sun, and there are blemishes in *The Faery Queene*. Sometimes the poet is trite and commonplace, prolix and over-elaborate; but for the most part he is truly inspired, and then he leads us into gardens of endless delight [158].

While this was a conscientious effort to justify *The Faerie Queene* in the English literary canon, it seems unlikely to inspire many children, attracted to story not style.

Clara Linklater Thomson, Our Inheritance *(1910)*

Clara Linklater Thomson's *Our Inheritance* (1910), an incisive overview of English literature, placed Shakespeare at the center with an expectation that children knew him and history. A photo of a room in his house in Stratford was one illustration. The other was G. F. Watts's *Una and the Red Cross Knight*, which appealed to boys and girls and established Spenser in the canon, the preservation of which was Thomson's objective: "We have tried in a little space to tell you something of its glories. The inheritance is yours. Will you not enter in and possess it?"[10] Four long literary histories, two English and two American, fully evaluated *The Faerie Queene*.

Andrew Lang, History of English Literature: from "Beowulf" to Swinburne *(1912)*

Andrew Lang's view of *The Faerie Queene* has special interest because of his influential collections of fairy tales and retold Spenser stories in *The Red Romance Book* (1905), discussed in Chapters 3 and 5. *History of English Literature: from "Beowulf" to Swinburne* (1912), 687 pages, would be intimidating for children, but its encyclopedic coverage helpful for older students.[11] Longmans priced the complete volume at 6s, or in five parts for specific periods at 1s. 4d. or 1s. 6d.

Spenser, principal author for non-dramatic literature of the Renaissance, was "after two centuries of verse tuneless or tentative, the second great English poet" (182) with affinity to Chaucer. Lang emphasized the "disturbed" religious circumstances in which Spenser lived, especially "the extreme Puritan exiles who, driven by the Marian persecution, had imbibed at Geneva the doctrines of Calvin." In "this troublesome world" Spenser was active in public affairs and never had "the personal leisure of a Wordsworth or Tennyson" (184–185). Moreover, his "nature was divided. With all his love of pleasure and of beauty he leaned, though not virulently, towards the puritan party, and, as a good patriot, loathed and detested Rome" (185). The *Shepherd's Calendar* had rival Protestant and Catholic clergy amidst its classical models. The "perfect poet" Cuddie complained "of public indifference and is advised to sing of redoubted knights" (186).

Discussion of *The Faerie Queene* began with religious conflict and Spenser's role as secretary to Lord Grey, "a bloody man" notorious for his 1580 massacre of six hundred disarmed prisoners at Smerwick, where Spenser was present. The poet, who defended such ruthless action, responded to horrified protests by presenting Lord Grey as Sir Artegal, "molested by the Blatant Beast, the public" (187). For all Spenser's recognition of classical authors, Lang deemed *The Faerie Queene* not an epic but in the tradition of medieval romance rewritten as Protestant apology:

> The original scheme is that of the "Morte d'Arthur," moralized, and intermingled with allegory. The poem is an allegorical romance adapted to the state of England, Ireland, and the Continent under Elizabeth, and to the war of the Reformation against the dragon of Rome and the Scarlet Woman of the Seven Hills, the seeming fair and inwardly filthy Duessa, who is occasionally meant for Mary Stuart. Such unity as the poem possesses is given by the

> conflict of Good, as Spenser understood it, against Evil, private and public, the vices, and the Church of Rome.
> There are people, says Spenser, who prefer to have Virtue "sermoned at large, as they use." But while Spenser insists on being taken as a moral preacher in his way, his true ideal is Beauty, and it is the gleam of Beauty that he follows as he wanders with knights and ladies through enchanted forests, and "awtres dire" [188].

This tension produced severe contradictions, especially in Book II. "The 'Faery Queen,' despite its moral intention, which is perfectly sincere, is the very Lotusland of poetry." Many faults stemmed from sheer prolixity: "Spenser soon lost hold of his main allegory … the romance becomes, like "Piers Plowman," a farrago of all that is in the poet's mind" that needed restraint (189). Nevertheless, Lang dismissed complaints about archaic words that "annoyed the critics of his time more than they vex us." Artificiality of "the language of no time" was like Homer's "no actual time: his own age is confused with the fairy age of chivalry, and the ages of the "Morte d'Arthur," and of Greek mythology. … That great and noble effort towards perfection, the spirit of chivalry, was his ideal" (190). Lang's final defense was that Spenser's

> blemishes were of his age; no pure and perfect work of immaculate art could arise in a poetry which was only emerging from a kind of chaos, too much learning being the successor of too much ignorance, and a divine genius being left at large with no control from sane and temperate criticism [190].

Yet his sonnets, *Epithalamium,* and *Prothalamion* win "the crown of the chief of English poets before Shakespeare" (191). Their beauty justified "the poets' poet," forgotten from the middle of the seventeenth century, but "his measures revived by Thomson," and his "magic book" restored by Keats (192).

W(illiam) H(enry) Hudson, An Outline History of English Literature *(1912/1941)*

W(illiam) H(enry) Hudson's *An Outline History of English Literature* (1912) was more elegantly written and critically sharper than most; numerous reprints for thirty years indicate its success. Hudson (1862-1918) was Staff Lecturer in Literature to the Extension Board of London University.[12] His approach was psychological, to understand writers' genius, the strength of personality, details of individuality, but informed by their place in history and as expression of national character. Hudson recognized literary influences, but "general life, politics, society" were the most profound effects on writers "We must never think of a book as though it were written outside the conditions of time and space. We must think of it as the work of a man who, living in a certain age, was affected according to the nature of his own personality, by the atmosphere and movements of that age" (6). A table named ten literary periods, "Pre Chaucerian" to "Tennyson," with "Approximate Dates" and "Historic Periods" (10).

In "Chapter VI The Age of Shakespeare (1558–1625)" Spenser was "the greatest non-dramatic poet of an age which found its most natural literary expression in the drama." A key biographical detail was posting to Ireland, "in miserable exile among a lawless people whom he loathed" (56). His 'voluminous minor poetry' alone would have assured his "pre-eminence among contemporary English poets." Subjects in the *Shepheardes Calender* were "his unfortunate love ... sundry moral questions, ... and the religious issues of the day from the standpoint of strong Protestantism" (57).

However, "Spenser's fame rests mainly" on *The Faery Queene* (57). Others appreciated the "poets' poet" and placed Spenser outside time in an imaginative world entered for aesthetic pleasures; Hudson urged the epoch in which he lived and wrote:

> [T]he traditional materials of chivalry; giants, dragons, dwarfs, wizards, knights of superhuman prowess and courage, and distressed damsels of marvelous beauty, provide its chief characters; enchantments, tournaments, love passages and endless fighting are the staple of its plot. But Spenser's genius was fed by the Reformation as well as by the love of mediaeval romance and the culture of the Renaissance, and unlike his brilliant Italian master Ariosto, who wrote only to amuse, his own great work is inspired by a high moral and religious aim. In other words, *The Faery Queene* is not simply a romance; it is a didactic romance, the poet throughout using his stories as vehicles of the lessons he wished to convey. He carries out his purpose by turning romance into allegory [58].

Referring to Aristotle's twelve cardinal virtues, Hudson specified types for the six principal knights. Arthur was "the incarnation of Divine Power" who aided all in triumphs over its foes. To this "ethical allegory" Spenser added 'historical ... directly concerned with the political and religious problems of the age.' Book I

> represents the work of the True Religion in rescuing Humanity from the power of the great dragon, Satan, while the friends and foes whom the knight meets are the forces which oppose the True Religion in the divine work of deliverance. But Spenser identifies True Religion with English Protestantism, and the foes of True Religion with the foes of England— the Papacy, and Rome's political allies, especially Spain and Mary of Scots; and so the two lines of allegory run together [59–60].

Spenser's "allegory is sometimes confused, inconsistent, and obscure" and "taxes the attention and detracts from the human interest of the poem"; however, "the allegory must never be altogether ignored"; it was the reason Spenser wrote *The Faery Queene* (60).

Defects were: "extreme artificiality ... a rather languid storyteller ... little dramatic power. ... The old machinery of romance seems almost to collapse in places under the stress of the new spiritual meanings with which it is loaded." Yet a "wonderful sense of beauty ... pictorial quality ... pure essential poetry" justified a place in the canon (60). And "more than any other single work of the time it represents the combination of the spirit of the Renaissance with the spirit of the Reformation ... and it everywhere testifies to the strenuous idealism and moral earnestness of Protestantism" (61). These waned until eighteenth-century revival of medieval romance and chivalry (196) and subsequent use of the Spenserian stanza.

Amy Cruse, English Literature through the Ages *(1914),* The Shaping of English Literature *(1927)*

Amy Cruse (b.1879) in *English Literature through the Ages: Beowulf to Stevenson* (1914) matched others in scale, 592 pages and 66 illustrations, mostly portraits.[13] She read literature in historical context with substantial attention to biography and storytelling, and focused on "great literary masterpieces ... representative of a particular period, a certain class of writers, or a common literary tendency" (5) that would serve as markers on a long road that could be followed and in time bypaths.

"The Renaissance Period" was "Chapter XII. Utopia" to "Chapter XXI. Ecclesiastical Polity." An introductory note described circumstances after Chaucer's death: "The old sources of stimulus—religion and romance—worked languidly and ineffectually. In all our literary history there is no period so unproductive as the fifteenth century" (99). This lethargy needed awakening:

> The nations of Europe had reached such a spiritual and mental condition as made them ready for change. They had outgrown the teaching that the Middle Ages could give; medieval ideals no longer awoke their enthusiasm; they were waiting for a new teaching and new ideals [99].

Key factors in the New Learning were discoveries of Copernicus and Columbus, Greek learning and literature, and

> religious ideals of the Continental reformers that reached England, and were taken up with the strongest enthusiasm. ... One book, and that a great one, the Protestant Reformation gave us—Tindale's translation of the Bible. The value and influence of this—speaking only from the literary standpoint—can hardly be over-estimated [100-101].

Framing the period with Thomas More—who sought gradual reform only to be martyred for his religion—and Richard Hooker—whose *Laws of Ecclesiastical Polity* brought dignity and calm to heated religious debate—made religion dominant, the context in which Spenser lived and wrote.

"Chapter XVII The Faerie Queene" described Spenser as secretary to Lord Grey in Ireland: "The state of the country was terrible. Death in warfare, death from an ambushed foe, death by treachery, death by pestilence, death by starvation, death at the hands of the public executioner—these were so common that men had almost ceased to look upon them with horror" (143). Unlike others, Cruse gave no indication of Grey's brutal massacres and Spenser's complicity. Instead she described his situation at Kilcolman and singular perseverance in the momentous year 1588—the Armada, execution of Mary Queen of Scots, Sidney's death, and Shakespeare in London: "Amid scenes of strife and misery and crime, and poverty in its most revolting forms, without, as far as we can tell, companionship or encouragement, Spenser worked on" (144). Cruse discerned escapism.

Compared with a recreation of ordinary life and people in Chaucer's *Canterbury Tales*, Spenser's *Faerie Queene* was "more highly imaginative," a far cry from London origins; Spenser showed a "love of the "strange and unusual" that set him apart.

> Beauty of form, of colour, of sound, and above all, moral and spiritual beauty he loved with a great passion. Lovely shapes flitted before his eyes. He saw the white radiance of truth, the enchanting grace of courtesy, the grave loveliness of temperance with such a rapture of realization that he must needs make for himself some image to embody his conception and receive his worship. These images turned to living men and women beneath his hand, but they were not the men and women of common earth. Theirs must be a country of mystery and wonder; and Fortune was good to Spenser in leading him to his lonely Irish home. For certainly not in England could he have found a region which would have helped his imagination to picture that country as wild Ireland helped it. There he found the dark background against which his visionary men and women showed like forms of light; there were the forests "not perceable with power of any starr," the "wilderness and wastful deserts" where they adventured like fairy knights and ladies in the days when the world was young, yet with the grace and dignity of high-born courtiers of the great Queen. There, too, was the bestial crew of savage and treacherous foemen, who should test the knight's valour and the lady's purity [145–146].

Cruse followed this exuberant and glittering romantic analysis with a didactic one:

> Yet there was a stern Puritan strain in Spenser's nature that made it impossible for him to abandon himself entirely to these seductive dreams of beauty. He could not justify himself in his own eyes if he produced a work which had no high moral purpose. His conception of a poet—a conception common to his time—was that he should be first of all a great teacher. To this end he fashioned his work. It was to be, essentially, an exposition of spiritual and moral truth [146].

The Faerie Queene was an allegory of virtues and vices, and of present circumstances, a manifestation of Elizabethan political involvement to make a "double allegory."

> All this is very perplexing, and if the reader tries conscientiously to keep the different threads clear in his mind as he reads, his enjoyment of the poem will be sadly marred. But he need not do this. Spenser himself often forgets all about his allegory and loses himself in the sheer delight of the story. The best way to read the *Faerie Queene* is to consider it simply as a beautiful fairy story, and disregard altogether the allegorical intention. Then nothing but pure pleasure can result [147].

Others urged this approach—but not after such a stirring case for Spenser's religious purpose. Declaring "it would be impossible here even to outline all the stories," she quoted Spenser's letter to Raleigh, identified the Knight of Holiness as St. George and Una as Truth, and quoted two stanzas describing the lady. Gertrude Demain Hammond's "Una is rescued by a Troupe of Fauns and Satyrs" (150) was the only illustration, taken from Dawson's *Stories from the Faerie Queene Retold from Spenser* (1909), published by Harrap, and discussed in Chapter 3. This sylvan scene and mythical creatures supported Cruse's argument for fairy tale. Summary of Book I took less than two pages. A single paragraph noted: "The second book deals in a similar manner with the adventures of Sir Guyon, the Knight of Temperance; the third with those of Britomart, the maiden Knight of Chastity" (152).

Chapter XVII returned to Spenser's biography—marriage to Elizabeth, "the glorious marriage hymn Epithalamion," three more books of the *Faerie Queene* written before the attack and fire at Kilcolman by "rebels," and Spenser's death a few months later in London. Cruse suggested "many cantos" might have been lost in the fire, but "even in its incompleteness it suffices to give Spenser a place in the front rank of our poets" (153). *English Literature through the Ages* was an evocative history "not designed as a substitute for the actual text of the works dealt with" (6). They should be read, at least in selections. My copy was a prize for Form IV Upper.

English Literature through the Ages addressed the tension between esteem for *The Faerie Queene* as canonical literature and difficulty in making it accessible. *The Shaping of English Literature: and the Readers' Share in the Development of Its Forms* (1927) studied readers' response from Saxon times to the end of the eighteenth century.[14] "Chapter XXXI. Poor Folks' Books" and "Chapter XXXII. Children's Books" recognized areas not established as fields of literary study until decades later.

"Chapter XV A General Reader in the Days of Elizabeth" was a case study of response to *The Faerie Queene*. Cruse began with Robert Laneham's letter of 1575, cited in Chapter 1, that recorded books preferred by Captain

Cox. Then she imagined a poor law student—her general reader—visits booksellers / publishers in St. Paul's Churchyard and Paternoster Row. Because of limited means, he can only look longingly at books offered by John Day—Hakluyt's *Principall Navigations*, Peele's *The Old Wives' Tale*, and Books IV-VI of *The Faerie Queene*. The student's response to the latter was intense and poignant. A poster announcing it

> especially made his mouth water, for he has at home the first three books of the poem, published six years before, and they have given him great delight. But alas! he cannot spare the four shillings or thereabouts that he knows he must pay for the poem, a copy of which he can see lying on the other side of the stall. Stealthily he makes his way toward it, takes it up, and reads eagerly page after page, forgetful of his surroundings; until he is interrupted by the bookseller's impatient query whether he wishes to buy the book. He laughs, shakes his head, and slaps his empty pockets, while worthy John Day smiles grimly [129].

Even after he joins a group of young men laughing at a new jest book, "the spell of *The Faerie Queene* is still upon him" (130). When he passes the stall of Richard Tottel, purveyor of law books, he considers exchanging one of his; then he thinks of the few books of delight he already possesses:

> song-books, jest-books, books of riddle, cheap romances, a Bible and a Prayer Book; Marlowe's *Faustus*, Greene's *Friar Bacon and Friar Bungay*, Lyly's *Euphues*, Painter's *Palace of Pleasure*, Fenton's *Tragical Discourses*, North's translation of Plutarch, Foxe's *Book of Martyrs*, *A Gorgeous Gallery of Gallant Inventions*, Spenser's *The Shepheard's Calender*, More's *Utopia*, Lodge's *Rosalynde*; half a dozen French and Italian *novelle*; copies of school and university classics [130].

The student considers selling but is unwilling to part with any; moreover, his books are so worn sale would be unlikely. At Henry Bynneman's bookstall near St. Paul's, he lingers to read again Du Bartas's *Divine Weekes and Workes*. This leads to action. "Du Bartas's monotonous rhyming lines seem to-day to have lost their charm for him—perhaps because the rhythms of *The Faerie Queene* still linger in his head." Even though he will have little money for dinner, he "cheerfully" pays approximately four shillings for "that alluring *Faerie Queene*" and "goes off with a light heart and a light purse, but with the prospect of an evening of delight before him" (131). Cruse's engaging story established differences between price and readership.

Not surprisingly, "poor folks" and "children," classes of expanding literacy, did not purchase Spenser. Even when religious works and Puritan tracts became dominant, Cruse recognized the popularity of ballads, broadsides, and old romances. In spite of exceptions, lower classes became more ignorant and less religious in the first half of the eighteenth century, until publications by John and Charles Wesley reached and changed many, including a small class of informed readers.

Puritan ascendancy in the seventeenth century made the Bible the chief book.

> Foxe's *Book of Martyrs*, the sermons of Puritan divines, and tracts and pamphlets denouncing the practices of those who still remained in the outer darkness of the Catholic Church made up the rest of their reading. Life was a stern business in those days for the children of the Saints [295].

Warnings against delight in idle tales and things of this world were severe; chapbooks—ballads, shortened old romances, and traditional fairy tales—were popular. John Bunyan's *The Pilgrim's Progress* (1678), for two hundred years a part of households in England and America, was the other Protestant text. The Restoration was a period of such license that it inspired a new literature, notably James Janeway's *A Token for Children* (1671) and stories of worthy children who died young and thus did not go to Hell. Again there was a reaction: John Newbery introduced an era of books for children that celebrated rewards in this world. Writers as different as Sarah Fielding, Oliver Goldsmith (*Little Goody Two Shoes*), and Sarah Trimmer contributed.

William J. Long, Outlines of English and American Literature *(1917)*

Outlines of English and American Literature: An Introduction to the Chief Writers of England and America, to the Books They Wrote, and to the Times in which They Lived (1917) promised a monumental survey.[15] William J. Long (1867–1952), in 557 pages, included selections for reading and bibliography for each chapter, a general bibliography, and index. Seven chapters, 341 pages, were about English literature; four chapters, 200 pages, were devoted to American writers. This unusually close parity was marked by the pun in Long's last chapter "The All-America Period." That patriotic view of a distinctly American literature expressed an attitude not automatically in sympathy with an English canon. Long's bold evaluation of Spenser was not altogether positive.

He first compared Chaucer and Spenser, "great poets" yet "in aims, ideals, methods, they are as far apart as two men of the same race can be" (66). Long, who asserted little is known about Spenser, described his birth in London and education at Cambridge where he "steeped himself in Greek, Latin and Italian literatures" concurrent with "a revival of interest in Old English poetry, which accounts largely for Spenser's use of obsolete words and his imitation of Chaucer's spelling" (66–67). After acknowledging "the political and religious turmoil of the times of Mary and Elizabeth," Long asserted,

"For all this turmoil Spenser had no stomach; he was a man of peace, of books, of romantic dreams" (66). He went to Ireland, "an expectant adventurer who accompanied Lord Grey in his campaign of brutality. To the horrors of that campaign the poet was blind, his sympathies were all for his patron Lord Grey, who appears in *The Faery Queen* as Sir Artegall, 'the model of true justice'" (67). A footnote justified "blind" by claiming "barbarism" was characteristic of the time as were pirates; English "use of horrible methods" to put down the Irish rebellion was compared to the "notorious Duke of Alva in the Netherlands." Long claimed a detachment for Spenser not commensurate with early modern England, but with nineteenth-century Romanticism:

> In character Spenser was unfitted either for the intrigues among Elizabeth's favorites or for the more desperate scenes amid which his lot was cast. Unlike his friend Raleigh, who was a man of action, Spenser was essentially a dreamer, and except in Cambridge he seems never to have felt at home. His criticism of the age as barren and hopeless, and the melancholy of the greater part of his work, indicate that for him, at least, the great Elizabethan times were "out of joint." The world, which thinks of Spenser as a great poet, has forgotten that he thought of himself as a disappointed man [69].

Implicit is affinity with poets like Keats whom Spenser inspired.

Criticism of Spenser's works reinforced contradiction, "two discordant elements, which we may call fashionable poetry and puritanic preaching" in *The Shepherd's Calendar*. Conventions of pastoral yielded to responses to "religious controversy that was rampant" and need for flattery: in May "rival pastors of the Reformation, who end their sermons with an animal fable; in summer they discourse of Puritan theology" (70). Although Long judged it "an amateurish work" with experiments in meters (69), he promised the patient reader would find "on almost every page some fine poetic line, and occasionally a good song" (70).

Discussion of *The Faery Queen* began with storytelling: "Let us hear one of the stories of this celebrated poem, and after the tale is told we may discover Spenser's purpose in writing all the others" (71). Long quoted Sir Guyon, or Temperance, the last canto of Book II (71–73). Eleven cantos preceded this story: "So leisurely is Spenser in telling a tale!" Long listed other episodes. A quoted stanza described "the fair huntress Belphœbe, who is Queen Elizabeth in disguise. Now Elizabeth had a hawk face which was far from comely, but behold how it appeared to a poet." Of the canto about Britain's ancient kings, Long observed, "So all is fish that comes to this poet's net; but as one who is angling for trout is vexed by the nibbling of chubs, the reader grows weary of Spenser's story before his story really begins" (73). Moreover, "Other books of *The Faery Queen* are so similar in character to the one just described that a canto from any one of them may be placed without change in any other."

> It is impossible to outline such a poem, for the simple reason that it has no outlines. It is a phantasmagoria of beautiful and grotesque shapes, of romance, morality and magic. Reading it is like watching cloud masses, aloft and remote, in which the imagination pictures men, monsters, landscapes, which change as we view them without cause or consequence. Though *The Faery Queen* is overfilled with adventure, it has no action, as we ordinarily understand the term. Its continual motion is without force or direction, like the vague motions of a dream [74].

Long asked, "What was Spenser's object?" and answered his "professed object was to use poetry in the service of morality by portraying political and religious affairs of England as emblematic of a worldwide conflict between good and evil" (74). A few examples of allegory in Book I might delight "those who are fond of puzzles," but "the beginner will wisely ignore all such interpretation." Spenser's allegories "are too shadowy to be taken seriously" and "as a chronicler of the times he is outrageously partisan and untrustworthy" (75). "A Criticism of Spenser" stressed contrast between substance and style:

> his matter is: religion, chivalry, mythology, Italian romance, Arthurian legends, the struggles of Spain and England on the Continent, the Reformation, the turmoil of political parties, the appeal of the New World—a summary of all stirring matters that interested his own tumultuous age. His manner is the reverse of what one might expect under the circumstances. He writes no stirring epic of victory or defeat, and never a downright word of a downright man, but a dreamy, shadowy narrative as soothing as the abode of Morpheus [75–76].

A stanza of description exemplified the melodious stanza Spenser invented and later poets used. He imitated medieval romance but was unsuccessful in his refashioning.

Lest anyone reading *Outlines of English Literature* have missed his frequently damaging evaluations, Long reiterated:

> As Spenser's faults cannot be ignored, let us be rid of them as quickly as possible. We record then: the unreality of his great work; its lack of human interest, which causes most of us to drop the poem after a single canto; its affected antique spelling; its use of *fone* (foes), *dan* (master), *teene* (trouble), swink (labor), and of many more obsolete words; its frequent torturing of the King's English to make a rime; its utter lack of humor, appearing in such absurd lines as,
> Astond he stood, and up his hair did hove [76].

Undaunted by what would probably strike most readers as a negative warning, he persisted "Such defects are more than offset by Spenser's poetic virtues." First was "the moral purpose which allies him with the medieval poets in aim, but not in method." Medieval romancers regarded virtue as a means to an end, but Spenser's view was "virtue is not a means but an end, beautiful and desirable for its own sake; while sin is so pictured that men avoid it because of its intrinsic ugliness. This is the moral secret of *The Faery Queen*." Spenser's "sense of ideal beauty" was "perhaps his greatest poetic quality ... the poet-painter of the Renaissance" wrote descriptions as Italian painters created ceilings, "having set beautiful figures moving to exquisite music" (77). Positive evidence was a list of poets Spenser influenced. The case for excellence was largely aesthetic, albeit Spenser's declared purpose was moral.

Without its allegory *The Faerie Queene* was too much of the matter of Roman Catholic medieval romances, to which Puritan origins of American literature were antithetical. American literature was unlike any other because it began not with stories of fairies and heroes but with "historical records, with letters of love and friendship, with diaries or journals of exploration, with elegiac poems ... chronicles of human experience" (343).

Herbert Bates, English Literature *(1918)*

Although published in the same year Herbert Bates's *English Literature* (1918) was startlingly different.[16] Both intended literary history be used "in connection" with "a course in the reading of literature" (v), with each chapter serving as a lesson and ending with "Questions for Review." Bates gave less biographical material and more attention to works. Each of four books was followed by "Recommended Reading" and "List of Authors and Their Works"—a helpful table that included "Events in History and Letters," "Author," and "Particular Works." Bates (1868-1929), an Englishman, urged admiration of *The Faerie Queene*. The only color illustration was the frontispiece, F. J. H. Ford's "Una and the Lion," from Lang's *The Red Romance Book* (1905), also published by Longmans, Green. The longest quotation (six stanzas modernized from Book I, Canto 3) described Una's meeting the lion (148-150).

"Book II The Great Awakening" began with "The Revival of Learning" that emphasized increased knowledge of antiquity, printing, widespread reading of the Bible, exploration, and a new independence of thought. In "Chapter 3 The Elizabethan Outbreak: Poetry" Spenser was the principal poet, Chaucer's successor, still writing at a time of dependence upon "the feudal system of patronage." The caption for a small portrait characterized: "The author of *The Faery Queene*. His face is strong and thoughtful, not that of a weak dreamer" (144). Deeply affected by World War I, Bates found neither detachment nor escapism:

Much of *The Faery Queene* is not the stuff of dreams, but was from experiences in Ireland. There were still lonely forests, savage bands of unruly men with cudgels, wild lords who captured strangers, knights who fought on horseback—everything but dragons and enchanters, and if these themselves were not there, never was there any land so abounding in wild tales of them [148].

Literary antecedents were medieval (moral allegory, romance, Chaucer's poetry) and new (Renaissance tone and spirit, openness, consciousness of the new). Allegory was similar to Bunyan's *Pilgrim's Progress*, "a moral in the form of a story, each character representing some quality or idea," yet *The Faery Queene*, also political allegory, was "less simple." After quoting parts of Spenser's letter to Raleigh, Bates advised

> The best thing for the reader to do is to forget the allegory except when it forces itself upon his attention. We must read the story merely as a story of knightly deeds in enchanted forests, a tale of adventure, yet a tale "where more is meant than meets the ear." We need not trouble ourselves about the plot, or about underlying meanings [147–148].
>
> The poem is too richly imaginative for continuous reading. One should read a little at a time. And he should read it not for the story, but for the scenes in the story; not for the plot, but for delight in the poem itself [150].

Literary histories consistently recognized inaccessibility and difficulty, yet still urged reading because of poetic gifts: "Spenser's representative work is *The Faery Queene*. Every student should read at least one long selection from it. He should make sure that he sees clearly the peculiar quality of Spenser's verse, which was reflected later in Milton, in Keats, and even in Tennyson and Arnold." A "peculiar charm" was "rare mingling of sweetness and stateliness ... the gift of creating for the reader a golden atmosphere, an enchanted vision." Nevertheless, Spenser's lack of "Chaucer's gift of telling a story with simple directness" and "Shakespeare's dramatic genius," meant *The Faery Queene* "had a tendency to overload with detail," albeit this was characteristic of the age (152–153). Three of seven questions at the end called for answers about style.

Long wrote at length of American literature as a separate well-formed national tradition; Bates relegated it to "Chapter XVII. American Literature," the last of seventeen in "Book IV—Modern Literature" following "Chapter XVI. Foreign Influences that have affected English Literature." Both were unusual. Influences were from Latin, Greek, French, Italian, Spanish, German—"this Teutonic element is not the Teutonism of Prussia" (541), Scandinavian—"the English, almost Norse themselves" (544), Dutch, Slavonic, Celtic, and Oriental—from the Crusades but also British possessions in India. Each enriched the "English" tradition. The situation with the United States was different, literatures with much in common (language, race, traditions, institutions) that developed concurrently but differently. Bates praised American writers who inherited the tradition and did "not merely imitate ... aims not at identity, but at similarity" (552). Exemplars were Walt Whitman and

Mark Twain (552). Nevertheless, "In spite of the uplifting of the general level, there are few elevated peaks" (553).

Bates finished with the Great War, which the United States entered late, being "dominated by a spirit of materialism, of 'common sense' business, a spirit as selfish, as narrow, and as gross, in its own way, as that which deadened the inspiration of England in the eighteenth century" (553). World War I changed America's place from a "young" country to "a part of the modern world, a mature world, a world that has known and lived and suffered, a world emerging lacerated but transfigured from the spiritual agonies of a terrible war." Hope lay in the lesson that "the great things of the world ... are not material things, but spiritual—ideals, ideals of human freedom and of human welfare." America awakened late but in "such unselfish, sacrificing surrender of material welfare to the call of the ideal, lies the remedy for inert content and complacent toleration. In the pursuit of the ideal lies the hope of literature" (554). This was a rousing peroration, a pragmatic argument for literature like *The Faerie Queene*; it continues.

Epilogue

In the last half-century *The Faerie Queene* was retold anew. Sandol Stoddard Warburg's *Saint George and the Dragon* (1963), an ambitious translation into modern verse, sought "to move very gradually from the sounds and rhythmic patterns which are already familiar to us toward those special and much more beautiful constructions which are Spenser's own."[1] She briefly identified sixteenth-century England as "the perfect place and time ... perfect form ... and poet" for the legend. Although Warburg listed scholarly approaches to the poem's "truths ... historical, political, religious, philosophical, psychological ... layers upon layers of human wisdom and value," her objective was to initiate reading Spenser's poetry. Pauline Baynes's illustrations, drawings printed in red ink, imitated medieval illumination and added constant interest. All but six openings in 134 pages had one, often more, small pictures typical of medieval romance; placement varied, some continuous across pages. Four full-page illustrations were combat against dragon (7, 116) and Saracen (18, 50).

Margaret Hodges's *Saint George and the Dragon* (1984), illustrated by Trina Schart Hyman, won the 1985 Caldecott Medal after being named in 1984 a Notable Children's Book and *New York Times* Best Illustrated Children's Book.[2] The book was more enthralling romance adventure than promotion of Spenser to the canon. Elegant verbal and visual work were opposite in each opening of this thirty-two-page book. Hodges (1911–2005) expressed an Edwardian respect for Spenser's text, simplifying his complexity without loss of his tone and style. Language, sentence structure, and paragraphing were accessible with some adaptation of Spenserian imagery adding verbal richness [8, 24, 32]. The focus was exciting adventure, heroic perseverance, and the triumph of good over evil without details of the saint's legend or of Spenser's Protestant allegory. There was a vision: "Joyful angels were coming and going between heaven and the High City" (11); six central openings (14–25) were devoted to slaying the dragon; the final three were celebratory. Hyman's brilliant illustrations were vigorous in the protracted central combat, but gentle for rest and celebration. All pages were framed with decorative borders. Stylistic details effectively recalled medieval manuscripts and also echoed Art Nouveau, especially interlace of flowers.

The Questing Knights of The Fairie Queen (2004) by Geraldine McCaughrean (b. 1951) was very different.[3] This prolific British author's large book (8½ × 11 inches, 144 pages) retold Spenser's six books. Jason Cockcroft's dramatic and profuse illustrations enlivened in a romantic style—handsome knights like Golden Arthur (32) and creative monsters (13, 29, 40–41, 140–141).

McCaughrean did not replicate Edwardian support of Spenser's canonical status as a great poet with chivalric and religious idealism. Quite conversationally, she challenged readers: "Yes, yes. I hear you. You want to be a knight. Questing sounds glamorous and thrilling, doesn't it? But to be a good knight—to be a Queen's Knight? Ah...! Tell me, what does it take?" Armor and horse were easy to obtain, while character was more exacting. Her "recipe" had "six or so sacred ingredients.... Holiness, Courage, Justice, Moderation, Love, Courtesy ..." Few "can see it through. Don't take this the wrong way, but do you have any of the knightly virtues? ... Forewarned is forearmed, so they say" (8). A chatty—jokey—style, current idiom, and wry response were early established. Instead of turning Spenser's poetic language into elegant prose, McCaughrean made it idiomatic, contemporary, flippant. Discharge from Error's mouth is "dead meat" (14). The old man in Orgoglio's castle answers with childlike resonance: "Dunno! ... Dunno nothing, me. Blind Ignoramus dunno nothing!" (35). After felling Arthur, Firebrand turns to Guyon and sneers, "'Nah nah-nah nah!'" (54). When Artegall makes his initial judgment about the treasure chest, "'Told you so! Told you so!' Amidas jeered at his brother" (117). Artegall is not the Savage Knight but the "Scruffy Knight" (103), little more dignified than "Shaggy Bag" who steals Amoret; the Blatant Beast is "The Blaring Beast." McCaughrean, who commented on an Amazon book site that she "adapted indigestible classics," allowed little chivalric idealism.

Perhaps the most telling adaptations for today's children were of Britomart, the warrior maiden, and Talus, "a man of iron"—to offer observations about gender and technology and justice. Book Three Chapter 1 was titled "Of Knights and Knighties"—a rejection of a tendency not to distinguish gender (as in "actor") and a pun ("nighties"). McCaughrean rejected Spenser's Britomart who enjoyed male action and found female domestic activities boring. Her quest was purely personal, not commitment to serving others (81). At the tournament Britomart merely inquired of Artegall, but he charged competitively: "Could men not even manage to hold a conversation without resorting to swords and maces and pikes? She leveled her magic lance and prised the Scruffy Knight out of his saddle like a cork out of a bottle" (104).

Confronted with adulation accorded victorious knights—ladies want them as champion—Britomart's response is "'Arg! No thank you!'" Britomart has a "giggle" with Amoret to whom she revealed her sex—"'Oops'" (101). Artegall captive to Amazons was in "pinafore and frock," and reversed roles complement embroidery stitches and "backhand slash" (124). Britomart "decreed" new laws for Amazonia "tongue tucked firmly into her cheek with concentration," and Artegall "ticked her statues one by one like a teacher checking homework" (124). Male smugness leads him to assert "'God never meant women to hold sway over men!'" (124). All are horrified at his obtuseness; however, Britomart, ever a conciliatory woman, tries to save him by qualifying that Faerie Land is different.

Talus is the "one man at Cleopolis who is never troubled by the pangs of love—or even of indigestion. Talus feels no pain. But then Talus is not made of flesh and blood. Lucky Talus, some say" (113). Spenser's iron man sustained a medieval debate between Justice and Mercy with one character to judge and the other to execute. McCaughrean advised greater fusion, with a subversive observation: "Justice is seldom about Right and Wrong. It is more often about keeping things as they are" (118). Talus, who has neither voice nor mouth, flails at all—and pleases Artegal. When the Queen asks him to stop killing her Amazons, Talus "looked around at her out of his no-eyes. The tilt of his head said, *Pity? What is that?*" (124).

Since social justice is a prominent issue, McCaughrean's exploration raised serious questions. Yet "no-eyes" could evoke robots: "Oil oozed from his ankles, like sweat, rust-proofing the hinges of his wet feet. His eyes were twin holes, iron filings for lashes. He flexed the hollow pipes of his twelve fingers" (114). This was an inversion of the Tin Man in *The Wizard of Oz*, who frequently needed an oilcan. Talus was also characterized by a sound effect, obvious in different typeface and a delight for children to imitate: "Talus moved with unhurried strides—**chunk, chunk, chunk**. The knurled screws on the side of his head whirled in search of sound. The holes in his no-face sniffed the air" (114).

Edwardians idealistically urged young readers to behave like knights of old. McCaughrean's didacticism was to have Calidore explain his quest taught him "That courtesy is not the preserve of knights.... Without it a knight is no better than a Wild Man: and Courtesy makes a Wild Man fit to champion a Queen. I found as much Courtesy among shepherds as among gentlemen" (139). In the final episode at Cleopolis Arthur deems his squire Timian worthy to be dubbed. The moral is: "Of course, we can be knights, you and I" (144).

In the United States Roy Maynard's *Fierce Wars and Faithful Loves* (1999) and Toby J. Sumpter's *The Elfin Knight* (2910), made the poetry of Book I and

Book II of *The Faerie Queene* accessible schoolbooks for older children.[4] Both men described successful teaching of Spenser with texts "Updated and Annotated": spelling was modernized; changed meanings and retained archaisms were glossed, and occasional brief interpretations provided. Maynard followed each canto with "Sword Play" (matching words) and "Review Questions." Sumpter's exercises asked for identification and explanation of short passages. His play of nine scenes was an Appendix (265–282).

Maynard's Introduction quoted C. S. Lewis: "Beyond all doubt, it is best to have made one's first acquaintance with Spenser in a very large—and preferably illustrated—edition of *The Faerie Queene*, on a wet day, between the ages of twelve and sixteen" (9). A theologian, D. Gene Edward Vieth, commented: "In today's cultural, aesthetic, and educational wars, Spenser is a mighty ally for the 21st century Christians" (cover). Sumpter's Introduction observed "Edmund Spenser is an unsung hero in Christian literature" compared with Dante, Milton, and Shakespeare—"I suspect he is far too Christian for our modern taste buds" (9). The cover quoted C. S. Lewis's comment that the poem must first be enjoyed as a fairy tale though it is much more. Recognizing the influential twentieth-century Christian apologist / literary critic of *The Faerie Queene*, Maynard and Sumpter boldly reclaimed Spenser as Protestant advocate.

Ben Shealy retold *Faerie Queene, Book One* (2013) "in modern American idiomatic prose" with an attempt "to retain some sense of that antique language":

> Our hope is that this retelling will be read out loud to children and that eventually those who read this story will read the original poem.
> Sin is ugly and wicked and is so portrayed in this story. The imagery, action, and recurring themes of this tale will delight, caution and inspire young hearts. Older hearers might be enchanted too![5]

This reaffirmed Edwardian commitment to delight and teaching, hopes for later knowledge, and acknowledgment of adult hesitancy. Large print and picture book size, 8 × 10 inches, supported the family experience advocated. The only aid was a list of characters, "first introduced in canto." To a readable and full text Anne Shealy contributed twelve grisaille illustrations. Ten were portraits; Una was the first (3) and Red Cross Knight the last (151). "House of Pride" was a tall castle (43) and a leafy "Tree of Life" had abundant fruit (135). Without depiction of action attention was upon character. Noteworthy was "Sans-Loy, Sans-Joy, Sans-Foy," three Saracen heads (23)—reminiscent of Van Dyke's *Charles I*. "Gluttony" riding a pig (33) was the deadly sin readily understood by children.

While Spenser's *The Faerie Queene* was intensely of its time, these recent children's books recognize its continuing significance and appeal.

Chapter Notes

Preface

1. Velma Bourgeois Richmond, *The Popularity of Middle English Romance* (Bowling Green, OH: Bowling Green University Popular Press, 1975).
2. Velma Bourgeois Richmond, *The Legend of Guy of Warwick* (New York: Garland, 1996, paperback repr. London: Routledge, 2015).
3. See especially Eamon Duffy, *The Stripping of the Altars: Traditional Religion in England 1400-1580* (New Haven and London: Yale University Press, 1992), and Christopher Haigh, *English Reformations: Religion, Politics and Society under the Tudors* (Oxford: Clarendon, 1993).
4. Velma Bourgeois Richmond, *Shakespeare, Catholicism, and Romance* (New York and London: Continuum, 2000, repr. London, New Delhi, New York, Sydney: Bloomsbury, 2015).
5. J. B. Priestly, *The Edwardians* (New York and Evanston, IL: Harper & Row, 1970), 290.

Chapter 1

1. For a detailed discussion of changing audiences for the most popular romance see Velma Bourgeois Richmond, *The Legend of Guy of Warwick* (New York: Garland, 1996).
2. Richard C. McCoy, *The Rites of Knighthood: The Literature and Politics of Elizabethan Chivalry* (Berkeley, Los Angeles, and London: University of California Press, 1989); Sydney Anglo, ed., *Chivalry in the Renaissance* (Woodbridge: Boydell, 1990).
3. See, for example: Eamon Duffy, *The Stripping of the Altars: Traditional Religion in England, c.1400-c.1580* (New Haven, CT: Yale University Press, 1992); Christopher Haigh, Ed., *English Reformation Revised* (Cambridge: Cambridge University Press, 1987) and *English Reformations: Religion, Politics, and Society under the Tudors* (Oxford: Oxford University Press, 1993); Norman Jones, *The English Reformation: Religion and Cultural Adaptation* (Malden, MA: Blackwell, 2002); Ethan Shagan, *Popular Politics and Identity in Early Modern England* (Cambridge: Cambridge University Press, 2003); Ronald Corthell, Frances E. Dolan, Christopher Highley, and Arthur Marotti, eds., *Catholic Culture in Early Modern England* (Notre Dame, IN: University of Notre Dame Press, 2007).
4. Christopher Highley, *Catholics Writing the Nation in Early Modern Britain* (Oxford: Oxford University Press, 2008).
5. See, for example, Velma Bourgeois Richmond, *Shakespeare, Catholicism and Romance* (New York and London: Continuum, 2000); Richard Dutton, Alison Findlay, and Richard Wilson, eds., *Theatre and Religion: Lancastrian Shakespeare* (Manchester: Manchester University Press, 2003); Claire Asquith, *Shadowplay: The Hidden Beliefs and Coded Politics of William Shakespeare* (New York: Public Affairs/Perseus, 2005); Joseph Pearce, *The Quest for Shakespeare: The Bard of Avon and the Church of Rome* (San Francisco: Ignatius, 2008); Piero Boitani, *The Gospel According to Shakespeare*, trans. Vittorio Montemaggi and Rachel Jacoff (Notre Dame, IN: University of Notre Dame Press, 2009).
6. E. M. W. Tillyard, *The English Epic and Its Background* (Oxford: Oxford University Press, 1954), 262-293.
7. Donna B. Hamilton, *Anthony Munday and the Catholics, 1560-1633* (Aldershot: Ashgate 2005); "Anthony Munday's Translations of Iberian Chivalric Romances: *Palmerin of England*, Part I as Exemplar," in *Catholic Culture in Early Modern England*, 281-303.
8. Mary Frances Corinne Patchell, *The Palmerin Romances in Elizabethan Prose* (New York: Columbia University Press, 1947) is a helpful early study.
9. Tiffany Jo Werth, *The Fabulous Dark Cloister: Romance in England after the Reformation*

255

(Baltimore: The Johns Hopkins University Press, 2011), 4. All quotations are from this edition and page references are given in parentheses. Frances E. Dolan, *Whores of Babylon, Catholicism, and Seventeenth-Century Print Culture* (Ithaca, NY: Cornell University Press, 1999) identifies significant attitudes toward gender and religion by a pejorative term applied to Catholics and especially women. Alex Davis, *Chivalry and Romance in the English Renaissance* (Cambridge: D. S. Brewer, 2003) argues vitality and continuity. Helen Cooper, *The English Romance in Time: Transforming Motifs from Geoffrey of Monmouth to the Death of Shakespeare* (Oxford: Oxford University Press, 2004) with a rich thematic structure is more comprehensive.

10. Andrew King, *The Faerie Queene and Middle English Romance: The Matter of Just Memory* (Oxford: Clarendon, 2000) and "Sir Bevis of Hampton: Renaissance Influence and Reception," in Jennifer Fellows and Ivana Djordjevíc, eds., *Sir Bevis of Hampton in Literary Tradition* (Cambridge: D. S. Brewer, 2008), 176–191.

11. Richard Mallette, *Spenser and Discourses of Reformation England* (Lincoln, NE, and London: University of Nebraska Press, 1997).

12. Velma Bourgeois Richmond, *The Popularity of Middle English Romance* (Bowling Green, OH: Bowling Green University Popular Press, 1975) identified this as the essential theme in a variety of texts.

13. Jennifer Fellows, ed., *The Seven Champions of Christendom (1596/7): Non-Canonical Early Modern Texts* (London: Ashgate, 2003) is the original text. An eighteenth-century chapbook version, printed by J. Cotton and J. Eddowes, *The History of the Seven Champions of Christendom*, is available in facsimile (Portland, OR: Richard Abel, 1967).

14. Velma Bourgeois Richmond, *The Legend of Guy of Warwick*, 198–201.

15. Velma Bourgeois Richmond, *Chivalric Stories as Children's Literature: Edwardian Retellings in Words and Pictures* (Jefferson, NC: McFarland, 2014).

16. Quoted in Ronald S. Crane, *The Vogue of Medieval Chivalric Romance during the English Renaissance* (Menasha, WI: George Banta, 1919), 12. See also Richmond, *The Popularity of Middle English Romance*, 9–15, and "The Humanist Rejection of Romance," *The South Atlantic Quarterly* 77 (1978), 296–306.

17. Shulamith Shahar, *Childhood in the Middle Ages*, trans. Chaya Galai (London and New York: Routledge, 1990), 214.

18. Roger Ascham, *Toxophilus*, ed. Edward Archer, *English Reprints* (1869), 19.

19. Roger Ascham, *The Scholemaster*, ed. Edward Arber (London: Constable, 1927), 80.

20. Quoted from Crane, *The Vogue of Medieval Chivalric Romance*, 13.

21. Crane, *The Vogue of Medieval Chivalric Romance*, 20.

22. David H. Richter, ed., *The Critical Tradition Classic Texts and Contemporary Trends* (New York: St. Martin's, 1989).

23. Harold Gardiner, *Mysteries' End: An Investigation of the Last Days of the Medieval Religious Stage* (New Haven: Yale University Press, 1946) charts the systematic suppression of a vital Catholic community experience.

24. Ronald S. Crane, "The Reading of an Elizabethan Youth," *Modern Philology* 44 (1913–1914), 3; see Cooper, *The English Romance in Time*, 444, n101.

25. The text is from English Poetry 1579–1830: Spenser and the Tradition, http://spenserians.cath.vt.edu/TextRecord.php?textsid=33432. Bibliographical information is in Dale B. J. Randall & Jackson C. Boswell, *Cervantes in Seventeenth-Century England*, 131–132.

26. Lewis Spence, *A Dictionary of Medieval Romance and Romance Writers* (London: George Routledge & Sons; and New York: E. P. Dutton, 1913) and William S. Walsh, *Heroes and Heroines of Fiction: Classical, Mediæval, Legendary* (Philadelphia and London: J. P. Lippincott Co, 1915).

27. References that follow are from Dale B. J. Randall and Jackson C. Boswell, *Cervantes in Seventeenth-Century England*. Notes give specific details for the text cited and its place in this compendium.

28. Robert Burton, *The Anatomy of Melancholy*, Part 2, section 2, p. 353, cited in Randall and Boswell, item 52, p. 43.

29. John Taylor, *The Great O Toole* (1622), sig. A4r-v, cited in Randall and Boswell, item 66, p. 51.

30. Quotations are from Peter Heylyn, *Cosmographie in Four Bookes* (1652), cited in Randall and Boswell, item 243, p. 151. There is a recent facsimile (London: Bloomsbury, 2003).

31. *Bartholomew Faire: Or Variety of Fancies Where You May Find a Faire of Wares and All to Please Your Mind. With the Severall Enormityes and Misdemeanous Which Are There Seene and Acted*, p. 4, cited in Randall and Boswell, item 165, p. 102.

32. William London, *A Catalogue of the Most Vendible Books in England* (1657), sig. C2r, cited in Randall and Boswell, item 310, p. 202.

33. Peter Talbot, *A Treatise of Religion and Government with Reflexions upon the Cause and*

Cure of Englands Late Distempers and Present Dangers (1670), p. 148, cited Randall and Boswell, item 515, p. 304.

34. Thomas Brown, *The Late Convert Exposed; or, The Reasons of Mr. Bays's Changing His Religion Considered in a Dialogue. Part the Second* (1690), pp. 47–48, cited in Randall and Boswell, item 878, p. 480.

35. Samuell Croxall, 24–25, cited in Gillian Lathey, *The Role of Translators in Children's Literature: Invisible Storytellers* (New York and London: Routledge, 2010), 28. I am indebted to Lahey's analysis of their translations of Aesop, 26–29.

36. Elizabeth Godfrey (pseudo. Jessie Bedford), *English Children in the Olden Time* 1907 (Williamstown, MA: Corner House, 1980), 209–210. All references are to this reprint with page references given in parentheses.

37. Juliet Dusinberre, *Alice to the Lighthouse: Children's Books and Radical Experiments in Art* (New York: St. Martin's, 1987), 279–280, citing Stuart Dodgson Collingwood, *The Life and Letters of Lewis Carroll* (London, 1898), 107.

38. F. J. Harvey Darton, *Children's Books in England: Five Centuries of Social Life*, 1932; Brian Alderson, rev. 3d ed. (Cambridge: Cambridge University Press, 1982), 93. All references are to this edition with page references given in parentheses.

39. Humphrey Carpenter and Mari Prichard, *The Oxford Companion to Children's Literature* (Oxford and New York: Oxford University Press, 1984), 173.

40. Cornelia Meigs, ed., *A Critical History of Children's Literature: A Survey of Children's Books in English from Earliest Times to the Present* (New York: Macmillan, 1953), 46–51, 121.

41. Mary F. Thwaite, *From Primer to Pleasure in Reading: An Introduction to the History of Children's Books in England from the Invention of Printing to 1914 with an Outline of Some Developments in Other Countries*,1963, rev. American ed. (Boston: Horn, 1972), 100n2, 137. She also refers to Eliza W. Bradburn, *Legends from Spenser's Fairy Queen for Children* (1829), which I have been unable to find; however, Bradburn's *The Story of Paradise Lost* (1830) is in the British Library and available online. This suggests choice among Puritan masterpieces.

42. *The Home Treasury of Old Story Books* (London: Sampson, Low, Son, and Co., 1859).

43. *Bo-Peep Story Books* (New York: Leavitt & Allen [1852].

44. Victor E. Neuburg, *The Penny Histories, The Juvenile Library* (London: Oxford University Press, 1968) is a fine introduction to chapbooks as children's literature with several facsimiles. The romance example is *The History of Guy of Warwick*. Alison Lurie and Justin G. Schiller, *Classics of Children's Literature 1621–1932*, A Garland Series (London and New York: Garland, 1977), has facsimiles of chapbooks. Michael Patrick Hearn's introduction to Richard Johnson's *The History of Tom Thumbe* (1621) lists ten notable editions, the last in 1934. Hearn's introduction to two examples of *The History of Jack & the Giants* (c.1711–1730) lists eight notable nineteenth-century versions and three twentieth-century ones. The other facsimiles were of *Robin Hood's Garland* (1789) and three fairy tales—*Little Red Riding Hood, Beauty and the Beast*, and *Jack and the Beanstalk*—from Henry Cole's *The Home Treasury* (1845), but not *The Faerie Queene* that was also offered. Margaret Spufford, *Small Books and Pleasant Histories: Popular Fiction and Its Readership in Seventeenth-century England* (Athens: University of Georgia Press, 1981) is a broad and richly detailed study of texts and contexts. Spufford's appendix annotated the trade-list of William Thackeray (1689)—"Small godly books," "Small merry books," and "Double books"—to identify 217 items purchased by Samuel Pepys and bound as collections of *Penny Merriements*, three volumes; *Penny Godlinesses*, one volume; and *Vulgaria*, four volumes. They are in the Pepys Library, Magdalene College, Cambridge. Velma Bourgeois Richmond, *The Legend of Guy of Warwick* details chapbook and children's version of this most popular romance. John Simons, ed., *Guy of Warwick and Other Chapbook Romances: Six Tales from the Popular Literature of Pre-Industrial England* has examples dating from the eighteenth and nineteenth centuries: *Guy of Warwick* (two versions), *The Seven Champions of Christendom, Parismus, Valentine and Orson*, and *The Seven Wise Masters of Rome*.

45. F. J. Furnivall, *Captain Cox His Ballads and His Books, or, Robert Laneham's Letter* (London: Ballad Society, 1871).

46. Louis B. Wright, *Middle Class Culture in Elizabethan England* (Chapel Hill: University of North Carolina Press, 1934), 86–87. See Lori Humphrey Newcomb, *Reading Popular Romance in Early Modern England* (New York: Columbia University Press, 2002), 149–156

47. Margaret Spufford, 73, makes this point and cites her knowledge of current parallel activity, 82n89.

48. Francis Kirkman, "Epistle" in Jerónimo Fernández's *The Honour of Chivalry; or, The Famous and Delectable History of Don Bellianis of*

Greece (1664), sig. A3v-4r, cited in Randall and Boswell, item 440, pp. 267-268.

49. Roger Thompson, ed., *Samuel Pepys' Penny Merriments* (New York: Columbia University Press, 1976), 95. This book of eighty extracts indicates the variety and flavor of seventeenth-century chapbooks and reproduces thirty title pages. A similar approach was used in John Ashton, *Chapbooks of the Eighteenth Century*, 1882, repr. (New York and London: Benjamin Blom, 1966). Ashton, who based his collection on chapbooks published in Aldermary and Bow Churchyard, gave some chapbooks in their entirety and summarized others. Included are an alphabetical list of titles and notes of sources and versions. See also Tessa Watt, *Cheap Print and Popular Piety* (Cambridge: Cambridge University Press, 1991) and Lori Humphrey Newcomb, *Reading Popular Romance*, 156-157.

50. *The Lucubrations of Isaac Bickerstaff, Esq.* (London, 1754), 2: 244-245.

51. Laurence Sterne, *The Life and Opinions of Tristram Shandy Gentleman* (New York: Modern Library, [1950]), 480.

52. F. J. Harvey Darton, *Children's Books in England: Five Centuries of Social Life*, 214.

53. Dated 16 October 1797 in Earl Leslie Griggs, ed., *Collected Letters of Samuel Taylor Coleridge* (Oxford: Clarendon Press, 1956), 1: 354, cited by Gillian Lathey, *The Role of Translators in Children's Literature*, 64.

54. Cited by David Vincent, *Literacy and Popular Culture England 1750-1914*, 198.

55. Vincent, 210-214.

56. Cited by Vincent, 165, 309n45, from J. Bowd, "The Life of a Farm Worker," *The Countryman* 51, pt. 2 (1955), 293-294.

57. Cited by Vincent, 222-223, 321n141, from J. Eldred, *I Love the Brooks* (London, 1955), 45.

Chapter 2

1. Carol Belanger Grafton, arranger, *Walter Crane: Illustrations and Ornamentation from The Fearie Queene* (Mineola, NY: Dover, 1999). All references are to this edition with page references given in parentheses.

2. Walter Crane, *Of the Decorative Illustration of Books Old and New*, 1896 (London: Bell & Hyman, 1979). All quotations are from the reprint, and page references are given in parentheses.

3. J. E. Rabbeth, *The Story of Spenser's Faerie Queene* (London: George Bell & Sons, 1887). All quotations are from this edition, and page references are given in parentheses.

4. Wikipedia includes reference to Macleod, http://www.sacred-texts.com/neu/eng/sfqj.

5. *Knights and Enchanters: Three Tales from The Faerie Queen* (Salisbury: Brown & Co., and London: Simpkin, Marshall & Co., 1873), 3. All quotations are from this edition, and page references are given in parentheses.

6. M. H. Towry, *Spenser for Children*, 1878 (London: Chatto & Windus, 1885). All quotations are from the later edition, and page references are given in parentheses.

7. Spenser wrote of "Sir Guyon," the French name. Towry's "Sir Guy" might have been intended to point the connection to Sir Guy of Warwick, Spenser's inspiration. See Velma Bourgeois Richmond, *The Legend of Guy of Warwick* (New York and London: Garland, 1996), 165-166. An unpublished "Corrected Historie of Guy Earle of Warwick" (1621) by John Lane, was written in Spenserian stanzas, 213-219. Guy's story was a favorite for Victorian and Edwardian children, not least in chapbooks.

8. Sophia H. Maclehose, *Tales from Spenser Chosen from The Faerie Queene*, 1889 (Glasgow: James Maclehose & Sons, 1902). All quotations are from the fifth edition with page references given in parentheses.

9. R. A. Y., *The Story of the Red Cross Knight*, 1885 (London, Edinburgh, and New York: T. Nelson & Sons, 1891). All quotations are from the later printing with page references given in parentheses.

Chapter 3

1. Humphrey Carpenter, *Secret Gardens: A Study of the Golden Age of Children's Literature* (London: George Allen and Unwin, 1985) and Jacqueline Rose, *The Case of Peter Pan, Or, The Impossibility of Children's Fiction* (Philadelphia: University of Pennsylvania Press, 1984) are influential readings.

2. Mary Macleod, *Stories from the Faerie Queene*, 1897, 3d ed. (London: Gardner, Darton & Co., 1903). All quotations are from this edition, with page references given in parentheses.

3. Mary Macleod, *The Red Cross Knight and Sir Guyon* (London: Wells, Gardner, Darton & Co., 1908).

4. E. Edwardson, *The Courteous Knight and Other Tales Borrowed from Spenser and Malory* (Edinburgh and London: T. Nelson & Sons, 1899). All quotations are from this edition, with page references given in parentheses. My copy was a first prize awarded by the School Board

of Thurso at The Miller Institution, for English, Higher Grade, Class II, in 1908-09.

5. Children's versions were quite varied. It was one of the earliest titles in an inexpensive (one penny) paper booklet, W. T. Stead, *The Adventures of Reynard the Fox*, Books for the Bairns #5 (London: "Review of Reviews" Office, July 1896). It was the major item in an extravagant collection, F. J. Havey Darton, ed., *A Wonder Book of Beasts* (London: Wells Gardner Darton & Co., 1909), 90-219. E. Louise Smythe, *Reynard the Fox*, Eclectic School Readings (New York, Cincinnati, and Chicago: American Book Co., 1903) was an American schoolbook.

6. W. T. Stead, *The Red Cross Knight, Parts I and II*, Books for the Bairns #53 and #54 (London: Review of Reviews Office, 1900). All quotations are from these editions, and page references are given in parentheses. See Sally Wood, *W. T. Stead and His "Books for the Bairns"* (Edinburgh: Salvia, 1987), especially for bibliographical information; Estelle Wilson Stead, *My Father: Personal and Spiritual Reminiscences* (London: Thomas Nelson, 1918); Frederick Whyte, *The Life of W. T. Stead*, 2 vols. (London: Jonathan Cape, 1925); Roger Lockhurst, ed., *W. T. Stead Newspaper Revolutionary* (London: British Library, 2012).

7. Bound issues indicate individual efforts to preserve. Those in my collection combined from five to eleven books; some had special interests: Christmas stories, fairy tales, histories, and legendary stories.

8. N(aomi) G. Royde-Smith, *Una and the Red Cross Knight and Other Tales from Spenser's Fairy Queene* (London: J. M. Dent & Co.; and New York: E. P. Dutton & Co., 1905). All quotations are from this edition, and page references are given in parentheses.

9. Jeanie Lang, *Stories from the Faerie Queene*, Told to the Children Series (London: T. C. & E. C. Jack & New York: E. P. Dutton, 1906), [iii]. All quotations are from this edition and page references are given in parentheses.

10. R(obert) W. Grace, *Tales from Spenser* (London: T. Fisher Unwin, 1909). All quotations are from this edition and page references are given in parentheses.

11. Samuel Smiles, *Self-Help: With Illustrations of Conduct and Perseverance* (London, John Murray, 1913), 437. There were editions in many languages; I quote an Edwardian reprint, price one shilling, appropriate for a book that originated as lectures to humble workers in an evening class.

12. Velma Bourgeois Richmond, *Chivalric Stories as Children's Literature: Edwardian Retellings in Words and Pictures* (Jefferson, NC: McFarland, 2014), especially 8-10.

13. My copy was a prize given at Dr. Williams' School for Form IIIa. "Honour before Honours" was the motto on the citation.

14. Lawrence H. Dawson, *Stories from The Faerie Queene Retold from Spenser* (London: George G. Harrap & Co., 1909), v. All quotations are from the 1911 printing, and page references are given in parentheses.

15. Harrap's characteristic publishing history records interest: First published in the Romance Series March 1909. Reprinted February 1911. Reprinted in the Told Through the Ages Series: December 1909; April 1911; February 1912; July 1914; October 1917; October 1919; August 1921; April 1923; May 1925; July 1927; September 1928; October 1930; March 1935; March 1945.

16. See Velma Bourgeois Richmond, *Chivalric Stories as Children's Literature*, 149-155

17. A. J. Church, *The Faery Queen and Her Knights: Stories Retold from Edmund Spenser* (London: Seeley & Co., 1910). All quotations are from this edition, and page references are given in parentheses.

18. Emily Underdown, *The Gateway to Spenser: Tales Retold from "The Faerie Queene" of Edmund Spenser* (London, Edinburgh, Dublin, and New York, 1911), 7. All quotations are from this edition, and page references are given in parentheses.

19. Emily Underdown, *Stories from Spenser: Retold from "The Faerie Queene" of Edmund Spenser* (London, Edinburgh, Dublin, and New York, 1912). All quotations are from this edition, and page references are given in parentheses.

20. Records of the publisher are at Reading University, UK.

21. Andrew Lang, ed., *The Book of Romance* (London, New York, and Bombay: Longmans, Green, & Co., 1902), v, viii. Quotation is from the 1903 reprint.

22. Andrew Lang, ed., *The Red Romance Book* (London, New York and Bombay: Longmans, Green, & Co., 1905), vi. All quotations are from this edition with page references given in parentheses.

23. W. J. Glover, *Tales from the Poets* (London: A. and C. Black, 1915), 92. All quotations are from this edition with page references given in parentheses.

24. M. Dorothy Belgrave and Hilda Hart, *Children's Stories from the Poets*, The Raphael House Library of Gift Books, ed. Edric Vredenburg (London, Paris, New York, 1915). All quotations are from this edition with page references given in parentheses.

25. Christine Chaundler, *My Book of Stories from the Poets* (London, New York, Toronto and Melbourne, 1919). All quotations are from this edition with page references given in parentheses.

26. H(élenè) A(deline) Guerber, *The Book of the Epic: The World's Great Epics Told in Story* (London: George G. Harrap, 1919). All quotations are from this edition with page references given in parentheses.

Chapter 4

1. Edward Brooks, ed., *The Story of the Faerie Queene* (Philadelphia: The Penn Publishing Co., 1902). All quotations are from this edition with page references given in parentheses.

2. Velma Bourgeois Richmond, *Chaucer as Children's Literature: Retellings from the Victorian and Edwardian Eras* (Jefferson, NC: McFarland, 2000), 156–161.

3. Calvin Dill Wilson, *The Faery Queen, Book First* (Chicago: A. C. McClurg & Co., 1906), v. All quotations are from this edition and page references are given in parentheses.

4. Grace Adele Pierce, *The Red Cross Knight and The Legend of Britomart (the Lady Knight): Being Tales from Spenser's "Faerie Queene" Done into Simpler English* (New York: John Martin's House, 1924). All quotations are from this edition; since pages are not numbered, my references give a Roman number for the Adventure and Arabic for the page in each part.

5. Abbie Sage Richardson's *Stories from Old English Poetry*, c. 1871 (Boston: Houghton Mifflin & Co., 1891). All quotations are from this edition with page references given in parentheses.

6. She chose stories from Shakespeare's romances, similar comedies, and British history. Other early modern dramatists—John Lyly and Robert Greene—were sources for three stories. See Velma Bourgeois Richmond, *Shakespeare as Children's Literature: Edwardian Retellings in Words and Pictures* (Jefferson, NC: McFarland, 2008), 115–130.

7. See Velma Bourgeois Richmond, *Chaucer as Children's Literature*, 65–70.

8. Abbie Sage Richardson was the occasion for a notorious trial of her first husband, Daniel McFarland, whom she left for Albert David Richardson, journalist and Union spy. McFarland shot and killed Richardson in a second attempt. Henry Ward Beecher married Abbie Richardson just before he died. McFarland was acquitted.

9. Carolyn Sherwin Bailey, *Stories of Great Adventures*, For the Children's Hour Series (Springfield, MA: Milton Bradley Co., 1919), 219–220.

10. *The Delphian Course: A Systematic Plan for Education, Embracing the World's Progress and Development of the Liberal Arts*, 10 vols. (Chicago: The Delphian Society, 1913), 1: x-xi.

11. *The Delphian Course*, 8: 106.

12. Thomas Bailey Aldrich, ed., *Young Folks' Library*, 20 vols. 1901–02 (Boston: Hall & Locke, Co., rev. ed. 1910), xiii. Quotations are from this edition, and page references are given in parentheses.

13. Charles Welsh, *The Key to the Treasure House: A Book of Reference Containing Complete Indexes, A Pronouncing Vocabulary, Notes on Literary Sources, and on Names, Places, Events, References, and Allusions in the Young Folks' Library* (Boston: Hall & Locke Co., 1902), 2–3. Quotations are from this edition, and page references are given in parentheses.

14. Robert Newton Linscott, *A Guide to Good Reading with Practical Directions for the Use of The Children's Hour in the Home* (Boston: Houghton Mifflin Co., 1912), 20.

15. Eva March Tappan, *A Short History of England's Literature* (Boston, New York, Chicago, Dallas, Atlanta, San Francisco: Houghton Mifflin Co., 1905/1933). Reference is from the revised edition.

16. William Patten, ed. *Heroes and Heroines of Chivalry*, vol. 4, *The Junior Classics*, 10 vols. 1912 (New York: P. F. Collier & Son Co., 1918), 9. All quotations are from the reissue, and page references are given in parentheses.

17. *Our Wonder World: A Library of Knowledge* (Chicago and Boston: Geo. L. Shuman Co., 1914), v. Quotations are from the 1929 reprint of *Every Child's Story Book*, vol. 5, and page references are given in parentheses.

18. *Our Wonder World: A Library of Knowledge, Story and History*, vol. 8 (Chicago and Boston: Geo. L. Shuman Co., 1914). All quotations are from this edition, and page references are given in parentheses.

19. William Brown Forbush, ed., *Classic Tales and Legendary Stories*, vol. 3, *Young Folks' Treasury*, eds., Hamilton Wright Mabie, Edward Everett Hale, and William Brown Forbush (New York: The University Society, 1919), v. All quotations are from this edition, and page references are given in parentheses.

20. Dorothy Loring Taylor, *Olive Beaupré Miller and the Book House for Children* (Chicago: Chicago Review Press, 1986), is a biography and well-illustrated bibliographical sur-

vey, 93–104, which describes uncertainties in distinguishing the many editions. Much of my discussion is indebted to Taylor.

21. Olive Beaupré Miller, ed., *The Latch Key of My Book House*, vol. 6 (Chicago: The Bookhouse for Children, 1921, 1925). All quotations are from this edition, and page references are given in parentheses.

22. Olive Beaupré Miller, ed., *Halls of Fame of My Book House*, vol. 12 (Chicago: The Bookhouse for Children, 34th printing, 1951). All quotations are from this edition, and page references are given in parentheses.

23. Curiously the addenda "More Short Stories from Life" of nine pages, in smaller print, preceded the indexes. Within a long list with names, nationalities, dates, and titles were longer entries for established English major authors—Blake, Byron, Milton, Charles Kingsley, George MacDonald, John Ruskin, Swinburne, Thackeray. Longer entries for many Americans were writers who did not achieve canonical status; the most notable exception was Carl Sandburg.

24. Olive Beaupré Miller, ed., *From the Tower Window of My Book House*, vol. 5 (Chicago: The Bookhouse for Children, 1921). All quotations are from this edition, and page references are given in parentheses.

25. Although a long undervalued artist, Crane is now increasingly recognized as an early fantasy artist. See http://babylonbaroque.wordpress.com/category/donn-p-crane/.

26. Olive Beaupré Miller, *From the Tower Window of My Book House*, vol. 10 (Lake Bluff, IL: The Book House for Children, 1963). All quotations are from this edition—many dates are given, but seem to be reprints from 1950s—and page references are given in parentheses.

27. Olive Beaupré Miller, ed., *In Shining Armor of My Book House*, vol. 11 (Chicago: The Book House for Children, 1950). All quotations are from this edition, the 33rd printing, and page references are given in parentheses, 3.

28. James Baldwin, *The Book Lover: A Guide to the Best Reading*, 1884, 14th ed. (Chicago: A. C. McClurg & Co., 1902), 5. All quotations are from this edition and page references are given in parentheses.

29. Mary E. Burt, *Literary Landmarks: A Guide to Good Reading for Young People, and Teachers' Assistant* (Boston and New York: Houghton, Mifflin, & Co., 1897). All quotations are from this edition and page references are given in parentheses.

30. John Harrington Cox, *Literature in the Common Schools* (Boston: Little, Brown, & Co.,

1909), vii. All quotations are from this edition and page references are given in parentheses.

31. Montrose J. Moses, *Children's Books and Reading* (New York: Mitchell Kennerley, 1907).

32. Frances Jenkins Olcott, *The Children's Reading* (Boston and New York: Houghton Mifflin Co., 1912), xii-xiii. All quotations are from this edition and page references are given in parentheses.

Chapter 5

1. Henry Newbolt, *The Teaching of English in England: Being the Report of the Departmental Committee Appointed by the President of the Board of Education to Inquire into the Position in the Educational System of England* (London: His Majesty's Stationery Office, 1924), 374.

2. D. Laing Purves, ed., *The Canterbury Tales and Faerie Queene with Other Poems of Chaucer and Spenser, Edited for Popular Perusal with Current Illustrations and Explanatory Notes* (London and Edinburgh: William P. Nimmo, 1884), clearly linked the first two great English poets.

3. Zaidee Brown, ed., *Standard Catalog for High School Libraries* (New York: The H. W. Wilson Co., 1929), has no entry for Edmund Spenser.

4. Hubert M. Skinner, *Readings in Folk-Lore: Short Studies in the Mythology of America, Great Britain, The Norse Countries, Germany, India, Syria, Egypt, and Persia; With Selections from Standard Literature Relating to the Same* (New York, Cincinnati, Chicago: American Book Co., 1893). All quotations are from this edition, and page references are given in parentheses.

5. Clara L. Thomson, *Tales from The Faerie Queene* (Shaldon, South Devon: The Norland Press, 1902). All references are to the corrected second edition (London: Horace Marshall & Son, nd.), v.

6. See Velma Bourgeois Richmond, *Chivalric Stories as Children's Literature: Edwardian Retellings in Words and Pictures* (Jefferson, NC: McFarland & Co., 2014) 326–340.

7. *Stories from "The Faerie Queene,"* Arnold's Tales of Old Romance Series (London: Edward Arnold, (1902).

8. Alfonzo Gardiner, ed., *St. George of Merry England, from Spenser's "Faerie Queene,"* The "A. L." Bright Story Readers, No. 32 (Leeds, Glasgow, & Belfast: E. J. Arnold & Son, c. 1908), back cover. All quotations are from this edition, and page references are given in parentheses.

9. Lack of reference to Chap. XIV, which gives the end of the story, was apparently an oversight.

10. The role of Notes was explained in the parallel blurb given for "The Books for the Upper Classes ... The Books in this Series are to be used as Alternative Literary or Continuous Readers—one or more each term. The Notes at the end of each book make the Series unequalled for Silent Reading.
"They are printed in bold, clear type on an Imperial 16 mo page (size 5½ × 7¼ inches), and all are suitably illustrated."

11. *Tales from the Faerie Queene*, Longmans' Continuous Story Readers (London, New York, Bombay, and Calcutta: Longmans, Green, & Co., 1910). All quotations are from this edition, and page references are given in parentheses.

12. Andrew Lang, ed., *The Red Romance Book* (London, New York, and Bombay: Longmans, Green, & Co., 1905). All quotations are from this edition, and page references are given in parentheses.

13. Mary E. Litchfield, *Spenser's Britomart: From Books III, IV, and V* (Boston and London: Ginn & Co., The Athenæum Press, 1896). All quotations are from this edition, and page references are given in parentheses.

14. Arthur Burrell, ed. *Selections from The Faerie Queene* (English Literature for Schools (London: J. M. Dent & Sons, 1914), 5. All quotations are from this edition, and page references are given in parentheses.

15. Minna Steele Smith, *Stories from Spenser* (Cambridge: Cambridge University Press, 1919). All quotations are from this edition, and page references are given in parentheses.

16. For discussion of *Minstrel Tales*, see Velma Bourgeois Richmond, *Chivalric Stories as Children's Literature*, 313–316; for *The Canterbury Pilgrims*, see Velma Bourgeois Richmond, *Chaucer as Children's Literature: Retellings from the Victorian and Edwardian Eras* (Jefferson, NC: McFarland, 2000), 181–185.

17. M(ary Sturt and E(llen) C(atherine) Oakden, *The Knights of The Faerie Queene: Tales Retold from Spenser*, The King's Treasuries of Literature #115 (London: J. M. Dent & Sons and New York: E. P. Dutton & Co., 1924), 6. All quotations are from the 1931 reprint, and page references are given in parentheses.

18. Henrietta Christian Wright, *Children's Stories in English Literature* (London: Ward & Downey, 1890). All quotations are from this edition and page references are given in parentheses.

19. C. Linklater Thomson, *A First Book in English Literature, Part III Lyndsay to Bacon* (London: Horace Marshall & Son, 1906). All quotations are from this edition and page references are given in parentheses.

20. *The Greenwood Tree: A Book of Nature Myths and Verses*, Arnold's Literary Reading Books (London: Edward Arnold, 1903).

21. *In Golden Realms*, Arnold's Literary Reading Books (London: Edward Arnold, 1902), 145. All quotations are from this edition and page references are given in parentheses.

22. *In the World of Books*, Arnold's Literary Reading Books (London: Edward Arnold, 1902). All quotations are from this edition and page references are given in parentheses.

23. *Tales of Many Lands, Book II, Steps to Literature* (London: Edward Arnold, 1905), 9–11. All quotations are from this edition and page references are given in parentheses.

24. Publisher's blurb included as end papers.

25. *Stories from English and Welsh Literature, Book III, Steps to Literature* (London: Edward Arnold, 1905), 63. All quotations are from this edition and page references are given in parentheses.

26. *Stories from the Literature of the British Isles, Book IIIA, Steps to Literature* (London: Edward Arnold, 1905), 26–27. All quotations are from this edition and page references are given in parentheses.

27. Publisher's blurb included as end papers.

28. *Tales that Are Told, Part VI, The Royal Treasury of Story and Song* (London, Edinburgh, Dublin and New York: Thomas Nelson & Sons, 1909), 15–19. All quotations are from this edition and page references are given in parentheses.

29. Veronica Franklin Gould, *G. F. Watts The Last Great Victorian* (New Haven and London: Yale University Press, 2004), 95. Prinsep, subsequently a lieutenant general in command of the Eleventh Bengal Lancers, was also the idealized knight in Watts's *Aspiration*, another painting of a knight sometimes included in schoolbooks.

30. *The Morning Star, Book III, Highroads of Literature* (London, Edinburgh, Dublin, and New York: Thomas Nelson & Sons, 1915), 9. All quotations are from this edition and page references are given in parentheses.

Chapter 6

1. Henry Gilbert, *Stories of Great Writers*, "In Days of Old Series" (London, Edinburgh, New York: T. C. & E. C. Jack, 1914).

2. Abby Sage Richardson, *Familiar Talks on English Literature* 1881, rev. ed. (Chicago: A. C. McClurg & Co., 1894), vi. All quotations are from the third edition, and page references are given in parentheses.

3. Dorothea Beale, *Literary Studies of Poems, New and Old* (London: George Bell & Son, 1902), [iii]. All quotations are from the Classic Reprint Series (London: Forgotten Books, 2015) and page references are given in parentheses.
4. Eva March Tappan, *A Short History of England's Literature*, 1905, 2d rev. ed. (Boston, New York, Chicago, Dallas, Atlanta, San Francisco: Houghton Mifflin Co., 1933). All references are from the revised (including the title) edition printed in 1933.
5. H(enrietta) E. Marshall, *English Literature for Boys and Girls* (London and Edinburgh: T. C. & E. C. Jack, 1909). All quotations are from this edition and page references are given in parentheses.
6. John Clare, "Free—A Proper History Book for Every School," *The Daily Telegraph*, September 21, 2005, p. 25.
7. Zaidee Brown, ed., *Standard Catalog for High School Libraries: A Selected List of 2600 Books* (New York: The H. W. Wilson Co., 1929), 127.
8. The judgment "sad to say" was not atypical for Edwardian stories for children: Mary was usually viewed more sympathetically than Elizabeth. See Velma Bourgeois Richmond, "Elizabeth I in Imperial Britain: A Myth for Children," in Christa Jansohn, ed., *Queen Elizabeth I: Past and Present*, Studien zur englischen Literatur 19 (Münster: Lit Verlag, 2004), 211–231.
9. All quotations are from the American edition, Edward Parrott, *The Pageant of English Literature* (New York: Sully & Kleinteich, 1914), iii.
10. Clara Linklater Thomson, *Our Inheritance* (Cambridge: Cambridge University Press, 1910), 39.
11. Andrew Lang *History of English Literature: From "Beowulf" to Swinburne* 1912 (London, New York, Bombay, Calcutta: Longmans, Green & Co., 1913). All quotations are from the third edition, and page references are given in parentheses.
12. W(illiam) H(enry) Hudson, *An Outline History of English Literature* 1912, repr. (London: G. Bell & Sons, 1941). The book was frequently reprinted; the new edition of 1930 added "The Age of Hardy (1887–1928)" written by A. C. Ward. All quotations are from a reprint of 1941 with page references given in parentheses.
13. Amy Cruse, *English Literature through the Ages: Beowulf to Stevenson* (London, Calcutta, and Sydney: George G. Harrap & Co., 1914). All quotations are from this edition and page references are given in parentheses.
14. Amy Cruse, *The Shaping of English Literature: And the Readers' Share in the Development of Its Forms* (London, Bombay, Sydney: George G. Harrap, 1927). All quotations are from this edition and page references are given in parentheses.
15. William J. Long, *Outlines of English and American Literature: An Introduction to the Chief Writers of England and America, to the Books They Wrote, and to the Times in which They Lived* (Boston, New York, Chicago, London, Atlanta, Dallas, Columbus, and San Francisco: Ginn & Co., 1917). All quotations are from this edition and page references are given in parentheses.
16. Herbert Bates, *English Literature 1918* (Longmans, Green & Co., 1923). The first edition April 1918 was reprinted and then followed by a new edition September 1919 that was frequently reprinted. All quotations are from the October 1923 reprint, and page references are given in parentheses.

Epilogue

1. Sandol Stodard Warburg, *Saint George and the Dragon: Being The Legend of the Red Cross Knight from The Faerie Queeene by Edmund Spenser* (Boston: Houghton Mifflin Co., 1963), [v]. All quotations are from this edition, and page references are given in parentheses.
2. Margaret Hodges, *Saint George and the Dragon: A Golden Legend Adapted from Edmund Spenser's Faerie Queene* (New York and Boston: Little Brown & Co., 1984).
3. Geraldine McCaughrean, *The Questing Knights of The Fairie Queen* (London: Hodder Children's Books, 2004). All quotations are from this edition and page references are given in parentheses
4. Roy Maynard, *Fierce Wars and Faithful Loves, Book I of Edmund Spenser's The Faerie Queene* (Moscow, ID: Canon Press, 1999), and Toby J. Sumpter, *The Elfin Knight: Book II of Edmund Spenser's The Faerie Queene* (Moscow, ID: Canon Press, 2010). All quotations are from this edition, and page references are given in parentheses.
5. Ben Shealy, *Faerie Queene, Book One* (New York: Atelerix, 2013), Library of Congress Summary and v. All quotations are from this edition, and page references are given in parentheses.

Bibliography

Books

Brooks, Edward, ed. *The Story of the Faerie Queene*. [A. G. Walker illustrations unidentified.] Philadelphia: Penn, 1902.
Church, A(lfred). J. *The Faery Queene and Her Knights: Stories Retold from Spenser*. Illustrated in Color. London: Seeley, 1910.
Dawson, Lawrence H. *Stories from the Faerie Queene Retold from Spenser*. 1909. Told through the Ages Series. Illustrated by Gertrude Demain Hammond. London: George G. Harrap, 1909, repr. 1948.
Edwardson, E. *The Courteous Knight and Other Tales: Borrowed from Spenser and Malory*. Illustrated by Robert Hope. Edinburgh and London: T. Nelson & Sons, 1899.
Grace, R. W. *Tales from Spenser*. Illustrated by Helen S. Kück. London: T. Fisher Unwin, 1909.
Hodges, Margaret. *Saint George and the Dragon*. Illustrated by Trina Schart Hyman. New York and Boston: Little, Brown, 1984.
Knights and Enchanters: Three Tales from The Faerie Queene. Salisbury: Brown & Co.; and London: Simpkin, Marshall & Co., 1873.
Lang, Jeanie. *Stories from The Faerie Queene*. Told to the Children Series. Illustrated by Rose Le Quesne. London: T. C. & E. C. Jack; and New York: E. P. Dutton, 1906.
Maclehose, Sophia H. *Tales Chosen from The Faerie Queene*. Glasgow: James Maclehose & Sons, 1889/1902.
Macleod, Mary. *The Red Cross Knight and Sir Guyon: From Spenser's "Faerie Queene."* Illustrated by A. G. Walker. London: Gardner, Darton, 1908.
_____. *Stories from the Faerie Queene*. Illustrated by A. G. Walker. London: Gardner, Darton, & Co., 1897; 3d ed. 1903.
Maynard, Roy. *Fierce Wars and Faithful Loves. Book I of Edmund Spenser's Faerie Queene*. Moscow, ID: Canon, 1999.
McCaughrean, Geraldine. *The Questing Knights of The Færie Queen*. Illustrated by Jason Cockcroft. Hodder Children's Books. London: Hodder Headline, 2004.
Pierce, Grace Adele. *The Red Cross Knight and The Legend of Britomart [The Lady Knight]*. Illustrated by Henry Pitz. New York: John Martin's House, 1924.
R. A. Y. *The Story of the Red Cross Knight*. Illustrated by E.M.M.S. London, Edinburgh, and New York: Thomas Nelson & Son, 1891.
Royde-Smith, N(aomi). G. *Una and the Red Cross Knight and Other Tales from Spenser's Faery Queene*. Illustrated by T. H. Robinson. London: J. M. Dent; and New York: E. P. Dutton, 1905.
Shealy, Ben. *Faerie Queene Book I*. Illustrated by Anne Shealy. New York: Atelerix, 2013.
Smith, Minna Steele. *Stories from Spenser*. Cambridge: Cambridge University Press, 1919.
Stead, W. T. *The Redcross Knight*, Part I and Part II. Books for the Bairns Series # 53 and 54. Illustrated by Brinsley Le Fanu. London: Review of Reviews Office, 1900.
The Story of St. George and the Dragon, or, The Redcross Knight, from Spenser's Faerie Queene, The Penny Poets #18, The Masterpiece Library. London: Review of Reviews Office, 1895?.
Sumpter, Toby J. *The Elfin Knight Book II of Edmund Spenser's The Faerie Queene*. Moscow, ID: Canon, 2010.

Towry, M. H. *Spenser for Children.* Illustrated by W(alter). J. Morgan. 1878. London: Chatto & Windus, 1885.

Unterdown, Emily. *The Approach to Spenser: Prose Tales with Extracts.* Edinburgh, Dublin, and New York: Thomas Nelson, 1925.

———. *The Gateway to Spenser: Tales Retold from "The Faerie Queene."* Illustrated by F(rank). C. Papé. London, Edinburgh, Dublin, and New York: Thomas Nelson & Sons, 1911.

———. *Stories from Spenser: Retold from "The Faerie Queene."* London, Edinburgh, Dublin, New York: Thomas Nelson & Sons, 1912.

Warburg, Sandol Stoddard. *Saint George and the Dragon: Being the Legend of the Red Cross Knight from The Faerie Queene by Edmund Spenser.* Illustrated by Pauline Baynes. Boston: Houghton Mifflin, 1963.

Wilson, Calvin Dill. *The Faery Queen: First Book.* Old Tales Retold for Young Readers. Chicago: A. C. McClurg, 1906.

Collections

Bailey, Carolyn Sherwin. *Stories of Great Adventure.* For the Children's Hour Series. Springfield, MA: Milton Bradley, 1919.

Belgrave, Dorothy M. and Hilda Hart. *Children's Stories from the Poets: Tales of Romance and Adventure Told in Prose.* The Raphael House Library of Gift Books. Illustrated by Frank Adams. London, Paris, and New York: Raphael Tuck & Sons, 1915.

Chaundler, Christine. *My Book of Stories from the Poets.* Illustrated by A. C. Michael. London, New York, Toronto, and Melborne: Cassell, 1919.

Glover, W(illiam) J(ohn). *Tales from the Poets.* Illustrated by Sybil Tawse. London: A. & C. Black, 1915.

Guerber, H(elène) A. *The Book of the Epic.* Illustrated by various artists. London: George G. Harrap, 1919.

Lang, Andrew, ed. *The Red Romance Book.* Illustrated by Henry J. Ford. London, New York and Bombay: Longmans, Green, & Co., 1889.

Richardson, Abbie Sage. *Stories from Old English Poetry.* Boston: Houghton, Mifflin, & Co., 1891.

School Books

READERS

Burrell, Arthur, ed. *Selections from The Faerie Queene.* English Literature for Schools. London: J. M. Dent & Sons, 1914.

Gardiner, Alfonzo. *St. George of Merry England from Spenser's "Faerie Queene."* The "A. L." Bright Story Readers # 32. Leeds, Glasgow, & Belfast: E. J. Arnold, 19—.

Litchfield, Mary E. *Spenser's Britomart: From Books III, IV, and V.* Boston and London: Ginn & Co., 1896.

Smith, Minna Steele. *Stories from Spenser.* Cambridge: Cambridge University Press, 1919, repr. 2014.

Stories from "The Faerie Queene." Arnold's Tales of Old Romance Series. London: Edward Arnold, 1908?.

Sturt, M(ary)., and E(llen). C. Oakden, *The Knights of the Faerie Queene: Tales Retold from Spenser.* The King's Treasuries of Literature #115. London & Toronto: J. M. Dent & Sons; and New York: E. P. Dutton, 1924.

Tales from the Fairy Queen. Longmans' Continuous Story Readers, Junior Series. London, New York, Bombay, and Calcutta: Longmans, Green, 1910.

Thomson, Clara L(inklater). *Spenser: The Faerie Queene, Book I.* The Carmelite Classics. London: Horace Marshall & Son, 1905.

———. *Tales from the Faerie Queene.* Illustrated by Helen Stratton. Shaldon, South Devon: Norland, 1902.

GRADED SCHOOL BOOKS

Arnold's Literary Reading Books. 8 vols. London: Edward Arnold, 1902-11. *In Golden Realms: An English Reading Book for Junior Forms,* 1902; *Chips from a Bookshelf: An English Reading Book for Junior Forms,* 1908, ed. H(orace). B(aker). Browne.

Highroads of Literature. Illustrated by Famous Paintings. London, Edinburgh, Dublin, New York: Thomas Nelson & Sons, 1913–1920. Book III. *The Morning Star,* 1915?.

The Royal Treasury of Story and Song. 7 vols. London, Edinburgh, New York: Thomas Nelson & Sons, 1907-09. VI. *Tales That Are Told.*

Steps to Literature. 7 vols. Edward Arnold, 1905. I. *Tales of the Homeland,* III. *Stories from English and Welsh Literature*, IIIA. *Stories from the British Isles*, VI. *Glimpses from World Literature.*

Pedagogy and Librarians' Advice

Baldwin, James. *The Book Lover: A Guide to the Best Reading*. 1884. Chicago: A. C. McClurg, 1902.
Burt, Mary E. *Literary Landmarks: A Guide to Good Reading for Young People and Teachers' Assistant with a Carefully Selected List of Seven Hundred Books*, rev. ed. Boston and New York: Houghton Mifflin & Co.; and Cambridge: Riverside, 1897.
Cox, John Harrington. *Literature in the Common Schools*. Boston: Little, Brown, 1908.
Moses, Montrose J. *Children's Books and Reading*. New York: Mitchell Kennerley, 1907.
Olcott, Frances Jenkins. *The Children's Reading*. Boston and New York: Houghton Mifflin; and Cambridge: Riverside, 1912.

Literary Histories

Bates, Herbert. *English Literature*. Illustrated. London, New York, Toronto, Calcutta, Bombay, Madras, 1918/1923.
Beale, Dorothea. *Literary Studies of Poems Old and New*. London: George Bell & Son, 1902.
Cruse, Amy. *English Literature through the Ages*. Illustrated by Paintings. London, Calcutta, Sydney: George G. Harrap, 1914.
———. *The Shaping of English Literature*. London: George G. Harrap, 1927.
Hudson, W(illiam). H(enry). *An Outline History of English Literature*. 1912. New ed. 1930, repr. London: G. Bell & Sons, 1941.
Lang, Andrew. *History of English Literature from "Beowulf" to Swinburne*. London: Longmans, Green, 1902.
Long, William J. *Outlines of English and American Literature*. Illustrated. Boston, New York Chicago, London, Atlanta, Dallas, Columbus, San Francisco: Ginn, 1917
Marshall, H(enrieta). E. *English Literature for Boys and Girls*. Illustrated by J. R. Skelton. London and Edinburgh: E. C. & T. C. Jack, 1909.
Parrott, Edward. *The Pageant of English Literature*. Illustrated by J. M. W. Turner, et al. New York: Sully & Kleinteich, 1909.
Richardson, Abby Sage. *Familiar Talks on English Literature*. 1881. Chicago: A. C. McClurg, 1892.
Tappan, Eva Mash. *A Brief History of English Literature*. 1905. London: George G. Harrap, 1914.
Thomson, C(lara). L(inklater). *Our Inheritance* Cambridge, UK: Cambridge University Press, 1910.

Index

Numbers in ***bold italics*** indicate pages with illustrations.

Adams, Frank 129–130
Adams, Henry 169
Addison, Joseph 111
Aeneas *see* Virgil
Æschylus 175
Aesop 15, 16, 22
"A.L." Bright Story Readers 181, 190, ***191***, 192–193, 261*n*8
Aldrich, Thomas Bailey 160–162, 260*n*12
Alice in Wonderland 17
Allen, J.C. 25, 194–196
Amadis of Gaul 11–12, 15, 20
"Ambrose Merton" 18–19
The Anatomy of Melancholy 14
Andersen, Hans Christian 99, 164, 190, 193
Anglo, Sydney 255*n*2
An Apology for Poetry 11
The Approach to Spenser 11
Aquinas, Thomas 208
Arabian Nights 121, 154, 163, 166, 178, 190, 193
Arcadia 7, 13, 20, 21
Ariosto, Ludovico 5, 7, 106, 208, 239
Armada 241
Arnold, Edward 3, 181, 182, 188–190, ***191***, 192–193, 210–217, 261*ch*5*n*7, 262*ch*5*n*20, 262*ch*5*n*21, 262*ch*5*n*22
Arnold, Matthew 102–103, 169, 232, 248
Arnold, Thomas 102–103
Art Deco 168, 172
Art Nouveau 26, 44, 75, 77, 85, 91, 101, 105, 120, 122, 147, 152, 186, 188, 251
Artesia 20
Arthur 8, 10, 11, 12, 13, 19, 28, 29, 58, 93, 106, 133, 142, 157, 162, 164, 165, 179, 180, 182, 190, 192, 205, 210, 211, 216, 245; *see also* Faerie Queene (characters)
Arthur of Britain 12
Arts & Crafts Movement 25, 29, 146, 148
Ascham, Roger 10–11, 256*n*18, 256*n*19
Ashley, Robert 12, 15, 19, 22
Ashton, John 258*ch*1*n*49
Asquith, Claire 255*ch*1*n*5
Augustine, Saint 10, 15

Bacon, Francis 176, 207
Baden-Powell, Robert 100; *see also* Boy Scouts
Bailey, Carolyn Sherwin 140, 157–158, 260*n*9
Baldwin, James 174–175
Barbour 210, 216
Barrie, James 57
Bartholomew Faire 15, 256*n*31
Bates, Herbert 224, 247–249, 263*n*16
Batten, John Dixon 28
Baum, L. Frank 29
Baynes, Pauline 250
Beale, Dorothea 224, 227, 263*ch*6*n*3
Beardsley, Aubrey 26, 101
Bede 213
Belgrave, Dorothy M. 3, 128, ***129***, 130, 259*n*24
Bellianis, Don 20, 22, 257*n*48
Belloc, Hilaire 9
Beowulf 133, 157, 162, 177, 180, 182, 183, 206, 210, 213, 215, 237, 240
Bevis of Hamtoun 5, 8, 10, 11, 12, 13, 15, 16, ***18***, 19, 21, 22, 82, 190, 192
Bible 16, 56, 100, 103, 104, 113, 177, 178, 179, 198–199, 240, 243, 244, 247
Blake, William 25, 261*ch*4*n*23
Bluebeard 23
Bo-Peep Story Books 19, 257*n*43
Boadicea 46
Boitano, Piero 255*ch*1*n*5
Bolland, John 192
Books for the Bairns 3, 57, ***78***, 79–***82***, 83–***84***, 85, 181, 259*n*5, 259*n*6
The Book Lover 174–175, 261*n*28
Book of Martyrs 243, 244
The Book of Romance 125–126, 259*n*21
The Book of the Epic 133, 134–139, 260*ch*3*n*26
Boswell, Jackson C. 14, 256*n*25, 256*n*27, 256*n*28, 256*n*29, 256*n*30, 256*n*31, 256*n*32, 256*n*33, 257*n*34, 257*n*48
Bowd, James 23, 258*ch*1*n*56
Bradamante 126
Bradburn, Eliza W. 257*n*41
A Brief History of English Literature see *A Short History of English Literature*
Brooks, Edward 57, 140, 141–144, ***143***, 260*n*1
Brown, Thomas 15

267

Brown, Zaidee 261*ch*5*n*3, 263*n*7
Browne, W. 186, 257*n*34
Browning, Elizabeth Barrett 103
Browning, Robert 101, 103, 130, 164
Brunhilde 121
Bunyan, John 3, 7, 16, 17, 23, 100, 147, 163, 165, 166, 175, 179, 244, 248
Burne-Jones, Edward 25, 26, 28
Burns, Robert 216
Burrell, Arthur 182, 199, 262*ch*5*n*14
Burt, Mary E. 176, 261*n*29
Burton, Robert 14, 256*n*28
Bynneman, Henry 243
Byron, George Gordon 28, 130, 261*n*23

Caedmon 213, 229
Caldecott, Randolph 168
Calvin, John 8-9, 237
Campion, Edmund 7
The Canterbury Tales see Chaucer, Geoffrey
Capgrave, John 13
Carpaccio, Vittore 201
Carpenter, Humphrey 17, 257*n*39, 258*ch*3*n*1
Carroll, Lewis 17, 257*n*37
Catherine of Aragon 10
Catholicism see Popery
Caxton, William 5, 192, 200
Cervantes, Miguel de 14, 85, 164, 166, 176, 178, 180, 216
chapbooks 1, 17, 18-23, 78, 162, 257*n*44, 258*n*49
Charlemagne 196, 112, 162, 180
Charles I 15
Chaucer, Geoffrey 2, 5, 11, 12, 13, 23, 24, 28, 29, 35, 39, 59, 76, 93, 116, 128, 130, 142, 144, 146, 154, 157, 159, 162, 166, 169, 170, 175, 176, 178, 180, 181, 188, 190, 199, 200, 202, 205, 209, 210, 213, 219, 220, 223, 225, 228, 230, 232, 233, 234, 235, 237, 239, 240, 241, 244, 247, 248, 261*n*2
Chaundler, Christine 3, 130-***131***, 132-133, 260*n*25
Chester, Norley see Underdown, Emily
Children's Books and Reading 178, 261*n*31
The Children's Hour 141, 162-163
The Children's Reading 178-180, 261*n*32
Children's Stories from the Poets 128-***129***, 130, 259*n*24
Children's Stories in English Literature 182, 205-207, 262*n*18
chivalry 30, 33, 43, 55, 64-65, 72, 82, 99-100, 102, 111-112, 117, 119, 120, 135, 142, 169, 199
Church, A(lfred). J. 3, 17, 57, ***58***, 112-***114***, 115, 162, 259*n*17
Church, Dr. Ralph 27
The Cid 144, 162, 216
Clare, John 263*n*6
Clarke, Mary Cowden 178
Claxton, John 235
Cockcroft, Jason 251
Cole, Charles 19

Cole, Henry 18-19, 257*n*44
Cole, Herbert 85
Cole, William 22
Coleridge, Samuel 22-23, 186, 209, 258*n*53
Colet, John 230
Columbus 240 4
Cooper, Helen 9, 256*n*9, 256*n*24
Copernicus 240
Copley, John Singleton 28
Corneille, Pierre 216
Corthill, Ronald 255*n*3
Cosin, John 15
The Courteous Knight and Other Tales 57, 75-***76***, ***77***-78, 258*ch*3*n*4
Courthorpe, William John 232
Cox, Captain 19, 243, 257*n*45
Cox, John Harrington 177-178, 261*n*30
Crane, Donn P. 170-171, ***172***
Crane, Ronald 11, 20, 21, 24, 256*n*16, 261*n*25
Crane, Walter 25-26, 147, 258*n*1, 2
Cranmer, Thomas 8
Croxall, Samuel 16, 257*n*35
Crusades 248
Cruse, Amy 224, 240-244, 263*n*13, 263*n*14
Cundall, Joseph 19

Dalziel 19
Dante 115, 175, 176, 197, 201, 227, 253
Darton, F.J. Harvey 17, 58, 257*n*38, 258*n*52, 259*n*5
Davis, Alex 256*n*9
Dawson, Lawrence H. 3, 57, 106-***107***, 108-112, 133, ***134***, 259*n*14
Day, John 243
de Chatelain, Mme. 19
The Delphinian Course 140-141, 158-159, 260*n*10, 260*n*11
Dent, J.M. 26, 85, 182
De Quincey, Thomas 216
De Ribadineira, Pedro 13
Dering, Edward 11
Dickens, Charles 164
Djordjevic, Ivana
Dolan, Frances E. 255*n*3, 256*n*9
Dowden, Edward 186
Drake, Francis 170
Dryden, John 15-16, 28, 168, 225
Du Bartas 243
Duffy, Eamon 255*pref.n*3, 255*ch*1*n*3
Dürer, Albrecht 93
Dusinberre, Juliet 17, 257*n*37
Dutton, E.P. 85, 189, 182
Dutton, Richard 255*ch*1*n*5

Edgeworth, Maria 190
Edward VII 217
Edwardson, E. 57, 75, ***76***, ***77***, 78, 250*ch*3*n*4
Eldred, John 23, 258*n*57
The Elfin Knight 252-253, 263*Epi.n*4
Eliot, Charles William 158
Elizabeth I 6, 10, 15, 50, 56, 86, ***114***, 115, 116,

133, *134*, 138, 147, 155, 169, 170, 182, 184, 192, 225, 228, 230, 235, 236, 242, 244, 245, 263, 263n8
Elsie Dinsmore 161
Emerson, Ralph Waldo 175
English Literature 224, 247-249, 263n16
English Literature for Boys and Girls 224, 229-*233*, 234, 263ch6n5
English Literature through the Ages 224, 240-242, 263n13
Epithalamion 225, 235, 238, 242
Erasmus, Desiderius 8, 10
Etty, William 28
Evans, Edmund 36

The Faerie Queene (characters & places): Acrasia 28, 32, 33, 37, 38, *63*, 64, 73, 86, 91, 114, 135, 136, 183, 184, 188, 203, 207, 226; Adicia 43, 71, 138; Æmylia 40; Agapé 115; Alma 37, 64, 184, 188; Amavia 91, 117, 184; Amazons 42, 46, 66, 70, 137, 153, 204, 252; Amoret 28, 34, 35, 40, 45, 48, 68, 108-109, 116, 121, 137, 152, 156, 183, 196, 215, 251, 252; Amyas 40, 68, 69, 142; Angela 38, 46, 147; Archimago 26, 30, 32, 33, 36, 48, 52, 53, 56, 62, 81, 86, *92*, 93, 101, 109, 126, 127, 130, 132, 133, 135, 146, 148, 184, 189, 192, 194, 202, 211, 213, 220, 221, 231; Artegal 33-35, 38, 40, 41, 42-44, 50, 60, 65, 66, 69-71, 98, 106, 108, 109, 110, 111, 112, 113, 115, 116, 135, 136, 137, 138, 144, 147, 151, 153, 157, 179, 189, 194-196, 198, 202, 203-204, 215-216, 227, 237, 244, 251, 252; Arthur 26, 28, 31, 33, 36, 37-38, 40, 43, 45, 47, 49, 54, *58*, 60, 61, 62, 64, 65, 68, 69, 73, 74, 75, 81, *82-83*, 86, 87, 91, 97, 103, *105*, 109, 110, 111, 112, 113, 115, 117, 120, 123, 127, 132, 135, 136, 137, 138, 139, 144, 145, 149-150, 156, 172, 184, 185, 188, 189, 192, 201, 202, 203, 204, 205, 206, 207, 211, 213, 214, *218*, 221, 228, 231, 236, 239, 251; Astrea 32, 69, 207; A-te 152; Belgé 111, 113, 138; Belphoebe 40, 46, 47, 50, 68, 108, 110, 137, 186, 188, 208, 210, 245; Blandamour 152, 156 6; Blatant Beast 44, 49-50, 71, 72-73, 75, 76, 77-78, 98, 109, 116, *118*, 119-120, 121, 122, 123, 124, 128, *129*-130, 137, 138, 144, 179, 204, 205, 237, 251; Bower of Bliss 32, 33, 38, 61, 63, 64, 65, 87, 94, 135, 155, 158, 162, 179, 189, 203, 208 209; Braggadochio 32, 34, 37, 41, 45, 61-62, 66, 69, 73, 87, 113, 137, 156, 157, 188, 210; Briana 71, 77; Britomart 9, 26, 28, 29, 33-35, 36, 38, 40-41, 45, 46, 47, 64-66, *67*-68, 70, 94, 98, 106, 108, 109, 110, 112, 113, 115, 116, 117, 121, 123, 135, 136, 138, 144, 146, 151-154, 155-156, 160, 162, 179, 182, 183, 189, 194-196, 197-199, 201, 202, 203-204, 207, 215-216, 227, 231, 251-252; Burbon 43, 71, 115; Busirane 34, 36, 40, 46, 48, 68, 121, 136, 152, 198, 215; Calepine 120, 123, 138; Calidore 45, 49, 60, 71-73, 77-78, 98, 106, 109, 111, 112, 116, 118, 119, 120, 121, 123, 124, 128, *129*-130, 135, 138, 139, 199, 202, 204-205, 152; Cambel 36, 38, *39*, 45, 46, 47, 94, 95, 96, 128, 135, 154-155; Cambina 32, 46, 76, 94, 96, 155, 156; Canace 36, 38, 46, 47, 75, 76, 128, 154, 155, 156; Castle Joyous 65, 215; Charissa 49, 54, 83, 91, 104, 135, 171, 172, 211; Claribel 72, 94, 98; Clarinda 42; Coelia 54, 83, 103-104, 150; Contemplation 55, 61, 83, 104, 135, 150; *see also* New Jerusalem; Coridon 72, 98, 130, 139, 204; Crudor 71, 77, 204; Cymocles 37, 63, 64, 74, 117, 135, 203; Cymoent 40-41, 156, 189; Despair 48, 54, 61, 127, 132, 150, 184, 186, 194, 196, 221; Diamond 38, 94, 96, 128, 154; Dolan 70, 158; dragon 31, 35, 36, 45, 48, 49, 51, 55, 60, *78*, *83-84*, 87, *88*, *89*, 91, 93, 94, 97, 98, 101, 104, 110, 113, 117, 120, 122, 123, *124*, 127-128, 132, 133, 135, 145, 150, 171, 174, 182, 184, 185, 186, 188, 189, 192, 193, 196, 198, 201, 202, 206, 213, 214, 217, *219*, 221, *222*, 231, 232, 237, 247, 250; Duessa 31, 53, 54, 60, 61, 71, 73, 80, 81, 86, 87, 91, 93, 97, 101, 103, *107*, 108, 109, 121, 123, 127, 132, 138, 145, 147, 148, 152, 156, 170, 172, 183, 184, 192, 211, 213, 220-221, 231, 237; Emilia 68, 69; Error 26, 30, 37, 52, 81, 87, 101, *124*, 135, 148, 185, 220, 231, 251; Faerie Queene *see* Gloriana; Fidelia 54, 87, 104, 211 7; Fidessa *see* Duessa; Florimel 34, 35, 36, 40-41, 45, 47, 48, 65, 66, 69, 70, 97, 98, 108, 110, 116, 122, 123, 137, 144, 155, 157, 189, 190, 226; Fradubio 101, 145-146, 172, 188; Fraelissa 146, 172; Furor 32, 63, 73, 135, 184, 186; George (Saint) 2, 6, 8, 28, 29, 37, 48, 55, 57, 61, 89, 91, 93, 94, 97-98, 100, 104, 108, 117, 135, 145, 150, 185, 186, *187*, 211, 212, 213, *219*, 221, 231 242 (*see also* Red Cross Knight); Gereones 36, 138; Glaucé 33, 34, 38, 40, 46, 47, 65, 66, 109, 137, 151, 153, 195, 207, 215, 216; Gloriana 9, 28, 35, 44, 47, 48, 50, 51, 54, 55, 60, 61, 80, 81 86, 87, 91, 94, 97, 98, 100, *105*, 111, 113, *114*, 115, 116, 117, 130, 133, *134*, 135, 136, 137, 138, 139, 145, 147, 149, 173, 192, 202, 203, 205, 207, 211, 213, 220, 221, 228, 236; Grantorto 42, 43, 69, 71, 115, 138, 204; Grill 38; Guyon (Guy) 8, 9, 29, 32-33, 34, 35, 36, 37-38, 41, 45, 57, 60, 61, *62*, *63*, 64, 65, 70, 73, 74-75, 86, 87, 91, 94, 98, 106, 108, 109, 110, 112, 113, 116, 117, 122, 135-136, 144, 151-152, 156, 157, 158, 162, 179, 181, 183, 184, 185, 186, 188, 189, 199, 200, 201, 202, 203, 206, 208-209, 226, 231, 245, 251; House of Holiness 49, 54, 61, 97, 132, 145, 184, 189, 211, 213-214; House of Pride 26, 30, 36, 53, 79-80, 81, 101, 106, *131*, 132, 135, 151, 184, 185, 186, 253; Ignorance 54, *218*, 221, 232, 251; Irena 42, 43, 69, 71, 138; Isis 43, 70; Kirk-rapine 52, 112, 127; lion 28, 31, *44*, 55, *50*, 53, 60, 87, 93, 97, 109, 115, 123, 126, 130, 132, 135, 144, 148, 185, 186, 188, 192, 194, *196*, 213, 221, 223, 226, 247; Lucifera 26, 30, 53, 80, 86, 91, 101, 135, 146, 170, *172*, 185, 202, 206, 220; Malbecco 66, 152; Malecasta

65; Mammon 33, 37, 64, 73, **74**, 75, 76, 87, 94, 110, 113, 117, 158, 179, 184, 188, 189, 208, 209, 226; Marinel 34, 35, 40–41, 45, 47, 69, 94, 98, 137, 152, 156, 157, 189 (*see also* Florimel); Masque of Cupid 34, 40, 48, 68, 136, 152, 198, 215; Meleger 37, 184; Melibee 72, 130, 139, 204; Mercilla 43, 71, 138, 204; Mercy 54–55, 104 8; Merlin 31, 38, 43, 47, 65, 82, 123, 127, 151, 195, 207, 215; Mordant 61, 117, 188; Munera 69; New Jerusalem 55, 61, 83, 91, 104, 113, 135, 150, 187; Occasion 63, 185; Ollyphant 40, 152; Orgoglio 31, 48, 60, 81, **82**, 86, 87, 103, 132, 135, 145, 150, 171, 183, 184, 188, 202, 211, **218**, 231, 251; Palace of Pride *see* House of Pride; Palmer 32, 38, **62**, **63**, 64, 75, 87, 91, 108, 109, 122, 136, 152, 158, 179, 189, 200, 205, 207, 208, 220, 223; Paridell 152, 153; Pastorella 45, 72, **77**, 94, 98, 109, 130, 139, 144, 204; Phædria 64, 73, 135, 186, 188; Philotime 33, 188; Placidas 40, 68, 69; Poena 40, 68, 144; Pollenté 69; Priamond 38, 94, 96, 128, 154; Priscilla 138; Proteus 48, 122, 137, 157; Pyrocles 32, 33, 37, 63, 64, 74, 113, 117, 123, 203; Radigund 42–43, 66, 70, 113, 137, 139, 204, 252; Red Cross Knight 2, 6, 8, 9, 26, 27, 28, 29, 30–32, 33, 35, 36, 37, 38, 45, 48, 49, **50**–56, 57, **58**, 60–61, 71, 72, 75, 76, 80–85, 87, **88**, **90**, 97–98, 100–104, 106, **107**–108, 110, 112, 115, 116, 117, 121, 122, 123, **124**, 126–128, 130, **131**, **134**, 135, 136, 144, 145, 146, 148–151, 156, 157–158, 162, 170, 171, 172, 179, 181, 182, 183, 184, 189, 192, 193–194, 199, 201, 202–203, 205, 206, 209, 210, 211, 212, 213, 217, 220, 221, 226, 227, 228, 231, 236, 253 (*see also* George [Saint]); Ryence 33, 38; Samient 43, 71; Sanglier 42; Sansfoy 52, 80, **90**, 101, 102, 115, 123, 126, 132, 148, 170, 184, 211, 220, 253; Sansjoy 31, 53, 80, 87, 102, 121, 127, 132, 194, 211, 220, 253; Sansloy 31, 48, 52, 53, 102, 127, 132, 148, 185, 211, 221, 253; Satyrane 31, 34, 40, 41, 53, 66, **67**, 81, 113, 127, 132, 136, 152, 156, 201, 211; satyrs 31, 81, 108, 113, 120, 127, 150, 171, 186, 232, 242; Scudamour 34, 35, 40, 66, 68, 109, 115, 137, 152, 153, 195, 196, 200, 215; Serena 77, 109, 119, 120, 123, 138–139, 204; Seven Deadly Sins 26, 31, 48, 53, 73, 80, 101–102, 135, 144, 146, 170, **172**, 185, 202, 206, 220 253; Speranza 54, 211 9; Squire of Low Degree *see* Amyas; Sultan 43, 71, 138; Talus 29, 36, 42, 43, 69, 70, 71, 98, 108, 138, 153, 203, 204, 207, 251, 252; Terwin 54; Timias 40, 45, 46, 47, 48, 49, 93, 108, 110, 120, 123, 137, 139, 146, 252; Tree of Life 55, 61, 253; Triamond 36, 38, **39**, 45, 46, 94, 95, 96, 128, 135, 154–155; Tristram 72, 78, 138; Trompart 32, 37, 41, 62; Turpin 42, 139; Una 26, 28, 29, 30, 32, 35, 37, **44**, 45, 47, 48, 49, **50**–56, 60, 61, 73, 80, 81, 83, 84, 85, 87, 91, 93, 97, 100, 101, 103, 104, 108, 112, 113, 115, 116, 120, 121, 122, **124**, 126–128, 130–**131**, 132, 135, 145, 146–151, 157, 158, 170, 171, 173, 179, 182, 183, 184, 186, 189, 192, 193–194, **196**, 201, 203, 210, 211, 213, 214, 217, **219**, 220, 221, 223, 226, 231, 242, 247, 253; Verdant 38; Well of Life 55, 61, **83**, 113, 206

Faerie Queene, Book One 253, 263*Epi.n*5
The Faery Queen, First Book 140, 144–154, 260*n*3
The Faerie Queene and Her Knights 57, **58**, 112, **114**, 115, 162, 259*n*17
Fairfax-Mucklay, Louis 26
Familiar Talks on English Literature 224–226, 262*n*2
Faustus 20
"Felix Summerly" 18; *see also* Cole, Henry
Fellows, Jennifer 256*n*13
Fernández, Jerónimo 20
Fielding, Sarah 244
Fierabras 162
Fierce Wars and Faithful Loves 252–253, 263*Epi.n*4
Findlay, Alison 255*n*5
A First Book in English Literature 182, 207–210, 262*n*19
Forbush, William Byron 165–166, 179, 260*n*19
Ford, H(enry) J. 3, 125–128, 181, **196**, 247
Fortunatus 20
Four Sons of Aymon 11, 19
Foxe, John 243, 244
Francis I 6
Friar Bacon 20, 21
Frithiof 157, 162
Frobisher, Martin 170
Froissart, Jean 58, 85, 210
From the Tower Window **167**, 170–**172**, 173–174
Furnivall, F.J. 58, 257*n*45
Fuseli, Henry 28

Galahad 91, 115, 210
Gardiner, Alfonzo 181, 190, **191**–193, 261*n*8
Gardiner, Harold 256*n*23
The Gateway to Spenser 57, 116–**118**, **124**–125, 218, 220, 259*n*18, 259*n*19
Gawain and the Green Knight 177
Generydes 10
Geoffrey of Monmouth 198, 215, 216
George V 217
giant **18**, **82**, **218**; *see also* Orgoglio
Gilbert, Henry 224, 262*n*1
Gilbert, John 3, 28, **219**
Glimpses of World Literature 216–217
Glover, W.J. 128, 259*n*23
Godfrey, Elizabeth (Jessie Bedford) 17, 257*n*36
Godwin, William 22
The Golden Legend 13, 192, 200
Goldsmith, Oliver 244
Goodrich, Samuel 19
Gould, Veronica Franklin 262*n*29
Grace, R(obert) W. 57, 99–**105**, 259*n*10
Grafton, Carol Belanger 17, 25, 257*n*36, 258*ch*2*n*1

Index

Grahame, Kenneth 57, 229
The Great O'Toole 15
The Great War *see* World War I
Greene, Robert 243, 260*n*6
The Greenwood Tree 211–212, 262*n*20
Grey, Lord 50, 147, 155, 159, 169, 199, 235, 237, 241, 244
Griggs, Earl Leslie 258*n*53
Grimm Brothers 164, 190, 11193
Grissel 19
Guerber, H(élène) A. 3, 106, 133, **134**–139, 260*n*26
A Guide to Good Reading ... The Children's Hour 260*n*14
Gulliver's Travels 17, 163, 164, 166, 178, 179
Guy of Warwick 1, 5, 8, 9, 10, 11, 12, 13, 19, **21**, 22, 82, 190, 192, 229, 255*ch*1*n*1, 257*n*44, 258*ch*2*n*7

Haigh, Christopher 255*Pref.n*3, 255*ch*1*n*3
Hakluyt, Richard 243
Hale, Edward Everett 165
Hales, John W. 58–59, 142
Halls of Fame 168–170, 261*n*22
Hamilton, Donna B. 7, 255*n*7
Hammond, Gertrude Demain 3, 106, **107**–109, 133, **134**, 242
Hanson, Charles Henry 205
The Happy Warrior 102, 125
Harrap, George G. 106, 133, 134, 259*n*15
Hart, Hilda 3, 128, **129**–130, 259*n*24
Harvard Classics 158
Havelok 8, 162
Hawkins, John 170
Hawthorne, Nathaniel 179
Hazlitt, William 23, 175, 186
Hearn, Michael Patrick 257*n*44
Heliodorus 13
Henry V 192
Henry VIII 6, 10, 230
Herodatus 175
Herrick, Robert 176
Heylyn, Peter 14–15, 256*n*30
Hiawatha 177
Highley, Christopher 255*ch*1*n*3, 255*ch*1*n*4
Highroads of Literature 182, 217, **218**–**219**, 220–**222**, 223, 262*n*30
History of English Literature 224, 262*n*11
Hodges, Margaret 250, 263*Epi.n*2
Holcroft, Thomas 23
The Home Treasury of Old Story Books **18**, 19, 257*n*42, 257*n*44
Homer 13, 160, 166, 175, 180, 188, 210, 216, 238
Hooker, Richard 8, 240, 241
Hope, Robert 75, **76**, **77**
Horn Childe 8
Hudson, William Henry 224, 238–240, 263*n*12
Hunt, Leigh 186
Huon of Bordeaux 11, 15
Hyman, Tina Schart 250–251, 263*Epi.n*2
Hyrde, Richard 10

In Golden Realms 210–212, 262*n*21
In Shining Armor 171–174, 261*n*27
In the World of Books 211–212, 262*n*22
Ipomedon 10
Irving, Washington 210

Jack, E.C. 57, 93, 229
Jack, T.C. 57, 93, 229
Jack and the Beanstalk 19, 257*n*44
Jack the Giant Killer 19, 82, 164, 257*n*44
Jacobus de Voraigne *see* *The Golden Legend*
Janeway, James 17, 244 12
Jansohn, Christa 263*n*8
Jesuits 7, 13, 20
Joan of Arc 46
Johnson, Evelyn C. 164, 260*n*18
Johnson, Richard 9, 21, 22, 28, 162, 192, 257*n*44
Jones, Norma 255*ch*1*n*3
Journeys Through Bookland 163
The Junior Classics 141, 163, 260*n*16

Keats, John 160, 179, 245, 248
Kelmscott Press 25, 148
The Key to the Treasure House 161–162, 260*n*13
King, Andrew 8, 256*n*10
King Horn 8
Kingsley, Charles 186, 190, 261*n*23
Kirkman, Francis 20, 22, 257*n*48
Knights and Enchanters 3, 30–35, 258*n*5
The Knights of The Faerie Queene 182, 201–205, 262*n*17
Kück, Helen S. 101, **105**

Lamb, Charles 22, 163, 165, 166, 176, 178, 210, 211, 232
Lancelot 10, 66
Lane, John 258*n*7
Laneham, Robert 19, 242, 257*n*45
Lang, Andrew 3, 125–128, 181, 193–194, **196**, 224, 237–238, 247, 259*n*21, 259*n*22, 262*n*12, 263*n*11
Lang, Jeanie 3, 57, 93–**95**, **96**–99, 259*n*9
Lang, Leonora (Mrs. Andrew) 116, 125, 126–128, 193–194; *see also* Lang, Andrew
Langland, William 206, 238
The Latchkey 168–170, 261*n*21
Lathey, Gillian 257*n*35, 258*n*53
Latimer, Hugh 208
Le Fanu, Brinsley 3, **78**, 79–**82**, 83–**84**
Leicester 135, 236
Le Quesne, Rose 94, **95**, **96**–97
L'Estrange, Roger 16
Lewis, C.S. 60, 253
Linscott, Robert Newton 162, 260*n*14
Litchfield, Mary E. 182, 197–199, 262*n*13
Literary Landmarks 176, 261*n*29
Literary Reading Books for Junior Forms 182, 210–212, 262*n*20, 262*n*21, 262*n*22
Literary Reading Books Related to Empire 216

Index

Literary Reading Books Related to Europe 216
Literary Studies of Poems Old and New 224, 227, 263ch6n3
Literature in the Common School 177–178, 261n30
Locke, John 16
Lockhurst, Roger 259n6
Lodge, Thomas 243
London, William 15, 256n32
Longfellow, Henry Wadsworth 75, 133, 160, 161, 175, 177, 205, 213, 216
Long, William J. 224, 244–247, 263n15
Longmans 125, 181, 237, 247
Lope de Vega 176
Lowell, James Russell 103, 161, 170, 179, 186
Lubbock, John 175
The Lucubrations of Isaac Bickerstaff 22, 258n50
Lurie, Alison 257n44
Lybeaus Desconus 10
Lyly, John 176, 243, 260n6
Lyndsay, David 207

Mabie, Hamilton Wright 165
Mabinogion 162, 213
Macaulay, Thomas B. 59, 235
Maclehose, Sophie 3, 29, **44**–50, 181, 258n8
Macleod, Mary 3, 17, 28, 57, 58–**62**, **63**, **67**, **74**–75, 140, 141, **143**, 162, 165, 180, 258ch3n2, 258ch3n3
Maeldune 183
Mallette, Richard 256n11
Malory, Thomas 11, 26, 57, 75, 76, 183, 198, 210, 211, 213
Mandeville, John 210
Mantegna, Andrea 188
manuscripts 5, 8, 19, 23
Marlowe, Christopher 176, 205, 228, 243
Marotti, Arthur 255n3
Marshall, H(enrietta) E. 224, 229–**233**, 234, 263ch6n5
Marshall, Horace 181, 183
Mary Stuart (Queen of Scots) 50, 86, 135, 138, 147, 228, 231, 236, 239, 241, 244, 263n8
Mary Tudor 10, 182, 237
Maynard, Roy 252–253, 263Epi.n4
McCaughrean, Geraldine 251–252, 263Epi.n3
McClurg 136
McCoy, Richard 255ch1n2
Meigs, Cornelia 17, 257n40
Michael, A.C. **131**, 132
Miller, Olive Beaupré 166–**167**, 168–171, **172**–174, 260n20, 261n21, 261n22, 261n23, 261n24, 261n25, 261n26, 261n27
Milton, John 2, 5, 7, 28, 58, 59, 133, 142, 165, 176, 179, 186, 197, 208, 225, 248, 253, 261n23
minstrels 31, 91, 154, 202, 215
Montaigne, Michel 15
Montelion 20
morality plays 12, 17
More, Thomas 10, 13, 223, 241, 243

Morgan, Walter J. 36, 37, 38, **39**, 40, 41, 43
The Morning Star **218**–**219**, 220–223, 262n30
Morris, R. 58
Morris, William 25, 116, 148
Morte d'Arthur 11, 75, 208, 237, 238
Moses, Montrose J. 178, 261n31
Mother Goose 168, 169
Mother Hubberd's Tale 75, 210
Mucha, Alphonse 105
Munchausen, Baron 163, 165
Munday, Anthony 7
Muscular Christianity 100
My Book House 141, 166–**167**, 168–171, **172**–174, 260n20, 261n21, 261n22, 261n23, 261n24, 261n25, 261n26, 261n27
My Book of Stories from the Poets 130–**131**, 132–133, 260ch3n25
mystery plays 12, 17

Nashe, Thomas 11
Neilson, William A. 158
Nelson, Thomas 3, 57, 93, **95**, **96**, 116, 182, 205, 217–**218**, **219**–**222**, 223, 224, 229
Nennius 213
Nesbit, E. 57, 163
Neuburg, Victor E. 257n44
New World 14–15, 240, 245
Newbery, John 244
Newbolt, Henry 181, 261n1
Newcomb, Lori Humphrey 257n46
North, Thomas 243
Norton, Charles Eliot 161

Oakden, E(llen) C. 182, 201–205, 262n17
Olcott, Frances Jenkins 178–180, 261n32
Oliver of the Castle 11
Orientalism 31, 70, 71, 89, **90**, 101, **107**, 108, 121, 193
Orlando Furioso 7, 11, 13
Ornatus 20
Our Inheritance 224, 236–237, 263n10
Our Island Story 229
Our Wonder World 164–165, 260n18
An Outline of English Literature 224, 238–240, 263n12
Outlines of English and American Literature 224, 244–247, 263n15

The Pageant of English Literature 224, 234–236, 263n9
Painter, William 243
Palace of Westminster (Parliament) 28, 217
Palmerin 15, 20
Papé, Frank C. 3, 57, **118**, 120–123, **124**, 220, 221, 258n18
Parismus 20, 22, 23, 257n44
Parrott, Edward 224, 234–236, 263n9
Partenope 10
Patchell, Mary Frances Collins 255ch1n8
Patten, William 163, 260n16
Paynell, Thomas 10

Pearce, Joseph 255*ch*1*n*5
Penny Merriments see Pepys
Pepys, Samuel 21, 257*n*44, 258*n*49
Percy, Bishop Thomas 58, 130, 192
Perrault, Charles 22, 190
"Peter Parley" 19
Philip II of Spain 86, 138, 236
Pierce, Grace Adele 140, 146–154, 260*n*4
Piers Plowman 238
The Pilgrim's Progress 3, 16, 17, 23, 60, 79, 100, 141, 147, 158, 163, 175, 178, 244, 248
Pitz, Henry 147, 148
Plato 175
Plutarch 179, 243
Poets' Corner 218
Poole, Thomas 22
Pope, Alexander 225
Popery 10–11, 13, 16, 37, 86, 135, 146, 217, 231, 237, 239, 244; *see also* Archimago
Potter, Beatrix 57
Pre-Raphaelite 28, 65, 91, 94, *95*, 108, 127, 186, 196
Prideaux, Mathias 12–14, 256*n*25
Priestly, J.B. 4, 255*Pref.n*5
Pritchard, Mari 17, 257*n*39
Prosopoia see Mother Hubbard's Tale
Protestantiam 2, 5, 86, 100, 103, 133, 139, 162, 170, 179, 180, 193, 197–199, 208, 230, 231, 235, 237, 239, 240–242, 245, 246, 250, 253
Prothalamion 235, 238
Puritan 7, 11, 15, 17, 142, 155, 198, 199, 207, 208, 228, 235, 237, 241, 244, 245, 247
Purves, D. Laing 261*n*2
Pyle, Howard 148
Pynson, Richard 5

The Questing Knights of The Faerie Queene 251–252, 263*Epi.n*3
Quiller Couch, A.T. 201
Quixote, Don 13, 14, 15, 16, 21, 23, 85, 115, 125, 141, 144, 163, 164, 166, 175, 178, 179, 216

Rabbeth, J.E. 24, 27, 258*ch*2*n*3
Rackham, Arthur 120
Raleigh, Walter 6, 50, 56, 155, 158, 170, 176, 186, 192, 198, 202, 208, 223, 225, 226, *233*, 235, 236, 242, 245, 248
Randall, Dale B.J. 14, 256*n*25, 256*n*27, 256*n*28, 256*n*29, 256*n*30, 256*n*31, 256*n*32, 256*n*33, 257*n*34, 257*n*48
Raphael 212
R.A.Y. 2, 30, *50–56*, 258*n*9
Readings in Folklore 182–183, 261*n*4
The Red Cross Knight and Sir Guyon 57, 73–*74*, 75, 258*ch*3*n*3
The Red Cross Knight and the Legend of Britomart 140, 146–154, 260*n*4
The Red Cross Knight, Parts I & II 57, *78–82*, 84–85, 181, 259*n*6
The Red Romance Book 125–128, 181, 193, *196*, 237, 247, 259*n*22, 262*n*12

Religious Tract Society 16
Reynard the Fox 13, 75, 259*n*5
Richard Coeur de Lion 8
Richardson, Abbie Sage 140, 154–157, 176, 224–226, 260*n*5, *n*8, 262*n*2
Richmond, Velma B. 255*Pref.n*1, 255*Pref.n*2, 255*Pref.n*3, 255*Pref.n*4, 255*ch*1*n*2, 255*ch*1*n*4, 255*ch*1*n*5, 255*ch*1*n*6, 257*n*44, 258*n*7, 259*n*12, 259*n*16, 260*n*2, 260*n*6, 260*n*7, 261*n*6, 262*n*16, 263*n*8
Richter, David H. 256*n*22
Riviére, Briton 3, 38, 331, *222*
Robert the Bruce 216
Robin Hood 19, 21, 93, 133, 157, 162, 164, 229, 257*n*44
Robinson, T(homas). H(eath). 3, 57, 85, 87–*88*, *89*, *90*, *92–93*
Robinson, W. Heath 85
Robinson Crusoe 17, 163, 164, 166, 178
Roland 13, 157, 162, 174, 177, 210, 216, 229
Rose, Jacqueline 258*ch*3*n*1
Rossetti, Dante Gabriel 28, 130, 215
The Royal Prince Readers 217,
Royal Treasury of Story and Song 182, 217, 262*n*28
Royde-Smith, N(aomi) G. 57, 85–*88*, *89*, *90*, *92*–93, 180, 234, 259*n*8
Ruskin, John 100–101, 161, 175, 261*n*23

Saint George 2, 3, 9, 21, 22, 24, 29, 48, 140, 163, 164, 182, 192, 200, 214, 231
Saint George and the Dragon (Hodges) 250–251, 263*Epi.n*2
Saint George and the Dragon (Warburg) 250, 263*Epi.n*1
St. George of Merry England Retold from Spenser's "Faerie Queene" 181, 190, *191*–193, 261*n*8
Saint Paul 11
Sandford and Merton 161
Schiller, Justin G. 257*n*44
The Scholemaster 11, 256*n*19
Scott, Sir Walter 28, 126, 163, 164, 178, 199, 210, 224
Selections from The Faerie Queene 182, 199, 262*n*14
The Seven Champions of Christendom 9, 15, 16, 22, 23, 28, 162, 192, 257*n*44
Seven Wise Masters of Rome 20, 257*n*44
Seymour, Mary 205 17
Shagan, Ethan 255*n*3
Shahar, Shulamith 256*n*17
Shakespeare, William 2, 7, 17, 22, 28, 29, 47, 58, 65, 97, 106, 116, 137, 158, 162, 165, 166, 169, 175, 176, 177, 178, 180, 181, 197, 201, 210, 213, 216, 224, 225, 228, 230, 235, 236, 239, 241, 248, 253
The Shaping of English Literature 224, 240, 242–244, 263*n*14
Shealy, Anne 253, 263*Epi.n*5
Shealy, Ben 253, 263*Epi.n*5

Shelley, Percy Bysshe 28, 218
A Short History of English Literature 162, 224, 227–228, 260*n*15, 263*ch*6*n*4
Sidney, Sidney 6, 7, 11, 13, 20, 21, 56, 138, 155, 169, 176, 206, 207, 210, 223, 225, 228, 235, 236, 241
Siegfried 142, 162, 174, 180, 188, 216
Simons, John 257*n*44
Skinner, Hubert M. 182–183, 261*n*4
Smiles, Samuel 100, 259*n*11
Smith, Minna Steele 182, 200–202, 262*n*15
Smythe, E. Louise 259*n*6
Socrates 208
Spence, Lewis 256*n*26
Spenser for Children 3, 29, 35–44, 178, 258*n*6
Spenser Redivivus 3, 23–24
Spenser: The Faerie Queene, Book I 181; *see also Tales from the Faerie Queene* (Thomson)
Spenser's Britomart: From Books III, IV, and V 182, 197–199, 262*n*13
Spufford, Margaret 257*n*44, 257*n*47
Standard Catalog for High School Libraries 229, 261*n*3, 263*n*7
Statius 13
Stead, Estelle Wilson 259*n*6
Stead, W(illiam) T. 57, 79–85, 181, 259*n*5, 259*n*6; *see also* Books for the Bairns
Steele, Richard 22
Steps to Literature 182, 212–217, 262*n*23, 262*n*24, 262*n*25, 262*n*26, 262*n*27
Sterne, Lawrence 22, 258*n*51
Stevenson, R(obert) L. 240
Stories from English and Welsh Literature 213–214, 262*n*25
Stories from Old English Literature 140, 154–157, 176, 224, 226, 260*n*5
Stories from "The Faerie Queene" (Arnold) 181, 188–190, 261*n*7
Stories from the Faerie Queene (Lang) 3, 57, 93–**95**, **96**–99, 259*n*9
Stories from the Faerie Queene (Macleod) 28, 57, 58–**62**, **63**, **67**, **74**–75, 140, 141, **143**, 162, 165, 180, 258*ch*3*n*2
Stories from the Faerie Queene Retold from Spenser (Dawson) 57, 106–**107**, 108–112, **134**, 259*n*14
Stories from the Literature of the British Isles 215–216, 262*n*26
Stories from Spenser (Smith) 182, 200–202, 262*n*15
Stories from Spenser (Underdown) 57
Stories of Great Adventures 140, 157–158, 260*n*9
Stories of the Great Writers 224, 262*n*1
"The Story of Britomart and Artegal" 194–196, 262*n*11
The Story of Spenser's Faerie Queene 3, 24, 27–28, 258*ch*2*n*3
The Story of the Faerie Queene 140, 141–**143**, 144, 260*n*1

The Story of the Red Cross Knight 3, 30, 50–56, 258*n*9
Stratton, Helen 186, **187**–188, 261*n*5
Stringer, Agnes 120
Strudwick, John Melhuish 28
Stubbs, George 28
Sturt, M(ary) 182, 201–205, 262*n*17
Sumpter, Toby J. 252–253, 263*Epi.n*4
Swift, Jonathan 166, 178
Swinburne, Algernon Charles 237, 261*n*23
Swiss Family Robinson 165
Sylvester, Charles 163

Tabart, Benjamin 22
Talbot, Peter 15, 256*n*33
Tales from Spenser 57, 99–**105**, 259*n*10
Tales from Spenser Chosen from The Faerie Queene 3, 29–30, **44**–50, 181, 258*n*8
Tales from the Faerie Queene 6, 181, 183–**187**, 188, 234, 261*n*5
Tales from the Fairy Queen 181, 193–**196**, 197, 262*n*11
Tales from the Poets 128, 259*n*23
Tales of the Homeland 212
Tales of Many Lands 212, 262*n*23
Tales that Are Told 217, 262*n*28
Taliesin 205
Tappan, Eva March 162–163, 224, 227–228, 260*n*15, 263*ch*6*n*4
Tasso, Torquato 5, 176, 208
The Tatler 22
Tawse, Sybil
Taylor, Doris Loring 260*n*20
Taylor, John 15, 256*n*29
The Teaching of English in England 181, 261*n*1
Tell, William 229
Tennyson, Alfred Lord 65, 101, 102, 116, 150, 160, 164, 199, 201, 211, 216, 229, 234, 239, 248
Thackeray, William M. 164, 257*n*44
Thomas of Erceldoune 9
Thompson, Roger 258*n*49
Thoms, William J. 18–19
Thomson, Clara L(inklater) 181, 182, 183–**187**, 188, 207–210, 224, 236–237, 261*n*5, 262*n*19, 263*n*10
Thwaite, Mary F. 257*n*41
Tillyard, E.M.W. 255*n*6
Tom Hickathrift 19, 21, 82 19
Tom Thumb 19, 21, 164, 257*n*44
Towry, M.H. 3, 29, 35–44, 59, 178, 258*n*6
Toxophilus 10
Traquair, Phoebe Ann 28–29
Trimmer, Sarah 244
Tristram 11, 142
Tristram Shandy 22, 258*n*51
Turner, J.M.W. 161
Turpin 13
Twain, Mark 160, 249
Tyndale, William 240

Una and the Red Cross Knight with Other Tales from Spenser 57, 85–**88**, **89**, **90**, **92**–93, 180, 234, 259n8
Underdown, Emily 3, 57, 116–**118**, **124**–125, 218, 220, 259n18
Union Jack 192, 231
Upton, John 3, 24, 27–28, 258ch2n3
Urania 7
Utopia 13, 240, 243

Valentine and Orson 12, 22, 130, 257n44
Vieth, D. Gene Edward 253
Vincent, David 258n54, 258n55, 258n56, 258n57
Virgil 13, 205, 210
Virgin Mary 9, 15
Vives, Juan Luis 10

Wagner, Richard 121
Walker, A.G. 3, 58, 59, 60, 61, **62**, **63**, 64, 65, **67**, 68, 69, 70, 73, **74**, 140, 141–142, **143**, 144, 258ch3n2, 258ch3n3, 260n2
Wallace, William 13
Walsh, William S. 256n26
Warburg, Sandol Stodard 250, 263Epi.n1
Waterhouse, John William 65
Watt, Tessa 258n49
Watts, G(eorge). F. 3, 28, 64, 102, 121, 201, 210, 217, 236, 262n29
Webster, Thomas 214
Wells Gardner Darton 57, 58

Welsh, Charles 161–162, 260n13
Werth, Tiffany Jo 7, 9, 255n9
Wesley, Charles 243
Wesley, John 243
Wharton, Thomas 8
Whitman, Walt 248
Whittier, John Greenleaf 169
Whittington, Dick 21, 164
Whyte, Frederick 259n6
Wilson, Calvin Dill 140, 144–154, 260n3
Wilson, Richard 115, 255ch1n5
Wilson, Woodrow 170
Wise, T.J. 25
Witham, Rose Adelaide 228
The Wonderful Wizard of Oz 29
Wood, Sally 259n6
Wordsworth, William 102, 225
Working Men's College 175
World War I 4, 102, 185, 217, 224, 234, 247, 249
Worth, Lady Mary 7
Wright, Henrietta C. 182, 205–207, 262n18
Wright, Louis B. 237n46
Wycliffe, John 10, 206
Wynkyn de Worde 5

Young Folks' Library 141, 160–162, 269n12
Young Folks' Treasury 141, 165–166, 260n19
Young People's Home Library 141

Zangwill, Israel 170

www.ingramcontent.com/pod-product-compliance
Lightning Source LLC
Chambersburg PA
CBHW051212300426
44116CB00006B/543